Governance in Contemporary Germany
The Semisovereign State Revisited

Throughout the 1970s and 1980s, West Germany was considered to be one of the world's most successful economic and political systems. In his seminal 1987 analysis of West Germany's 'semisovereign' system of governance, Peter Katzenstein attributed this success to a combination of a fragmented polity, consensus politics and incremental policy changes. However, unification in 1990 has both changed Germany's institutional configuration and created economic and social challenges on a huge scale. This volume therefore asks whether semisovereignty still exists in contemporary Germany and, crucially, whether it remains an asset in terms of addressing these challenges. By shadowing and building on the original study, an eminent team of British, German and American scholars analyses institutional changes and the resulting policy developments in key sectors, with Peter Katzenstein himself providing the conclusion. Together, the chapters provide a landmark assessment of the outcomes produced by one of the world's most important countries.

SIMON GREEN is Lecturer in German Politics, University of Birmingham. He has worked extensively on German politics, in particular immigration and citizenship policy, and his book *The Politics of Exclusion: Institutions and Immigration Policy in Contemporary Germany* was published in 2004.

WILLIAM E. PATERSON is Professor of German Politics, University of Birmingham, and chairman of the German–British forum. He has written widely on German and European politics, and in 1999 was awarded an OBE for scholarship in German studies.

Contributors: Andreas Busch, Roland Czada, Kenneth Dyson, Klaus H. Goetz, Simon Green, Wade Jacoby, Charlie Jeffery, Peter J. Katzenstein, Charles Lees, William E. Paterson, Thomas Saalfeld and Wolfgang Streeck.

Governance in Contemporary Germany

The Semisovereign State Revisited

Edited By

Simon Green and William E. Paterson

CAMBRIDGE
UNIVERSITY PRESS

CAMBRIDGE UNIVERSITY PRESS
Cambridge, New York, Melbourne, Madrid, Cape Town, Singapore, São Paulo

Cambridge University Press
The Edinburgh Building, Cambridge, CB2 2RU, UK

Published in the United States of America by Cambridge University Press,
New York

www.cambridge.org
Information on this title: *www.cambridge.org/9780521848817*

© Cambridge University Press 2005

First published 2005

Printed in the United Kingdom at the University Press, Cambridge

A catalogue record for this book is available from the British Library

Library of Congress Cataloguing in Publication data

Governance in contemporary Germany: the semisovereign state revisited
edited by Simon Green and William E. Paterson.
   p. cm.
  Includes bibliographical references and index.
  ISBN 0 521 84881 4 — ISBN 0 521 61316 7 (pb.)
1. Germany—Politics and government—1990–
2. Germany—History—Unification, 1990. I. Green, Simon, 1971–
II. Paterson, William E. III. Title. JN3971.A91G65 2005
320.443'049—dc22 2004065037

ISBN-13 978-0-521-84881 - 7 hardback
ISBN-10 0-521-84881 - 4 hardback
ISBN-13 978-0-521-61316 - 3 paperback
ISBN-10 0-521-61316 - 7 paperback

Contents

Figures

Tables

Contributors

ANDREAS BUSCH is Reader in European Politics and a Fellow of Hertford College, University of Oxford

ROLAND CZADA is Professor of Politics at the University of Osnabrück

KENNETH DYSON is Research Professor in the School of European Studies, Cardiff University

KLAUS H. GOETZ is Senior Lecturer in Government at the London School of Economics and Political Science

SIMON GREEN is Lecturer in German Politics at the University of Birmingham

CHARLIE JEFFERY is Professor of Politics at the University of Edinburgh

WADE JACOBY is Associate Professor of Political Science at Brigham Young University, Provo, Utah

PETER J. KATZENSTEIN is the Walter S. Carpenter, Jr Professor of International Studies at Cornell University

CHARLES LEES is Lecturer in Politics at the University of Sheffield

WILLIAM E. PATERSON is Professor of German Politics and Director of the Institute for German Studies, University of Birmingham

THOMAS SAALFELD is Senior Lecturer in Politics at the University of Kent

WOLFGANG STREECK is Professor of Sociology and Director at the Max Planck Institute for the Study of Societies, Cologne

Acknowledgments

We would like to thank Professor Edward Page FBA and Professor Peter Pulzer, as well as three anonymous referees, for their invaluable support and comments on this project as a whole. We are also grateful to Matthew Allen and Chantal Lacroix for their help with editing and indexing the manuscript. In particular, we are grateful to the ESRC Future Governance Programme and the School of Social Sciences at the University of Birmingham for supporting a workshop in April 2002, at which first drafts of the chapters included here were presented.

SIMON GREEN AND WILLIAM E. PATERSON
Birmingham

Abbreviations

ABM	*Arbeitsbeschaffungsmaßnahmen*
B90/*Die Grünen*	*Bündnis 90/Die Grünen* (abbreviated in English to the 'Greens')
BA	*Bundesanstalt für Arbeit*; from 2002 *Bundesagentur für Arbeit*
BAFI	*Bundesamt für die Anerkennung ausländischer Flüchtlinge*
BAMF	*Bundesamt für Migration und Flüchtlinge*
BAT	Best Available Technology
BDA	*Bundesvereinigung Deutscher Arbeitgeberverbände*
BDI	*Bundesverband der Deutschen Industrie*
CDU	*Christlich Demokratische Union Deutschlands*
CSU	*Christlich-Soziale Union*
DGB	*Deutscher Gewerkschaftsbund*
ECB	European Central Bank
EMU	Economic and Monetary Union
ERDF	European Regional Development Fund
ESDP	European Security and Defence Policy
EU	European Union
FDP	*Freie Demokratische Partei*
FRG	Federal Republic of Germany
GDP	Gross Domestic Product
GDR	German Democratic Republic
GRW	*Gemeinschaftsaufgabe Verbesserung der regionalen Wirschaftsstruktur*
IMK	*Innenministerkonferenz*
KMK	*Kultusministerkonferenz*
LFA	*Länderfinanzausgleich*
LZB	*Landeszentralbank*
NATO	North Atlantic Treaty Organisation
NGO	Non-governmental organisation

OECD	Organisation for Economic Co-operation and Development
PDS	*Partei des Demokratischen Sozialismus*
PISA	Programme for International Student Assessment
SAM	*Strukturanpassungsmaßnahmen*
SEA	Single European Act
SOP	Standard Operating Procedure
SPD	*Sozialdemokratische Partei Deutschlands*
TA	*Technische Anleitung*
THA	*Treuhandanstalt*

1 Introduction: Semisovereignty Challenged

Simon Green and William E. Paterson

The Semisovereign Model of Governance

In political science, every once in a while, a book is published which redefines the way scholars think about a social phenomenon, a policy, a concept or an institution.[1] It is, however, particularly rare for a book on the politics of a single country to have a similar impact: it is notoriously difficult to capture adequately the links between institutions, history, cultural environment and policy outcomes at the same time. More importantly, it is even more unusual for such a book to be accepted by the indigenous community of political scientists as one of the definitive accounts of that country.

Peter Katzenstein's 1987 book, *Policy and Politics in West Germany: the Growth of the Semisovereign State*, is just such a contribution. Conceived of as an illustration of the limits of domestic state power, it locates institutional structures and policy outcomes in the Federal Republic of Germany (or West Germany before 1990) within the country's specific historical and societal context. Its central argument is that policy in West Germany was defined by 'incremental outcomes', a pattern which, moreover, remained broadly constant across changes of government. This stood in direct contrast, for instance, to the much more dramatic changes introduced by Margaret Thatcher after the Conservatives came to power in the UK in 1979. The tendency towards incremental outcomes, so the argument continued, was conditioned by the 'semisovereign' structure of the state, which sees decentralised state institutions pitted, often individually, against strong centralised societal organisations.

How did this relationship between state and society work in practice? For Katzenstein, the decentralisation of the state (or as he calls it, 'The Taming of Power' (1987, p. 1)) was achieved through four main

---

[1] The authors would like to thank Matthew Allen for his comments and suggestions on an earlier version of this chapter.

structural factors. First, West Germany's federal constitution, with (at the time) eleven federal states (*Länder*), constituted a highly visible and *prima facie* limit on the power of the central government (*Bund*). Although the usual constitutional division of responsibilities, as in other federal states, has tended to favour the federation (cf. Bulmer 1989a), the *Länder* have still managed to retain an essential role in the polity, which is derived from two key sources. On the one hand, the *Länder* have a collective direct input into federal policy-making via the upper chamber of parliament, the *Bundesrat*. On the other hand, the (West) German constitution (the Basic Law) differentiates between the functions of formulation and implementation in federal domestic policy, with the latter role being assigned to the *Länder* in most areas. The *Länder*, certainly collectively, thus constitute an important potential check on the federal government's power, even if there is rarely any doubt over which of the two levels of government is *primus inter pares*.

Second, with its activist remit of competencies, the Federal Constitutional Court (*Bundesverfassungsgericht*) has exercised a strong influence on German policy-making over the decades. Throughout the life of the Federal Republic, its judgments have helped define the terms of debate in a whole range of issues, including in several instances the division of power between the federation and the *Länder*, as well as abortion and party finance. Since unification, the court has continued to hand down path-defining rulings in both domestic and foreign affairs (see Rudzio 2000, pp. 334–7). These have included judgments on abortion (again), the constitutionality of Germany's membership of the EU's Economic and Monetary Union (EMU), the participation of Germany's armed forces in missions abroad, the financial equalisation scheme between the *Länder* (*Länderfinanzausgleich*), fiscal policy and asylum policy. On several occasions, its opinion (which it has rarely been reluctant to give) has even been sought explicitly in order to resolve what elsewhere would be considered strictly political conflicts. Indeed, its influence stretches far beyond its judgments, as policies are frequently formulated with one eye firmly on the possible position that the court might be expected to take on an issue. The court is, therefore, a key and constant shaper of the parameters of the possible in German politics.

The third and fourth factors defining Germany's decentralised state are its strong tradition of bureaucratic independence, and the relative lack of direct power of the federal chancellor. Katzenstein notes both the strong hierarchical nature of the administration and the formal separation between the federal ministerial bureaucracy and the implementing level, which, as already noted, is usually located within the *Länder*. This combination produces a situation where 'federal ministries lack experience in the details of policy implementation and tend to focus more on policy formulation' (Katzenstein 1987, p. 22). Of course, this increases the reliance of federal ministries on the input of both interest groups and the *Länder* for the evaluation stage of the policy cycle, which in turn creates a symbiotic balance of mutual interdependence.

Finally, the formal power of the federal chancellor (*Bundeskanzler*) is strictly limited to appointing ministers and setting the general guidelines of policy (*Richtlinienkompetenz*) (Articles 64–5 of the Basic Law). Individual ministers, once appointed, are therefore independent in the political and practical leadership of their offices (the so-called *Ressortprinzip*). Certainly, the chancellor has more scope for leadership in foreign and European policy (Paterson 1998). But in domestic politics, the chancellor's scope for setting even the guidelines for policy are limited by his information deficit resulting from the *Ressortprinzip*, the dynamics of coalition politics and the practice for coalition partners to lay down the government's programme in advance in considerable detail by means of a 'coalition treaty' (Katzenstein 1987, pp. 22–3; see also Smith 1991). Indeed, for a chancellor to exploit the *Richtlinienkompetenz* fully and successfully, he would himself need to be able to offer policy solutions that are superior to those of his ministers. So far, only one chancellor has arguably been able to fulfil this criterion: Helmut Schmidt, who also stands out as being the only German political leader to have run both major spending and planning ministries at federal level before acceding to the highest political office.[2] Even the chancellor's powers of patronage within his own party are very limited, given the political need to distribute key offices of state on a regional basis.

By contrast, Katzenstein underlines the fact that societal interests are comprehensively and centrally organised. In particular, the national employers' and labour organisations still wield considerable power and influence in policy-making and cannot be ignored as actors: historically, it has been unthinkable for a federal government to push through radical changes in economic and labour-market policy against the expressed wishes of either of these two groups. Moreover, their role as the main peak organisations means that they can be consulted on policy proposals which go far beyond the formal delineation of their interests. Such large 'class-based' groups are complemented by powerful 'status groups', such

---

[2] Chancellor Schröder's leadership style in economic reform is discussed in more detail in chapter 6 by Kenneth Dyson. See also Patzelt (2003), as well as *Der Spiegel* (19 July 2004).

as doctors and farmers, who often have 'insider' status by virtue of their central role in policy implementation (Katzenstein 1987, pp. 23–30).

The resulting complex web of relationships, checks and balances both between and within state and society is, so Katzenstein argues, held together by three key institutions, which he identifies as 'nodes of the network': political parties, federalism and parapublic institutions. First, political parties, by virtue of the formal role they are accorded in Article 21 of the Basic Law, occupy a unique position, both in the context of German politics and in a cross-national comparison of party systems. Ever since the foundation of the Federal Republic in 1949, the party system (and hence government) has been dominated by two large parties, the Christian Democratic CDU/CSU and the Social Democratic SPD.[3] But rather than being simple class-based parties, the CDU/CSU and SPD have consciously defined themselves as mass organisations, with relatively large memberships and broad electoral bases, which bridge traditional electoral cleavages, especially class and religion. It is for this reason that these 'people's parties' (*Volksparteien*), but especially the CDU/CSU, serve as a close approximation to the ideal-type of 'catch-all party' identified by Kirchheimer (1966). Precisely because of their broad appeal, the *Volksparteien* must reconcile a wide range of interests within their ranks, including both employer and employee interests. This emphasis on cross-cleavage consensus within the two main parties is complemented by the requirements of coalition politics: not only has almost every government in the Federal Republic's history been a coalition, but the *Ressortprinzip* and the limited power of the chancellor provide the junior partner with a formal power which should not be underestimated.

The second node of the network is federalism, which, far from creating discrete arenas in which actors can conduct their politics independently of other levels, actively binds together the otherwise diffuse range of state actors. By design, (West) German federalism is intrinsically 'cooperative' in nature; in other words, it places a premium on consensus interactions both within the community of *Länder* and between the *Länder* and the federal government (Scharpf et al. 1976). This cooperative function of federalism is epitomised, on the one hand, by the horizontal and vertical financial equalisation schemes for the *Länder*, and, on the other, by the role of the upper chamber of parliament, the *Bundesrat*, in German politics. Via this body, the *Länder* can collectively veto any bill which affects either their direct policy competencies or,

[3] The CSU is the CDU's Bavarian sister party, and although the two parties are formally independent of each other, they operate together at federal level.

crucially, their implementation of policy. As most laws now involve the amendment of existing administrative implementation of policy, rather than the legislation of new areas, the *Bundesrat*'s role in federal policy-making has become gradually more important. In 2004, around 60 per cent of bills were subject to the *Bundesrat*'s absolute approval, making it a formidable veto player in public policy (Tsebelis 2002).

But federalism is important in other ways too. Since the late 1960s, the *Länder* and the federation have together been responsible for the so-called 'joint tasks', mainly consisting of infrastructure projects such as the construction of new universities, which have served to further the dependence relationship of the sub-national on the national level of government. In party-political terms, federalism matters too: all main parties are structured on a federal basis, thereby creating powerful regional leaders (*Landesvorsitzende*), without whose support any party leader at federal level risks becoming a 'lame duck'. Finally, the sub-national level is the main recruiting area for national politics: all five federal chancellors since 1966 had previously been either ministers or minister-presidents at *Land* level. The same goes for opposition parties: since 1972, the opposition party's chancellor candidate has been a serving *Land* minister-president at every federal election except 1983.

Katzenstein's third node of the policy-making network is the range of parapublic institutions that he identified in West Germany (Katzenstein 1987, pp. 58–80). The role of these parapublic institutions was to depoliticise controversial policy areas by turning them into areas of technical and administrative expertise. Key among this range of institutions was, of course, the politically independent *Bundesbank*, which, as guardian over the stability of Europe's largest currency, wielded significant power within both Germany and the European Union (EU). As Katzenstein notes (1987, p. 64), its independence is demonstrated by the fact that its actions have frequently frustrated both CDU- and SPD-led governments, although conversely, the limits of the *Bundesbank*'s power were also revealed when Chancellor Kohl pushed ahead with a 1:1 exchange rate for German Monetary Union in July 1990 against the expressed advice of the then *Bundesbank* president, Karl-Otto Pöhl. But the role of other institutions, including the Federal Labour Office, the Council of Economic Experts ('*Die fünf Weisen*'), and private and Church welfare associations, have also testified to the tradition of 'rationalist consensus' in (West) Germany's policy-making (Dyson 1982).

The importance of these nodes for understanding German politics and policies cannot be stressed too highly. For Katzenstein's nodal concept captures perfectly how the structure-agency debate in political science is played out in the German context. Thus, parapublic bodies and political parties can be both policy-making agents and part of the institutional structure, depending on the individual context (Hay 2002, p. 127; McAnulla 2002).

Inevitably, neither (West) Germany's institutions nor their patterns of interaction can be separated from the historical and geo-political environment in which they operated. The entire West German political system was constructed out of the physical and moral ruins left behind by National Socialism. In 1949, the year the Federal Republic of Germany (FRG) was founded, the overriding concern was to build a political and party system that would prove more stable than the Weimar Republic had been, while avoiding the centralisation and lawlessness of the Nazi dictatorship. Given the experiences of hyperinflation in the early 1920s, and of a centrifugal party system by the early 1930s, it is hardly surprising that the new republic's political classes were 'learning from catastrophes' (Schmidt 1989).

Equally, West German politics quickly came to be defined by the realities of the Cold War, both in terms of its physical security and, more importantly here, its domestic politics. The physical division of Germany into the capitalist West and communist German Democratic Republic (GDR) in 1949 meant that the challenge of socialism was more direct and immediate in the FRG than in any other western European country. Until the construction of the Berlin Wall in 1961 made travel between the two countries impossible (as opposed to just difficult), the two systems were in direct competition with each other. In consequence, the West German social market economy (*Modell Deutschland*) simply had to be seen to deliver a higher level of social welfare than the GDR. This maxim, which informed the positions of employers, employees and parties alike, persisted deep into the 1980s, when East Germany was still officially being touted as the world's tenth largest economy.

Neither West Germany's historical legacy nor the Cold War environment in which it found itself favoured a confrontational, 'Westminster' type of politics (cf. Lijphart 1984). Instead, what Gordon Smith has memorably described as the 'politics of centrality' was able to flourish (Smith 1976, 1982; also Paterson and Smith 1981). Governance by consensus, with the associated disappearance of the ideological distance between the main parties, became the norm for both the CDU/CSU and SPD. In addition, the role of the liberal FDP, which has formed governments with both the large parties, has been to provide a constant moderating, centripetal influence on policy when necessary (cf. Schmidt 1989). What is more, the pivotal role of parties in the (West) German polity has helped spread this pattern of consensus governance to other institutions, including the Constitutional Court: because its judges require two-thirds majorities in both houses of parliament, the CDU/ CSU and SPD have always co-operated extremely closely in their selection and appointment. This, in turn, has meant that the court has tended to be centrist in its judgments (Rudzio 2000, p. 341).

Overall, the effect of the decentralised state and centralised society, operating in an environment where consensus was the desired mode of governance, was to give a unity of intentions to its actors and institutions (Bulmer 1989b). This had the effect of helping to transform a fundamentally weak state into a strong one. From an early stage, it also facilitated the pooling of sovereignty in the form of the European Economic Community (EEC), which paradoxically contributed to West Germany's strength by aiding its international rehabilitation. Certainly, the pace of domestic policy change has never been breathtaking, as the centrality of the notion of incremental outcomes to the semisovereign model illustrates. Katzenstein himself notes that, 'within the constraints and opportunities that characterise the Federal Republic, incremental policy change . . . is a politically logical choice' (Katzenstein 1987, p. 351). But he also differentiates between incremental outcomes and policy stagnation: 'It is easy to mistake incremental change for incapacity to change . . . There is a world of difference between incrementalism and immobilism' (Katzenstein 1987, p. 350). Indeed, the German polity's capability to innovate from within was clearly demonstrated by the Grand Coalition of 1966–9, and more recently by the successful integration of the environmental agenda into mainstream politics from the mid-1980s onwards, as Charles Lees' analysis in chapter 10 shows. Above all, the events of 1989–90 showed how exogenous pressures could produce change on a massive scale, although, as chapter 2 illustrates, unification was accompanied by a characteristically incremental institutional adaptation.

In terms of policy outputs, the semisovereign model of governance, which in its inclusivity and consensual focus constituted the political equivalent of the 'Rhineland' model of capitalism, served West Germany extraordinarily well (Conradt 2001; Harding and Paterson 2000). West Germany pursued an economic policy of the 'middle way', located between the extremes of Anglo-Saxon market and Scandinavian welfare capitalism (Schmidt 1987, 1989). By the late 1980s, the country was one of the most successful economies with one of the highest standards of living in the world. Driven by the strength of an export-led economy, West Germany could afford generous pensions, enviable health care and excellent public services. Moreover, the relatively high productivity of labour meant that West German employees could enjoy longer holidays, shorter working weeks and more generous pensions than their counterparts in other industrialised countries: the notion of a thirteenth monthly salary, common in German industry and public service, remains wishful thinking for employees in most other countries. The West German model was seen as a success externally (Paterson and Smith 1981), an achievement made all the more remarkable given the political and economic devastation that the country had suffered as a result of the Second World War. This feature made a huge impression in the UK, where an infinitely smaller scale of devastation was routinely invoked as an explanation of post-war economic failings.

It is this evident success that has made semisovereignty an indispensable point of reference in debates about governance in Europe. This is particularly evident in three respects. First, the institutionalised role for interest groups in (West) Germany as a system of private-interest governance has represented a clear alternative to the privatisation wave of the 1980s. Second, Katzenstein was one of the first scholars to show that federalism in Europe could be a source of strength, and not just a way for heterogeneous ethnic and cultural groups to co-exist under the auspices of the nation-state. Using the West German case, he demonstrated how federalism could produce democratically legitimated policy change, even if this tended to be only incremental. In doing so, the semisovereign model of governance refuted the conventional wisdom of the time about the inherent superiority of the unitary state. It also foresaw the trend towards greater decentralisation of power, either via federalism or via the broader process of devolution, which has taken place over the past fifteen years in previously highly centralised countries such as France, Spain and the UK. Indeed, in his later work, Katzenstein argues forcefully that the benefits from sharing sovereignty at the national and sub-national levels can apply equally to sharing sovereignty at the supranational, European level (Katzenstein 1997a). Finally, the concept and role of parapublic institutions in a political system appears to have been enthusiastically embraced by other European countries in the 1990s. The *Bundesbank*'s model of institutional independence was directly 'exported' to the European level in the form of the European Central Bank (Bulmer et al. 2000, pp. 40–2). Even the Bank of England's operational independence, granted in May 1997, was influenced by the perceived success of the *Bundesbank* model of central bank autonomy.

Among scholars, Manfred Schmidt (2002a, pp. 177–8) quite explicitly employs the semisovereign model in his instructive cross-national comparison of constitutional structures and veto players, while Reutter (2004) uses it to contextualise the policy changes under the SPD-Green government from 1998 to 2002. More broadly, the importance of the model of semisovereign governance is reflected in the fact that Germany is included almost by right in any significant study of comparative government and governance (e.g. Lane and Ersson 1999; Pierre and Peters 2000, especially p. 38; see also Tsebelis 2002).

Unification and the Challenge to Semisovereignty

Given (West) Germany's undoubted past economic and political success, as well as its importance in comparative political studies by virtue of its sheer size and economic power, it is only natural to explore the question of how the semisovereign model of governance has fared in post-unification Germany, both in terms of structures and outcomes. This question, which forms the central theme of this book's analysis, has become particularly germane in the light of Germany's generally weakening economic performance after the immediate post-unification boom. Whereas West German Gross Domestic Product (GDP) grew by an average of 2.8 per cent in real terms between 1970 and 1980, this rate slowed to 2.3 per cent between 1980 and 1991, and to 1.3 per cent for united Germany between 1991 and 2000. Indeed, in 2001, 2002 and 2003, real GDP effectively ground to a halt, with growth rates of just 0.8 per cent, 0.2 per cent and −0.1 per cent respectively.[4]

While the slowdown in Germany's economic growth since 1992 has been unmistakable, its performance has languished in other areas too: unemployment has increased rapidly since 1990, and in 2003 remained stubbornly high at around 10 per cent of the workforce, or over four million in total, with considerable regional variation. When combined with an increasingly ageing population (and a sharp rise in early retirements), plus a long-term decline in the birth rate, this has contributed to a rapid increase in social expenditure, including unemployment benefit, health and pension costs, which has jumped from 29.3 per cent of GDP in 1990 to 33.6 per cent in 2001. Higher welfare expenditure has also impacted on the cost of labour in Germany: hourly labour costs in Germany are now 13 per cent higher than in the USA, 43 per cent higher than in the UK and 59 per cent higher than in Spain (*The Economist*, 7 December 2002), although Germany admittedly fares better on a comparison of unit labour costs. The volume of red tape and bureaucracy, which had baffled outside observers of West Germany even before unification, has reached almost epidemic proportions since

---

[4] Unless otherwise stated, all economic data are taken from the Statistisches Bundesamt (http://www.destatis.de).

1990, with over 3,400 legislative acts passed by the federal level alone between 1990 and 1998 (*Der Spiegel*, 21 September 2002).

Even though the fact that other European countries have also increased their welfare expenditure since the 1990s has meant that Germany remains broadly on the 'middle way' internationally (Schmidt 2000a), the country's economic performance since unification has, by most standards, been disappointing. This has given a sense of urgency to the question of what (if any) reforms might be needed to the structures of *Modell Deutschland*. However, so far, progress has been painfully slow. Since the late 1990s, notably pre-dating the change of government in 1998, commentators have been lining up to berate the sclerosis that was perceived to have gripped the German public policy agenda: even incremental change *à la* Katzenstein no longer seemed possible. Thus, already in 1997, the term *Reformstau* (reform blockage) was the word of the year for the Society for the German Language. More recently, *Der Spiegel* news magazine entitled its issue coinciding with the federal election on 22 September 2002 'The Blocked Republic' (*Die blockierte Republik*) (*Der Spiegel*, 21 September 2002). Elsewhere, *The Economist* asked 'Is Deutschland AG Kaputt?' in its post-election survey of Germany, aptly entitled 'An Uncertain Giant' (*The Economist*, 7 December 2002). Academic and non-academic commentators too have highlighted the parlous economic situation in which Germany currently finds itself (e.g. Padgett 2003; Kitschelt and Streeck 2004a; also Steingart 2004).

What had happened? In truth, and this is borne out by most of the chapters in this volume, most of Germany's structural and economic problems pre-date unification. As in other countries, economic growth in West Germany had already slowed from the mid-1970s onwards, to the extent that an influential volume in 1992 described the country's economic performance as the 'fading miracle' (Giersch et al. 1992). Already back in 1985, the year's first issue of the magazine *Der Spiegel* bore the title *Die Sklerose der deutschen Wirtschaft* ('The Sclerosis of the German Economy', quoted in Bulmer and Humphreys 1989, p. 181). The long-term implications of slowing birth rates in West Germany had also already been the subject of lively public debate in the mid-1980s. In 1988, Fritz Scharpf famously characterised West Germany's system of co-operative federalism as a 'joint decision trap' (Scharpf 1988), in which intractable conflicts tend to lead to 'non-decisions' (Bachrach and Baratz 1963). At the end of the 1980s, Bulmer and Humphreys (1989, p. 195) declared that 'the West German model faces its toughest challenge' in the 1990s. Perhaps most presciently, given the nature of political conflicts in recent years, Manfred Schmidt in 1989 summarised the problems of co-operative federalism thus: 'West Germany's federalism also tends to obstruct all policy initiatives that are targeted to the solution of highly complex problems, including mass unemployment stemming from cyclical and structural factors, and which are inherently unamenable to treatment in terms of policy initiatives of a purely distributive nature' (Schmidt 1989, p. 79).

But these problems may well not have developed in the same way and on the same timescale had the GDR's communist regime not collapsed in November 1989. As it was, unification the following year set off an unprecedented period of sustained drain on resources and thereby on German macro-economic policy. The unexpectedly desolate state of the economy in the new *Länder* has necessitated net transfers on a staggering scale, which by 2002 totalled no less than the equivalent of around € 800 billion (cf. *The Economist*, 7 December 2002). These have been financed through a mixture of taxes and (mostly) debt, which has doubled from just under € 600 billion in 1991 to € 1.224 trillion in 2001 (*Der Spiegel*, 20 January 2003). As a result, Germany's annual interest payments (in absolute terms) more than doubled in the space of just seven years, from DM 64.3 billion (€ 32.2 billion) in 1990 to DM 136 billion (€ 68 billion) in 1997.

With most of the transfers being spent on consumption rather than investment, unification has arguably resulted in one of the biggest state-financed consumer spending sprees in history. Yet perhaps surprisingly, no party has seriously questioned these fiscal transfers. Two reasons may be identified for this. First, the creation of equality of living conditions across the country remains a constitutionally defined policy goal. Second, as is discussed below, eastern German voters are more likely than their western counterparts to switch parties between elections, thereby making a reduction in net transfers electorally extremely hazardous.

What is more, this extra expenditure has meant that Germany has not been able to comply with the budget deficit criteria of the EU's Stability and Growth Pact, which it had ironically helped to establish in the mid-1990s: in 2002 and 2003, it returned the worst budget deficits in the EU, at −3.5 per cent and −3.9 per cent respectively. In turn, this 'double whammy' of higher debt and higher taxes has created hitherto unheard-of external and internal pressure to reduce public expenditure and Germany's still relatively generous social welfare provision. Even though painful measures were announced in Chancellor Schröder's Agenda 2010 on 14 March 2003, progress has been difficult, as the various actors (including from within the SPD) have used their positions to frustrate and dilute the federal government's agenda.

Crucially, the massive exercise in Keynesian deficit spending represented by unification has so far been slow to produce much in the way of results, principally because eastern productivity levels remain too low to justify the wage settlements achieved by western unions in the immediate aftermath of unification. Accordingly, the east remains economically weak, and its real GDP, despite growing rapidly in the early 1990s, has since stagnated. Significantly, the early increases in real GDP failed to produce increases in employment in the east, where average unemployment, excluding work-creation measures, was 17.5 per cent in 2001, more than double the rate in the west. This in itself has created even more pressure on Germany's beleaguered public-finance system, producing a vicious circle of lower economic growth, higher public expenditure and higher taxes, leading to lower economic growth again.

But public finances have not been the only area in which unification has had a major impact. Much of the unions' considerable influence was derived from West Germany's well-established system of industry-wide collective wage agreements. However, with the glaring imbalance between wages and productivity in the east, many employers there have withdrawn from such agreements, paving the way for more flexible wage settlements. Consequently, the proportion of businesses participating in collectively bargained agreements in the east is only about half the level in the west (see chapter 2), a development which has prompted Stephen Padgett to talk of 'post-modern' interest group structures in the east (Padgett 1999). Even the state is contributing to this trend: Berlin left the public-sector employers' association in early 2003 in order to avoid having to take over wage settlements agreed via collective bargaining. On top of all this, the demographics of eastern Germany's population growth are even more unfavourable than in the west: whereas, on average, each woman bears 1.7 children in western Germany, which is still well short of the notional 2.1 needed for a population to sustain its size, the corresponding figure in the east is just 0.8, far lower than in any EU member state (Schmid 2001). Such a low fertility rate will only serve to exacerbate Germany's long-term demographic problems, and in particular potentially bankrupt its 'pay-as-you-go' pension system, in which employers and employees pay for those currently drawing a pension (see *Die Zeit*, 9 January 2003).

In terms of institutions, too, unification has brought about changes. Not only have the federal government's worsening public finances put pressure on its relations with the sub-national level, but the addition of five new *Länder* has added new patterns of interest divergence to inter-*Länder* relations (Jeffery 1999): whereas before 1990, the *Länder* could mainly be divided along two north–south and rich–poor axes, the five new eastern states have added large–small and east–west cleavages. With the per capita GDP of the richest eastern state (Brandenburg) in 1997 still less than 75 per cent of that of the poorest western state (Lower Saxony) (Rudzio 2000, p. 358), the constitutionally prescribed goal of uniform living conditions among all the *Länder* has been difficult to maintain. Indeed, in recent years, the southern states of Bavaria, Baden-Württemberg and Hesse have been openly espousing a new system of 'competitive federalism', a theme which Charlie Jeffery explores in detail in chapter 4. Overall, this means that it has been much harder to create stable coalitions of interests among the *Länder* since unification.

In principle, this increasing heterogeneity of interests in the federalist node of Germany's policy-making network could be counterbalanced by an increasing role for the second of Katzenstein's three nodes, political parties, which of course operate at both national and sub-national levels of government. But parties, too, have found it difficult to adapt to the changed circumstances of post-unification Germany. On the one hand, partisan 'de-alignment' (the weakening of traditional patterns of party support) has been in evidence in western Germany since the 1980s, but as with *Modell Deutschland*, unification has added a whole new dimension to a transformation which would otherwise probably have taken place in a much more gradual manner. The reason for this lies in the fact that, while the western electorate has been de-aligning, the eastern electorate has been 'non-aligned', with practically no discernible stable patterns of electoral support (Dalton 2003). As a result, voters in Germany, but especially in the east, have shown a remarkable propensity to change their allegiances from one election to another. This feature was particularly important in every *Bundestag* election since 1990: as Wade Jacoby notes in chapter 2, the winner (as defined by the largest party nationally) on each occasion was the party which 'won' the east. It is arguably no surprise that 1998 saw the first election to produce a complete change of government in Germany since 1949 (cf. Green 1999).

This trend has been compounded by fundamental differences in the structure of the party system between west and east. Since the 1980s, a 'two-plus-two' party system has operated in the west, consisting of the CDU/CSU, the SPD, the smaller liberal FDP and the ecologist Greens. By contrast, the party landscape in the east has consisted of three more-or-less equal players: the CDU, SPD and ex-communist PDS, the last of which has regularly polled at or over 20 per cent at regional elections, as well as being represented in the *Bundestag* (albeit with a considerable variation in its parliamentary strength) ever since unification. These differences reflect a quite different political culture in eastern and western Germany, with voters in the new *Länder* for instance generally favouring a higher degree of state intervention (see chapter 3 in this volume, pp. 72–3). Such changes in the structures of party competition theoretically make it harder for the two larger *Volksparteien* to act as integrating forces (cf. Padgett 2001).

One critical combined effect of the divergence of *Länder* interests and the changing party system for policy-making has been to frustrate the creation of dependable majorities for the federal government in the *Bundesrat*. The 1990s saw a proliferation of possible coalition permutations at sub-national level outside the standard government–opposition split at federal level. These have included grand coalitions of CDU and SPD, so-called 'traffic light' coalitions of SPD, FDP and Greens, and coalitions with the ephemeral, but nonetheless momentarily influential regional parties which periodically achieve representation at state elections (for instance, *Arbeit für Bremen*, which gained representation in the 1995 Bremen election). Moreover, with the exception of a few months between October 1990 and May 1991, and again from October 1998 to February 1999, the federal government has been unable to command a regular majority in the *Bundesrat* at any time since unification, prompting Manfred Schmidt to characterise Germany as a 'grand coalition state' (M. Schmidt 2002b).

Finally, parapublic institutions too have changed. Although unification created the biggest parapublic institution of all, the *Treuhandanstalt*, whose remit was to privatise the GDR's economic infrastructure between 1990 and 1994, it was, by definition, only short-lived. A second critical change to Germany's arsenal of parapublic institutions was the transfer of monetary policy responsibility from the *Bundesbank* to the European Central Bank (ECB) on 1 January 1999. Although the ECB, as noted above, is overtly modelled on the *Bundesbank* (and is even located in the same city), its responsibility is of course for the entire euro–zone, in which Germany in 2004 was just one of twelve members. A significant component of the semisovereign state has, therefore, been Europeanised. Third, there was a general trend to privatisation during the 1990s, especially in the former state-owned telecommunications and rail industries. The cumulative effect of these changes on the operation of semisovereignty is discussed by Andreas Busch in chapter 5.

In addition to the endogenous pressures on semisovereignty created by unification, Germany's entire international environment has been fundamentally transformed since 1990. Politically, unification ended the country's formal *external* semisovereignty, an aspect which was deliberately not covered in Katzenstein's 1987 analysis (but see Katzenstein 1997a). In foreign policy terms, West Germany's security requirements had been met by other countries (principally the United States). However, in the post-Cold War world, this position as a 'consumer' of security can no longer be taken as a given. Demands on Germany to become a 'producer' of security have increased (Longhurst 2004), which the country has found difficult to meet given its comparatively low expenditure on defence (Paterson 2003, p. 214). Similarly, participation in the process of European integration is no longer part of the broader aim of regaining international credibility, but now is a rational policy decision like any other (albeit broadly unchallenged at elite level), in which Germany's willingness hitherto to bear most of the EU's financial burden can no longer be taken for granted in the coming years.

In economic terms, the process of globalisation, which developed yet further during the 1990s, has also only served to expose the German model's post-unification difficulties further. One of West Germany's principal perceived strengths was that, despite its reliance on exports, its economic structures were to a considerable degree cocooned from global pressures, even though certain critical events such as the 1970s' oil shocks did highlight the limits of independence. Thus, large and medium-sized German companies famously not only financed, but also, in the case of larger firms, held stakes in each other. The resulting insulation from global capital markets protected firms from having to maximise returns in the short term. This, of course, also benefited the social market economy, in which the principle of equal contributions by both employers and employees to the welfare funds was well established and, in the absence of global competitive pressures, affordable. However, with the recent trend towards liberalisation of capital flows and trade, not least via the establishment of the EU's single market in 1993 and the completion of the GATT Uruguay Round of tariff reductions in 1995, this insulation has become impossible to maintain (Hall and Soskice 2001). The degree to which Germany is now embedded in the global economy was graphically illustrated in the aftermath of the terrorist attacks of 11 September 2001, which helped end the tentative economic recovery that had begun the previous year. Today, joint German–US conglomerates (e.g. Daimler-Chrysler, DresdnerKleinwortBenson), German companies listed on the New York Stock Exchange (e.g. SAP, Siemens) and hostile takeovers (Mannesmann by Vodafone) are part and parcel of Germany's industrial landscape. In terms of semisovereignty, this trend has meant that the incentive for German capital to bear the high costs of the social market economy is decreasing (cf. Kenneth Dyson's analysis in chapter 6); correspondingly, for each year between 1991 and 2001, there have been net capital outflows from Germany, with the exception of 2000 (the year of the Mannesmann takeover by Vodafone) (Deutsche Bundesbank 2002, p. 48). With no moral or even physical imperative (in the form of the Iron Curtain) to bind industry to the German model, Wolfgang Streeck has noted that 'the patience of capital may erode in the face of growing opportunities for migrating out of the ambit of national regulation and taking advantage of the greener, or at least easier-to-graze, pastures of less obligational economic systems' (Streeck 2001a, p. 4).

Significantly, the option of capital flight is not available to many small and medium-sized enterprises (the *Mittelstand*), which account for the majority of employment in Germany. In the current German system, many such companies are simply resigned to a constant struggle to remain competitive internationally.

Semisovereignty: From Asset to Liability?

Overall, post-unification Germany has been caught in a complex web of interrelated endogenous and exogenous factors, which have combined to create a serious challenge to the future viability of *Modell Deutschland*. The question of whether the semisovereign model of governance, with its wide dispersal of power within government, its powerful societal groups and non-partisan parapublic institutions, can rise to address this challenge, or whether immobilism and stasis are the inevitable outcome, forms this book's central line of enquiry.

On the face of it, things do not look good for the semisovereign model of governance. For one thing, the last significant revisions to the Federal Republic's institutional structure took place over thirty-five years ago, during the Grand Coalition between 1966 and 1969. Since then, it is difficult to avoid the conclusion that the dispersal of power within Germany's political system has prevented further structural reforms. Indeed, Manfred Schmidt's cumulative index of veto players places Germany equal to Switzerland, and second only to Austria among thirty-six major industrialised democracies in terms of limitations on central government's scope for action. As he notes, 'in Germany, there is a particularly large number of cooks stirring the political broth' (Schmidt 2000b, pp. 352–3; see also Czada 2003).

In addition, as Thomas Saalfeld discusses in chapter 3, Germany's system of staggered state and federal elections means that political parties are constantly campaigning; it is very rare for a twelve-month period to pass in German politics without either an important *Land*, federal or European election. More importantly, election-free periods following a federal poll, when national governments would normally push through their most unpopular proposals in the hope that the voters will have forgiven them by the time of the next election, are even rarer. As Sir Christopher Mallaby, former UK Ambassador to Bonn, was once overheard to comment, 'There is no such thing as a post-election moment in Germany'.

When combined with well-established trends in public opinion, which show that voters support reforms, as long as they do not affect their own individual situations, the main political parties have for many years been reluctant to grasp the nettle and make potentially unpopular decisions, most of which would have involved zero-sum re-distributive dynamics. As such, this is not surprising: the German miracle has been fading only gradually and millions of voters are still in a comparatively comfortable position, and hence with a great deal to lose through changes. Accordingly, since March 2003, when Chancellor Schröder announced Agenda 2010, many of whose changes are likely to hit lower income earners hardest, the SPD has suffered a series of heavy defeats at *Land* elections, as well as at the European election on 13 June 2004.

Even when reform proposals have been put forward, the cross-cleavage nature of the CDU and SPD's memberships and electorates has meant that the various factions have often been able to neutralise those proposals which are perceived as being most damaging to their clienteles in the short term. On top of that, opposition parties have a range of options open to them in order to veto proposals, ranging from organising a *Bundesrat* blockade to taking the law before the Constitutional Court and, in the case of citizenship policy, even organising a highly controversial petition campaign.

The deep problems that Germany has had in tackling the economic and structural challenges of unification raise an important point. Prior to unification, Katzenstein's analysis showed that semisovereignty, with its emphasis on consensus governance, actually made West Germany stronger. Yet the current situation, in which the political incentives to undertake major reforms are very low, prompts a new question, as posed by Wolfgang Streeck in chapter 7: in post-unification Germany, is semisovereignty an asset or a liability? Can the inherited, semisovereign mode of governance still provide real solutions to the issues facing Germany, or would it be better served by the 'kill-or-cure' approach of Thatcherism, as the German historian Dominik Geppert has asked (Geppert 2003)?

This question is highly germane for the future viability of semisovereignty as a model of comparative governance. If Germany is to remain a point of reference in international comparisons, its structures of governance must find a way of taking decisions which help reverse its economic under-performance of recent years. More importantly, the question is also of huge relevance for Germany itself. It currently faces a situation in which its post-1945 political structure, with its emphasis on continuity, no longer appears adequate to a rapidly changing world, with interdependent economies, an absence of a direct military threat and new patterns of work which go far beyond the traditional employer/employee relationship. At least part of the problem surely lies in the fact that Germans have found it understandably difficult to part with a successful model, as opposed to parting, as they did in 1945, with a model that had so patently failed. Here parallels may be drawn with the experience in recent years of Japan, as the other main defeated power in 1945 which achieved unparalleled economic success during the second half of the twentieth century only to find that this became unsustainable during the 1990s. Like Japan, Germany

appears to be stuck in a 'high equilibrium trap' – a situation in which the institutional and cultural legacies of a successful past shape the actor's interpretations of self-interest and of feasible strategies, as well as the choices available to them, in such a way as to prevent them doing what they would otherwise have to do in order to improve economic outcomes. (Kitschelt and Streeck 2004b, pp. 1–2)

Yet like Japan, Germany ultimately may have little choice: the country is falling behind in most international league tables, including, tellingly, in the OECD's PISA programme on educational attainment. As *The Economist* asked after the 2002 federal election: 'In Germany, compromise and consensus remain the order of the day. But can they still deliver the goods?' (*The Economist*, 7 December 2002).

That said, it should by no means be taken for granted that semisovereignty, or for that matter the Rhineland model of capitalism, is doomed to failure (Hall and Soskice 2001). The recent experience of Japan, where reform has been followed by a degree of economic recovery, indicates that it is possible to escape from the high equilibrium trap. As noted above, Katzenstein in his original analysis was at pains to emphasise that incremental change does not equal immobilism. Significant decisions, notably unification and membership of the euro, are still possible. The key question is whether semisovereignty is by itself capable of translating its default tendency towards incremental outcomes into more far-reaching, path-defining changes both in terms of entire policy fields and the institutions that govern them. The cross-party reform commission on the functioning of Germany's federal system, which was convened during 2003 and 2004, is an important indicator of the system's potential capacity for self-regeneration. Even though its failure in December 2004 constitutes a blow to attempts to streamline decision-making in the German polity, there can be little doubt that this setback is temporary and that there will be renewed political initiatives to take this agenda forward in the near future.

What is more, the 1998 federal election may, in retrospect, come to be identified as a critical juncture in terms of shifting the political class's expectations of public policy. Not only was the fourteenth *Bundestag* between 1998 and 2002 the first in which none of its members had seen regular active service during the Second World War, but Chancellor Schröder is the first post-war political leader to have no memory of the Nazi regime. The 'catastrophe' which informed many of the Federal Republic's institutional choices more than fifty years ago is, thus, passing from memory into history. Future generations of political and business leaders will quite simply not be weighed down by the shadows of the past, although they will continue to find it difficult to recalibrate the policy and institutional mix, which for so long provided unparalleled success, to meet the changed terms of international competition.

This volume, then, brings together a range of contributions to examine the applicability and future viability of semisovereign governance in Germany in detail. Its main focus lies on events from unification up to the 2002 federal election, although subsequent events, including the development of Agenda 2010 up to mid-2004, will also be addressed. The analysis is divided into two parts. First, Wade Jacoby in chapter 2 considers the process of institutional transfer to the east, thereby showing how semisovereignty itself helped burden the federal government with massive financial commitments. In chapters 3, 4 and 5, Thomas Saalfeld, Charlie Jeffery and Andreas Busch respectively then examine the development of each of the three policy-making nodes, namely political parties, federalism and parapublic institutions.

In the second part of the book, individual policy case studies are analysed along the lines originally employed by Katzenstein, who structured his discussion under the headings of context, agenda, process and consequences. Of the six original case studies, one (university reform) is not re-examined here, as its relevance (it was originally included as an example of co-operative federalism) has diminished in recent years. The remaining five original areas (economic management, industrial relations, social policy, immigration and administrative reform) are examined by Kenneth Dyson, Wolfgang Streeck, Roland Czada, Simon Green and Klaus Goetz in chapters 6–9 and 11 respectively. They are supplemented by studies of two new fields, environmental policy (chapter 10 by Charles Lees) and European policy-making (chapter 12 by William Paterson). The former is well established as a major area of domestic policy, while the impact of the EU on domestic policy is now so great that Germany's structures in this field have effectively become part of the internal arena. In chapter 13, Peter Katzenstein concludes the volume by providing a re-evaluation of the semisovereign model as a whole in the light of the analysis presented here. Together, the chapters provide a differentiated and nuanced perspective on governance in one of the world's most important countries, as well as a uniquely authoritative account of policy developments in key sectors over the past two decades.

2 Institutional Transfer: Can Semisovereignty be Transferred? The Political Economy of Eastern Germany

Wade Jacoby

Introduction: Can Semisovereignty be Transferred?

Peter Katzenstein's analysis of the 'semisovereign' West German state is one of the most enduringly popular conceptualisations of German politics.[1] This chapter asks whether Germans could transfer this widely admired model of policy-making to the new states in eastern Germany. The chapter frames German unification around the idea of 'institutional transfer', an idea explored more fully in the next section. The point of departure is the progressive crisis of the state socialist model in the German Democratic Republic (GDR), followed by the collapse of the GDR state, and the widespread hope among eastern Germans that their territories might not merely join the Federal Republic but also be remade in its image (McAdams 1993; Maier 1997; Hampton and Soe 1999).

It would be unrealistic to ask of a model that highlights incremental change to explain the most rapid period of institutional and policy change in the post-war period. In that sense, the question here is not so much whether the semisovereignty model predicts or explains the main contours of unification, but rather whether the political features it high-lighted – including incrementalism, political bargaining and societal engagement – survived the move to the east. This is no easy question, for there is no one answer valid across all policy domains. Clearly, institutional transfer has resulted in many similarities between the political economies of western and eastern Germany. The question, however, is whether these similarities are more than 'skin deep'. To do justice to this question, the investigation is limited to three policy areas in eastern Germany: active labour-market policy, regional development policy

---

[1] The author thanks the editors as well as Mark Vail and Matthew Wells for comments on an earlier version of this chapter.

and tax equalisation. All belong to the political economy, which was the central focus of Katzenstein's model. In addition, two other cases (wage bargaining and limits on labour migration) will be treated much more briefly. The original model's focus on parapublic institutions and federalism will be prominent, with party politics playing a subsidiary role.

The question, then, is whether semisovereignty, which developed in a particular historical and international context, could be actively transferred to a territory with different historical antecedents and international influences. There is no shortage of works that suggest that such transfer is simply impossible, and that all meaningful institutional developments are organic ones, native to a particular cultural and historical soil (e.g. Muniak 1985). Yet there were powerful political incentives to attempt such a transfer (and to persevere when difficulties appeared). And so the West German government did make the attempt. The results include some fascinating developments that are likely to matter to scholars of institutional change in advanced industrial states, especially those concerned with processes of intense regionalisation, globalisation, benchmarking and the diffusion of so-called 'best practices'.

Three themes on institutional transfer deserve initial emphasis and will be illustrated more fully below: first, institutional transfer requires not just transferring *technical designs*, but also the more difficult task of transferring *political compromises*; second, unintended consequences are so ubiquitous that the key issue is not necessarily how to minimise them, but how to cope with them; third, in a state where power is fragmented, a variety of actors can step forward (or not) to cope with these consequences. In eastern Germany, the search for subsequent solutions involved a combination of more institutional transfer but also of novel experiments that had no real West German antecedents. But in this search for solutions, the federation (*Bund*) was consistently the problem-solver of last resort. Though virtually every actor had strong incentives to solve problems, and some actors had the funds to make a contribution, only the federal government had both the incentives and the resources to stay deeply involved.

Variables and Cases

In this chapter, the question of whether specific experiments in eastern Germany worked well is investigated in conjunction with two other questions. First, were the old policy instruments in western Germany robust or modest? Second, to what extent could the federation externalise the costs of experimental solutions as opposed to underwriting them itself? This chapter assumes that when confronted by new problems in eastern Germany, the federal government prefers to mix two strategies: problem-solving and blame avoidance.

Robustness is a rough proxy for problem-solving potential. The semi-sovereignty model implies that policy innovation is usually incremental in Germany. This chapter defines robust policy instruments as ones that have existed for many years and that represent high levels of financial commitment. On the one hand, robust instruments might be helpful to politicians trying new experiments because they are well endowed in both human capital and budgetary terms. Thus, they may contain the slack resources and the expertise to try new approaches. On the other hand, if robust instruments equate to robust commitments, they may oblige the state to continue trying to solve problems even when its best attempts do not look promising. Robust instruments are likely to be a double-edged sword.

By contrast, the externalisation challenge allows clearer predictions. What is meant by 'externalisation' is the ability to push the costs of adjustment on to others, such as the *Länder*, municipalities, firms, social partners, parapublic institutions or the EU. If the federation cannot solve a problem, it should try to ensure that voters do not hold it responsible for that problem. The initial presumption is that the German semisovereign state will be quite good at off-loading tasks and external-ising costs – far better than, say, historically statist France (cf. Levy 2002). On balance, the worst situation for the federation is when robust instruments combine with high political salience to lock in its engage-ment even though externalisation is very difficult. The easiest external-isation should occur when modest tools exist at the federal level, the voting public accepts this, and a competent and willing third party is available.

A simple 'two by two' matrix results in four distinct combinations, and this chapter looks at detailed case studies representing three of those combinations. The first two reflect cases in which the old (i.e. pre-unification) Federal Republic of Germany (FRG) had modest policy instruments. First, in active labour-market policy, the state lacked strong institutions to promote employment (Schmidt 2000a). The *Bundes-anstalt für Arbeit* (BA), or Federal Labour Office, was a parapublic insti-tution whose prevailing instruments were too weak to cope with the problems of eastern Germany. With federal-state approval, the BA transferred to the east labour-market policy 'crutches' that had existed in West Germany; however, in eastern Germany, the BA and the state turned these crutches into 'pillars' that support major segments of the under-employed population. The state has been only partially able to externalise these costs on to the social insurance funds, and has taken on significant new commitments in labour-market policies that are funded from taxes (and not from employers' and employees' social-security contributions).

The second case is regional policy, and it is also best seen as modest in terms of existing infrastructure. To be sure, this case displays somewhat more in the way of traditional instruments, as developed especially in the Ruhr since the 1970s. Yet it is important not to exaggerate the policy tools available to the state, as this policy area had become quite liberalised in the 1980s. As we will see, however, a significant political battle was waged between the state, the *Treuhandanstalt* (THA – the institution charged with overseeing the privatisation of companies formerly owned by the GDR), unions and employers over an eastern German regional policy. In the context of this fight, the federation could externalise many costs on to the supranational level of the European Union (EU); to receive these funds, however, it made important concessions in its rules over regional policy.

The third area – tax equalisation between the *Bund* and the *Länder* – is one in which the old Federal Republic had robust instruments that were very long-standing and well endowed. The old balance reflected federal efforts to buy increasing policy influence over the years in return for funds redistributed to poorer *Länder*. After 1989, very little innovation has occurred at all in this area; however, we do see that it was the federal government which provided the money to keep the old system intact. Thus, stasis has become very expensive, mostly because the federation has been unable to externalise many of the new costs in light of the electoral incentives to prop up the status quo as expanded to eastern Germany.

A fourth policy area, though not considered as a case below, helps complete the initial sketch of variation. Border controls are an area in which the old West German federal government had robust capacities that had been further reinforced both by the EU's Schengen Agreement and by the run-up to the eastern enlargement of the EU on 1 May 2004. While it is beyond the scope of this chapter to give an account of the complex immigration policy debates in Germany (see instead chapter 9 in this volume), one political economy aspect of the debate illustrates the thrust of the argument: in response mostly to pressure from Germany and Austria, the EU agreed to allow individual member states, if they so wished, to restrict for up to seven years the free movement of labour from those (mainly central and east European) states that joined the EU in 2004. This deal helped the federal government address fears of labour-market competition in eastern Germany and Bavaria. It did so, however, by externalising costs onto both the citizens of the aspirant

Table 2.1. *Sovereignty shifts across policy domains: the initial hypothesis*

		Federal government's ability to externalise costs	
		Easier	Harder
Government's policy instruments	Historically robust	Control of new immigration	Tax equalisation
	Historically modest	Regional development policy	Active labour-market policies

members in central and eastern Europe and, more worryingly, the weak states even further to the east (e.g. Ukraine) whose borders have been hermetically sealed by their western neighbours at some cost in both commerce and political stability (Jacoby 2002). Here, a robust instrument went hand in hand with externalisation.

Table 2.1 maps the cases along the two lines of variation just indicated. First, what is the capacity of traditional instruments (two were modest; two, robust)? Second, what possibilities exist for the federal government to externalise costs (in two, very good possibilities existed for it to externalise costs, and in two others it had modest or low possibilities)?[2]

The *Bundesregierung*, or federal government, deserves emphasis both because it plays such a crucial role in the discussion of semisovereignty and because post-unification federal governments of varying hues have had incentives to make institutional transfer work in eastern Germany. Eastern Germany is electorally significant for both major parties, and both the SPD and CDU/CSU must strive hard to do well there. In all four all-German elections, the party that won eastern Germany also won the country, including the 2002 election where the national margin of victory was a mere 7,000 votes (see Table 2.2). This pattern gives any party in government the incentive to be the problem-solver of last resort in the region, providing, of course, that such costs cannot easily be externalised.

---

[2] It is only partially true that the federal government cannot externalise the costs of employment promotion. But, as Streeck (2001b) has noted, many of these costs have indeed been externalised onto the welfare state. In this case, the burden is borne far more by those employed than by taxpayers. Details of the significant new exposure of the federal government in this domain that justifies its placement here appear below. Vocational training is an alternative policy area in which historically weak central-state instruments have been expanded significantly at great cost and without much externalisation of these costs (see Jacoby 2000, chapter 6).

Table 2.2. *Federal election results for the CDU and SPD in eastern Germany since 1990 (per cent)*

	Year election held			
Party	1990	1994	1998	2002
CDU	42	38.5	27	28
SPD	24	31.5	35	40

Source: The Economist, 14 March 2002, p. 55; http://www.btw2002.de, accessed 5 December 2002.

Transfer as More than Colonisation, Set-up and Extension

'Institutional transfer' was a concept that seemed to match so well with the actual process of institutional change in eastern Germany that many used it without knowing that it had once been prominent in discussions of de-colonisation (Hamilton 1964). The idea has entered the debate about eastern Germany in three different ways. One common usage considers transfer simply as a tool wielded by western German actors to colonise the east – a technique for cutting off indigenous innovation in eastern Germany (Unger 1993, pp. 221–8). But this variant of the concept has two fatal flaws. First, it blends out the enthusiasm – however superficial their knowledge might have been – of eastern Germans for West German institutions. Second, western German cash transfers to eastern Germany have run at around € 100 billion per year – something of a reversal of the normal financial relationship between metropole and colony. This use, thus, ignores those aspects of transfer that appeared, from the eastern German perspective, to be desirable.

A second approach treats transfer simply as the *formal* process of establishing institutions and practices in the east (e.g. Johnson 1995). Other problems may still abound, such arguments run, but the transfer itself was quickly and easily implemented. Here, transfer is narrowed to a purely formal process that consists of one or a few legislative acts or executive decrees in 1990 and, perhaps, 1991. For example, an excellent study by Robischon et al. (1995) of institutional continuity in the health, research and telecommunications sectors during unification shows that, in all three sectors, efforts to transfer 'reformed' West German structures to the east were blocked by the veto positions of other players in the sector. As a result, in all three cases, the state and unification treaties foresaw the 'one to one' duplication of the western system. Thus, the authors' focus is decidedly on the process of negotiating the formal design of the institutions, and this makes transfer technocratic and, thus, politically less interesting.

The third approach casts transfer not as colonisation or technocratic rule-making, but as one ideal-type for institutional change. Lehmbruch (1996a) reserves the concept to describe only those sectors – such as health care – where West German regulatory governance was *extended* to eastern Germany. He separates this transfer process from three other modalities of institutional change: first, 'indigenous' innovation in the GDR before the signing of the Unity Treaty established the basic political institutions of parliament, federalism and local government; second, those sectors where eastern German interests have successfully resisted or modified transfer attempts; and third, the institutional 'borrowing' processes that have occurred in eastern Europe.

This chapter uses an even broader notion that locates examples of institutional transfer *within* each of Lehmbruch's three other modalities. It does so for three reasons. First, it is implausible that some *policy areas* are shaped only by exogenous processes (transfer) while others are shaped only by endogenous ones (innovation). Rather, in any given sector, one finds a mixture of exogenous and endogenous changes. Second, while GDR decision-makers did have recourse between January and July 1990 to 'older German traditions' in redesigning institutions (and, thus, according to Lehmbruch, had no need for transfer), they were clearly influenced by West German structures even then; thus, those poised to use institutional transfer in eastern Germany hardly needed to wait for formal economic or political union as the starting gun. Finally, the comparative perspective reveals many processes in eastern Germany to be extreme variants of those in other post-Communist states. 'Borrowing' in eastern Europe *is* complicated, but it still can be fruitfully compared to transfer in eastern Germany (Cox 1993; Jacoby 2002).

This chapter, thus, draws on a broader notion of institutional transfer developed in a previous work on the creation of unions, works councils, employer associations, and secondary and vocational schools in eastern Germany (Jacoby 2000). Three themes from that work are relevant to the current chapter. First, institutions are more than just designs; rather they are also political compromises, which are much harder to 'transfer' than the institutional architecture itself. For example, even the extraordinarily comprehensive transfer of West German structures has not been able to compensate for the challenges of transferring industrial relations to a new setting. Second, unintended negative consequences abound and create new problems for existing actors. Third, these new problems may shift the competencies of key actors because these actors may have different interests in compensating for unexpected institutional failures. In some cases, social partners stepped into the breach – witness the well-nigh frenetic activity of some unions in eastern Germany – but, in many cases, only the federal government had both the incentives and the resources to build new programmes.

One specific set of unintended consequences will be of special relevance below: the transfer of the West German wage-bargaining system, which the Kohl government supported and encouraged as a tool to increase eastern standards of living, and to stem migration flows to the west, has also kept eastern German firms under intense cost pressure (Schröder 2000).[3] This cost pressure has led to a de facto flight from the employers' associations which, in many firms' eyes, do not represent their interests in collective wage bargaining: eastern German unit wage costs were 159 per cent of western levels in 1991, and in 1997 were still 125 per cent of those in western Germany (Bach et al. 1998, p. 55). The resulting unemployment cost trade unions dearly in terms of employed membership. The two social partners, which represent ever smaller shares of capital and labour in eastern Germany, have thus had considerable difficulty defending the integrity of their core mission: setting wages. Informal deals abound in which employers pay less than contract wages with the complicity of the works councils; this also strains ties between unions and the works councils concerned (Jacoby 2000). Moreover, the situation is not getting appreciably better. In fact, economic growth in the new *Länder* was negative (GDP in the east decreased by 0.5 per cent in 2001 after posting strong gains in the early and mid-1990s). Productivity has remained at about two-thirds of western levels since 1997 (Bach et al. 2002; *The Economist*, 14 March 2002).

Given the significant problems in the wake of institutional transfer, what steps has the federal government taken to shore up, invent or abandon particular policy instruments? Obviously, a full inventory of institutional transfer is beyond the scope of this chapter. The next three sections do, however, present case studies that show a range of efforts by the federation to externalise the costs of adjustment in eastern Germany. We start with a case in which it had only an intermediate level of success (financing active labour-market policies), move next to a case of reasonably high externalisation (financing regional development policy), and conclude with an abject failure of externalisation (financing tax

---

[3] Eastern wages remain, even to this day, below those in the west.

equalisation). In the first two cases, externalisation efforts rested on historically modest policy instruments, while in the final case, the instruments were quite robust.

Active Labour-Market Policies: From Crutches to Pillars

Though eastern Germany lost 3.9 million jobs between 1990 and 1993, unemployment in 1993 numbered 'only' about 1.15 million. This huge gap between actual job losses and official unemployment can be accounted for by the range of labour-market policies that were transferred to the east.[4] Migration to western Germany, early retirement, short-time work, employment-creation companies and retraining all absorbed a share of these workers, and the special conditions that prevailed in the aftermath of unification have been well documented (Knuth 1997). Thus, institutional transfer in one area – industrial relations – helped drive huge labour-market problems that were addressed, in part, by the transfer, and then expansion, of relatively minor West German policy instruments. What had been minor 'crutches' soon became major 'pillars'. In addition, various actors also created new instruments. In both cases, the federal government played a key role, though flanked by the parapublic Federal Labour Office (*Bundesanstalt für Arbeit*, BA) and from 2002, its successor organisation, the Federal Labour Agency (*Bundesagentur für Arbeit*).[5]

German active labour-market policy traditionally has been pro-cyclical because it is funded from the same source as passive measures. During a recession, passive measures, such as unemployment benefit, which the state is legally obliged to provide, 'crowd out' the optional (i.e. non-statutory) active measures. In eastern Germany after 1989, this pattern did not hold – a situation made possible only by heavy subsidisation of active measures by both the BA and the federal government (Knuth 1997). Early on, the BA bore the brunt of the new costs, and here the federation was indeed able to externalise some significant costs. In 1992, for example, the BA covered two-thirds of the extra costs and the federal government one-third, but as the programmes grew, so, too, did state exposure. The new measures placed up to thirty people in job-creation schemes for every hundred unemployed persons when the previous high in western Germany had been only seven per hundred

---

[4] The key 'active' components of eastern German labour-market policies have been retraining and employment companies.

[5] Another parapublic agency, the *Treuhandanstalt*, also helped insulate the state from blame, as it was a perennial target of animosity. See chapter 5 in this volume, p. 101.

(Knuth 1997, p. 73), although this ratio has since come down. In addition, for every hundred unemployed persons in the east in 2001, there were also ten workers on retraining programmes. When all active measures are combined, twenty-four workers were on active programmes in the east for every hundred persons who were unemployed. Moreover, there were 187,000 potential workers in the 'silent reserve' who are not officially looking for work (Bach et al. 2001, pp. 6, 9–12).

Figures 2.1 and 2.2 give a fairly comprehensive picture of the labour-market policies – both passive and active – that resulted from the crash of the eastern economy. Since 1990, there have been four key programmes designed to absorb potential workers. Figure 2.1 plots each individually (along with official unemployment), while Figure 2.2 gives the picture of the cumulative effects of these measures over time.[6]

At first glance, there is a sharp downward trend in eastern German labour-market programmes – from nearly two million participants in 1992 to about 400,000 for most of the period since 1997. This initial impression contains an important element of truth, but it must be amended to note that one programme – short-term work – had a relatively brief moment on the stage, and has since dwindled to become very small, while another programme – *special* early retirement programmes for the east – ended entirely in 1998. In other words, not all crutches became pillars, for some were, indeed, phased out (though the *standard* early retirement programmes have continued in the east at great additional cost). On the other hand, the two other crutches – retraining and employment promotion – have become pillars, and both are active measures. In 2002, the major new eastern German instrument for employment promotion – section 249h of the 1993 Employment Promotion Law (*Arbeitsförderungsgesetz*, AFG) – was continued under the new name of *Strukturanpassungsmaßnahmen* (SAM), or structural adjustment measures. This programme allowed the state to subsidise wage costs up to the level that the BA would pay in unemployment benefits. The various SAM programmes run alongside a continued reliance on work-creation measures (*Arbeitsbeschaffungsmaßnahmen*, ABM).

If the pattern of expanding historically modest policy instruments is plausible, we need to look outside the narrow eastern German context for the data on externalising costs. Most costs borne by the federation come not from funding new programmes directly (though some of this occurs), but from covering BA deficits. For this reason, it is important

---

[6] Note therefore that the measures that involve large numbers of people have more space between the lines on Figures 2.1 and 2.2, while those measures that affect fewer people have correspondingly little space between the lines.

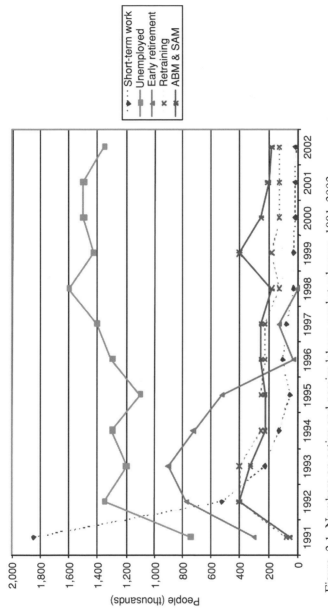

Figure 2.1. Numbers on active and passive labour-market schemes, 1991–2002

Source: Bundesanstalt für Arbeit 2003; Bach et al. 2001, p. 5.

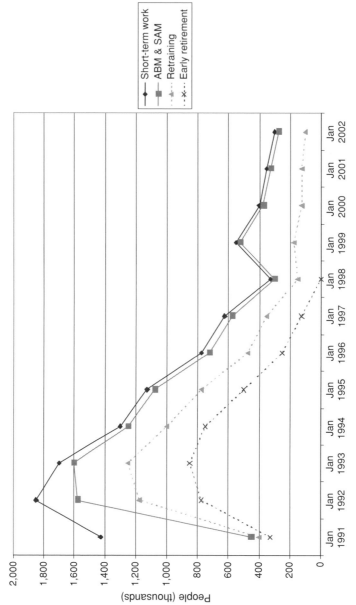

Figure 2.2. Absorption effects of selected labour-market policies, 1991–2002
Source: Bundesanstalt für Arbeit 2003; Bach et al. 2001, p. 5.

not to attribute to the BA costs that it agrees to cover, but that it does not actually pay. BA deficits can be incurred in the west as well as the east, and, clearly, we can see trends towards new active labour-market instruments in the west as well. By 1998, all-German labour-market schemes covered about 1.7 million potential workers, divided between ABM (430,000), retraining (402,000) and early retirement (809,000) (Vail 2003, p. 64; Wingens and Sackmann 2000).

In addition, since 2002, the Schröder government has asserted much more control over BA programmes as well as the financing of them. With its electoral reputation purportedly riding on the reduction of unemployment (though its failure to reduce unemployment significantly did not cost it the 2002 election), control was something the re-elected government could not do without, even if that control came at a price. So, while the insurance funds administered by the BA are typically financed by equal employer and employee contributions, federal subsidies now make up a very substantial overall contribution to the total BA budget – in 1999 it was about 30 per cent of total spending (Vail 2003, p. 50; Bundesanstalt für Arbeit 2001). Thus, the expansion of active policies in the east has now linked up with the growth of the role of the state in a reforming parapublic institution.

What are the contours of this increasing state role? First, as part of the third volume of the Social Security Code (*Sozialgesetzbuch III*) of 1 January 2002, the government's *JOB-AQTIV Gesetz*[7] instituted new procedures requiring employment offices to create individual profiles for job-seekers. It also required the recipients of unemployment benefits actively to seek work or to face, after twelve weeks, the termination of benefits. One fascinating aspect of this programme is that state leverage *increases* (in that it orders the BA to change policies), but in a manner designed to *decrease* BA (and, thus, state) costs.[8]

Second, in response to the striking imbalances between the high demand for youth apprenticeships and the stagnant supply of apprenticeships, the SPD-Green government has targeted youth employment more vigorously (Jacoby 2000). One of its first new initiatives upon taking office in 1998 was the *Sofortprogramm zum Abbau der Jugendarbeitslosigkeit* (JUMP), or Immediate Programme to Reduce Youth Unemployment. Here was another instance in which active labour-market

---

[7] JOB-AQTIV stands for *Job-Aktivieren, Qualifizieren, Tranieren, Investieren, und Vermitteln*, or Job Activating, Qualifying, Training, Investing, and Finding Work.

[8] At the same time, as Streeck (2001b) has pointed out, many towns in the east rely heavily on labour loaned to them by the local *Arbeitsamt*, or employment office, to carry out vital functions.

costs could be partially externalised, for the EU Social Fund covers € 300 million of the € 1 billion annual costs (Vail 2003, p. 50). Of the remaining costs, however, 90 per cent were covered by federal revenues (primarily through the Federal Ministry of Economics and Labour), and not through the BA. The EU Social Fund is distributing € 12 billion to Germany during the budget period 2000–6, of which € 6 billion are earmarked for eastern Germany. These funds enable programmes to be implemented that are not covered in Germany's Employment Promotion Law (Bundesministerium für Arbeit und Sozialordnung 2000, p. 29).

Third, total federal spending on labour-market policies is substantial; it is also rising. During 2000 – when the total number of unemployed persons dropped by 225,000 (all net gain was in the west) – the federation spent more than ever on active labour-market policies (DM 44.1 billion, approximately € 22.6 billion) (Bach et al. 2001). Every additional 100,000 unemployed persons cost the insurance funds about € 1.5 billion, and in recent years, the BA has repeatedly gone to the government to pay for shortfalls in its own budget (*Frankfurter Allgemeine Zeitung*, 11 September 2001). Additional federal spending has gone to pay the taxes and social-security contributions for low-wage workers who do not have to pay these at all if they are employed in so-called € 400 jobs (Heineck and Schwarze 2001).[9] This shift moves funds from the general revenues (i.e. tax revenues) into the social-insurance funds, which used to be financed solely from employer and employee contributions (cf. chapter 8 in this volume).

Finally, the government has passed laws allowing workers in firms with fifteen or more employees to shift unilaterally their full-time job to a part-time one. Many firms objected to this perceived intrusion of the state into the domain of employment bargaining. In addition, the new co-determination law relaxed procedures whereby workers can establish works councils. By contrast, however, business interests have looked with approval on the notion of state-financed wage subsidies for low-wage workers, calling for programmes of up to € 10 billion in annual spending (Vail 2003, pp. 51–2).

In sum, the SPD-Green government has used behavioural rules, targeted programmes, funds for cost overruns and regulatory changes

---

[9] The level below which social-insurance contributions and taxes were not collected from those in 'mini-jobs' used to be € 318 per month. From April 2003, this limit was increased to € 400 per month, with employers paying a contribution that amounts to 25 per cent of the wage to cover taxes and social-security contributions; above this level, social-security contributions for employees are gradually increased until, at the level of € 800 per month, they must be paid in full. Employers pay the usual 21 per cent social-security contributions on employee earnings above € 400 per month.

to gain increased leverage over active policies. The upshot of these trends in eastern Germany, in conjunction with changes in the west, is that the state does seem to be playing a more significant role both in the funding of active labour-market policies and in shifting the rules and regulations of labour markets in some novel ways. None of the changes identified so far has been revolutionary, but, in total, they support both the notions of pre-1989 labour-market 'crutches' being turned into enduring 'pillars', as well as novel experiments in response to prolonged labour-market problems. Modest policy instruments have become much more widely used. And while some of the new costs could be externalised to the BA or the EU, the federal government's contributions to active labour-market policies increased very substantially over the period.

Regional Policy: New Rules for New Money

One of the great ironies of unification is that a state that traditionally had low public employment in spite of high state spending (Schmidt 2000a) came, overnight, to own an entire economy. The Kohl government's first instinct was to divest itself of its newly acquired property by selling it to private investors. In order to make rapid privatisation politically sustainable, the state found it had to support the promise of equal wages in east and west. Yet rising wages in the east made investment there less attractive; even greatly depressed *Treuhandanstalt* asset prices could not lure sufficient investors (Sinn and Sinn 1992). The state, it became clear, would have to help promote investment. Yet the main regional-policy instrument in Germany, the *Gemeinschaftsaufgabe Verbesserung der regionalen Wirtschaftsstruktur* (GRW), was quite restrictive in the activities it would fund. These restrictions played a key role in the east, for they not only shaped the kind of aid offered, but they also compelled the unions and the *Länder* to cast about for new solutions.

Could the transfer of West German regional-policy structures compensate for problems that accompanied the transfer of the western wage-bargaining system? If not, could innovation in regional policy help? This section shows that the Federal Republic's existing regional-policy instruments were quite modest, and that subsequent innovation was mostly as a consequence of both the problems in the east and the availability of EU money that came with strings attached. The federation could significantly externalise costs, but only if it agreed to change its rules.

In 1989, GRW restrictions included two that distinguished it from the European Regional Development Fund (ERDF). First, the GRW focused on stimulating investment through capital subsidies to firms, but generally eschewed the ERDF's additional effort to exploit 'endogenous potentials', through promoting vocational training or research and development. Second, the GRW focused on export-driven growth, and so tended to support large firms (Conzelmann 1998, p. 4; Dyson 1997). After privatisation, these rules privileged subsidised greenfield investment in massive industrial parks by large western German firms (Lichtblau, 1995; Nägele, 1996). In response, two developments require emphasis. First, the unions began a campaign to promote a regional policy focused on restructuring old GDR firms. Second, the federal government, responding to developments at both the EU and *Länder* levels, later reformed the GRW in 1996. The rest of this section covers each in turn.

Besides an existing policy mix geared towards promoting large firms and export-led growth, there were other inauspicious bases for an eastern German regional policy. Social actors were weak and firm boundaries were still unclear, so there was little pressure from inside eastern Germany to force early state attention to regional policies. Western German corporate interests were generally aligned towards preventing the growth of a large state-subsidised economy in the east. Moreover, given sectoral overcapacity, few had strong incentives to invest there. The preferred initial strategy of most western firms was to acquire the best industrial and real-estate assets at modest prices and then to favour state subsidies for individual worker retraining over subsidies for remaining state firms. As noted above, the precondition of this strategy was the acceptance by the eastern German population of positions in training and the secondary labour market. Privatised firms shed labour at a tremendous rate throughout 1991 and 1992, while the THA's firms were restructured very little, as the organisation's leadership maintained that 'privatisation is the best method of restructuring' (cf. Czada 2000). The *Treuhandanstalt* used union involvement with the employment and training companies to diminish protest while successfully resisting union calls for structural or regional policy (Knuth 1997).

In the early period after unification, the unions issued many calls for coherent regional and industrial policies, but they appeared to devote few resources to developing them (Karrasch 1995). As job losses continued and new investment remained low, however, the unions began to pitch a more activist policy to the THA and *Land* governments. In this, the unions recognised that maintaining employment was the best way to preserve labour's power. While early developments brought unions many new members, job losses meant membership losses and, ultimately, organisational weakness.

In 1992 IG Metall, the Metalworkers' Union, counterattacked before it was too late; however, its first step, the ATLAS Programme in Saxony, was a big disappointment.[10] ATLAS was an amalgamation of non-privatised THA firms about which Saxony's Ministry of Economics could make proposals to the *Treuhandanstalt*, subject to input from labour and the employers. But ATLAS had no real decision-making competence, and the *Land* Saxony, the THA and IG Metall all manoeuvered to shift the burdens and the blame (Kern 1994; Lichtblau 1995). In 1993, IG Metall proposed an industrial holding company that would remove key firms from THA control and restructure them under the joint auspices of the social partners (Kern 1994, p. 18). The *Land* showed interest, but the strike of spring 1993 shifted attention away from regional policy for several months. In the wake of the 1993 strike, IG Metall overcame most of the scepticism that had previously existed in the union towards regional policy (Author interview, Frankfurt 1993). Union officials pushed specific proposals for saving and restructuring existing firms. Furthermore, the union began developing the organisational skills to participate in discussions about specific restructuring plans. Given the SPD's weakness in eastern Germany, the lack of funds at the *Land* level and employers' worries about sectoral overcapacity, unions took the lead in calling for regional policies.

Events in Chemnitz elucidate both the possibilities and limits of trade-union involvement in regional policy. In response to huge job losses in Saxony's machinery-building region, IG Metall successfully exerted pressure on the relevant employers' association to form, in 1992, a sectoral 'interest association' called the *Interessenverband Chemnitzer Maschinenbau* (ICM) (Bluhm 1993; Preusche 1993). The ICM was unlike anything previously seen in western Germany, as it brought together the union, employers, chamber of commerce, city government, Technical University and trade college to co-ordinate employment promotion. Contentious wage and working-time issues were left out of the ICM's ambit. Moreover, while the textile machinery sector was originally excluded, the unions later won its admission in order to make the interest association a *regional* instead of a merely *sectoral* body. The ICM had some immediate success in making joint purchases, thus saving on input costs for the predominantly small and medium-sized local firms. For IG Metall, these market advantages of joint action were a complement to the political advantages of tying together smaller firms into a

---

[10] ATLAS stands for *ausgesuchte Treuhandunternehmen, vom Land angemeldet zur Sanierung,* or selected THA companies that have been registered for restructuring by the *Land* government.

larger 'community' of interests. 'As individual firms, ours are simply too small to command political attention', remarked the leader of the local chamber of commerce, who added, 'we have to stay together' (Author interview, Chemnitz 1993).

But by 1998, the lobbying and co-ordination functions the union valued in the ICM had taken a backseat to firms using the ICM to capture subsidies (especially from the EU). Meanwhile, many smaller firms – in 2002 the ICM had forty-six member firms – were not members of the employers' associations, and used the ICM to provide services while avoiding the contract wages that were negotiated by the relevant employers' association and that, *de iure*, members of the employers' association have to pay. Finally, when, in 1998, the union leadership proved unable to reverse these trends in the direction of a 'subsidy mafia', it renounced its membership.

The unions also had a tense relationship with the SPD, who have traditionally been the party closest to the unions. Chemnitz's original CDU administration took a consistently neo-liberal approach to employment policy, and used subsidies almost exclusively to promote new start-ups. The unions first attempted to mobilise their works councils, but this effort was difficult because eastern works councils have been loath to engage in extra-firm 'politics' (Kädtler et al. 1997). In response, the unions felt obliged to develop new competencies. In Chemnitz, they promoted particular infrastructure developments to the municipal administration, sought private investors for local firms, and even once challenged the SPD electorally. Accusing the SPD of failing to counter the city's administration's policies actively, IG Metall and the DGB (the German Federation of Unions) in Chemnitz organised a party list to run in the 1994 municipal elections. The platform of this '*linkes Wählerbündnis*', or association of left-wing voters, was the protection of remaining firms and their employees (*Chemnitzer Freie Presse*, 6–7 November 1993). Ultimately, however, the SPD offered the union candidates places on their election list (including the number one position) in exchange for the unions dropping their separate list.

The prospect of unions competing against parties to promote regional policies is a departure from West German patterns. However, isolated challenges from unions, while serving as a marker for the level of frustration in some locales, were obviously inadequate to change the prevailing conservatism in German regional policy. In order to move to more robust forms of experimentation, it proved necessary to reform the GRW system. Necessary (though likely not sufficient) for this reform was the confluence of growing pressure from *Länder* governments and the EU Commission. The EU's new resources for eastern Germany increased incentives for the federal government to relax the tight restrictions of the GRW. The federal government had been allowed to channel all EU aid from 1990 to 1993 through the GRW, but beginning with the 1994–9 budget period, the EU Commission pushed for more flexible rules. Ultimately, the federal government relented in 1996 and allowed a loosening of controls (Conzelmann 1998, p. 5). The 1996 reforms allowed both more funding of small and medium-sized firms (as opposed to large firms more likely to be export motors) and a much broader range of programmes designed to spark 'endogenous growth'. The JUMP Programme mentioned above and financed by the EU Social Fund is an example of such a programme.

However, 'pressure' from the *Länder* and the EU is an incomplete explanation for the GRW reforms. Another reason the federal government agreed to loosen GRW rules was to ensure its control (especially through the Federal Economics Ministry) over rapidly increasing ERDF aid (Conzelmann 1998, p. 5). By 1996, other ministries, drawn by the new EU monies and frustrated by the conservatism of the Economics Ministry, called for ERDF aid to flow around the GRW into new instruments in which they could participate. Indeed, the Economics Ministry did lose some control over ERDF funds to new players (especially the Federal Transport and Environment Ministries) even after it went into damage control and agreed to GRW reforms. The result was a dispersal of state control (across three ministries) plus an accommodation with a different policy style. One motive for the shift was the possibility of externalising costs. Thus, institutional transfer came, first from West Germany, and then from the EU, because of the conjunction of obvious domestic difficulties, external policy models and new resources. As a result, the federation's policies shifted and control fragmented, so that new problems led to more federal *spending*, but not to more federal *control*. This outcome contrasts starkly with that in labour markets, where *both* federal spending *and* control rose sharply.

Tax Equalisation: An Expensive Status Quo

In the fiscal domain, unlike the two areas just discussed, the West German state had historically robust instruments of intervention, and had, indeed, been developing them since the reformulation of West German tax law after the end of the Second World War. The problem for the federal government, however, was that the German *Länder* had tools of their own, which they used either to limit the federation's intrusions into domains they saw as their own or to oblige it to share costs with them. The result, as we shall see, was that the federal government had little chance to externalise any of the costs of adjustment in eastern Germany.

Every federal system needs a fiscal architecture to make meaningful its rules and division of competencies. The Federal Republic is unusual in that its states cannot set their own tax rates, and in that the richer *Länder* must share some of their tax receipts with poorer *Länder* through a system of tax equalisation called the *Länderfinanzausgleich* (LFA) (see also chapter 4 in this volume). The LFA has long made an important difference in the amount of money that each state has to spend. In 1951, for example, the poorest state, Schleswig-Holstein, had DM 112 (€ 57) per person from its own revenues. However, because of the LFA (though this was still uncodified at that point), the state was able to spend DM 153 (€ 78) per capita, an increase of 36 per cent (Renzsch 1991, p. 14). The system grew more redistributive and expensive in subsequent decades. With unification, the system was, after some delay, extended to the east at great expense. Because the federal government could neither externalise those expenses, nor justify politically the permanent exclusion of the east from a well-established system, it ended up paying the lion's share of the costs.

The LFA system is not in the German constitution, but rather emerged from a Weimar antecedent, and from the fact that the *Länder* are obliged by the constitution to perform certain obligations, and to attempt to equalise 'living conditions' across the country. For the poorest *Länder*, however, the money available was often not enough to meet these obligations. Without the LFA, these states would have almost no discretionary spending. As a consequence, prior to the formal creation of the LFA in 1955, the poor states were more obliged to call for federal help to meet their obligations. The richer states feared that the federal government would usurp state competencies (at least in the poorer states) in exchange for its financial support. Indeed, the federation clearly did use poor states to carve out more influence throughout the 1950s and 1960s (Renzsch 1991).

In response to the federal government's direct 'categorical grants' to the minister-presidents of the financially weaker states, the richer states exercised 'pre-emptive solidarity' to keep the *Bund* from intervening too strongly (Renzsch 1991, p. 99; Adelberger 2001, pp. 61–2). The result in the 1950s was a system of 'horizontal' redistributions from richer to poorer states. The richer states tried unsuccessfully to deny any legal basis for 'vertical' federal payments to poor states, in order to stop the erosion of state competencies (Renzsch 1991, p. 129). A reform of the LFA in 1969 resulted in the inclusion of value-added/sales tax in the LFA formula in a way that made the system more redistributive. The 1969 reform also strengthened states *as a group*, since *individual states* lost their ability to cut side deals with the federation, thereby diminishing the divide-and-conquer tactics the government had perfected over the preceding twenty-five years (Renzsch 1991, pp. 258–9). Yet the reform also carved out a new space, first, for vertical redistribution in the form of 'joint tasks' shared by the federal government and the *Länder*, and, second, for 'mixed financing' to underwrite such tasks. The richer states saw here a way to garner some federal money, and, thus, achieve some financial compensation for the inroads the federal government had made into their policy domains.

With unification it seemed that the LFA system, largely untouched since 1969 and under attack from both rich states and the Constitutional Court, would have to be changed. If the five eastern states had joined the LFA system under the then existing rules, redistribution would have had to rise from DM 3.5 billion (€ 1.8 billion) per annum to DM 20 billion (€ 10 billion) in order to deal with the financial inadequacies in eastern Germany. Had the LFA remained unreformed, *every* western German *Land* but Bremen would have become a net payer!

In response to this dilemma, the federal government and the western states put off admitting the new *Länder* to the LFA until 1995 (Renzsch 1994; Burchardt 1992; Hüther 1993; Hickel 1992). Instead, they set up and financed more or less equally the Fund for German Unity. The fund distributed the debt inherited from the GDR, and limited the western German states' liability for rebuilding eastern Germany (Renzsch 1991, p. 276). For example, the western states used the fund to argue that eastern Germany should have a separate system for value-added tax that would distribute the revenues from this tax raised *in their territory* on a per capita basis, but that would not have access to these tax revenues raised from the entire territory of unified Germany. The Unity Treaty of 31 August 1990 set the East German access to the revenues raised from value-added tax at 55 per cent for 1991, and proposed to increase it slowly to 70 per cent by 1994. Here was a transfer or extension of institutions, but without full benefits.

Of course, the GDR government, which negotiated this treaty, showed little capacity to counter the disadvantages for the new states that would emerge on its territory. And as the first wave of layoffs came in the summer of 1991, the newly elected minister-presidents in the eastern *Länder* saw plainly that they had no realistic foundation for public finance. At that point, the old *Länder* relented and reversed the decision on value-added tax to allow all eastern German states full access on the same per capita basis that western German states had. Moreover, the federal government responded with a new programme, *Aufschwung*

Ost, which provided about DM 12 billion (€ 6.2 billion) a year in 1991 and 1992 for new investment and employment in eastern Germany (Sally and Webber 1994). Thus, early in the unification period the eastern states had partial access to pieces of the old system plus a series of special programmes to help with their special problems. All looked ahead anxiously to 1995 when the new states would enter the LFA, reformed or not. Yet only minor changes in the LFA were enacted in 1995, when the system was renewed until 2005. This raises the key question: who footed the bill for extending a staggeringly expensive LFA to the five new states?

The answer, it turned out, was mostly the federal government. In order to make possible the inclusion of the five new states, it chose to pay most of the new costs. The financially weaker western states were guaranteed the extension or *even the improvement* of conditions under which they had access to LFA monies. There were some small changes in the way richer states paid into the system, but on the side of the recipients, nothing significant in the formula changed. Thus, instead of using the financial crisis for fundamental reforms, virtually no reforms occurred. Instead, the federal government increased its direct payments to states. Where, prior to unification, the federal government's vertical payments had been about 60 per cent of the *Länder*'s horizontal ones, by 1992 vertical transfers had already outstripped the horizontal transfers. Yet this slight 'bump' was nothing compared with what came next. As can be seen from Figure 2.3, vertical redistribution had jumped by

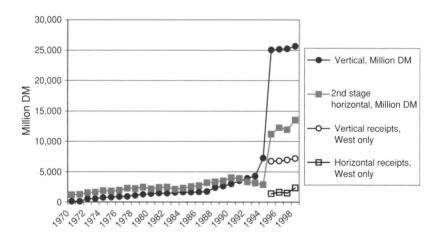

Figure 2.3. Transfers under the LFG arrangement, 1970–98
Source: Adelberger 2001, p. 71.

almost 500 per cent by 1995 (from less than DM 5 billion (€ 2.6 billion) per year in the early 1990s to around DM 25 billion (€ 12.5 billion) from 1995 onwards). The vast majority of the new vertical transfers went to the new *Länder*, although vertical transfers to western German states increased significantly; indeed, they almost doubled (from around DM 4 billion (€ 2.1 billion) to around DM 7 billion (€ 3.6 billion)).

What political manoeuvrings produced this deal (Adelberger 2001; Renzsch 2001; Schneider 1999; Vesper 1998; Gunlicks 2000; Ziblatt 2001; Färber and Sauckel 2000)? Essentially, the rich states feared that the poor *Länder* would form a coalition with the federal government – the old political constellation of the 1950s and 1960s. They tried to head off that possibility by offering the poor states revenue sharing that was as attractive as that proposed by the federation in its initial offer. The difference was that the richer states, led by Bavaria, proposed that the federal government absorb most of the costs, rather than splitting them with the rich states. Their proposal was especially generous to the eastern German states, offering them about 120 per cent of average per capita taxes. In the end, the federal government agreed because Chancellor Kohl had made such a commitment to the Fund for German Unity that he could not accept a breakdown of the system that paid for it, and so, ultimately, went along with a proposal quite close to that from the rich states.

This pattern – minor concessions by current recipients coupled with increased federal payments – was repeated in negotiations in June 2001. Even though only five states paid into the LFA (while eleven were beneficiaries), the sides reached an agreement to extend the current LFA system from 2005 until 2019.[11] Two institutional factors pushed the states towards a deal. First, the Constitutional Court had ordered the parties to find a more just system in response to the case brought by Bavaria, Baden-Württemberg and Hesse (cf. chapter 4 in this volume, pp. 88–9). Second, if the *Länder* could not broker a consensus, manoeuvring would shift to the *Bundestag*, where more parties would be involved. After regulating the system for four years (1991–5) and then ten more (1995–2005), the *Länder* moved to strike a long-term bargain. This time, the richer states did better, achieving, first, permission to keep the first 12 per cent of revenues over the national average, and, second, a cap on their total contribution. Bavaria will gain an estimated € 200 million per year from these new arrangements. Yet, neither the poorer states of western nor those of eastern Germany lost the benefits they had

---

[11] Details in this section are drawn from various German press sources, and from author interviews in Germany in May and June 2001.

formalised during the 1995 negotiations. Why not? When the negotiations seemed in trouble, Chancellor Kohl stepped in with a package of DM 13 billion (€ 6.7 billion) to compensate the poorer *Länder* for the funds the richer would be allowed to retain. Thus, even Bremen, a poor *Land*, was offered an additional DM 70 million (€ 35.9 million) per year. All in all, this accord was very expensive for the federal government.

Conclusion: Semisovereignty in Eastern Germany and Europe

Since 1990, both major parties have twice won and twice lost the eastern vote. The CDU won in 1990 and 1994; the SPD, in 1998 and 2002. And in each case, the government that won eastern Germany also won the general election. One general conclusion valid across the cases is that in the tight and volatile electoral context of post-unification politics, the search for votes tugs the *Bund* into problem-solving in the east, but at the same time, the existing institutional configuration of the German state powerfully shapes the distribution of the costs that result.

A virtue of semisovereignty is that the federal government does not have to face problems alone. This chapter has shown that it did have strategies for attempting to externalise some of the staggering and unexpected costs of German unification. Whether these strategies worked, however, turned on particular combinations of institutional and electoral factors. Cost externalisation strategies worked least well in tax equalisation, where historically robust instruments delivered veto points to hamper reforms while electoral incentives pushed first Chancellor Kohl and then Chancellor Schröder to deliver significant new federal spending. Yet in another case of robust instruments – state limits on migration – the German government had little trouble externalising costs. Here, Schröder convinced other EU member states that Germany should be allowed to suspend the free movement of labour for up to seven years for citizens from the new member states of central and eastern Europe. While this externalisation did little to diminish unemployment in eastern Germany (and Bavaria), it was sold as a barrier against even worse conditions. If, as Schattschneider (1960) famously argued, voters in a republican system are, at best, semisovereign, then eastern Germans are at least inside the political community and can, thus, motivate their national politicians to avoid harming them in ways that eastern Europeans can only dream of.

In the cases where modest prior instruments prevailed, the federal government also had varied success in externalising costs. In the active portion of labour-market policy, it has taken on significant new costs, and has also continually covered BA budget shortfalls. While the federation leaned on the social-insurance funds during the early years after unification, it has increasingly created new federally funded programmes as well as new interventions in BA procedures to attack high unemployment. In regional development policy, the federal government has long been able to rely on significant EU resources for investment and social programmes in the east; however, in order to gain long-term access to these programmes, it did relax its relatively tight rules on regional development policies.

More generally, semisovereignty is not well established in the eastern German political economy. Based upon the cases considered, the argument can be made that the primary reason for this is that the federal government has both more incentives to attack problems and more resources for solving them than do social actors. To be sure, the federation has not approached problems alone. Parapublic institutions, such as the BA, the *Treuhandanstalt* and the eastern *Länder*, have made some significant contributions. In addition, the public sectors in the eastern *Länder* have significantly more employees than western *Länder* of roughly comparable size.

How do these struggles compare with other European countries? In France, even as state spending as a percentage of GDP remained stable, there has been a massive 'redeployment' of funds from old state instruments like industrial policy to such matters as early retirement and active labour-market policies (Levy 2002). But if the highly sovereign French state created a very different but still highly sovereign state in less than two decades since the U-turn of 1983, the semisovereign German state was much less able to reproduce semisovereignty. This is perhaps not so surprising since the state must do much more than hand over tasks to other state agencies; rather, it must engage in a co-ordination game with *Länder*, parapublic agencies, unions and employers. The weakness of unions and employers in eastern Germany is particularly alarming since they are counted on to perform so many tasks in the German political economy (Hall and Soskice 2001). This chapter has argued that when others actors buckle under the weight of problems, the federal government has powerful incentives to step in. Thus, one essential premise of semisovereignty – a strong society – has not yet emerged in eastern Germany. Until it does, the federation is likely to continue to increase gradually its financial exposure to a variety of problems that it is used to seeing solved by others. Whether it can solve these problems is another matter, but for now the electoral logic of German politics obliges it to try.

3   Political Parties

Thomas Saalfeld

Political parties, as Strøm (2000, p. 180) maintains, are generally 'the most important organisations in modern politics'. Along with co-operative federalism and parapublic institutions they constitute one of the three crucial 'nodes' of the 'semisovereign model of governance' Katzenstein (1987) developed to analyse patterns of policy-making in the Federal Republic of Germany. Not only do parties in this model serve as links between citizens and elected officials at the regime level (cf. Poguntke 2002; more generally Müller 2000), they also connect the various tiers, arenas and corporate actors in the Federal Republic's decentralised state contributing to a peculiar mix of competitive and co-operative elements (cf. Holtmann 2000; Leonardy 2001; Renzsch 2000). As for political parties, this model is generally characterised by 'the conjoining of the party-run state with statist parties' (Katzenstein 1987, p. 377) and, more specifically, by a number of structural attributes that he believes to have profoundly influenced the formulation of centrist policies, which tend to be adjusted incrementally and largely irrespective of the party-political composition of the federal government of the day (Katzenstein 1987, p. 39).

This chapter seeks to map and analyse continuities and change of relevant structural attributes of the German party system at all three levels conventionally emphasised in the literature: (1) party in public office, (2) party as organisation and (3) party in the electorate, following the triad famously suggested by Key (1964). These continuities and changes will be analysed in relation to their implications for governing and public policy-making and against the backdrop of changes in the organisational environment within which the Federal Republic's political parties operate. These changes are due to a number of factors, amongst them (1) longer-term socio-economic and technological change affecting the citizens' party identification, the role of parties as intermediaries between civil society and state and the organisation of parties (in Germany as in other advanced industrial societies) and (2) Germany's unification in 1990 (cf. Saalfeld 2002). The chapter will attempt to assess whether *changes* in the party system since the second half of the 1980s have compounded the tendency to incremental policy change observed by Katzenstein (1987) or whether, alternatively, important traditional characteristics of the German party system, considered to be an asset until the 1980s, have *persisted* but come to be seen as a liability since.

Since the mid-1990s, comparative research on the influence of political structures on public policy has made significant advances, especially through the development of veto players theory. This theory can provide the micro-political foundations of parts of Katzenstein's argument from a rational-actor perspective. The present chapter relies on Tsebelis' (2002) model of 'veto players' as an organising framework for the assessment of continuity and change in the Federal Republic's party system and an analytical tool to establish the importance of these developments for the policy process, especially with regard to the difficulties of moving away from the status quo in policy terms.

In a nutshell, the main argument of this chapter is that the German party system has changed in response to socio-economic change and unification. Yet, these changes have not fundamentally challenged Katzenstein's (1987) analysis, although a number of subtle changes are important and an analysis of the distribution of voter preferences would provide an important additional perspective. A brief account of Katzenstein's analysis of the Federal Republic's party system in the second section will be followed by a section on the persistence of the German party state – despite the erosion of party identification and party membership. In the fourth section, a very concise and informal summary of the main elements of Tsebelis' (2002) theory of veto players will be offered, which serves as an organising framework for the subsequent sections. The fifth and sixth sections will analyse continuity and change in the Federal Republic's party system in respect of the number of partisan veto players and their ideological distance. In the seventh section, some relevant aspects of the role of parties in the *Bundesrat* will be analysed. The eighth section will deal with the cohesiveness of veto players, especially in the *Bundesrat*. This will be followed by a section demonstrating the importance of the 'electoral connection' as an explanatory factor for the persistence of the status quo in Germany's policy process. The main results will be summarised in the final section.

Katzenstein on the Federal Republic's Parties

In addition to the internationally remarkable interpenetration of state and parties in Germany, Katzenstein highlights three properties of the

Federal Republic's parties and party system that he considers to be crucial in shaping the nature of party conflict and co-operation, ultimately promoting policy continuity, or 'centrality' as Gordon Smith (1976) once put it in a similar vein. First, he argues that the structure of the Federal Republic's major parties, the centre-right Christian Democrats (CDU/CSU) and the centre-left Social Democrats (SPD), as catch-all parties with highly organised memberships, 'encourages centrist political solutions', as both contain strong and well-organised wings 'that prevent much movement away from the political center' (Katzenstein 1987, p. 39).

Second, the third and smallest of the three 'relevant' (Sartori 1976, p. 121) parties between 1961 and 1983, the liberal – and politically centrist – Free Democrats (FDP), played a pivotal role representing segments of the Federal Republic's middle class and functioning as a 'kingmaker' and moderating force in coalitions with one of the two larger parties. 'The FDP', as Katzenstein (1987, p. 39) puts it, 'knows that its survival depends on maintaining its middle ground between the two major parties'. The Federal Republic's party system, he maintains (1987, p. 44), 'has become a system of party blocs in which, given the closeness of federal elections, the FDP determines which bloc will pre-vail'. At the time of the publication of his book, the Green Party had just begun to make significant inroads mainly into the SPD's voter clientele. Katzenstein noted the party's potential for changing the logic of party competition, but it was too early to make more than informed guesses as to their future impact. Nevertheless, he suggested that they had 'sub-stantially broadened the range of issues addressed in politics and that the process of political bargaining within and between blocs has become more fluid and complex' (Katzenstein 1987, p. 44).

Third, and closely linked to this point, Katzenstein (1987, p. 40) notes that government by coalition had reinforced the centralist tendencies in the structure of the Federal Republic's party system, and that the preva-lence of government by coalition with a high degree of continuity resulting from the central role of the FDP 'encourages incremental policy change'. Finally, Katzenstein suggests that the institutional rules of the *Bundestag* as a parliament – and the main platform for the policy-related activities of the 'parties in public office' – emphasises committee work and legislative specialisation rather than adversarial confrontation. These institutional factors, he argues, 'reinforce these tendencies and tend to produce consensual political outcomes, as the high proportion of unanimously passed bills illustrates'. The opposition in the *Bundestag*, he observes, 'seeks to exercise control through co-operation in legislation rather than confrontation in debate' (Katzenstein 1987, p. 43).

In addition, he emphasises the extent to which the Federal Republic's parties are embedded in the political system as a whole. Referring to the 'established' parties, he speaks of a 'conjoining' or 'interpenetration' of statist parties and the party-run state. *Bundestag* and *Bundesrat*, for example, appoint the judges of the Federal Constitutional Court; yet, in practice, their appointment is the result of inter-party bargaining. However, once appointed to twelve-year non-renewable terms, the judges serve as ultimate controls over the political parties. A similar interpenetration can be observed in other constitutional bodies. Since the 1970s, Katzenstein claims, the diverse territorial interests represented in the *Bundesrat* have increasingly been subordinated to the dynamics of party competition in the federal capital. At the same time, political parties have also been colonised by the Federal Republic's system of co-operative federalism forcing on the government majority in the *Bundestag* as elected chamber a bargaining process common to coalition partners. In contrast to other political systems elsewhere, German federalism can provide the opposition with significant institutional leverage that may compel the government to negotiate rather than relying on its parliamentary majority using – in Scharpf's (1997) terminology – hierarchical co-ordination or unilateral action as its main decision-making mode. The resulting policies often look as if they have been formulated by a broad, inclusive coalition – the 'grand coalition' structure referred to by M. Schmidt (2002b). Similarly, the parties have gradually penetrated the higher echelons of the civil service. Conversely, the lower echelons of the civil service have penetrated the political parties, as the former are strongly over-represented amongst the parties' candidates for elected office. The semisovereignty of the German state is, as Katzenstein argues, further demonstrated by the system of party finance. Private interests attempt to influence the parties' policies through donations, but parties also receive substantial public subsidies. Finally, he claims, the Federal Republic's political class consists of officials 'who are sustained neither by capitalist riches nor the state's power. They administer a "cartel" of big, publicly subsidised party bureaucracies. They play a complex game of electoral conflict and policy co-operation which connects mass participation and the representation of societal interests with collaboration among elites and the governance of state institutions' (Katzenstein 1987, pp. 376–81, at p. 381).

Persistence of the Party State

The interpenetration of party and state in the Federal Republic has persisted since the publication of Katzenstein's study and allowed the 'established' parties to maintain their grip on state bodies, despite a decline in party identification at the electoral and a significant decline in membership at the organisational level. In line with other advanced industrial societies, the Federal Republic's electorate has changed significantly since the 1970s. Like elsewhere in western Europe and North America, the years of economic affluence after the Second World War, the expansion of the welfare state (especially education), socio-economic change and technological change (especially the electronic mass media) have contributed to changes in social and political values, the emergence of new political demands, declining party identification, increasing volatility, the growing attractiveness to citizens of 'non-institutionalised' forms of political participation and the growing role of electronic mass media as channels of direct communication between elected officials and citizens (Dalton and Wattenberg 2000). These developments weakened political parties – in the Federal Republic and elsewhere – in relation to the electorate and to their membership organisations (see Dalton 2000; Saalfeld 2002; Scarrow 2000).

It is one of the puzzles identified by comparative students of political parties that the 'parties in public office' have been able to maintain, or even enhance, their strength to a point where scholars begin to speak about a 'primacy of party in government' (Thies 2000) compared with parties in the electorate and as organisations. Again, the Federal Republic is not exceptional in this context (cf. Bowler 2000; Katz and Mair 2002; Strøm 2000; Thies 2000).

Standard indicators of partisan control at the parliamentary and governmental level (cf. Bowler 2000; Strøm 2000) include, for example, the share of members of a parliament that have been elected without a party label ('independents'). With the exception of the first *Bundestag* (1949–53) there have never been any members *elected* without an established partisan label; even the three successful independent candidates of the first *Bundestag* were elected with the support of a party and/or joined a party after their election (Schindler 1999, pp. 284–6). The number of members of the *Bundestag changing* their partisan affiliation during a parliamentary term has declined after considerable movement in the context of the consolidation of the Federal Republic's party system during the 1950s (Schindler 1999, pp. 907–30). As far as *party voting* is concerned, there has not been a significant reduction. If recorded votes are taken as a valid indicator (it is the only empirical indicator available over a longer period of time), the opposite has been the case. Although there has been a slight decline of voting cohesion of the SPD between 1983 and 1990, the cohesion of CDU/CSU and FDP members in recorded votes has improved markedly since the 1970s (Saalfeld

1995). *Party control of the parliamentary agenda*, measured as the percentage of government bills that become law, has not declined dramatically, although it has been reduced to approximately 70 per cent from the relatively high levels of around 80 per cent during the 1970s. Nevertheless, the levels during the 1990s (1990–8) roughly represent the levels of the first two *Bundestag* terms (1949–57; Schindler 1999, pp. 2388–9; Deutscher Bundestag 2002), although – as a result of institutional constraints rather than a loosening of partisan control – the percentage has always been relatively low compared with the United Kingdom or France. Further indicators include the *number of cabinet terminations due to internal dissent* within the government parties and the number of cabinet terminations due to lack of parliamentary (i.e. sufficient party) support. Compared with other western democracies, such events have remained relatively rare in Germany (Strøm 2000, pp. 198–9). If anything, cabinet terminations as a result of dissent within the government parties had been considerably more frequent in the 1950s than in the period since the publication of Katzenstein's (1987) work. The same picture emerges if one looks at cabinet stability, which was relatively low in the 1950s and has increased since (Saalfeld 2000a).

Beyond the parliamentary and governmental arenas, Wagschal (2001) demonstrates that the 'conjoining' of state and parties has persisted since the publication of Katzenstein's (1987) book, both in terms of the composition and *modus operandi* of a number of the Federal Republic's political and other public institutions. Germany's federalism has continued to have a strong partisan dimension. Party 'control' of the *Bundesrat* has become more problematic since unification, predominantly (if not exclusively) resulting from the diverse coalition patterns in the eastern German federal states, frequently cutting across the national government–opposition divide, as well as more territorial competition (see chapter 4 of this volume). Nevertheless, empirical evidence suggests that – in the absence of government control of a supporting majority of votes in the *Bundesrat* (as has been the case for much of the time since unification, see below) – the national opposition has regularly attempted to use the *Bundesrat* to block government legislation, especially in the run-up to national elections. In other words, the higher the electoral stakes at the national level and the closer these elections are, the stronger the level of partisan control of the *Bundesrat* (cf. Wagschal 2001, p. 874; Zohlnhöfer 1999, pp. 343–4). The major political parties have continued to control appointments to other institutions such as the Federal Constitutional Court and the *Bundesbank*'s Central Council. Nevertheless, neither of the two major parties has prevailed in the nomination process, encouraging a replication and reinforcement of 'grand coalition' politics and policies of the middle way observed as a result of Germany's federalism at these levels (Wagschal 2001; M. Schmidt 2002b).

Thus, despite significant indications of partisan decline at the electoral and organisational levels (see below), the main political parties have managed to protect their privileged political position in the German state and – as a result of institutional rules reducing the probability of majoritarian control of core institutions – maintained a decision-making process that is based on compromises between the major parties or, failing that, non-decisions and retention of the status quo. There are competing explanations of this paradox in comparative party research. One important argument is that the decline of the parties in the electorate has been overstated, at least in the German case. Despite a decline since the 1970s, voter turnout in German federal elections has never fallen below 77.8 per cent (1990) and remained relatively high by international standards (for data see Forschungsgruppe Wahlen 2002, p. 84).[1] A strong focus on chancellor candidates in *Bundestag* election campaigns and a moderate increase in 'chancellor candidate effects' as an independent variable explaining voter choice since the 1994 elections notwithstanding, the effect of candidate voting remains clearly weaker than the explanatory leverage of party identification (measured as standardised regression coefficient), despite the undeniable decline of party identification and the fact that candidate voting is strongest amongst voters with low levels of party identification (Brettschneider 2001, pp. 372, 388).

In their influential cartel party thesis, Katz and Mair (1995) have argued – albeit controversially (see Kitschelt 2000; Koole 1996) – that, especially in political systems with generous levels of public subsidies for political parties, parties have moved towards the ideal-type of so-called 'cartel parties'. Under this model, professional organisations are predominantly driven by office-seeking motivations and collude like cartelists to acquire state resources (especially state funding) in order to restabilise their organisational environment, which had become increasingly uncertain as a result of smaller membership numbers, looser ties with collateral organisations and declining party identification on the part of many voters. This explanation has immediate appeal given the relatively generous levels of state funding the Federal Republic's political parties apportion themselves, their parliamentary parties and their foundations (von Alemann 2000, pp. 144–6; Saalfeld 2000b). Nevertheless, this perspective can be criticised as insufficiently emphasising the extent to which

---

[1] By contrast, turnout at *Land* elections in general has displayed a marked decline since unification.

German parties are still rooted in civil society and as exaggerating the 'etatisation' of the main parties (Padgett 2001, pp. 64–8).

Scholars in the rational-choice tradition have offered alternative explanations. Thies (2000), for example, illustrates his explanation with an analogy between parties and firms where members of the party in government 'are the owner-operators . . . who attempt to sell their products to consumer-voters. In this effort, brand loyalty (party loyalty/party identification) is nice if you can get it, but is not strictly necessary for the health of the firm, which need only keep its sales up, relative to its competitors' (Thies 2000, p. 256). In this view, parties exist, and – despite looser ties with the electorate – continue to be important, largely because of their capacity to solve collective-action problems at the electoral and the parliamentary level – and not because of their strength as organisations. This account finds a high degree of support in the literature on the rise of 'electoral-professional' parties (cf. generally Panebianco 1988; Jun 2002; Padgett 2001).

Parties as Veto Players: Lessons from Comparative Politics

Subsequent to the publication of Katzenstein's (1987) book, veto players theory has become an influential approach in the comparative study of the link between political institutions and policy choices. The empirical findings of this body of scholarship are largely compatible with Katzenstein's empirical findings, although veto player models originating in rational-choice theory place a stronger emphasis on the preferences, strategies, cohesiveness and agenda-setting powers of political parties. Veto players theory was first developed to explain variations in different political systems' capacity to change the policy status quo. In the meantime, the veto players framework has been used to analyse variation within countries as well (e.g. Bawn 1999). In this chapter, Tsebelis' (1995, 1999, 2002) veto players theory will be used as an analytical framework. The focus on a single country will allow the unitary-actor assumption in Tsebelis' theory to be relaxed, political parties to be disaggregated and a closer look to be taken at empirical variations in their cohesiveness.

Tsebelis (1995, p. 301) defines a veto player as 'an individual or collective actor whose agreement (by majority rule for collective actors) is required for a change in policy'. He (1995, p. 302) distinguishes between *partisan veto players*, the parties forming a government, and *institutional veto players*, collective or individual actors such as second chambers with real veto powers (like in the Federal Republic) or presidents, if they can veto parliamentary legislation (like in the United

States). One of the main interests of veto players approaches is the question of policy stability and change. Tsebelis (1995, 1999, 2002) demonstrates that a government's ability to change the status quo decreases with the number of, and ideological distance between, (partisan and institutional) veto players, even where they have a preference for change.[2] A further important variable is the internal cohesion of collective veto players such as political parties. The more cohesive collective actors are, the stronger is the impact of the number and ideological distance of veto players on the stability of the policy status quo.

There is some disagreement about the appropriate operationalisation of the variable 'veto player' (in other words, counting rules for veto players; cf. M. Schmidt 2002a, p. 177; Tsebelis 2002, p. 231). Nevertheless, it is undisputed that the Federal Republic, similar to, for example, Belgium, Switzerland or the United States, is a country with a relatively large number of veto players, especially when the federal government does not control a majority in the *Bundesrat*, the de facto (if not in a strict constitutional sense) second legislative chamber.

Basic Properties of the Party System and the Number of Partisan Veto Players

The typical number of partisan veto players (two) has remained unchanged since the publication of Katzenstein's (1987) book.[3] This has been possible because the two major parties have largely defended their share of the vote with at least one of them attaining a minimum of 40 per cent of the vote. Although the 2002 *Bundestag* election was the first election since 1953 in which neither of the two major parties surpassed the 40 per cent mark, the aggregate share of CDU/CSU and SPD has remained relatively constant since 1990. The biggest drops in the CDU/CSUs' and SPD's combined share of the vote occurred in 1983 and 1987 with the rise of the Greens eating into the electoral strength of the SPD (Table 3.1).

The stability and centrality of coalition cabinets in the Federal Republic was facilitated by the rapid concentration of the party system during the first half of the 1950s, which is illustrated in Tables 3.2 and 3.3. In the

---

[2] In the formal exposition of his argument, Tsebelis (1999, p. 594) is more cautious and merely proposes that policy stability does not decrease. The empirical evidence he discusses (1995, 1999) shows that stability tends to increase with the number of, and ideological distance between, veto players.

[3] Disregarding a brief period in 1990 (prior to the first all-German elections) when the CDU/CSU-FDP coalition was enlarged to include the East German Social Union (DSU) for three months after unification.

Table 3.1. *Share of the main parties in elections to the* Bundestag, *1949–2002 (per cent of the vote)*

Election	CDU/CSU	SPD	FDP	Greens	PDS	Others	CDU/CSU + SPD
1949	31.0	29.2	11.9			27.8	60.2
1953	45.2	28.8	9.5			16.5	74.0
1957	50.2	31.8	7.7			10.3	82.0
1961	45.3	36.2	12.8			5.7	81.5
1965	47.6	39.3	9.5			3.6	86.9
1969	46.1	42.7	5.8			5.5	88.8
1972	44.9	45.8	8.4			0.9	90.7
1976	48.6	42.6	7.9			0.9	91.2
1980	44.5	42.9	10.6	1.5		0.5	87.4
1983	48.8	38.2	7.0	5.6		0.5	87.0
1987	44.3	37.0	9.1	8.3		1.4	81.3
1990	43.8	33.5	11.0	3.8	2.4	5.4	77.3
1994	41.4	36.4	6.9	7.3	4.4	3.6	77.8
1998	35.1	40.9	6.2	6.7	5.1	5.9	76.0
2002	38.5	38.5	7.4	8.6	4.0	3.0	77.0

Source: Forschungsgruppe Wahlen 2002, p. 84.

1949 *Bundestag*, there were several smaller parties to the right of the CDU/CSU; the Communist Party (KPD) was positioned to the left of the SPD. However, even in the relatively fragmented *Bundestag* elected in 1949, the parties at the extreme poles of the party system were relatively weak. By 1961 this multiparty system had effectively shrunk to three 'relevant' parties in Sartori's (1976, p. 121) terminology. The 'effective number of parties' in parliament (Laakso and Taagepera 1979) decreased from 3.99 in 1949 to 2.39 in 1957 and remained at the level of a 'two-and-a-half party system' until 1987, when the Greens began to make a stronger numerical impact. Nevertheless, Table 3.3 demonstrates that the fundamental numerical properties of the Federal Republic's party system have not changed dramatically since the publication of Katzenstein's book in 1987. Despite a certain re-fragmentation through the advent of the Greens (first elected to the *Bundestag* in 1983) and the Party of Democratic Socialism (PDS, represented in the *Bundestag* as a group or parliamentary party 1990–2002), the effective number of parties in the *Bundestag* has remained below 3.0. Because of this development, the Federal Republic's multiparty system has remained one of 'moderate pluralism' since the late 1950s, with the centripetal dynamics in party competition and policy-making terms predicted by Sartori (1976).

Table 3.2. *Left–right placement[a] of parties and party strengths (per cent of seats) in the Federal Republic of Germany, 1949–2002[b]*

Election	KPD	PDS	GR	B90	SPD	FDP	CDU/CSU	Z	GB/BHE	DP	WAV	BP	NR
1949	3.73				32.59	12.94	34.83	2.49		4.23	2.99	4.23	1.49
1953					31.01	9.86	50.10		5.54	3.08			
1957					34.00	8.25	54.33			3.42			
1961					38.08	13.43	48.50						
1965					40.73	9.88	49.40						
1969					45.16	6.05	48.79						
1972					46.37	8.27	45.36						
1976					43.15	7.86	48.99						
1980					43.86	10.66	45.47						
1983			5.42		38.76	6.83	49.00						
1987			8.45		37.42	9.26	44.87						
1990		2.57		1.21	36.10	11.93	48.19						
1994		4.46	7.29		37.50	6.99	43.75						
1998		5.38	7.03		44.54	6.43	36.62						
2002		0.33	9.12		41.63	7.79	41.13						

Notes: [a]For explanations on the left–right placement of parties see Saalfeld (2000a, pp. 41–3). [b]Measurement at the beginning of each government's term; 1949–90: appointed Members for Berlin excluded; 2002: two individual PDS Members (0.33 per cent) elected without recognised party status. *Abbreviations:* KPD: Kommunistische Partei Deutschlands; PDS: Partei des Demokratischen Sozialismus; GR: Grüne; B90: Bündnis 90; SPD: Sozialdemokratische Portei Deutschlands; FDP: Freie Demokratische Partei; CDU: Christlich Demokratische Union Deutschlands; CSU: Christlich-Soziale Union in Bayern; Z: Zentrum; GB/BHE: Gesamtdeutscher Block/Bund der Heimatlosen und Entrechteten; DP: Deutsche Partei; WAV: Wirtschaftliche Aufbau-Vereinigung; BP: Bayernpartei; NR: Nationale Rechte.

Sources: Saalfeld 2000a, pp. 41–3; Forschungsgruppe Wahlen 2002, p. 83.

Table 3.3. *Party system characteristics, 1949–2002*

Election	Number of parties in parliament	Effective number of parties in parliament (Laakso and Taagepera Index)	Share of anti-system parties	Aggregate volatility (Pedersen Index)
1949	9	3.99	4.9	
1953	5	2.77	0.0	19.3
1957	4	2.39	0.0	9.2
1961	3	2.51	0.0	14.3
1965	3	2.38	0.0	7.7
1969	3	2.24	0.0	6.7
1972	3	2.34	0.0	6.0
1976	3	2.31	0.0	4.1
1980	3	2.44	0.0	4.6
1983	4	2.51	0.0	8.4
1987	4	2.80	0.0	6.0
1990	5	2.65	0.0	9.1
1994	5	2.91	0.0	8.9
1998	5	2.90	0.0	8.4
2002	4	2.80	0.0	7.2

Notes: The PDS was counted as a party in parliament although it was not recognised as a full parliamentary party according to the Bundestag's rules of procedure in 1990 and 1994. The same is true for the group of the 'National Right' in the first Bundestag. It is contentious in the German debate whether the PDS should be considered an anti-system party opposed to liberal democracy. Since the Constitutional Court has not banned it, it is not treated as such, whereas the 'National Right' (including members of the Socialist Reich Party [SRP]) and the Communist Party (KPD) in the first Bundestag (1949–53) are treated as anti-system parties, because they were banned in 1952 and 1956 respectively.
Source: Calculated from Schindler 1983, pp. 34–9; 1994, pp. 80–2; Kürschners Volkshandbuch 1995, p. 37; Presse- und Informationsamt der Bundesregierung, 21 October 1998, p. 859; Saalfeld 1997, p. 68; Forschungsgruppe Wahlen 2002, p. 38.

The small numerical 'size' of the party system with two dominant and moderate centre-left and centre-right parties and a varying number of smaller parties has kept the number of 'partisan veto players' in government down to two. It also created favourable circumstances for stable coalition government (Laver and Schofield 1990, pp. 148–9). Some brief (usually transitory) interludes notwithstanding (for details see Saalfeld 2000a), the Federal Republic has almost constantly had two partisan veto players since 1957, as the federal cabinets have predominantly consisted of one of the two major parties, the CDU/CSU or SPD, plus one smaller party.

Despite the appearance of stability in terms of the number of partisan veto players, the 1983 elections brought 'a fundamental change in the dynamics of the party system at the federal level' (Lees 2001, p. 131). Although the FDP had defended its role as the party controlling the overall median legislator in the *Bundestag* in the 1983 elections, its role as 'kingmaker' choosing between the two major parties as coalition partners effectively ceased to exist (cf. Saalfeld 2002, p. 111). The rise of the Greens had weakened the SPD's presence in the *Bundestag* to such an extent that a social-liberal option was numerically no longer feasible. This development has arguably led to the emergence of a 'two-bloc' structure of a centre-left bloc of SPD and Greens on the one hand, and a centre-right alternative of CDU/CSU and FDP on the other, at least at national level. The FDP's attempt to regain its 'place in the sun' in the 2002 elections by boosting its own vote and keeping its coalition options open until after election day failed and was not endorsed as a credible strategy by the party's potential voters. Around two-thirds of all respondents to pre-election surveys in September 2002 preferred the party to commit itself unequivocally to a particular coalition partner (predominantly the CDU/CSU). In sum, therefore, coalition politics of two partisan veto players in the elected legislative chamber, the *Bundestag*, have remained the norm of the Federal Republic's politics, but the triangular structure of the period 1961–83 (as observed by Katzenstein in 1987) has effectively been replaced by a two-bloc structure. Coalition compromises between the two partisan veto players occur no longer in the ideological space between a major centre-right or centre-left party and the centrist FDP, but between two centre-left or, alternatively, two centre-right parties. This need not lead to less centrist and incremental policies, however, as the federal cabinets are constrained by their constituent parties' overall ideological position (which may – or may not – be centrist, see below) and the extent to which the ideological position of one of the opposition parties has to be accommodated during times when the majority of the *Bundesrat*, effectively the second legislative chamber at the national level, is not controlled by the governing parties.

Ideological Distance Between Partisan Veto Players

Tsebelis' (2002) veto players theory predicts that the ideological distance between partisan veto players is important for the government's ability to move the policy status quo, as long as there are at least two veto players.

In other words, even if there are a large number of partisan veto players, the impact of this number will remain relatively modest, as long as they have similar policy preferences. Tsebelis thus formalises the observation made by Katzenstein (1987) who argues that the ideological differences between the parties forming coalition cabinets in the Federal Republic have been relatively small given the fact that the centrist FDP usually coalesced with one of the major parties, which themselves were relatively centrist. Nevertheless, as Figure 3.1 demonstrates, there have been variations in the ideological proximity of coalition parties over time. Figure 3.1 and Table 3.4 need to be read together. The bar in the column marked '1949', for example, denotes the first coalition cabinet under Konrad Adenauer formed after the election in 1949. It consisted, as Table 3.4 indicates, of CDU/CSU, FDP and the German Party (DP), a conservative regional party in northern Germany, which was later largely absorbed by the CDU. Thus the coalition consisted of three veto players. The horizontal line delineates the political 'centre'. The length of the bar indicates the ideological distance between the (relatively speaking) most left–wing party in the coalition according to overall left–right scores extracted from the data provided by the Party Manifesto Group (Budge et al. 2001), the CDU/CSU, and the most right-wing party, the DP. It stretches from −11.56 on the left (CDU/CSU) to 28.57 on the right (DP).[4] Whatever reservations one might have about assigning labels such as 'left' and 'right' to aggregate manifesto data, there is little doubt that the scores reflect significant policy differences with a high degree of accuracy.

Figure 3.1 suggests that the ideological distance between the partisan veto players has tended to be relatively small since 1961, with the exception of the 1972 *Bundestag* where a move of the FDP to the right foreshadowed the difficulties the two coalition partners would encounter over economic policy in the following decade. In addition, the parties' positions remained close to the political centre. Thus, despite the

---

[4] This is not as implausible as it may appear at first glance, as the early CDU/CSU had relatively state-friendly and labour-friendly policies as far as the economy and the welfare state are concerned. The 1953 and 1957 elections saw a sharp move of the DP to the left. This is largely due to the 'saliency method' used by the Party Manifesto Group to construct the left–right indicators. An increased emphasis on welfare measures in support of ethnic German refugees and expellees from eastern European countries, a clientele courted by a number of right-wing parties in the early Federal Republic, meant that welfare measures became more salient in the DP's election manifesto, which is why it had a 'left-wing' score. Simultaneously, the CDU/CSU moved sharply to the right in the 1957 election campaign, especially as a result of its stance regarding rearmament and western integration, which was opposed by some of the nationalist 'right-wing' parties (formally moving their position towards a more 'left-wing' one), because it made reunification unlikely in an international environment increasingly influenced by the Cold War.

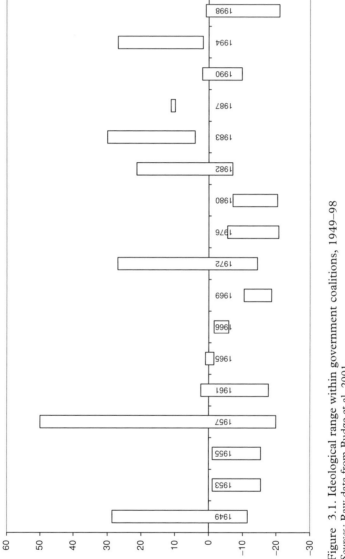

Figure 3.1. Ideological range within government coalitions, 1949–98
Sources: Raw data from Budge et al. 2001.

Table 3.4. *Overall ideological positions of parties in coalition cabinets, 1949–98 (based on overall ideological scores calculated from election manifestos)*

Year	Coalition cabinet	Greens	SPD	FDP	CDU/CSU	GB/BHE	DP
1949	CDU/CSU-FDP-DP		−18.37	**6.54**	**−11.56**		**28.57**
1953	CDU/CSU-FDP-DP-GB/BHE		−23.46	**−1.12**	**−6.61**	**−13.33**	**−15.48**
1955	CDU/CSU-FDP-DP		−23.46	**−1.12**	**−6.61**	−13.33	**−15.48**
1957	CDU/CSU-DP		−25.00	0.00	**50.00**		**−20.00**
1961	CDU/CSU-FDP		−2.91	**−17.76**	**2.33**		
1965	CDU/CSU-FDP		−5.92	**0.94**	**−1.60**		
1966	CDU/CSU-SPD		**−5.92**	0.94	**−1.60**		
1969	SPD/FDP		**−10.43**	**−18.67**	−5.08		
1972	SPD/FDP		**−14.44**	**26.92**	5.14		
1976	SPD/FDP		**−20.79**	**−5.53**	14.53		
1980	SPD/FDP		**−20.35**	**−7.13**	21.21		
1982	CDU/CSU-FDP		−20.35	**−7.13**	**21.21**		
1983	CDU/CSU-FDP	−24.39	−7.17	**4.00**	**29.93**		
1987	CDU/CSU-FDP	−22.97	−13.88	**11.22**	**9.89**		
1990	CDU/CSU-FDP	−15.97	−31.18	**1.89**	**−9.87**		
1994	CDU/CSU-FDP	−20.32	−18.15	**1.66**	**26.81**		
1998	SPD/Greens	**−21.00**	**0.87**	3.28	27.91		

Note: Government parties are highlighted in bold.
Source: Party policy positions from Budge et al. 2001.

appearance of the Greens and a certain re-polarisation of the party system since the early 1970s in general (Padgett 2000, pp. 60–1; Saalfeld 2002), moderate, ideologically compact centre-right and centre-left coalitions remained the norm of post-unification politics, as Figure 3.1 illustrates. In this sense, Katzenstein's (1987) analysis still holds to a large extent for the partisan veto players in the *Bundestag*. It follows from veto players theory that – *ceteris paribus* – the relatively small ideological distance between partisan veto players especially in the 1965, 1966, 1969 and 1987 coalitions would generally have facilitated changes to the status quo in policy-making. Indeed, the periods immediately following the formation of the 1966, 1969 and 1987 coalitions were characterised by strong reform drives. Generally, the small number of, and relatively small ideological distance between, partisan veto players should have facilitated changes in the policy status quo. However, the *ceteris paribus* assumption does not account for the role of the *Bundesrat* as institutional veto player during much of the Federal Republic's history.

The *Bundesrat* as an Institutional Veto Player, the Party System and 'Grand Coalition' Politics

The dimension 'party in public office' includes partisan conflict and co-operation in the *Bundesrat*, effectively the second legislative chamber. The interpenetration of party government, essentially based on a competitive 'logic', and a federal system strongly relying on negotiation and co-operation (even in the absence of consensus) has been identified as one of the problems of the Federal Republic's political system (Lehmbruch 1976; Katzenstein 1987; Scharpf 1988). Problems for policy innovation can arise, in particular, if the (usually) two partisan veto players in the elected chamber are joined by a third, institutional veto player, the *Bundesrat*. The *Bundesrat* becomes a veto player for laws requiring *Bundesrat* consent (*Zustimmungsgesetze*), when the parties forming the federal government do not control a majority in the *Bundesrat*.[5] In this case, the governing parties may need to win the support of (depending on the distribution of votes in the *Bundesrat*) at least one federal state (*Land*) government fully or partially controlled by one of the opposition parties. Not only is the number of veto players then increased by one, the ideological distance within the enlarged set of veto players is also likely to increase. The constitutional veto powers of the *Bundesrat*, especially in the case of 'consent laws', will then increase the scope for policy gridlock, or *Reformstau*. What is crucial here from a theoretical perspective is the importance of *party ideology* as a key variable influencing the scope for gridlock, although a territorial dimension (regional interests which are largely independent of party ideology and strategy) may also play an important role. The latter dimension is discussed in greater detail in chapter 4 of this volume.

Table 3.5 provides a numerical summary, and Figure 3.2 a visual breakdown, of the percentage of months the government parties on the one hand and the opposition party or parties on the other nominally controlled a majority of votes in the *Bundesrat* between September 1949 and September 2002. As Table 3.5 shows, in slightly less than one-third (200) of the 637 months in this period, the government parties nominally had control of a majority of the votes in the *Bundesrat*; in just less than one-quarter of the total time, the opposition party or parties nominally controlled the *Bundesrat*. 'Nominal' rather than 'real' control refers to the fact that, in practice, the national government parties may not be able to control the voting behaviour of 'friendly' federal states

---

[5] This does not necessarily mean that the *Bundesrat* is controlled by the opposition parties, however. A number of federal states may be governed by one or more of the national opposition parties plus one or more of the governing parties at the national level.

Table 3.5. *Majority of government and opposition parties in the* Bundesrat, *1949–2002*

Decade	Months with government parties controlling *Bundesrat* majority		Months with opposition parties controlling *Bundesrat* majority		Total months (100%)
	N	% of total	N	% of total	
1940–9	0	0.00	0	0.00	4
1950–9	2	1.67	0	0.00	120
1960–9	93	77.50	0	0.00	120
1970–9	0	0.00	76	63.33	120
1980–9	87	72.50	33	27.50	120
1990–9	18	15.00	36	30.00	120
2000–2	0	0.00	5	15.15	33
Total	200	31.40	150	23.55	637

Source: Calculated from Schindler 1999 and (for the period after 1996) various editions of *Zeitschrift für Parlamentsfragen.*

when territorial conflicts of interest between federation and federal states cut across party lines and the parliamentary government–opposition divide in the *Bundestag*. For 45 per cent of the time, the control of the *Bundesrat* was 'mixed'. 'Mixed' *Land* governments are those including at least one of the national government parties plus one of the national opposition parties, such as the SPD-CDU government formed in Brandenburg after the 1999 election in that state (cf. Figure 3.2). At that time the SPD was in government at the national level, whereas the CDU was in opposition. In such cases, the coalition agreements at *Land* level usually contain a 'coalition clause' setting out rules for the behaviour of the state in contested *Bundesrat* votes.[6]

A look at the changes per decade (Table 3.5 and Figure 3.2) demonstrates that the federal governments had long periods of control during the 1960s and 1980s, whereas the opposition party or parties nominally controlled a majority of the *Bundesrat* during substantial periods in the 1970s. When the *Bundesrat* is an institutional veto player, the ideological position of at least one of the national opposition parties will need to be taken into account, at least in the case of bills for which *Bundesrat* consent is mandatory. This need not always be the major opposition party (the SPD between January 1991 and September 1998 and the CDU/CSU since September 1998). Depending on the majorities, it

---

[6] The usual practice is that the respective federal state will abstain, if the coalition parties at the federal-state level cannot agree whether a government proposal should be accepted or rejected.

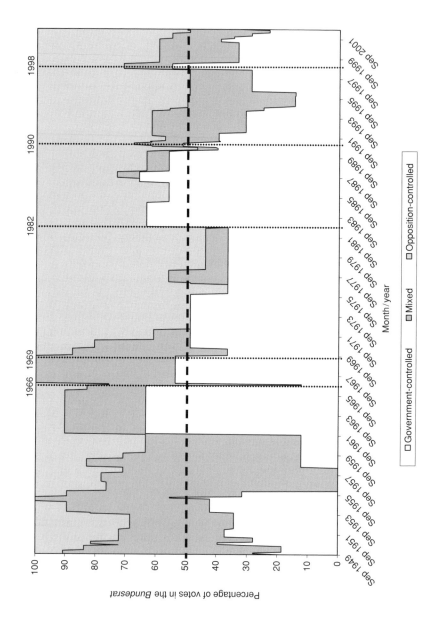

Figure 3.2. Numerical control of the *Bundesrat*, 1949–2002
Source: See Table 3.5.

may be sufficient for the federal government to sway a minor opposition party in a single federal state: for instance, the Schröder government persuaded the FDP in Rhineland-Palatinate, which was in a coalition with the SPD there, to support its citizenship bill in 1999 (see chapter 9, p. 207). In most cases, however, the federal government will have to take the preferences of the main opposition into account. For this reason, Manfred Schmidt (2002b) describes the Federal Republic as a 'grand coalition state', that is a state run by the two major German parties.

Figure 3.3 illustrates the increase of the ideological distance between veto players when the federal government formally loses control in the *Bundesrat*.[7] In March 1991, for example, the Kohl government lost its majority in the *Bundesrat*. The figure demonstrates the dramatic increase of the ideological distance between veto players as the overall ideological position of the SPD now had to be accommodated in controversial legislation requiring *Bundesrat* consent. The distance was reduced to the distance between the two government parties in October 1998 after the new SPD-Green cabinet under Gerhard Schröder had been sworn in. Once Schröder's government lost its majority in the *Bundesrat* in April 1999 (the formal election of a new CDU-FDP state government in Hesse replacing the previous SPD-Green coalition), the gap widened again as now the CDU/CSU's policy preferences had to be accommodated in important domestic legislation. This demonstrates that a loss of control in the *Bundesrat* may have significant consequences for the ideological distance between partisan and institutional veto players rendering changes in the policy status quo more difficult.

For much of the time since the publication of Katzenstein's (1987) book, policy-making in the Federal Republic has been characterised by the absence of government control of the *Bundesrat* and, therefore, by the de facto grand coalition structure observed by Manfred Schmidt (2002b), if and when the veto players act cohesively.

Cohesiveness

A further feature of the party system emphasised by veto players theory is the cohesiveness of political parties. Katzenstein (1987) recognised the

---

[7] The increasing ideological distance that needs to be bridged is represented by the lines in the graph assuming that the government parties have to accommodate the major opposition party of the time. Of course, it may be possible that the federal government needs to accommodate the position of a smaller opposition party, which may or may not be ideologically closer. Following the logic and argument of the 'grand coalition state' thesis (M. Schmidt 2002b), however, the ideological position of the major opposition party was used in the graph to illustrate the increase in the ideological distance between veto players.

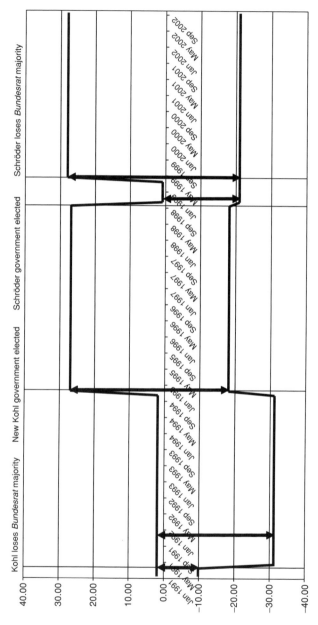

Figure 3.3. Ideological distance on a single left–right continuum with and without *Bundesrat* as institutional veto player, January 1991–September 2002
Sources: See Tables 3.4 and 3.5.

importance of this variable when referring, amongst others, to the internal structure of the Federal Republic's main parties. In this section it will be argued that – notwithstanding a voluminous literature on party change including the debate on 'electoral-professional' (Panebianco 1988) and 'cartel' parties (Katz and Mair 1995) – there is a great deal of continuity in the development of the Federal Republic's political parties as relatively cohesive organisations. Many of the changes reported in the recent literature pre-date the publication of Katzenstein's (1987) book and have been observed at least since the 1970s in the context of the consolidation and development of the 'catch-all' party model (von Beyme 2000). The parties' programmes, milieux, religious and class connotations have decreased in importance since the 1960s, while the 'proximity (or symbiosis) between the party establishment and the state' intensified (Puhle 2002, p. 71, see pp. 68–71). Campaigns have become more professionalised and centralised (cf. Padgett 2001). The internal weight of the 'party in public office' and the parliamentary parties has increased (Saalfeld 2002; generally in advanced industrial societies, see Katz and Mair 2002). Much of the evidence cited in the third section above suggests that the Federal Republic's parties in parliament (especially the centre-right and right-wing parties) have become more cohesive at the parliamentary level since the late 1960s.

Despite the decreasing reliance of the parties on mass membership and relatively long-term links with collateral organisations (such as trade unions and interest groups; see Poguntke 2002), party leaders in public office still need – and cultivate – organisations providing them with certain capabilities and resources such as: information about the electorate and their preferences; a 'brand name' potentially enhancing a political entrepreneur's legitimacy and credibility; mobilisation of supporters in elections and other campaigns; financial resources and economies of scale; and development and implementation of policy in various institutions to which the party gains access (cf. generally, Strøm and Müller 1999, pp. 14–15; Aldrich 1995).

This explains why the Federal Republic's catch-all parties – despite their developments of elements of electoral-professional and cartel parties – have sought to maintain relatively large membership parties and an extensive network of internal associations and groups. Poguntke (1994, pp. 211–12) therefore warns of 'attributing parties too hastily to the sphere of the state', despite the fact that the 'most conspicuous change over the past three decades has been a substantial loosening of ties between parties and society', indicated, for example, by lower membership numbers (cf. Saalfeld 2002) and looser ties with collateral organisations (Poguntke 2002).

In their internal life, German parties have been compared with the 'garbage-can model' in organisational research (von Alemann 2000, p. 126) referring to a considerable amount of organisational complexity and, as Wiesendahl (2000) maintains, 'organisational anarchy'. Article 21 of the Basic Law stipulates that parties must have a vertical, democratic organisation which ensures a chain of delegation from the grass-roots organisations to the national leadership, independent arbitration, accountability of elected party leaders to party conferences and a strong regional decentralisation of the parties (von Alemann 2000, p. 128). In all parties, power is further decentralised by the elaborate system of associations (referred to as *Vereinigungen* in the two major parties) representing specific socio-economic interests (for example, young members, students, women, employees, retired people, small business, farmers), policy-related working groups (*Arbeitsgemeinschaften*) dealing with issues such as local government, agricultural policy or various aspects of welfare policy. The associations within, and the parliamentary representatives of, the main parties are often closely linked with important interest groups. Especially in the two major parties, Germany's plurality of interest groups is, therefore, reflected within the parties and has continued to favour centrist policies, although the power of the trade unions, in particular, has been weakened in both the CDU/CSU and SPD since the 1990s (Trampusch 2003a, p. 22).

Poguntke (1994, p. 210), therefore, describes German parties as organisations characterised by 'horizontal and vertical fragmentation', arguing that they 'are closer to a stratarchic than to an oligarchic model' and that they are, 'as a result of the extensive legal regulation of party politics . . . also fairly similar as regards the main structure of their hierarchy of decision making bodies'. This internal decision-making structure has persisted. Even party leaders with strong electoral appeal cannot survive in office and implement reform policies if they cannot generate a broad consensus within their parties, especially amongst mid-level party elites in the various associations and regional organisations. The fall of Helmut Schmidt in 1982 is a case in point (Jäger and Link 1987, pp. 201–21). Gerhard Schröder's effort to generate such a consensus within his party for reforms of labour-market and welfare policies in April/May 2003 provides a further example of the importance government leaders place on the consensus within their own parties. In other words, the cohesiveness of the Federal Republic's parties cannot be taken for granted by party leaders. It has to be achieved through persuasion, negotiation and compromise, which, as far as the two major parties are concerned, favours the persistence of a politically centrist status quo.

Unification has generally not reduced the cohesiveness of the Federal Republic's parties significantly. The western German parties managed to extend their organisations to the east. A number of prominent party leaders in eastern Germany were imports from the west. Empirical studies have not found a new west–east cleavage in parliamentary voting behaviour as far as recorded votes are concerned (Saalfeld 1995). With the exception of the PDS, the parties in eastern Germany are weak in terms of membership and organisation (Saalfeld 2002), which means that their 'weight' within the all-German parties is relatively low. They rely more heavily on prominent candidates than do their western German counterparts and are even more vulnerable to short-term issues in the run-up to elections.

One attempt to reconcile these divergent observations – the co-existence of centralisation at the level of the parties in public office and continued decentralisation of intra-party decision-making – is Wiesendahl's (2000, p. 120) argument that German parties are 'organised anarchies' comprising 'two incompatible organisational spheres, each with their independent rationales, resources and routines. The two spheres are prevented from clashing by loose coupling [of a] pre-modern membership party at the ground and the modernised electoral professional service party at the top'. This, combined with the proximity between party establishments and state and the delaying or blunting of electoral sanctions, 'may eventually limit the parties' capabilities for reform and their effectiveness as mediators, and favour corruption, clientelism, and lack of imagination' (Puhle 2002, p. 71). Yet, the decentralised system of intra-organisational bargaining may also have positive effects as it can facilitate intra-organisational learning through the diffusion of successful practices, which have been tried at lower, or other, levels of the organisation (e.g. Schmid 1990).

Party politics plays an important role in the composition of the *Bundesrat*. In some of the literature, there is a tendency to describe the *Bundesrat* as an institutional veto player whenever the parties forming the federal government do not control an outright majority there. Yet, the oppositional parties in the *Bundesrat* are by no means always in control or always cohesive as *Land* interests may conflict with the interests of the national parties. Table 3.5 (see p. 63) provides information on the share of *Bundesrat* votes the parties included in the federal government controlled in the *Bundesrat* between 1949 and September 2002 (by decade). The table demonstrates the low levels of even nominal government control since the beginning of the 1990s and, more importantly in the context of cohesiveness of veto players, the great numerical importance of the votes of the 'mixed' federal states between 1949 and the early

1970s and since 1990, in other words, those periods when the *Bundesrat* was controlled by neither the government nor the opposition. In a wider historical perspective the clear confrontation between government and opposition observed by Katzenstein (1987) appears to have been an aberration of the 1970s and 1980s. At any rate, the confrontation between national government and national opposition parties in the *Bundesrat* is not always clear-cut, and the lack of a clear government–opposition pattern in the *Bundestag* has increased as a result of party system change following unification, which has extended the SPD's range of coalition options in eastern Germany and nationally. This means, however, that there is considerable scope for the federal government to exploit the presence of a significant number of votes from 'mixed' states, that is, a lack of cohesiveness of the *Bundesrat* as an institutional veto player, even if the government does not control a majority in this chamber and if it chooses to change the status quo in a policy area where *Bundesrat* consent is mandatory. This theme is discussed further in chapter 4 (pp. 91–2), but suffice it to say that a large number of case studies demonstrate that federal governments under Kohl and Schröder have learnt how to use this room for manoeuvre, although their ability to do so may depend on the electoral cycle (cf. Zohlnhöfer 2000, p. 724; also König 1998, p. 486; Krause-Burger 2000, pp. 122–7).

The Changing Electorate: Increasing Uncertainty in the Bargaining Environment

Elected politicians can be modelled as actors attempting to maximise three different kinds of benefits: (1) the number of votes for themselves and/or their parties at elections, (2) private benefits from government office and (3) influence on public policy. These goals are often not entirely compatible, hence difficult choices and trade-offs may be necessary. Although party leaders may primarily value office benefits, which they can convert into private goods, their organisations' activists will not nominate them if they neglect policy, and they will not be elected if they do not care for votes and their voters' policy preferences (Müller and Strøm 1999, p. 14). Since both the ability to control policy-making and the attainment of elected office largely depend on votes, electoral considerations and strategies must be taken into account when seeking to explain the persistence of status quo policies in the Federal Republic. This aspect is sometimes not given sufficient weight in policy studies of an institutionalist nature emphasising the structural aspects of the policy process. It will be argued in this section that three electoral factors

constrain the main parties' abilities to depart from the status quo in key
policy areas: (1) the centrism and status quo orientation of large parts of
the Federal Republic's electorate and (2) the increasing amount of
electoral uncertainty in general, which is (3) exacerbated by the fre-
quency of regional electoral contests with increasing levels of volatility (and, hence, uncertainty) and far-reaching implications for
policy-making at the national level.

Figure 3.4 demonstrates that the voters' preferences have remained
centrist in the 1990s. The raw data were taken from the ALLBUS survey
(1996). The figure plots the self-placement of a representative sample of
German voters in 1996 on a left–right scale from one (extreme left) to
ten (extreme right) distinguishing between western and eastern
Germans. The preferences in both parts of the country constitute a
relatively symmetric unimodal distribution with the scale's middle value
of five as the mode and a slightly positive skew, which is stronger in the
eastern part of the country. This will continue to create electoral incentives for centrist policies on the part of vote-seeking and office-seeking

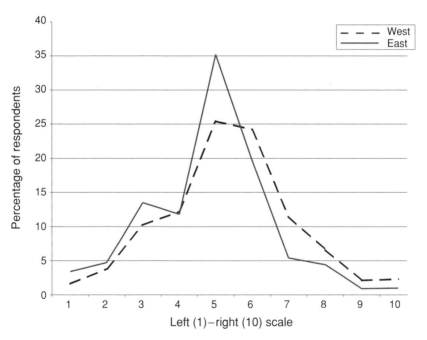

Figure 3.4. Left–right preference distribution in the German
population, 1996
Source: Calculated from ALLBUS 1996.

parties. There is no significant demand for extreme left-wing or extreme right-wing policies, which explains why populist parties challenging the centrist consensus from the right have depended on protest votes for some sporadic regional successes, and why the PDS does not have a realistic option to present itself as a radical alternative challenging the status quo from the left.

Although Franke's (2003, p. 25) claim of a general left-wing bias in the preference distribution of German voters is borne out only by the eastern German data summarised in Figure 3.4, he is still persuasive in concluding that the main political parties have very strong electoral incentives to integrate politically centrist voters with predominantly welfarist political preferences. Reforms of the welfare systems aiming at the reduction or liberalisation of services carry a high risk of immediate electoral penalties in exchange for uncertain long-term benefits (Franke 2003, p. 26). The Federal Republic differs from the Anglo-Saxon democracies in this respect. An international comparison of popular attitudes towards the role of government in securing the welfare of people in 1992 demonstrates that West German and Norwegian voters are far more supportive of a strong role of the government in reducing income differences, providing jobs for all and providing a basic income than those in Australia and the United States (Matheson and Wearing 1999, pp. 141–9).[8] Given those expectations, the potential electoral costs facing a German government in reforms reducing the level of welfare are relatively high in international comparison.

Despite the overall centrism of the electorate, the supporters of different parties have different preference distributions on economic and welfare issues (Table 3.6). The 1996 ALLBUS survey includes questions about people's voting intentions and their attitude towards two fundamental issues of economic and welfare policy: for example, their preference for a reduction of taxes over increased welfare spending or vice versa. Overall, 43.5 per cent of the respondents favoured a reduction of taxes over an increase in welfare spending, whereas 29.6 per cent expressed the reverse preference order. About one-quarter was undecided. Amongst the voters of the CDU/CSU, FDP and Republikaner party there was a clear preponderance of those favouring the lowering of taxes. Amongst PDS voters, there was a clear preponderance of those favouring increased spending on welfare programmes. The supporters of SPD and Greens were split. Overall, therefore, the electoral costs of

---

[8] Earlier empirical investigations (e.g. Bean 1991; Papadakis 1993) demonstrate that these cross-national differences had been relatively stable since the 1980s.

Table 3.6. *Preferences for taxation and welfare spending, 1996 (broken down by voting intention and region)*

Voting intention	Reduce taxes	Increase welfare spending	Cannot tell
Federal Republic			
CDU/CSU	53.70	22.00	22.10
SPD	42.50	34.50	21.50
FDP	62.60	19.90	17.00
Greens	37.00	39.80	19.90
Republikaner	61.20	20.40	18.40
PDS	23.00	48.40	28.60
Total	43.50	29.60	24.70
Western *Länder*			
CDU/CSU	59.50	16.80	21.50
SPD	47.90	29.70	20.80
FDP	69.90	16.30	13.30
Greens	37.60	39.10	19.00
Republikaner	73.00	16.20	10.80
PDS	14.30	57.10	28.60
Total	50.70	23.40	23.40
Eastern *Länder*			
CDU	38.10	35.80	23.70
SPD	29.20	46.20	23.10
FDP	32.50	35.00	32.50
Greens	34.90	42.20	22.90
Republikaner	25.00	33.30	41.70
PDS	23.50	47.90	28.60
Total	28.00	42.80	27.60

Source: Calculated from ALLBUS 1996 (ZA No. 2800, V409 and V327).

reducing taxes at the expense of welfare spending would seem to be highest for the SPD, Greens and PDS.

Attitudinal and behavioural changes in the electorate have further increased the uncertainties and risks in the parties' electoral environment since the 1980s with significant potential implications for bargaining processes within and between parties. In a comparative study, Dalton (2000, pp. 25–33) found that the percentage of German citizens identifying with a political party or strongly identifying with a political party decreased significantly between 1972 and 1998. The Federal Republic is no exception to a general trend found in most advanced industrial societies. In the Federal Republic, signs of a significant drop in partisanship had first been discovered in the 1980s, but the trend became more pronounced in the elections of the 1990s (Dalton 2000). In the western part of the Federal Republic, the accelerated decrease of partisanship in the 1990s was particularly strong amongst younger and better-educated voters. The aggregate decline of party identification can be said to have accelerated through unification, as eastern German voters' attachments to (apart from the PDS, predominantly 'western') political parties have generally been lower than in the west (Roth and Jung 2002, pp. 15–17).

The main behavioural consequence of declining party identification has been higher electoral volatility. While *aggregate* volatility (that is, the average change in party vote shares between adjacent elections)[9] has increased since the early 1980s, it has remained below the levels observed between 1949 and 1961 (Table 3.3; see p. 57). Yet, volatility at the *individual level*, that is, the propensity of individual voters to switch parties, has increased significantly, especially since the 1990s, and makes German voters less reliable and predictable from the parties' perspective. Harald Schoen and Jürgen Falter (2001) demonstrate on the basis of panel data that over 30 per cent of the western German and nearly 40 per cent of the eastern German respondents said they had switched between parties from 1994 to 1998. Individual volatility was by no means limited to changes within the 'camps' of the government and opposition parties (in other words, exchanges of voters between CDU/CSU and FDP on the one hand and SPD and Greens on the other). Schoen and Falter estimate that over 18 per cent of the western Germans and nearly 15 per cent of the eastern Germans switched between government and opposition parties (in both directions) in September 1998, that is, from CDU/CSU or FDP to SPD or Greens, or vice versa. A similar picture could be observed in the 2002 election (Roth and Jung 2002, pp. 15–17) with strong evidence that volatility is particularly high in the eastern part of the Federal Republic where longer-term party identification is generally weaker and voters respond more strongly to candidate evaluations and short-term issues on the political agenda (Arzheimer and Falter 2002, pp. 30–3).

In the eastern parts of the Federal Republic this is a result of the fact that the largely superimposed party system has not 'bedded down' since unification. Party identification is lower. Yet, increases in electoral volatility are not restricted to the new *Länder*. The gradual erosion of the traditional electoral support bases of the two major parties has continued also in the west. The most important social cleavages in post-war German voting behaviour, class and religion, have continued to decrease

---

[9] The aggregate volatility ('Pedersen Index') is calculated as follows: $V_t = TNC_t/2$, where V_t is the aggregate volatility at time t and TNC_t is the total net change of the votes all parties have received in the election at time t (cf. Pedersen 1979).

in importance as the main parties' traditional socio-economic and religious support groups have declined in size: practising Roman Catholics for the CDU/CSU and unionised working-class voters for the SPD (Arzheimer and Falter 2002, p. 31; Roth and Jung 2002, pp. 16–17).

As chapter 1 of this volume has already indicated, the effect of this growing electoral uncertainty is amplified by the frequent occurrence of regional elections with significant consequences for national politics. Not only do incumbent federal governments face voters every four years, but there is a constant stream of *Land* elections in the period between national elections. On average, there are four *Land* elections per year, which often have (at least partially) the character of a mid-term vote on the national government's record (Franke 2003, p. 27). These elections have a decisive impact, first, on the parties' access to public office in the federal states and, second, on the composition of the *Bundesrat* as a de facto second legislative chamber. Empirical research on the precise interaction between national and regional motives in the voters' behaviour is somewhat inconclusive (cf. Jeffery and Hough 2001, p. 93; Decker and von Blumenthal 2002, p. 164). It may be sufficient in our context to highlight that – because of the large number of important *Land* elections following national elections – federal governments have very little 'breathing space' to carry out unpopular measures and very little time to persuade electorates. Electoral penalties can follow very quickly.

In combination, these electoral incentives and uncertainties constitute formidable obstacles for the main parties in changing the status quo in policy terms. Growing volatility can be expected to lead to a larger degree of electoral uncertainty in the bargaining environment that the political parties face in coalition formation. This may lead to a reduced ability, and willingness, to accept the possible short-term electoral costs of reform programmes. A more uncertain electoral environment can thus be expected to have a negative impact on cabinet stability and party co-operation which has been central to the consensual policy style associated with the Federal Republic's 'grand coalition state' (M. Schmidt 2002b). In a strategic environment characterised by a high degree of electoral uncertainty, the costs of co-operation and the incentives for coalition termination for the sake of short-term electoral gain may be considerable, and there may be fewer incentives for the parties to compromise in policy terms (the theoretical underpinnings of this argument can be found in Lupia and Strøm 1995; Mershon 1999). The bargaining environment becomes tougher and resembles more a one-shot 'Prisoners' Dilemma' than a situation characterised by a high degree of electoral certainty, repeated interaction and incentives for the parties to engage in long-term co-operation, for example through deferred reciprocal compensation (cf., generally, Sartori 1987, p. 229; Scharpf 1997, pp. 128–30).

Conclusions

The fundamentals of the Federal Republic's party system and 'grand coalition structures' have remained remarkably stable considering the 'exogenous shock' of unification and also when compared with the dramatic changes of some party systems in other advanced industrial societies (witness for example Italy, or the spectacular rise of populist right-wing parties in a number of European democracies). Two-party, ideologically compact and centrist minimal-winning coalitions, based on politically moderate centre-left and centre-right parties, persist. Although the FDP has lost its pivotal function in the 1980s and the dynamics of the German coalition system have moved from a triangular to a two-bloc structure, the distribution of electoral preferences and the pluralism within both major parties has continued to create powerful incentives for centrist policies. Thus, a decade after publication of *Politics and Policy in West Germany*, Katzenstein (1997b, pp. 37–8) argues that coalition government and co-operative patterns across the government–opposition 'divide' have remained a crucial node in the policy process:

at both federal and *Länder* levels, the German state pools the powers of different coalition governments. The logic of coalition government is reflected also in the relations between the *Bundesrat* and the *Bundestag*. Political parties are themselves often statist in outlook, illustrated, for example, in their dependence on public funds . . . With or without the Free Democratic Party (FDP), Germany's party system is likely to continue the practice of coalition government and loyal opposition.

Parties have remained a crucial node in the Federal Republic's policy process. If we use Tsebelis' (2002) veto players model as an organising framework, the number of partisan veto players has remained constant since the mid-1980s, as has the ideological distance between them. *Ceteris paribus*, these observations would not seem to make policy gridlock inevitable. Yet, as Katzenstein suggested in 1987, the interpenetration of federalism and party government and the possibility for the opposition to block government initiatives in the *Bundesrat*, if they require *Bundesrat* consent and if the government does not control a majority of votes in the *Bundesrat*, exacerbates the tendency of the German policy process towards incrementalism. If and when the *Bundesrat* has veto powers, the ideological distance between veto players increases sharply.

At the same time, Tsebelis (2002) emphasises the importance of the cohesiveness of a veto player. Although the federal governments have usually not been able to 'control' a majority in the *Bundesrat* since unification in 1990, the *Bundesrat* majority has been far from cohesive. The heavy dependence of some poorer federal states on federal government support and the fact that many government coalitions in the federal states cut across the government–opposition divide at the national level has opened up strategic opportunities for federal governments. The latter have learnt to exploit these opportunities. The federal government's powers are also enhanced by its ability to set the policy agenda, for example by determining the timing of legislative proposals and formulating bills in a way that means that they (or important parts of them) do not require *Bundesrat* consent (cf. Zohlnhöfer 2003, p. 14).

Nevertheless, if and when the federal government does not control a majority in the *Bundesrat* and electoral competition between the major parties is intense, there is scope for gridlock and the results of the present chapter support the argument advanced in the Introduction to this volume, suggesting that the political and policy environment in which the Federal Republic's decision-makers operate has changed to an extent that the successful role of parties as nodes in the policy process observed until the 1970s must be seen in a more sceptical light today. Although Katzenstein (1987, p. 350) warns that it 'is easy to mistake incremental change for an incapacity to change', he does point out critically that 'it is possible that the incremental policy changes which have resulted from West Germany's political structures may, for a variety of reasons, have been more appropriate to the economic and social conditions of the 1970s than of the 1980s' (Katzenstein 1987, p. 5).

One of the main issues highlighted in this chapter is, however, that – in addition to the structural attributes of the party system – the 'electoral connection' is crucial for an understanding of the persistence of status quo policies. The Federal Republic's voter is centrist and supportive of the post-war policy status quo. Together with the greater propensity of voters to penalise 'their' parties and the greater electoral uncertainty faced by the parties, this has created incentives for parties to avoid necessary but unpopular reforms, as they would almost certainly involve short-term electoral costs in return for very uncertain long-term benefits. Such considerations have become more important as parties have attempted to maintain two different 'spheres', following Wiesendahl (2000) – the governmental and the membership spheres – through 'loose coupling'. The weakening links between party leaderships and civil society may indeed, as Puhle (2002, p. 71) puts it, 'limit the parties' capacities for reform and their effectiveness as mediators', persuading the German public of the necessity of policy change.

4   Federalism: the New Territorialism

Charlie Jeffery

Introduction: Federalism in Katzenstein's *Policy and Politics in West Germany*

Peter Katzenstein's treatment of federalism in *Policy and Politics in West Germany* (1987) was one of the classic accounts of co-operative federalism. It built on, reconciled and took forward what had hitherto been the pioneering texts: Fritz Scharpf et al. (1976) on *Politikverflechtung*, the interlocking of tiers of government in the policy process; and Gerhard Lehmbruch's *Parteienwettbewerb im Bundesstaat*, which explored how the dynamics of multi-tiered party competition could produce an equally interlocked 'all-party proportional government' through the interaction of different party majorities in *Bundestag* and *Bundesrat* (Lehmbruch 1976, p. 168). The arguments in Scharpf and Lehmbruch ran along parallel and largely unconnected trajectories. Parties did not really figure in Scharpf; Lehmbruch did not immerse himself in the institutional detail of the policy-making process. Each provided a brilliant but partial account. Katzenstein provided the linkage.

This linkage came in the juxtaposition of a 'decentralised state' with a 'centralised society' (Katzenstein 1987, p. 15). The decentralised state was a multifaceted antidote to Hitler. It was manifested in a strong Constitutional Court, the sectorised and regionalised operation of the civil service, ministerial autonomy under the *Ressortprinzip*, but above all federalism. West German federalism evolved in a way which was unusual. The division of powers was primarily functional, separating responsibilities for legislation, which was mainly carried out at the federal level, and implementation, which was mainly the responsibility of the *Länder* governments. This legislation–implementation split created an interlocking of tiers which was played out in the unique institution of the *Bundesrat*, a forum of *Länder* governments embedded in the federal legislative process. A series of constitutional amendments in 1969–70 elevated interlocked politics to a new plane by introducing federation–*Länder* joint policy planning and financing procedures

(*Gemeinschaftsaufgaben*, or Joint Tasks) for a series of high-cost policy fields for which the *Länder* were constitutionally responsible, but had insufficient financial capacity to modernise. These included regional economic development, coastal defences and university construction. Parallel reforms to territorial financial arrangements gave interlocking politics underpinning through the shared allocation of resources. *Despite* federalism – typically associated with territorial diversity of social preferences and differentiation of policy outcomes – the West German policy-making process ensured that more or less uniform standards of policy provision were delivered across the whole of West Germany.

The main message of Katzenstein's book was about the West German tendency to incremental policy change (or, more precisely, it set out to explain the failure of Helmut Kohl's *Wende*, after thirteen years of an SPD–FDP government, to deliver any notable and enduring changes in the substance of West German policy). Federalism, as Scharpf (1988) had made clear, was one of the main contributing factors, in particular through the 'joint-decision trap', the pathological tendency of joint decision-making procedures with high consensus requirements, such as the Joint Tasks, to inhibit policy adaptation to new circumstances.

But it was also the interaction of the federal state with the 'centralised society' which embedded the tendency to incremental change. West German society had a relatively simple pattern of social cleavages (as compared, say, with the Weimar Republic), and these were articulated and organised through a relatively small number of political parties. The party system was ideologically 'truncated' by the dual aversion to the ideas of the far right (as symbolised in the memory of the Third Reich) and the far left (as manifested in the German Democratic Republic). As a result, all significant parties were consensually oriented on a 'politics of centrality' (Smith 1976). They also organised and maintained a fairly stable pattern of nationwide support. There was one apparent exception, the Christian Social Union (CSU) in Bavaria. However, the CSU stood for election only in Bavaria while its 'big sister' party, the Christian Democratic Union (CDU), stood everywhere but in Bavaria; and the two together formed a joint parliamentary party in the *Bundestag* and jointly co-ordinated their priorities in the *Bundesrat*.

Put another way, there was only a highly limited territorial dimension to political discourse and party competition. The terms of partisan debate were uniform across tiers. The result – *pace* Lehmbruch – was that the CDU/CSU (or SPD) in the *Bundestag* and the CDU/CSU (or the SPD) in the *Bundesrat* were different manifestations of the same disciplined party-political organisations, despite being the products of different electoral processes. The effect, as Katzenstein (1987, p. 35) put it, was 'centripetal'. Combined with interlocking, co-operative federalism, the result was (Jeffery 1999, p. 138):

1 that all major party-political and federal-institutional actors were significantly involved in decision-making on most major issues;
2 that the boundaries between the federal level and the *Länder* and between the two party alignments were blurred; and
3 that decision-making (as a result) arose from multiple and simultaneous interactions along both the federal–*Länder* and party-political dimensions.

In these circumstances the number of potential veto points was inevitably high. It was unsurprising that the net effect was to inhibit significant policy change.

Federal systems have, broadly speaking, been more malleable elsewhere. One of Katzenstein's (implicit) reference points in discussing the factors underlying West German incrementalism was the United States. President Ronald Reagan's 'new federalism' in the 1980s had the purpose of disentangling the (much milder) US version of interlocking politics, cutting back the scope of uniform, federation-wide regulation, and allowing new room for policy innovation and variation in the states. This 'disentanglement' process has let loose a debate on how far the states are capable of acting as 'laboratories of democracy' (Osborne 1988), with fifty different locations for policy-making opening up space for a competition of ideas, facilitating innovation and helping to tailor policy outputs better to different territorial preferences (Jeffery 2002a, pp. 177–9).

The USA has not been alone in decentralising policy responsibilities. Canada also went through a period of disentanglement in the 1990s as fiscal crisis at the federal level led to withdrawal from a welter of joint funding arrangements, especially in social policy and education, which had been built up since the Second World War. A by-product, again, was greater scope for province-to-province diversity in public policy. More recent federation-making processes such as those in Belgium, Spain and, arguably, the UK have also had the purpose and effect of reducing the scope of nationwide policy standards in favour of greater territorial diversity (cf. de Rynck 2002; Moreno 2003; Adams and Robinson 2002). However, as Katzenstein (1987, p. 45) put it, because of the centripetal forces of co-operative federalism and the dynamics of territorially undifferentiated party competition, such 'far-reaching policy initiatives . . . which would place more responsibility back in the hands of state governments would not be possible in the Federal Republic'.

One could add that, unlike the cases noted above, there was in West Germany no noticeable demand anyway for a disentanglement of the policy process and for territorial differentiation of policy standards (cf. Grube 2001). Indeed, West Germans wanted what the Basic Law, in Article 72, said they should have: a 'uniformity of living conditions throughout the federal territory'. There was a much stronger normative commitment to equity and uniform standards than to the expression of territorial diversity. Significantly, as Katzenstein stressed (1987, pp. 46–8), this commitment to uniformity led the *Länder* to seek common nationwide standards even in areas where they had the possibility – i.e. under their exclusive legislative competence – to tailor-make their own distinctive standards, the classic example being the *Kultusministerkonferenz*, the Standing Conference of Ministers of Culture, which co-ordinates education-policy standards across the *Länder*.

Unification and the Decentralising Society

Almost twenty years on from *Policy and Politics*, what has changed?

Most obviously, it is harder now to see the post-unity Federal Republic as a 'centralised society'. The relative social homogeneity of the pre-unity Federal Republic has been riven by new patterns of territorial diversity. Most immediately this new diversity is about eastern Germany. Any perfunctory trawl through the relevant socio-economic indicators, such as those on GDP per capita and unemployment in Table 4.1, confirms the obvious: the objective needs of east Germans are different from those of west Germans. Overlying this is a collective sense of difference, an east German identity whose roots lie in the GDR past, and which has been recast and reaffirmed by the material dislocation of the post-unity era (Hough 2002, pp. 77–80). The net outcome is the emergence of eastern Germany as a 'space' for a distinctive territorial politics – more egalitarian, more statist – than in the west (Hough 2002, pp. 106–7).

But the territorial impact of unification cannot be limited just to an east–west dimension. Measures taken to address the socio-economic needs of the east – higher taxation generally, higher equalisation transfers within the federal system more specifically – have heightened territorial sensitivities about the allocation of resources. An era of budgetary restraint has added spice to the mix. Debate about the costs and benefits of social equity has become more vivid and, in part, polarised between donors and recipients. The figures on horizontal fiscal equalisation in Table 4.1 make the point clearly enough: over € 7.5 billion were transferred directly from richer to poorer *Länder* – the latter not just in the

Table 4.1. *Economic disparities among the German* Länder, *2001*

Land	GDP per head (€ thousand)	Unemployment rate (%)	Horizontal equalisation transfers (€ million)
Baden-Württemberg	28.75	4.9	−2,132
Bavaria	29.22	5.3	−2,298
Berlin	22.39	16.1	+2,654
Brandenburg	16.27	17.4	+500
Bremen	33.92	12.4	+402
Hamburg	42.88	8.3	−266
Hesse	30.56	6.6	−2,622
Lower Saxony	22.63	9.1	+954
Mecklenburg-Western Pomerania	16.29	18.3	+436
North Rhine-Westphalia	25.52	8.8	−269
Rhineland-Palatinate	22.75	6.8	+231
Saarland	22.96	9.0	+146
Saxony	16.79	17.5	+1,036
Saxony-Anhalt	16.18	19.7	+595
Schleswig-Holstein	22.57	8.4	+59
Thuringia	16.41	15.3	+575
Germany	25.08	9.4	±7,588

Note: Horizontal equalisation transfers are paid by *Länder* with above-average fiscal capacity to *Länder* with below-average fiscal capacity, with the aim of ensuring that all end up with at least 95 per cent of the average.
Sources: Statistisches Bundesamt at http://www.destatis.de/jahrbuch/jahrtab1.htm, http://www.destatis.de/jahrbuch/jahrtab13.htm, http://www.destatis.de/jahrbuch/jahrtab65.htm, http://www.destatis.de/basis/d/fist/fist023.htm, accessed on 19 August 2003.

east – in 2001 (cf. also the discussion in chapter 2 in this volume, pp. 39–43).

In these circumstances, rhetoric about 'our money' has in some places come to resonate strongly with territorial identity. Bavaria is the most obvious example. Bavaria shared Margaret Thatcher's response to German unification: 'Germany got bigger, but we didn't.' Being a smaller part of a larger, unified Germany has reduced Bavaria's 'weight' in the federal system. Unification has also increased Bavaria's obligations (Germany also 'got poorer', but Bavaria didn't: after unification Germany's average GDP per capita fell, widening the gap between affluent Bavaria and the average). It is no surprise in these circumstances that in Bavaria discourses of regional distinctiveness – based in traditions of statehood, political Catholicism and agrarian nostalgia – have become more prominent and have been instrumentalised as an argument for greater autonomy and self-reliance (or, in other words, less solidarity with the rest).

Other *Länder* – particularly those with better economic situations – have also, though less vigorously, hopped on the bandwagon of territorial politics. They have received (perhaps not always intended) support from their electorates. One thing that has become clearly evident since unification is the inability of the German political parties to renew their earlier status as institutions of nationwide integration. There is clearly an east–west dimension at play here. Only the CDU and SPD can generate an appeal which is broadly equivalent on both sides of the old east–west border (and even they are vulnerable to radical fluctuations in the east). The PDS is clearly a party of east German regionalism, while the Greens and the FDP are effectively restricted to their west German heartlands (though the FDP has more recently shown some signs of growing strength in the east).

But there is also a more general breakdown of the earlier, fairly predictable relationship between party competition at the federal level and party competition in the *Länder*. Pre-unity there existed a classic electoral cycle in which *Land* elections in mid-term were used as vehicles to 'punish' the (largest partner in the) federal-level coalition. This cycle seems to have broken down since unification. The main federal opposition party now gets punished as much as the main government party, and the beneficiaries tend to be fringe parties, often with a *Land*-specific identity (Jeffery and Hough 2001, pp. 86–94). Voting behaviour in *Land* elections displays wide variations from the pattern of voting behaviour in *Bundestag* elections in the same *Land*. Those variations have grown notably since unification, as Table 4.2 confirms.

Table 4.2 sets out indices of 'dissimilarity' for each *Land*. The indices measure the difference in votes cast for all the parties in a *Land* election as compared with the votes cast in that *Land* in the nearest *Bundestag* election. They are rough-and-ready measures of how far voters come to their decisions in federal and *Land* elections according to different criteria. In all but two western *Länder*, dissimilarity has grown since unification, and in all but one eastern *Land*, dissimilarity levels are high.[1] Voters do seem now to be coming to their voting decisions in *Land* elections in ways increasingly different from those in federal elections.

---

[1] These exceptions have simple explanations. Lower Saxony and Saarland were the fiefdoms of the two most prominent SPD politicians of the 1990s, Gerhard Schröder and Oskar Lafontaine, and, in the run-up to the change of federal government in 1998, became focal points for nationwide debate about the SPD. And Mecklenburg-Western Pomerania has held its elections on the same day as federal elections, which inevitably closes the dissimilarity 'gap'.

Table 4.2. *Indices of dissimilarity between federal and* Land *elections in Germany*

Land	Pre-1990	Post-1990
Baden-Württemberg	7.9	11.3
Bavaria	7.0	8.1
Bremen	10.4	14.9
Hamburg	9.9	18.6
Hesse	7.7	9.8
Lower Saxony	8.2	7.1
North Rhine-Westphalia	6.2	9.0
Rhineland-Palatinate	6.8	11.0
Saarland	10.8	8.5
Schleswig-Holstein	8.9	11.8
Berlin		14.2
Brandenburg		11.5
Mecklenburg-Western Pomerania		5.5
Saxony		16.0
Saxony-Anhalt		16.2
Thuringia		13.4
Federal Republic	8.4	11.7

Source: Hough and Jeffery 2003.

Put another way, there has been a growing 'territorialisation' of political discourse and party competition. This has necessitated innovation in coalition formation. Often the particular pattern of voting makes it impossible to build *Land* government coalitions which are 'congruent' with the standard party formations at national level: SPD-Green and CDU-FDP. The inclusion of 'outsiders' as coalition partners – e.g. the PDS, which in mid-2004 was in government with the SPD in Berlin and Mecklenburg-Western Pomerania, or the populist *Schill-Partei*, which coalesced for a time with the CDU and FDP in Hamburg – makes it more difficult to co-ordinate the activities of the main parties across the federal and *Land* levels. So do the CDU-SPD grand coalitions which have become a standard feature of *Land* politics since unification; the CDU (or SPD) nationwide becomes a harder party to manage and co-ordinate if in (quite) a number of *Länder* it is bound by coalition agreements with its nationwide, federal-level opponent. There is growing evidence, as a result, that the main parties themselves are becoming more territorial, more focused in the *Länder* on aggregating and articulating distinctive, *Land*-specific preferences, and less amenable to nationwide party discipline (cf. Detterbeck and Renzsch 2003).

In the context of post-unification differences between eastern and western *Länder*, the *Bundesrat* vote on 9 July 2004 on the proposed merging of unemployment benefit (*Arbeitslosenhilfe*) with income support (*Sozialhilfe* – cf. chapter 8 in this volume) constitutes a particularly good example of this dynamic. Despite a cross-party deal in the conciliation committee (*Vermittlungsausschuss*), the eastern *Länder* argued that this did not take enough account of their particular situations. In consequence, they refused, across party boundaries, to vote with their western counterparts. Although they failed to block the bill, this was the first time since unification that this trend towards territorialisation had expressed itself in such explicit east–west terms.

The discussion returns to this point later in the context of the *Bundesrat*. For now it suffices to say that the terms of partisan debate are no longer uniform across tiers and from one *Land* to the next. Some of the old 'centripetal' effect of party competition which Katzenstein and Lehmbruch noted seems to have been lost. The implication is that part of the 'formula' for incremental policy change in Germany – that of a centralised society – has been at the very least diluted. The next section looks at the implications of this territorial decentralisation and differentiation of interests, identities and party competition for the operation of the federal system.

Unification and the Unchanged Federal System

German federalism is still, indisputably, interlocked. There has been no substantial reform of the constitutional and institutional foundations of co-operative federalism. The post-unification round of constitutional revision left the federal system largely untouched (Jeffery 1995). The perennial debate about introducing change by redrawing territorial boundaries ran up against the buffers once again with the failure of the Berlin–Brandenburg merger in 1996 (Gunlicks 2003, pp. 199–202). And Solidarity Pacts marks one (1993) and two (2002) each failed to do much to reform the interlocked financial arrangements of German federalism (Jeffery 2003). There is, in other words, still the same set of factors at play which Katzenstein identified: functional division of powers, centrality of the *Bundesrat*, joint policy-making and fiscal interdependence. The system is still set up for federation and *Länder* to join forces to deliver standard levels of public service across the federal territory. However, that territory has changed, has become far more diverse than it used to be. There is now a mismatch between the form of federalism and the level of diversity of society.

In this situation the federal system has come under significant pressure for reform. Endless debates have resulted, which on the one hand are full of ideas about what should be done, but typically come to the conclusion on the other that nothing can be done (as evidenced in the failure of all substantial reform initiatives since unification). Failed reform breeds pessimism about the possibility of reform, creating a vicious circle of righteous impotence. Federalism is 'unreformable' (Abromeit 1996, p. 36), it has a 'depressing outlook' (Stolorz 1997). The most recent review of the reform debate concurs: 'a far-reaching reform of federalism is not to be expected in the near future' (Mardegant 2003, p. 13).

Such pessimism is exaggerated and misplaced, not least because it has a narrow notion of change focused solely on the scope for formal constitutional amendment. It is undeniably difficult to bring about formal constitutional amendment: two-thirds majorities for reform in both parliamentary chambers are needed, meaning that CDU/CSU, SPD and most of the *Länder* have to agree (Sturm 1999, p. 81). But political reform does not rely on constitutional amendment alone. Authors such as Arthur Benz have noted (1999, p. 56) that 'co-operative federalism is much more flexible and much more open to institutional adaptation and political change than is often assumed'. This inherent flexibility implies that the practice of federalism may depart from what is prescribed in constitutional texts, but may nonetheless still work effectively. This is precisely what happened during the 1950s and 1960s as a practice of intensive policy co-ordination and financial and operational interdependence between federation and *Länder* emerged which bore less and less relation to the initial vision of federalism set out in 1949 in the Basic Law.

The constitution did eventually catch up in the 1969–70 amendments which brought about the Joint Tasks and the interlocked fiscal arrangements which persist today. But it may be the case now that federalism in practice has moved once again beyond the constitution. What has been remarkable about the period since 1990 is a growing normative contestation about what the federal system is for and what purposes it should serve. It is clear what federalism used to be for. Co-operative federalism was not just a set of institutions and procedures but also a set of ideas which prized solidarity, consensus and the desirability of common standards across the federation. That set of ideas has increasingly come under challenge from a rival set focused on self-reliance, autonomy and differentiation of standards, as captured in the image of a more 'competitive' federalism. New ideas favouring this 'competitive' federalism have the potential to change the way the federal system – and with it the German policy-making process – works in practice.

Bavaria and the Propagation of Competitive Federalism

Ideas on competitive federalism are in origin Bavarian ideas. They emerged from a discomfiture with unification arising from the Bavarian combination of relative wealth and relatively strong territorial identity. The result has been an intensifying commitment by the CSU government to protect itself from the effects of co-operative federalism in the post-unity context in two ways: first, by limiting the hefty financial obligations implied by norms of solidarity (e.g. the € 2.3 billion paid in 2001 into the fiscal equalisation pot – see Table 4.1); and second, by (re-)asserting Bavarian distinctiveness in the face of norms of uniformity and equity. In practice, a Bavarian-style competitive federalism would:

1 favour a legislative division of powers between federation and *Länder* rather than a functional one;
2 in this way 'disentangle' the federation–*Länder* relationship by restoring competences to the *Länder* which have been sucked up into the federal ambit (and with it joint decision-making processes) since 1949, the 1969–70 'Joint Tasks' being the first to go;
3 reduce the level of minimum standards of common policy provision and uprate the scope for territorial variation (there are in Bavarian discourse a number of approving nods to the anti-centralist idea in the USA of the states as 'laboratories of democracy' and innovation. As a headline finding of the 2002 Commission of Enquiry of the Bavarian *Landtag* on reforming federalism put it: 'A competition among the *Länder* for the best political solutions will strengthen the capacity for innovation in politics' (Bayerischer Landtag 2002, p. 6));
4 'incentivise' the fiscal constitution by reducing the qualifying level for receipt of horizontal transfers and increasing the qualifying point at which financially stronger *Länder* are obliged to transfer surplus funds to weaker *Länder* (i.e. by reducing the obligation to solidarity, or, as the Bavarian *Landtag* (2002, p. 6) puts it, introducing the concept of 'solidaristic competition'!).

It would be easy to dismiss all this as Bavarian parochialism (and to underestimate it; there is a tendency among observers not to take Bavarian ideas very seriously because they dislike Bavarian politics). However, the Bavarian government is well organised, pursues a consistent line doggedly and invests heavily in publicising its messages. The result has been a widening acceptance of (parts of) the discourse of competitive federalism. Some of the key markers have been (cf. Jeffery 2002b):

- A joint campaign of Bavaria and Baden-Württemberg in 1996–7 focused on the theme of territorial diversity as the basis for innovation and economic success.
- A joint constitutional complaint by the same *Länder* (to which Hesse subsequently attached itself) in 1998 on the 'over-levelling' and disincentive effects of the fiscal equalisation process.
- A programmatic paper of all three of these *Länder* in 1999 on 'Modernising Federalism – Strengthening the Joint Responsibility of the *Länder*'. This provoked a counter-paper rejecting competitive federalism signed by nine of the other *Länder*. The other four – Hamburg and North Rhine-Westphalia in the west and Saxony and Thuringia in the east – have each shown sympathy with the 'competitive' agenda (the former two as net payers into fiscal equalisation, the latter as *Länder* – '*Freistaaten*' like Bavaria – which like to evoke a distinctive historical tradition and identity).
- The floating of radical ideas on the territorial differentiation of policy standards even in the heartlands of equitable provision: by varying cost-benefit packages in social insurance for health, unemployment and old age in order better to 'make clear the causal relationship between the policies of a *Land* and their impact on its citizens' (Bavaria; see Stamm 1998, p. 240); or by making welfare payments (*Sozialhilfe*) dependent on taking up some form of work or training provided by the state (the US-style 'workfare' model proposed by the minister-president of Hesse, Roland Koch (2001)). Perhaps unsurprisingly these ideas have provoked considerable opposition. There seems to be little appetite for such a challenge to inherited notions of solidarity which might make levels of social-policy provision dependent on where one happens to live (cf. Münch 1998, p. 78). But the fact that such a proposal could be made indicates how far the parameters of debate about federalism, solidarity and equity have moved on.
- Indeed, the discourse of 'competitive' federalism has become a general currency of debate about German politics, as reflected in statements and policy documents by former Federal President Herzog, the 'Schäuble-Lamers' duet, the FDP, the Friedrich-Naumann, Friedrich Ebert and Bertelsmann-Stiftungen, the BDI, the *Sachverständigenrat* and even the OECD (Jeffery 2002b, p. 186).

Changing Practices of Federalism: a New Capacity for Policy Change?

So how far have new ideas about federalism had an impact on how the federal system works in practice?

Formal Change

As was suggested earlier, there has not (yet) been much formal change. The post-unification constitutional reform process has tinkered at the margins by:

- reducing the requirement for federal legislation to kick in, instead of separate *Land* laws in specified fields, from that of maintaining 'uniform' living conditions to the apparently weaker standard of maintaining 'equivalence' of living conditions nationwide;
- making minimal relocations of competence from areas subject to federal legislation to exclusive *Länder* competence (Jeffery 1995);
- and making minor reforms to the fiscal equalisation process (prompted indirectly by the complaint to the Constitutional Court in 1998) which allow 'benefactor' *Länder* to keep a little bit more of their surplus before the obligation of solidarity to the weaker kicks in, and which give a little more incentive to recipient *Länder* to improve their economic performance (Jeffery 2004).

But in no sense have these limited changes bought off the discontent underlying pressures to reform the federal system. Future debates about the location of competences and the fiscal-equalisation process are more or less inevitable. By mid-2003, the best prospect in a generation for far-reaching reform had emerged in an agreement between the federal chancellor, Gerhard Schröder, and the minister-presidents of the *Länder* to establish a joint federation–*Länder* commission on the 'Modernisation of the Federal System', which began its deliberations in November 2003.

The commission had an ambitious agenda: to separate ('disentangle') the competences and the financial arrangements of the federal level and the *Länder*, to reduce the role of the *Bundesrat* in federal legislation, to 'strengthen the legislative powers of the *Länder* where they need more [capacity to] shape' outcomes, and to create the possibility for the *Länder* to 'deviate from current regulations in federal law through *Land* legislation' (MPK 2003). Clearly, these were ideas which matched closely the earliest, Bavarian visions of a more competitive federalism. Accordingly, clear divisions of interest quickly emerged between the federal government and the *Länder*. But they also emerged between richer and poorer *Länder*, with the former prioritising greater legislative autonomy, while the latter preferred to remain part of the federal legislative process as a means of maintaining common standards. Nonetheless, there was a broad consensus over the need to reduce the share of bills requiring the consent of the *Bundesrat* from 60 to about 35 per cent, in return for the federation conceding some competencies altogether to the *Länder*, such as disaster control.[2]

However, some influential commentators had been sceptical from the outset: 'In the end not much will come of it, or else everything will be crowded out by the next federal election campaign' (*Frankfurter Allgemeine Zeitung*, 11 August 2003). In fact, their fears were confirmed: on 17 December 2004, the commission collapsed ignominiously at the eleventh hour over competencies in education policy, thereby rendering meaningless all the progress made in other unrelated areas. Yet even if the commission had succeeded, its impact was always going to be limited. One of the central issues underpinning the organisational form of the federal system, the fiscal equalisation process, had been bracketed out of the discussions of the commission, even though any substantial reorganisation of competencies would have inevitable consequences for resource needs across the federation. Ultimately, while the commission's failure leaves the question of the reform of German federalism unanswered for the time being, it seems certain to return to the political agenda in the coming years.

The Länder *as Laboratories of Democracy?*

There are signs, though, in two other areas that the building blocks for the more disentangled, diversity-focused system the reform commission was meant to discuss are moving into place. First, where the *Länder* have had the opportunity outside of joint decision-making processes there have been significant examples of territorially distinctive policy portfolios, which might be seen as a German version of US 'laboratories of democracy' (cf. Blancke 2003). Most of these are linked to the regional economy, where some *Länder* are leading the way in experimenting with packages designed to attract inward investment, grow 'endogenous' innovative capacity, 'up-skill' the workforce and so on (Rosenfeld 2002). There are signs that these new regional economic policies are also beginning to 'spill over' into other policy fields with regional economic significance, e.g. higher education and 'cultural' policy more generally (Hertel 2001) and rural policy (Mehl and Plankl 2002). Some *Länder* are taking distinctive lines on policing and internal security, notably in Bavaria. And as mentioned above, more radical ideas about introducing territorial differentiation in social policy have entered

---

[2] For details of the debates of the commission and the papers presented to it for consideration, see the online archive available at http://www.bundesrat.de.

political debate. There appears, in other words, to be a growing appetite in the *Länder* for doing things differently in different locations.

The Bundesrat

Second, there has been a change in the way the *Bundesrat* works, though this has rather more to do with the differentiated judgements of *Länder* electorates than ideas about the benefits of competitive federalism. Nonetheless, the unpredictable patterns of *Land* election results have complicated processes of government formation and 'sent' into the *Bundesrat* coalition alignments which do not map closely onto those in the *Bundestag*. The obvious example concerns the SPD whose coalition promiscuity has led it into relationships with all the significant parties in German politics except the CSU (i.e. CDU, FDP, Greens and PDS, plus periodic arrangements with FDP and Greens at the same time and ephemeral movements like *Statt* in Hamburg). Many of these alignments have straddled the *Bundestag* government–opposition divide. In such circumstances it is no longer possible to achieve the level of *Bundestag–Bundesrat* co-ordination of federal and *Land* party positions as existed when Katzenstein wrote *Policy and Politics* (cf. Jeffery 1999, pp. 144–6). This invests the party governments represented in the *Bundesrat* with much more autonomy; or, to put it another way, they are now freer to pursue the territorial interests of their *Land* in the federal legislative process.

These changes in the way the *Bundesrat* works do not create a new federal paradigm. As long as there is no substantial relocation of legislative competencies to the *Länder*, *Bundesrat* consent will be needed for most laws. Federation and *Länder* will remain interlocked. However, the dynamics of decision-making in a more territorial *Bundesrat* are different. Though the nominal party majority in the *Bundesrat* has been the opposite of that in the *Bundestag* for most of the post-unity period (see Figure 3.2 in chapter 3 of this volume), it has proved rare for that majority to be mobilised as a de facto federal opposition. Accusations of an improper 'blockade' of the federal government's programme by the federal opposition wielding its *Bundesrat* majority were exaggerated during the Kohl chancellorship, and have been exaggerated under the Schröder chancellorship. Wolfgang Renzsch (1999) has shown convincingly that few of the failures of *Bundestag* bills which occurred after rejection by the *Bundesrat* in the 1994–8 legislative period were a result (simply) of the SPD using its *Bundesrat* majority. Mostly, cross-party alignments of *Länder* were involved, with the *Bundesrat* acting as a forum for (temporary and shifting) territorial coalitions which did not respect party sensibilities.

Similarly there have been examples under Chancellor Schröder – whose SPD-Green coalition in the *Bundestag* lost its parallel majority in the *Bundesrat* just four months after taking office – where the capacity of the CDU/CSU *Bundesrat* majority to blockade federal legislation has been much overstated. The classic example concerned the 2000 tax reform. Put bluntly, Schröder 'bought' the support of *Länder* government in which the SPD was in coalition with parties that did not form part of his *Bundestag* majority: the CDU (in Berlin, Brandenburg, Bremen), the FDP (in Rhineland-Palatinate) and the PDS (in Mecklenburg-Western Pomerania). Each was offered some kind of material territorial incentive to join the federal government ranks. Each accepted, despite a concerted effort on the part of the federal CDU to impose party discipline on its *Land* parties in Berlin, Brandenburg, and Bremen and reject the tax reform bill (*Der Spiegel*, 17 July 2000). A further example was the intense pressure placed on the SPD-CDU coalition in Brandenburg to support the Schröder government's bill for an immigration law (*Zuwanderungsgesetz*) in the *Bundesrat* in March 2002. Its formally split vote (with the SPD for and the CDU against) was carefully choreographed in such a way that the (SPD) president of the *Bundesrat* could interpret it as a vote in favour, a process to which the Brandenburg CDU acquiesced in the interests of saving its coalition with the SPD (Green 2004, pp. 125–7). The ploy almost paid off, except that the Constitutional Court ruled the voting procedure to be illegal in December 2002.

At that point in 2002, the SPD could rely on thirty-one out of sixty-nine total votes in the *Bundesrat*, with thirty-five votes needed to make a majority. One 'swing' *Land* could therefore swing an adverse majority behind the federal government. However, the SPD has fared so badly in subsequent *Land* elections that, by summer 2004, it could count reliably on just twenty-one votes in the *Bundesrat*: Berlin (SPD-PDS, four votes), Mecklenburg-Western Pomerania (SPD-PDS, three votes), North Rhine-Westphalia (SPD-Green, six votes), Rhineland-Palatinate (SPD-FDP, four votes) and Schleswig-Holstein (SPD-Green, four votes). With such an adverse majority it is near impossible for the federal government to peel off sufficient 'opposition' *Länder* through incentives or other pressures. It has therefore to work closely with the federal opposition in order to get anything done.

However, this is historically an anomalous situation and should not distract from the new 'fundamentals' of German federalism. German society is now more 'decentralised', more territorially differentiated than when Katzenstein wrote *Policy and Politics*. That new decentralisation has generated tensions which have steadily been picking open some of the entanglements which have tied together the federal level and the *Länder* in producing uniform, nationwide policy standards. It has opened up and maintained the pressure for the constitutional reform of the federal system. It has led the *Länder* to situations in which they can enact territorially distinctive policy portfolios. And it has introduced a more vigorous territorial dynamic to *Bundesrat* decision-making. Overarching these changes has been a normative reassessment of the purpose of federalism that has increasingly challenged inherited commitments to solidarity and equity.

In other words, as already predicted by Katzenstein (1987, p. 45), policy proposals which consist of the *Länder* taking on more responsibility again have now become possible, and, indeed, highly likely in the coming years. The *Länder* are emerging, blinking in the light, from the smoke-filled rooms of *Politikverflechtung* to take on new roles as policy 'laboratories'. The long-term effect will be to unlock a federal system whose structures are anachronistic and to re-match its operation to the now more decentralised society in which it is embedded, with greater territorial diversity of policy standards eroding the old, increasingly redundant commitment to uniformity of standards. Put another way, the old, 1987-era federal system examined by Katzenstein was appropriate to the centralised society of the time; the new, post-unity federal system is gradually becoming more appropriate to the more decentralised society of post-unification Germany.

5 Shock-Absorbers Under Stress: Parapublic Institutions and the Double Challenges of German Unification and European Integration

Andreas Busch

Introduction

The weakness of the (West) German 'semisovereign state' that Peter Katzenstein diagnosed in his book in 1987 was, according to his argument, not as insurmountable a disadvantage as one might have assumed. Quite the contrary: the profile of policy outcomes seemed to suggest that not having an almighty state could actually be an advantage. But the reason for these positive outcomes was not the state's weakness alone; it was the peculiar combination of a 'decentralised state' with a 'centralised society' that proved advantageous. It also helped to explain the central puzzle that West Germany presented when compared with similar cases of highly industrialised liberal democracies, namely the tendency towards only incremental policy change and the high degree of policy stability even after changes of government (Katzenstein 1987, pp. 4, 35).

Katzenstein argues that the 'decentralised state' and the 'centralised society' interact primarily through three 'nodes' in the policy network, namely political parties, co-operative federalism and parapublic institutions. In this chapter, the focus will be on the latter – and the question whether (and if so, how) their function in the German political system has changed. For the period since Katzenstein developed his hypotheses about (West) German politics in the mid-1980s has seen momentous changes in the history of the country. Above all German unification, but also further steps in European integration, certainly make it worthwhile to ask how far these developments have affected the 'parapublic institutions' that Katzenstein has portrayed as a vital ingredient of German politics.

How have these institutions developed during that period? Did their role change as a result of the challenges mentioned above? Have any structural changes occurred as a result of unification? Did different institutional patterns develop in western and eastern Germany? And how have any structural changes affected the patterns of interaction of the various actors? These are questions that will guide the analysis of this chapter. The empirical evidence for the analysis will be provided by case studies of three parapublic institutions and the role they have played since 1987. Their selection is guided by the criterion of the 'twin challenge' the German political system faced in the 1990s: that of German unification and European integration. While limiting the analysis in this way has the disadvantage of not allowing any statements about the development of parapublic institutions in general to be made, at least well-founded ones about the institutions covered here will be possible. Given the widely varying nature of these institutions and the contexts in which they operate, it seems unlikely that any generalisations would be possible anyway. Chapters 8 and 9 in this volume consider some other institutions from this class.

The next section will look in more detail into the parapublic institutions and their role in the German political system. The main section of the chapter will offer case studies on the *Treuhandanstalt*, the *Bundesbank* and the *Bundesanstalt für Arbeit*. The final section then offers reflections on the role of these German parapublic institutions 'under stress' in the changing circumstances of the 1990s and the present decade, arguing that their role diminished as their potential to absorb shocks decreased.

Parapublic Institutions: Shock-Absorbers in the Political System

Katzenstein's enumeration of parapublic institutions includes single institutions (such as the *Bundesbank*, the Council of Economic Advisers, the Federal Employment Office and the Science Council), classes of institutions (like the Labour Courts, churches, social-security funds and private welfare associations) and even rather abstract principles (such as co-determination, or *Mitbestimmung*). The term thus summarises a 'heterogeneous set' of institutions, as the author himself admits (Katzenstein 1987, p. 58), that does not map easily onto the categories that German constitutional and administrative law provide.[1] But in spite of the absence of a clear and encompassing definition, they share a

---

[1] The greatest organisational commonality between these institutions seems to be that many of them are organised under public law, mostly as *Anstalten des öffentlichen Rechts*. Therefore (and particularly in an Anglo-Saxon context) they are often mistaken as 'state institutions'; however, as this chapter will demonstrate, the state's influence on their operation is often quite limited and they operate with considerable independence.

common trait: namely that they bridge the gap between the public and private sectors, and that they carry out important policy functions.[2]

In organisational terms, parapublic institutions are often characterised by participation of the country's highly centralised economic and social interest groups in the affairs of a highly decentralised state. Granting access to policy-making to privileged groups is thus one hallmark of parapublic institutions. But besides this, two further elements characterise parapublic institutions:

1 a high degree of autonomy in policy-making (that takes place under the general supervision of the government, but that rules out interfering in details), and
2 a high level of expertise (which often surpasses that of the supervising government departments).

While the extent of each of these three elements varies across the parapublic institutions, it is by their *combination* that they manage to achieve positive effects for the political system. These can be described as reinforcing peace between the political left and the political right, thus inducing stability and limiting controversies in policy implementation. Functionally, parapublic institutions thus benefit the political system both in terms of politics and in terms of policy:

1 In terms of politics, they shelter governments from shocks by keeping many policy decisions 'at arm's length', thus removing direct accountability (which may have electoral advantages). By fostering compromise between all parties involved, they guard against adversarial politics.
2 In terms of policy, parapublic institutions provide continuity, because they are one or several steps removed from government, and are thus unlikely to change policies radically, for instance after a change in government. Smoother adjustment paths and less interruption are likely to result in superior policy outcomes.

To sum up, the delegation of important policies to institutions characterised by a (varying) mix of participation (for privileged groups), autonomy and expertise – parapublic institutions – can create advantages both for the political process and for the policies. By acting like

---

[2] The delegation of important policy functions to institutions over which the state has no direct control has a long tradition in Germany and dates back to the late nineteenth century (see, most recently, Manow 2002). Prominent examples include social-insurance institutions or placement services, in which tripartite co-operation has long been established between employers, trade unions and government in quasi-corporatist networks.

buffers, these institutions create positive externalities for both political actors and substantive policy decisions.

The Case Studies

Parapublic institutions fulfilled an important task in the West German political system up to the late 1980s. But how have they fared since? Based upon three case studies, the following section will look into the changes that have occurred in the years since Katzenstein's analysis.

In 1990, German unification was thrust upon a political system unsuspecting and largely unprepared for it. To cope with this challenge, what had seemed to be firmly established standard operating procedures of the political system were changed with amazing ease. New institutions sprang up, and none of them was more symbolic than the agency charged with privatising the, in former times, almost exclusively state-run economy of East Germany, the *Treuhandanstalt*. Not only was this an unprecedented institution in German history, but it also dealt with the problem of privatisation in a way that was unique among the central and east European countries.

The second case study chosen here was perhaps the most famous 'parapublic institution' in Katzenstein's list, and certainly the one that commanded most attention and respect not only in Germany, but also internationally, namely the *Bundesbank*, the country's central bank. It not only played an important role in the process of German unification, but was also totally transformed as a result of European integration. To any observer at the time of Katzenstein's writing in the mid-1980s, it would certainly have appeared completely beyond imagining that fifteen years hence the *Bundesbank*'s role in German politics would be completely changed.

Lastly, this section will deal with the Federal Employment Office as an example of a 'normal' case – at least compared with the seismic shifts that created or affected the other two institutions. But this, too, was an institution that faced new challenges as mass unemployment became a fixture of 1990s Germany – another case of a parapublic institution 'under stress'.

The Treuhandanstalt

If parapublic institutions are associated with tradition in the German political system and with an aversion to policy change, as has been argued above, then the *Treuhandanstalt* (literally the trustee agency), the institution charged with privatising the East German economy, is, in a way, not a typical case: a temporary institution, alien to many of the core principles of German political and economic governance, it played a central role during a decisive period, namely the four years following unification. But, upon closer inspection, it becomes clear that both organisationally and functionally, this was a typical parapublic institution, albeit a short-lived one built for a very special purpose.

The genesis of the *Treuhandanstalt* (THA) is as unique as the whole institution, for it was conceived of in principle and founded by the last Communist government of the GDR, and charged with the task of safeguarding the 'property of the people' (*Volkseigentum*) in March 1990 (Kemmler 1994, p. 94).[3] After the free elections later that month, the new, democratic government under Lothar de Maizière swiftly concluded a Treaty on Currency, Economic and Social Union with the Federal Republic, to come into effect on 1 July 1990. As part of the agreements, the mandate of the THA was altered in the *Treuhand* Act (which came into effect on the same day); it now required the agency to privatise East German enterprises. The 270 combines (*Kombinate*) were unbundled into some 12,000 joint stock or limited liability corporations of which the *Treuhandanstalt* held all the equity. Together, these firms employed some four million people – or 50 per cent of the total GDR working population of eight million. The sheer size of its holdings gave the THA and whatever it decided to do an immense political weight. It is, therefore, not surprising that it has frequently been likened to a 'shadow government in the east' (*Nebenregierung Ost*) (Czada 1993a, p. 153; see also H. Schmidt 1993, p. 110).

With respect to the three characteristics of 'parapublic institutions' identified above, the *Treuhandanstalt* can certainly be counted as such: it clearly possessed considerable *autonomy* in its actions, provided room for *participation* of organised societal interests (more on which below), and undoubtedly had a high degree of *expertise*.

Organisationally, the *Treuhandanstalt* was of a 'singular character' (Schmidt-Preuß 1997, p. 862): it was from a legal point of view not an enterprise, and it did not act like a state agency (*Behörde*). Located between the public and the private sectors, it was part of both in some respects. Although a corporation of public law (*Anstalt des öffentlichen Rechts*), it was legally empowered to discharge itself of its privatisation tasks according to 'entrepreneurial principles', thus enhancing its autonomy (sections 2 and 7 of the *Treuhand* Act). This autonomy has been compared by observers to that of the *Bundesbank*:

---

[3] This legacy remained visible throughout the life of the *Treuhandanstalt* because its fifteen regional offices coincided with the administrative structure of the *Bezirke* of the GDR.

The form, variety and scope of its activities give the impression that the *Treuhandanstalt* – like the *Bundesbank* – forms a third level in the federal structures of the State; this third level undertakes, for a limited time period and with technocratic autonomy, tasks – such as monetary policy – that neither the federal government nor the *Länder* are entrusted with. (Czada 1993a, p. 156)

At the top of the organisational structure of the THA was the executive, consisting of the president, the vice-president and six other members who were responsible for the conduct of business. They were appointed and supervised by the administrative council (*Verwaltungsrat*) which consisted of twenty members who had a role similar to the supervisory board of a German joint stock corporation. The members of the council were all appointed by the federal government. It is here that the contacts and networks vital for the fulfilment of the THA's task were represented, namely in members from both the federal and the *Länder* political levels as well as organised societal interests. The federal government appointed two permanent secretaries (*Staatssekretäre*) from the Federal Finance and Economics Ministries as well as one representative from each of the five new *Länder* and the state of Berlin.[4] The remaining representatives primarily came from industry and the trade unions. Here it is interesting to note that the CDU/CSU-FDP federal government appointed no fewer than four high-ranking trade union representatives to the council in order to compensate for the fact that the THA as a corporation of public law was exempt from the regulations concerning co-determination.[5] The council thus represented all the major interests the *Treuhandanstalt* needed to collaborate with in order to fulfil its task; it also allowed the THA to co-opt many important actors (Czada 1993a). In addition, there were advisory councils at each of the fifteen regional offices, comprising representatives of regional societal interests, and the *Bundestag* in October 1990 set up a subcommittee of the Budget Committee to monitor the conduct of the *Treuhandanstalt*.

From a resource and manpower point of view, the *Treuhandanstalt* was a remarkably small operation, with only 4,800 persons being employed at the headquarters and the fifteen regional offices at the peak of its operations in 1993. The latter were primarily charged with the privatisation of small and medium-sized enterprises in their region, while the 'big fish' were dealt with by the headquarters in Berlin. Altogether, the

---

[4] The seats of Brandenburg, Saxony, Saxony-Anhalt and Mecklenburg-Western Pomerania were filled by the respective minister-presidents themselves, indicating the high priority they ascribed to that task.

[5] The trade union representatives were Heinz Werner Meyer (head of DGB), Hermann Rappe (head of IG Chemie), Roland Issen (head of DAG) and Horst Klaus of IG Metall (Kemmler 1994, p. 199).

THA's task was certainly unparalleled, both in German history, and also in comparison with the other 'transition economies', namely to privatise practically a whole economy. As the title of one of the first academic books on the subject put it, the agency was 'daring to do the impossible' (Fischer et al. 1993). It was also an unenviable task, for its assets were an odd mixture, containing (in addition to the 12,000 firms mentioned above) some 20,000 small retail and catering outlets, 1,900 pharmacies, all East German cinemas, 390 hotels and no less than 62,000 square kilometres of land that amounted to 57 per cent of the whole area of the GDR (Kemmler 1994, p. 175). To arrive at well-founded valuations for these assets was, indeed, to perform an impossible task, especially since the *Treuhandanstalt* (at least initially) was short of qualified staff, and no reliable data on its assets were available. The situation was even further complicated, first, by the collapse of all East German exports to the traditionally strong markets in eastern Europe and Russia (a consequence of currency union with the Deutschmark), and, second, by the recession of 1992 and 1993 (a consequence of the high interest-rate policy of the *Bundesbank*). The gap between reality and the expectations that the Kohl government had raised with its talk of a 'second economic miracle' could hardly have been greater.

Nevertheless, when the *Treuhandanstalt* was dissolved in 1994, after four and a half years in existence,[6] it had managed to sell all but sixty-five firms from its portfolio. A total of 8,444 firms had been sold, and 3,718 liquidated; however, in terms of employment, the results of its activities were about three million redundancies (Kaser 1996, p. 61). Similarly bleak were the results in financial terms: initially, it had been estimated that the privatisation process would yield profits in the range of DM 500–600 billion (€ 256–308 billion). However, in reality, not only was there no profit, but there was a deficit of some DM 275 billion (€ 141 billion), according to figures provided by Federal Finance Minister Theo Waigel in 1994 (Deutscher Bundestag Plenarprotokoll 12/214; see also Kaser 1996, p. 62), a deficit which had to be covered by the taxpayer. So it was no wonder that criticism about the THA abounded: with a view to the job losses, the agency was accused of insufficiently committing itself to active restructuring, and of not pursuing an industrial policy. In fact, all the results had taken place in spite of previously unimaginable injections of public funds: in the Buna-Leuna-Bitterfeld chemicals triangle, only 2,700 jobs remained, although DM 30 billion (€ 15.4 billion) had

---

[6] Several successor organisations were created, the largest of which is the *Bundesanstalt für vereinigungsbedingte Sonderaufgaben*. Their tasks include the control of the more than 30,000 contracts between investors and the THA, privatisations of public lands and other similar tasks (Turek 1996, p. 666).

been spent since 1990; and a 50 per cent share of Carl Zeiss Jena was sold to its (West) German sister, Carl Zeiss Oberkochen, for the symbolic sum of only DM 1 (€ 0.51) after the THA and the Thuringia *Land* authorities had invested DM 1 billion (€ 510 million) (Flockton 1996, p. 227).

More disinterested observers, such as business consultant Roland Berger, consequently also stated that the THA had done 'an excellent job' (Kemmler 1994, p. 20), especially given that it had been, in the assessment of its President Birgit Breuel, 'absolutely overburdened' (H. Schmidt 1993, p. 108). Economically speaking, it is difficult to imagine how the *Treuhandanstalt* could have acted in a substantially different manner in principle – although one can always think of better solutions in the case of each individual decision. But the THA was acting under severe constraints – not the least of which were the consequences of the GDR adopting the Deutschmark at an early stage, which resulted in a de facto revaluation of 400 per cent, a markedly different situation from the other transition economies, all of which allowed their currencies to *devalue* (Kaser 1996, p. 64). While East Germans profited from this decision in the short run in terms of the value of their savings and their purchasing power, it became very costly in terms of job losses – particularly for the elderly and the comparatively less well-trained.

From the point of view of the political system, the *Treuhandanstalt* has certainly fulfilled its task very well. On the one hand, given the absurdly complex situation and the level of uncertainty it acted under, it is difficult to imagine any other strategy than one of pragmatic 'muddling through' to be appropriate – which is what the THA largely did (Czada 1993a, p. 171). In that sense, the THA, far from being 'alien' to the constitutional and institutional system of the Federal Republic (Wollmann 2001, p. 40), was actually rather typical of it. In addition, its special mix of extensive autonomy in each individual privatisation case, access to substantial financial resources and an embeddedness into the multilayered decision structures of the German political system proved up to the task at hand (Czada 2000, p. 470). Above all, it insulated the political system, and, in particular, the Federal Finance and Economics Ministries, from the negative fallout of many aspects of privatisation, since most of the criticisms were deflected to the *Treuhandanstalt*. As such, it played the role of a 'scapegoat' or 'lightning conductor' in a most excellent manner – a fact that did not go unnoticed by the SPD opposition, which was, however, unsuccessful in its complaints about it. This was also recognised by the government, as the following quotation from the then Federal Economics Minister Helmut Haussmann shows:

It is and remains historically correct that an intermediary institution such as the *Treuhandanstalt* was established. Even if the Federal Ministry of Economics had been directly involved in the privatisations and even if it had played a leading role, it would have been impossible for a ministry to carry out such a high number of privatisations. As a result, the *Treuhandanstalt* would have had to have been re-invented. One or two things about it would have been different, but the basic idea [*Grundansatz*] was correct. (quoted in Kemmler 1994, p. 20)

The parapublic institution *Treuhandanstalt* was a specific solution to most unusual circumstances in the first half of the 1990s. It classically fulfilled the tasks ascribed to parapublic institutions by Katzenstein – namely that of a political shock absorber and pacifier. However, the case also shows that while the German system may tend to shift certain tasks to parapublic institutions, these tasks need not always be associated with a low degree of policy change; this was certainly not so in the case of the *Treuhandanstalt*.

The Bundesbank

Contrary to the fleeting phenomenon of the *Treuhandanstalt*, the *Bundesbank* had been a fixture of (West) German politics for most of the Federal Republic's existence. It became almost the embodiment of many of the positive aspects of the country's macro-economic strategy and record. Certainly, the (West) German central bank was one of the best-known German institutions, both domestically and internationally. Largely credited with the enviable low inflation record of the Federal Republic, which ranks as the OECD champion of price stability in the post-war era (Busch 1993, 1995), it had claimed, and found, an important role in West German economic policy-making. Yet the 1990s were to transform its role completely.

As a parapublic institution, the *Bundesbank* is characterised by only two of the three features mentioned above: autonomy and expertise, the projection of both of which has always been central to the *Bundesbank*'s corporate identity. On the one hand, these have been achieved through a careful distancing from the government and on the other, through the highly professional management of its public relations with both economic experts and the public at large. The third feature, participation of societal interests, is, however, notably absent from the *Bundesbank*, which knows no quota system for allocating posts to representatives of societal interests such as business associations or trade unions.[7]

---

[7] It should, however, be mentioned that on the regional level (that of the *Landeszentralbanken*) there exist advisory councils manned by the banking industry, trade unions and

However, the federal mode of appointing the members of the *Bundesbank* council has always led to a wide range of societal interests and views being represented here at any point in time.

Organisationally, the *Bundesbank* has the status of a 'directly federal corporation of public law' (*bundesunmittelbare Anstalt des öffentlichen Rechts*) according to section 7 of the *Bundesbank* Act.[8] It is, therefore, free from ministerial and parliamentary control. The Act further stipulates that the *Bundesbank* conducts monetary policy with the aim of safeguarding 'the stability of the currency', and that, in doing so, it is free from directives of the government (sections 3 and 12). The constitutional and legal position of the *Bundesbank* is discussed in detail in Stern (1998).

The *Bundesbank*'s high standing is a result of its use, over the decades, of the powers rested in it. It has not been afraid to confront governments of various party-political compositions if it thought their economic policies were detrimental to its own task of keeping inflation down; nor, indeed, has it desisted in its criticisms if it was itself criticised by governments. The respective track record of skirmishes ranges from Adenauer in the late 1950s (on raising interest rates) to the grand coalition in the late 1960s, to the debate over revaluation of the Deutschmark, and to disputes with Chancellor Schmidt in the early 1980s, again over the level of interest rates (Sturm 1990, p. 265). In the 1990s, conflicts between the government and the *Bundesbank* centred around issues of budgetary consolidation and the planned revaluation of the central bank's gold reserves (Zohlnhöfer 2001a; Duckenfield 1999). On the international level, the *Bundesbank*'s importance grew as the Deutschmark developed into the de facto anchor currency of the European Monetary System and German interest-rate decisions affected many other countries (Busch 1994).

As a result, the *Bundesbank*'s power and independence became the subject of some mythology. It was dubbed the 'power upon Main' and 'the bank that rules Europe' (Marsh 1992). To many observers, it seemed a powerful shadow government (*Nebenregierung*) to the one in Bonn (Wildenmann 1969).[9] The 1990s, however, saw two conflicts in

business associations. But the *Bundesbank* emphasises that these councils are not official organs of the *Bundesbank* itself (Deutsche Bundesbank 1995, p. 22).

[8] I will not here discuss in any more detail the organisational structure of the *Bundesbank*. It is well described, for example, in Katzenstein (1987, pp. 61–2) and Kennedy (1991). Any changes in the structure since the early 1990s will be described below.

[9] The mythology surrounding the *Bundesbank*'s independence has even led some observers such as Hall (1986, p. 235) and Katzenstein (1987, p. 85) to state erroneously that the bank's independence was enshrined in the constitution. This is not the case – or, to be more precise, it was not at the time it was stated, when independence was only

which the *Bundesbank* had to surrender, and on issues it considered to be of central importance: once on the question of German monetary union in 1990, and then, two years later, on the question of the EU's programme for Economic and Monetary Union (EMU). The context of these defeats and the consequences thereof will be discussed in the remainder of this section.

After the opening of the Berlin Wall, political pressure mounted quickly as East Germans flooded into West Germany, creating huge problems for the administrations of both German states (Busch 1991; Kennedy 1991; Hartwich 1992; Marsh 1992). To alleviate the situation, the Kohl government decided in February 1990 to offer a German currency union to the GDR government, i.e. to introduce the Deutschmark into the GDR and make it the common currency of both states. This was an unexpected move: only days before, Finance Minister Waigel had rejected such a proposal from the SPD. The offer was made against the explicit recommendations of the *Bundesbank*, and the then *Bundesbank* president Karl-Otto Pöhl even briefly considered his resignation when he learned of the government's proposal about which – in a deliberate snub – he had not been informed in advance.

The *Bundesbank* feared that (what it considered to be a premature) currency union between the Federal Republic and the GDR might create inflationary pressure in the west, as East Germany required low interest rates to stimulate economic development. Once the principal decision had been taken by the government, however, the *Bundesbank* explicitly accepted it while emphasising that the responsibility lay entirely with the government.

The next decision to be taken was the rate of conversion between the Deutschmark and the East German mark. For free commercial transactions, the rate was about 1:4.5 at the beginning of 1990. Political considerations, however, dictated a rate that was closer to 1:1 – to indicate primarily that East Germans were not inferior to West Germans. The dilemma was clear: it was political logic against economic logic – and political logic prevailed as the government again chose the conversion rate against the clear wishes of the *Bundesbank*.

On the European level, discussions about a European Currency Union had been conducted in the second half of the 1980s. The *Bundesbank*, which had already been suspicious of the commitments emanating

granted by the *Bundesbank* Act and could easily have been withdrawn. It was only after the amendment of the Basic Law in 1992 (which incorporated the decisions of the Maastricht Treaty) that independence of the central bank and the primary goal of price stability were mentioned in the text of the constitution and thus gained constitutional quality (Stern 1998, pp. 180–3).

from the European Monetary System, was less than enthusiastic about it, though it had not openly opposed the idea. While one theory saw monetary union as a means to achieve tighter integration in other areas and therefore preferred a speedy implementation, the *Bundesbank* clearly favoured a competing theory according to which monetary union should only be the 'crowning' achievement after the successful completion of a series of prior steps and be achieved in conjunction with political union.

Again, the *Bundesbank* lost out. In 1992, moved forward more quickly by the very process of German unification that had led to the bank's first big defeat, the Maastricht Treaty was signed which led to the establishment of a European Central Bank and the Euro before the decade was out. Although the *Bundesbank*'s requirements were not met, it had no way of stopping these developments. Its independence was of no practical use, for technically (as in the case of German Monetary Union), these were decisions about the currency area that were not in the *Bundesbank*'s remit, but in the government's.

On the other hand, the government's victory (at least in the first case) was not a complete one, for the *Bundesbank* raised interest rates to record levels in the early 1990s to combat inflation and the debt financing of German unification, thus forcing the government to change its policy stance (Zohlnhöfer 2001a). And in the European case, the *Bundesbank* had managed to leave its imprint on large parts of the plans for the future European Central Bank which was largely modelled on its own organisational principles: with strong independence from political interference, a primary stated goal of maintaining price stability, and eventually even located in Frankfurt.

The organisational structure of the *Bundesbank* itself was also not left untouched by the developments in the 1990s. In two stages, it underwent major changes. Both were not uncontested, and mainly concerned the question of the federal dimension of the *Bundesbank*'s organisation. They consequently pitted the federal government against the *Länder*, and the members of the *Bundesbank*'s directorate against the presidents of the *Landeszentralbanken* (or the *Land* central banks).

Even before German unification had been completed, *Bundesbank* president Pöhl launched a proposal to centralise and streamline the *Bundesbank*'s organisational structure. To prevent the number of *Landeszentralbanken* (LZB) increasing from eleven to sixteen (one for each *Land*), he suggested creating eight combined LZBs. This was immediately met with strong resistance from a majority of the LZB presidents who feared the *Länder* would lose influence in that area. Eventually, however, a somewhat more modest reform was agreed, and the number of LZBs was limited to nine. Federal misgivings were overcome by cutting the maximum number of members of the *Bundesbank* directorate from ten to eight, thus preserving the relative power distribution between the two groups of members that make up the *Bundesbank* council.

After responsibility for the conduct of monetary policy had been taken over by the ECB in 1999, a more substantial reform was called for. Again, it pitted two principal solutions against each other: one with a more centralised character; the other with a more federal one (cf. Zentralbankrat der Deutschen Bundesbank 1999). The former opted for an eight-member executive (four of whom would be appointed by the federal government and four by the *Bundesrat*) in which the individual members would have regional responsibilities, but the LZBs would be abolished and replaced by administrative units under the leadership of regional directors who would not be members of the executive; the latter retained the previous structure (a directorate that together with the LZB presidents forms the *Bundesbank* council), but would cut both the numbers of the directorate (from eight to six) and LZBs (from nine to seven).

The *Bundesbank* directorate and the Finance Ministry preferred the first, the *Länder* and the LZBs the second solution. It took more than three years of debates and the report of a committee of experts (under the former *Bundesbank* president, Pöhl) finally to arrive at a solution. Ultimately, the more centralised model with an eight-member executive was adopted, changing the character of the *Bundesbank* substantially.[10]

Looking back over the past fifteen years of the *Bundesbank*, one could be tempted to argue that they cover both the *Bundesbank*'s zenith and its demise. The EU's Economic and Monetary Union (EMU) has robbed the *Bundesbank* of its main task, the conduct of monetary policy, and its attempts to expand into the field of banking regulation have been thwarted.[11] The *Bundesbank*, admired and at times vilified in German (and European) politics, will certainly play a less important role in the future. The combined effects of German unification and European integration have altered the environment for the formerly so powerful

---

[10] The eventual solution was only achieved because the CDU-governed *Länder* that had opposed the law passed by the *Bundestag* on 1 March 2002, boycotted the *Bundesrat* on the day in question (22 March 2002) because of the controversy over the new immigration law. Otherwise, there would have been a majority for a new round of negotiations as SPD-governed North Rhine-Westphalia had announced it would vote against the law.

[11] The *Bundesbank* had tried to take over responsibility for the Federal Banking Supervisory Office: however, on the same day the *Bundesbank* reform was passed (22 March 2002), a new integrated institution was, instead, created to combine the supervision of banking, insurance and securities.

institution completely. Some observers had already in the early 1990s thought of the *Bundesbank* as 'politically overrated' (Hartwich 1992, p. 272). On the other hand, one might argue that this German and quintessential 'parapublic institution' has now been exported successfully to the European level (see chapter 6 in this volume, p. 127).

The Bundesanstalt für Arbeit

The last of the parapublic institutions to be portrayed in this chapter is the Federal Employment Office, or *Bundesanstalt für Arbeit* (BA). There are two reasons for including it here: on the one hand, the BA was – unlike the *Bundesbank* and the THA – much less directly affected by the seminal challenges of European integration and German unification, and is, perhaps therefore, more 'normal' and representative for the development of this set of institutions as a whole; on the other hand, the substantial reforms of the BA initiated in 2002 may give an indication about the direction in which parapublic institutions may change in the future. This section starts by briefly describing the institutional structure of the BA prior to the recent reforms, before describing and discussing those.

The BA is, like the *Bundesbank*, organised as a public-law organisation that is directly responsible to the federation (*bundesunmittelbare Körperschaft des öffentlichen Rechts*), and as such is part of the indirect administrative structure of the state, or *mittelbare Staatsverwaltung*. The BA's organisation, tasks and instruments are governed by chapter 11 in the third volume of the Social Security Code (*Sozialgesetzbuch III*).[12] Organised into a three-level structure (the headquarters in Nuremberg, ten regional centres of *Landesarbeitsämter* and 181 local employment offices), the core principle of its organisation is tripartite representation in each of its organs – a tradition that goes back to the Weimar Republic. Consequently, the BA is a typical example of the German tradition of sectoral self-governance, in which considerable autonomy is devolved towards non-state institutions. Representatives of labour, employers and the state thus jointly administer the sectoral tasks of unemployment insurance, placement and employment counselling, and keep it at arm's length from direct influence of the federal government.

The most important organs of the BA prior to the reform were the *administrative council* (a 51-person-strong tripartite institution with seventeen representatives from each group), practically the 'legislative

---

[12] Prior to the introduction of the Social Security Code in 1998, the BA was governed by the Labour Promotion Act (*Arbeitsförderungsgesetz* or AFG).

organ' which sets the rules in the areas the BA governs autonomously; the *executive* with three representatives from each of the three groups; and the *president*, in charge of most of the day-to-day decision-making within the BA. While the former two organs would already appear to be lavishly manned, given their rather restricted tasks, tripartite representation is nevertheless faithfully replicated also on the two lower organisational levels, where on the *Land* level each regional employment office has its own administrative council with at least five representatives of each of the groups, similar to the local employment offices, where the number of representatives is at least three each.[13]

Over time, tripartite consensus led to the BA being used as an instrument for tasks that go well beyond the core area of labour-market policy (Trampusch 2002; see also chapter 8 in this volume). Examples include the administration and payment of child benefit and, more recently, the *Erziehungsgeld*. More generally, the BA was used by consensus of the parties involved to remedy economic structural problems (for instance, by generously extending early retirement) and repeatedly to plug holes in the federal budget and the pension system (for instance, by introducing pension contributions for recipients of unemployment benefits, in effect a cross-subsidy of the pension system by the BA). The BA thus classically fulfilled its task as a 'shock absorber' in the political system. But using this shock absorber had other consequences as well, for these were tasks of the whole state that should have been financed out of general taxation, but which were instead almost exclusively paid for by wage and salary earners contributing to the BA.[14]

The tradition of using the BA as a 'buffer' was continued – and even extended – after German unification. The BA poured enormous sums into the eastern German *Länder*: between 1990 and 2002, no less than € 242 billion were spent, of which € 91 billion (or 37 per cent) were unemployment benefits, and € 138 billion (or 57 per cent) expenses for active labour-market policy (Bundesanstalt für Arbeit 2003, p. 11). The BA thus spent about 40 per cent of its outlays in an area where only about 20 per cent of the population lived – a massive net transfer to the

---

[13] This replication of representation on the lower levels is, however, to a certain degree justified as the regional levels enjoy a considerable degree of independence in implementing measures of labour-market policy. While it is true to the spirit of *Selbstverwaltung* and may make reactions to specific local circumstances and challenges easier, it makes centrally co-ordinated strategies at the same time more difficult. But that is a well-known problem in a country where the federal government has to rely on implementation by the *Länder* for most administrative tasks.

[14] This means that approximately 15 per cent of the working population who are civil servants or self-employed did not contribute to these outlays.

east that drove up non-wage labour costs in all of Germany.[15] But even resources on so massive a scale could not engender the lasting economic upturn in the east many had hoped for.

In early 2002, a scandal about misrepresentation of placement statistics prompted a significant reform of the BA's organisational structure.[16] Characteristically, this took the form of a two-stage process, consisting of a package of immediate measures, combined with the setting up of a committee charged with the task of making further recommendations. The immediate reforms – which were rushed through the *Bundestag* and *Bundesrat* in only one month – amount to the most substantial reorganisation of the BA in its entire fifty-year history. The key provisions were an organisational shake-up of the BA structure, a strengthening of the role of private placement services and the pledge to reform the whole system root and branch by the year 2004.

Organisationally, the office of the president was abolished, and replaced by a three-member executive, which does not consist of civil servants, but which is being appointed for a five-year term. This new executive was now organised in accordance with private-sector practices (with clear lines and areas of responsibility) and also took over the (few) tasks of the former executive. The administrative council was charged with the task of controlling the executive, and substantially reduced from fifty-one to twenty-one members, but with continued tripartite representation. The BA was also renamed to *Bundesagentur für Arbeit*.

In addition to organisational changes, the role of private placement services in the labour market was enhanced to increase competition. The licensing of such firms was abolished, and vouchers for use in the private placement sector were introduced for long-term unemployed persons the BA could not place. A stronger 'customer orientation' was set as a goal for the provision of the BA's services, and transparency measures and 'benchmarking' between regional employment offices as well as performance-related pay were introduced (Hartwich 2003). Further recommendations were put forward in the report of the commission[17] on 'Modern Labour-Market Services' under the chairmanship

---

[15] BA contributions have consequently risen from 4.4 per cent of wages in 1990 to 6.5 per cent in 2000 (Trampusch 2002, p. 51). If it were not for the net transfers to eastern Germany, the rate could be lowered for West Germany to 5.0 per cent (Bundesanstalt für Arbeit 2003, p. 12).

[16] The fact that this occurred about six months before the general election of September 2002 and in a phase when labour-market results took a marked turn for the worse, thus threatening the chances of the incumbent government, added considerably to the controversy in the politics of the reform.

[17] Interestingly, the new chairman of the BA, Florian Gerster, was not appointed a member of the Hartz Commission, thus weakening his stance immediately after his installation.

of Volkswagen board member Peter Hartz (Hartz et al. 2002). Its thirteen main suggestions included measures for increasing placement efficiency and enhancing flexibility especially of the low-wage sector; part-time employment was to be particularly encouraged and partially subsidised by the BA; and the latter was in the future to be run by setting targets rather than by detailed prescriptions.

Most of these proposals – a detailed summary and critique of which can be found in the annual report of the Council of Economic Advisers (Sachverständigenrat zur Begutachtung der gesamtwirtschaftlichen Entwicklung 2002) – were put into law, albeit after some changes, with the support of the opposition parties (Hartwich 2003, pp. 132–5). Assessing whether they will have the desired positive effects on the German labour-market slump is beyond the scope of this chapter. At the time of writing (spring 2004), the results do not look promising so far. With regard to the consequences of the organisational changes within the BA, it is clear that the state's hand has been strengthened over that of the employers and trade unions, and partially against their expressed wishes. But what result that will bring is difficult to predict: while some scholars emphasise the 'quite revolutionary structural change' that lies in imposing a private-sector governance structure on the BA (Hartwich 2003, pp. 126, 139), others are markedly more reserved and point to the incremental decentralisation of labour-market policy that has been going on since the 1980s. Changing the rules at the top of the organisation will, in this assessment, have little impact on the way sectoral self-government works at the local level (Trampusch 2002). Initial signs (such as the sacking of the first chairman of the new board of the BA, Florian Gerster, over disputes concerning contracts with external consultants in January 2004) point to an increased politicisation of this parapublic institution. Gerster (a Social Democrat) was replaced by his deputy Weise (a Christian Democrat), even though the latter bore formal responsibility for said consultancy contracts. A coalition of disaffected trade unionists and business representatives was thus able to claim the political scalp of one of the Schröder government's most visible reformers – a symbolic victory. If such politicisation were to continue, it would severely endanger the BA's buffer function, which in turn might limit its usefulness for the political system.

Conclusions: Parapublic Institutions in a Changed Environment

Looking back on the case studies presented above, we can conclude that parapublic institutions do continue to play an important role in the political system of unified Germany. Indeed, as especially the case of the *Treuhandanstalt* after unification demonstrates, they very much belong to the standard policy repertoire of the Federal Republic: when faced with a new and hitherto unknown challenge, the response was the construction of a new parapublic institution, in which the various levels of the state worked with privileged societal interests to try to tackle the problem co-operatively. Similarly, the *Bundesanstalt für Arbeit* continues to display the characteristics of a parapublic institution throughout the period under investigation here – and maintains them even after the fundamental organisational reform of 2002, albeit on a somewhat reduced scale, as state influence over the BA has been strengthened. The most notable change has taken place in the case of the *Bundesbank*, which has been transformed as a result of the introduction of EMU. As was mentioned above, this can be interpreted either as the *Bundesbank*'s demise (particularly if one focuses on the disputes the central bank had lost against the federal government), or as its successful export to the European level, since the European Central Bank (ECB) is institutionally very much modelled on the *Bundesbank*. So, significant changes have taken place in some respects, and this section will focus on assessing these changes and looking for explanations.[18]

Parapublic institutions are, at the beginning of the twenty-first century, operating under circumstances that differ considerably from the ones emphasised in Katzenstein's 1987 study. It may be partly due to these changed circumstances that the policy outcomes associated with their role are now decidedly mixed (when parapublic institutions were once held to be major causes for policy success): they are ambiguous in the cases of both the *Bundesbank* and the *Treuhandanstalt*, but clearly not much cause for pride with respect to unemployment and the *Bundesanstalt für Arbeit*.

One particular change that has altered the foundations on which parapublic institutions operate is the relationship between state and society. In Katzenstein's original analysis, the weakness of the decentralised state was compensated for by its interaction with a centralised society. That centralised society, however, has been severely weakened in the Federal Republic in the past two decades. Hardly anywhere is this more evident than in the area that lies at the core of German corporatist networks, namely industrial relations (cf. chapter 7 in this volume). As

---

[18] Obviously, the conclusions offered in this chapter cannot claim to be generalised for all parapublic institutions – they have to restrict themselves to the cases studied here. The main reason for this is that recent and detailed studies for many of them are missing in the academic literature. Particular *desiderata* are studies on the role of the churches.

most parapublic institutions are characterised by privileged access for the 'social partners', namely employers and trade unions, they are directly affected by this change. Trade unions have lost four million members during the 1990s, and overall union density has dropped by one-third between 1980 and 1999 to just 18.6 per cent (Ebbinghaus 2002a). Moreover, although trade unions are still relatively strong in the declining 'blue-collar' industries, they are particularly weak in the 'white-collar' section of the economy that continues to grow: here union density is a meagre 12.6 per cent. Conversely, employers' organisations are also plagued by a decline in membership, which is particularly acute in the case of the small and medium-sized enterprises. One result of this is that big firms begin to dominate the associations more and more, and, thus, influence policy in their particular interest.

Both sides of the divide thus suffer from declining organisational capacity, which means that the gap grows between what is in their particular interest and what is in the interest of society as a whole. To halt their respective decline, these organisations are thus less inclined to compromise constructively. Instead, they try to provide their members with specific incentives for membership – and this can mean increased militancy. In the case of the trade unions, these tendencies have been exacerbated by mergers of unions (particularly in the service sector), which further weakened organisational capacities and put the need for finding a common identity above that of constructive co-operation in industrial relations.

The area of industrial relations is, however, only the most visible part of the decline of the 'centralised society'. It is not only unions that have seen declines in mass membership and organisational capacity: the same is true for political parties and churches, to name just two other prominent examples. These developments not only weaken these actors organisationally, they also result in declining financial resources, and above all in a reduction of the legitimacy which is so crucial for the effective operation of parapublic institutions. Put simply, the core institutions of Germany's 'centralised society' have lost much of their *Bindungskraft*, their power to organise and amalgamate interests at a high level. The underlying factors behind these developments, such as economic structural change (resulting from a shift from an industrial economy to one dominated by the service sector), increased societal heterogeneity and more individualisation, have thus affected the German political system in a special way. What is more, as chapters 3 and 4 in this volume have shown, the changes that have befallen parapublic institutions also affect the other two 'nodes' Katzenstein identified as linking state and society, namely political parties and co-operative federalism.

As this chapter has demonstrated, parapublic institutions continue to play a central role in the political system of unified Germany. But since 1990, they have had to cope with enormous new burdens and challenges from both German unification and European integration, while at the same time the societal foundations on which they rest have weakened. Parapublic institutions have thus come under considerable stress in the past fifteen years.

With their foundations and their operating environment changing, it becomes obvious that – with a view to policy outcomes – they have not operated as successfully as in previous decades. Obviously, their method of operation worked less well in the 'zero-sum' game situation during a time of low growth than it had in previous decades when higher growth rates made gains for all parties involved possible, with the dispute only being about relative gains.

Seen from the perspective of the political system, however, parapublic institutions have continued to fulfil their shock absorber function to a large degree. When German unification made massive fiscal transfers to eastern Germany necessary, it was parapublic institutions that enabled the political system to work like a 'problem atomizer' (Czada 1995), transferring money from their various funds and thus initially preventing the need for politically unpopular tax hikes. The degree to which this happened is, indeed, astonishing: no less than 75 per cent of the transfers to eastern Germany came from the coffers of the various social-security funds (Bundesanstalt für Arbeit 2003, p. 9).

But 'buffering' and postponing did not obviate the eventual need to face the truth. When the hoped-for self-sustaining economic upturn in the east did not materialise, costs mounted in the second half of the 1990s, and visibly so. At the same time, external constraints like the European Stability and Growth Pact put shackles on state deficits and an uncomfortable squeeze on state budgets both at the *Länder* and federal level.[19] Discontent with policy outcomes, not least in the labour market, has led to collective soul searching and calls for root and branch reform of the political system. However, even if these calls were less sweeping and unspecific than they generally are, it is unlikely that they would succeed because the German political system is not prone to radical changes – the original puzzle that, after all, prompted Katzenstein's original study of the 'semisovereign state'.

---

[19] It is no small measure of irony that it was a German government that insisted on the introduction of rigorous deficit limits as a precondition for EMU. Thus, the wounds can be seen as largely self-inflicted.

The fact that the German political system is difficult to categorise in the universe of political systems and that its functioning is often poorly understood certainly contributes to the criticism. For it consists of an almost *sui generis* combination of negotiation and competition elements of democracy for which Lehmbruch (1996b) has coined the phrase *korporative Verhandlungsdemokratie* (literally a corporative democracy based on negotiation). But contrary to, for example, the Swiss case in which parapublic institutions also play an important role in policy implementation (see Linder 1999, pp. 116–17), the German system is characterised by a far lower degree and tradition of *Konkordanz* between the political parties, which makes co-operation that much harder to attain.

But while many actors participate in German policy decisions and implementation, this does not necessarily mean that they all have the potential or willingness to act as 'veto players', as Merkel (2003) has shown. Indeed, reports of the 'deadlock' (Heinze 1998) in both German society and the German political system, as well as the hypothesis of incrementalism having turned into paralysis, may be premature as well as exaggerated. After all, game theory teaches us that strategic actors may opt for co-operation rather than veto if they find themselves in the situation of a repeated game from which they cannot escape. And their focus may be less on the 'consensus' that is often ridiculed in today's political debate in Germany, but on 'exchange'. Indeed, empirical studies that set out to test the hypothesis of the deadlocked German political system often find little evidence of it (Holtmann and Voelzkow 2000). In that political system, parapublic institutions are deeply embedded, and will remain so. Whether they can contribute to produce positive externalities depends, as the case studies here have shown, so much on circumstances that predictions about their future role are beyond generalisation.

6 Economic Policy Management: Catastrophic Equilibrium, Tipping Points and Crisis Interventions

Kenneth Dyson

Weak State, Incremental Bias: Semisovereignty in Comparative and Historical Context

Occasionally a book so successfully defines the central characteristics of a political system that it comes to inform the core assumptions, basic interpretations and agenda pursued in later studies. This applies with particular force to what are seen as its distinctive biases in economic policy management. It was Peter Katzenstein's (1987) seminal achievement to offer such an account of economic policy management in West Germany. Katzenstein's narrative was born out of a very different historical, institutional and ideational context from that of other countries such as France. The post-war reconstruction of West German economic policy was haunted by memories of the economic, social and political breakdown caused by hyperinflation in the 1920s and 1940s, by memories of the misuse of economic power by large firms and cartels, and by their association with the collapse into the barbarism of the Nazi period. Against this background, 'economic stability', the competitive market economy and 'social partnership' took on a deeply symbolic as well as practical value as guarantors of post-war liberal democratic stability. They decentralised and shared economic power (notably through competition policy and through co-determination in corporate governance), and put in place an institutional framework that was designed to prevent irresponsible political management of monetary and financial policy (in particular an independent central bank). The institutional expressions of this transformed system of economic policy management were the Federal Economics Ministry (especially its *Grundsatzabteilung*), the Federal Cartel Office, the *Bundesbank*, and the role of employee representation in the supervisory boards and the works councils of West German companies.

Katzenstein outlined a system of economic policy management that had worked well in the past, and that had been remodelled in the 1960s to take on Keynesian elements (notably by the Stability and Growth Law of Federal Economics Minister Karl Schiller). But it was facing new challenges for which it might not be well prepared. The new context in which Katzenstein was writing was Reaganism and Thatcherism and a new sense of ideological contest about economic policy. This loss of ideological initiative was accompanied by mounting debate about Germany's capacity to attract and retain investment (the *Standort Deutschland* debate). Since then – with the huge costs of German unification and the challenges of post-Fordism, globalisation and Europeanisation, as well as of labour-market reform – German economic policy has had to cope with deepening and more urgent problems.

In retrospect, Katzenstein's causal judgement about the economic policy performance of semisovereign Germany seems sound, indeed prescient. Germany was already exhibiting symptoms of relative economic decline, notably in growth, investment and employment performance (see Giersch et al. 1992). His portrait of semisovereignty seems likewise convincing. Power over economic policy is indeed shared, and there are collective-action problems in a system in which there can be strong incentives to act as policy veto players in defence of one's own interests.

The Context of Contested Beliefs and Policy Change: Catastrophic Equilibrium, Tipping Points and Crisis

Despite its strengths as an institutional account, Katzenstein's analysis of the change of German economic policy needs development in two ways. First, in its focus on consensus about the social market economy it underplays the element of contest amongst ideas. Second, its stress on incrementalism offers an inadequate analysis of policy change, failing to distinguish between, on the one hand, 'catastrophic equilibrium' and, on the other, the altered trajectory of change and transformation of the political economy that is linked to a 'tipping point' or a crisis intervention (on the distinction between these two concepts see Hay 1999). 'Incremental bias' tells us little about the nature of policy change, especially its trajectory.

From the 1990s, accounts began to converge around a new conventional wisdom about a German political economy caught up in a condition that is characterised here as 'catastrophic equilibrium' (e.g. Heinze 1998; Kitschelt and Streeck 2004a). This condition arises when mounting evidence of pervasive economic policy failures in growth and employment is not matched by mobilisation through narration of a crisis of the state that calls into question established policy paradigms, and that requires urgent, radical and painful structural transformation of the state and its relationship to the economy. The result is a blocked political economy, mired in *Reformstau* and 'gridlock'. Despite this bleak consensus, the semisovereign state is also consistent with periods in which other modes of policy change can lead to the displacement of leading economic policy ideas and new trajectories of development. In a context of contested ideas, exogenous shocks can trigger faster and more radical policy change by lending greater credibility to one set of arguments over another. Past examples are provided by the 1965–6 economic and political crisis and a new trajectory of Keynesian ideas associated with Karl Schiller, and later in 1973 the oil crisis and the empowerment of ordo-liberalism.

A bias to incrementalism may disguise the way in which one or more small changes may have unintentionally large transformational effects (a 'tipping point') or may be linked to an emerging crisis narrative that justifies more purposive radical intervention. The 'tipping point' highlights three characteristics of policy change: that policy ideas can prove contagious, spreading like epidemics; that they can reveal themselves in one dramatic moment; and that little causes can have big effects (see classically Granovetter 1978; Schelling 1978; more recently, Gladwell 2000). Examples of 'tipping points' include the perceived failures and collapses of Keynesian-style macro-economic co-ordination in the Concerted Action (*Konzertierte Aktion*) during the Schmidt chancellorship, and then of co-ordinated structural reforms in the Alliance for Jobs (*Bündnis für Arbeit*) during the Schröder chancellorship. In each case – under SPD-led governments – the effect was to empower ordo-liberal policy arguments. The final collapse of the Alliance for Jobs in March 2003 and Schröder's personal sponsorship of the highly controversial Agenda 2010 reform programme, seemed to have initiated a new trajectory of change, as many in the SPD and the trade unions recognised.

Katzenstein's account is problematic when seen from the perspective of the narrative content of German economic policy. Consensus around the social market economy exists essentially at the level of deep shared beliefs about the basic values of the German state. It is, however, less relevant to an understanding of economic management as a policy subsystem and the nature of core economic policy beliefs. Debate about German economic policy is structured around a set of advocacy coalitions contending for power over policy rather than around an epistemic community of policy professionals sharing normative and causal beliefs (cf. Sabatier and Jenkins-Smith 1993; Haas 1992). In short, there are contested beliefs about economic policy values, about causal mechanisms and about policy projects rather than a single shared belief system. Different advocacy coalitions are each held together by shared policy beliefs, but contest not just what should be done but how economic policy management should work.

In essence, three contending coalitions can be identified (Dyson 2002):

1 The ordo-liberal coalition, which gives primacy to the role of the state in providing a framework of economic stability, including rules for a competitive market;
2 The managed capitalism coalition, which emphasises the role of the state in protecting and promoting social solidarity so that the benefits and costs of economic adjustment are seen to be borne fairly;
3 The neo-Keynesian coalition, among whose key protagonists are the German Trade Union Federation (DGB) and former SPD leader and Federal Finance Minister Oskar Lafontaine, which gives primacy to the role of the state in demand management to optimise economic growth and job creation by using its fiscal instruments of taxation, public expenditure and deficit management.

As economic policy performance has declined since the 1980s, so the element of contest amongst these three coalitions has been more clearly revealed and the debate about economic policy has threatened to widen into a more profound debate about the structure and functioning of the German state. For the 'ordo-liberal' coalition, the requirement is powerful external pressures (e.g. strict interpretation of the EU's Stability and Growth Pact) combined with strong state actors willing and capable of pushing through major structural reforms of labour markets, the welfare state and fiscal policies. They look in particular to the Europeanisation of economic policy management as a catalyst, to a government that better reflects their policy ideas (typically with a strong FDP presence), and increasingly to political reforms to the federal system and to electoral timetables.

Ordo-liberal arguments were strengthened by a variable that is understated in Katzenstein's account – the role and impact of large firms on German economic policy. As Hirschman (1970) and Lindblom (1978) argue, firms are privileged in that their loyalty, voice and threats of exit have a disproportionate influence on governments – both federal and *Länder* – whose electoral prospects are bound up with investment, tax revenues and jobs. Hall and Soskice's (2001) account goes further in stressing the symbiotic relationship of a co-operative process of economic policy management not just to the macro-political framework but, more crucially, to the institutional structures of German capitalism and the firms that support them. The sustainability of this co-operative process rests ultimately on the loyalty of (large) key German firms and their continuing perception that its benefits in a high-productivity and committed workforce producing top-quality reliable goods outweigh its costs. In other words, the loyalty of German firms is a critical independent variable in economic policy change, and in whether the traditional virtuous circle of *Modell Deutschland* can be sustained.

A key change in the agenda of German economic policy in the 1990s has been the use of globalisation by firms as part of a discourse about reinforcing competitiveness through reduction in unit labour costs and more flexible labour, product and financial markets. As this chapter shows, globalisation has been a key feature of discursive change within economic policy, and has been taken up particularly by the Federation of German Industry (BDI), the *Bundesbank* and by ordo-liberal economists. But the pace-setting role has been played by major firms like Daimler-Chrysler and Deutsche Bank, which have repositioned themselves as global players. Ordo-liberalism has been strengthened by corporate emphasis on the mismatch between the requirements of competing in a global economy and the German regulatory culture. The implication is either a change in regulatory culture or the exit of firms.

In contrast, managed capitalism policy arguments were firmly linked to the welfare-state policy subsystem and its institutional arrangements of social partnership. In short, as chapter 7 in this volume emphasises, there is an important interactivity between economic policy management and the legacy of the Bismarckian welfare state. Political consensus has been maintained in the context of managing the costs of economic adjustment by externalising these costs to the welfare state. As employment helps finance the German welfare state, the result has been negative for the labour-market, and is reflected in higher and rising structural unemployment. This interactivity between policy subsystems is neglected in Katzenstein's account. Welfare-state reform is a vital component in dealing with the mounting problems of the German economy. This linkage was reflected in the importance that the Schröder government attached to a new expert commission on welfare reform following its victory at the 2002 federal election (see also chapter 8 in this volume). The problems of the welfare state are a second critical variable – alongside the loyalty of firms in a global economy – in shaping whether the virtuous circle of Model Germany can be sustained.

By 2003, the ordo-liberal coalition was clearly winning the policy argument in the context, first, of the discrediting of Lafontaine – and by association the neo-Keynesian case – and, then, of the collapse of confidence in a Schröder government whose attempts at structural reform through dialogue – principally in the Alliance for Jobs (*Bündnis für Arbeit*) – were linked to failure to deliver on growth and employment. This development indicated that 'tipping points' in policy argument are not linked so much to changes in federal government as to an internal loss of intellectual confidence in the face of worsening economic statistics and mounting public and private criticism. The Alliance for Jobs of the Schröder government was a 'tipping point' in that its perceived failure discredited managed capitalism policy arguments, and made it likely that a crisis narrative would develop in ordo-liberal terms. In this sense the collapse of the Alliance for Jobs could prove an unintentionally decisive event in the transformation of German economic policy.

Agenda Change and the Discourse of Competitiveness

Agenda change in German economic policy has been bound up both with wider international and European developments and with developments specific to Germany. Together they have conspired to push the issue of competitiveness to the top of the political agenda as the key to restoring strong economic growth and job creation. Central to this process is the way in which post-Fordism, globalisation, Europeanisation and population decline – and not least German unification – have been defined as problems of competitiveness and as evidence of growing institutional and policy 'misfit' between the requirements of these developments and the German political economy. These five developments and associated 'misfit' played little or no role in Katzenstein's account of economic policy management, essentially because they post-dated it.

Like other advanced industrial societies, Germany has been caught up in a long-term technological change away from Fordist large-scale production and organisation patterns towards more flexible forms of post-Fordist work and employment. Model Germany was in essence an account of highly effective Fordist organisation, with large, encompassing business, employer and trade union organisations working with the state to ensure efficient production in a framework of macroeconomic stability. The shift away from Fordist production broke the virtuous cycle of Model Germany. It had major implications for the capacity of the big-business and employer associations and the trade unions to represent sectors in an encompassing manner. Hence their legitimacy as partners of government has suffered, along with their status and power. In the post-Fordist world of work and employment, the emphasis is on flexibility. The role of government is to encourage self-employment, temporary and part-time employment, and flexible working hours as instruments of job creation. The problem is that the culture of German business and employer associations and trade unions is bound up with Germany's great comparative success in managing the Fordist production model. In addition, the regulatory culture of the German state is very closely linked to the same model (Dyson 1992). Germany's problems have to some extent been masked by a process of adapting new technologies to traditional industries such as engineering, and, thereby, revitalising them. However, this process has done little if anything to create jobs in new industries, especially those in the service sector. The result has been a comparatively poor performance in job creation, and high and rising structural unemployment.

The second motor of agenda change has been globalisation, again spurred on by technology, and manifested in increased economic inter-dependence through trade, investment and financial flows. In trade terms, the openness of the German economy – expressed as the percent-age of GDP accounted for by exports and imports – grew from 47.3 per cent in 1991 to 67.8 per cent in 2002 (Bundesministerium der Finanzen 2000, p. 10). Major German companies have redefined themselves as global players, and have sought, by a mixture of persuasion and threat of exit, to persuade federal and *Länder* governments to lighten tax and regulatory 'burdens' on them. The result has been sustained and suc-cessful political pressure to reduce business taxation, with important implications for fiscal policy. With the Annual Economic Report of 1997 the Kohl government adduced globalisation to legitimate a 10-point action programme of structural reforms (Bundesministerium für Wirtschaft 1997). Schröder also took up this theme in the 1998 federal election, although he stressed the need to marry modernising reforms with social justice. He was happy to be identified as the 'comrade of the bosses' (*Genosse der Bosse*), championing the theme of making Germany 'fit' for globalisation, and, in the tax reform of 2000, achieving substan-tial cuts in business taxation. He also sponsored the idea of biennial, productivity-oriented wage bargaining with the aim of reducing unit labour costs in the interest of increased competitiveness. Whilst polit-icians might vary in their preferred choice of policy instruments, the underlying agenda change was that none could escape the association of globalisation with an assertive discourse of competitiveness from the German corporate sector.

From the mid-1990s, the discourse of competitiveness was given new momentum by the US economic miracle, the decline of German prod-uctivity growth since 1990, and the large and growing productivity gap between the USA and Germany from 1996. Domestic critics, especially ordo-liberals, adduced the US model of productivity growth and job creation to justify a domestic agenda of structural supply-side reforms to liberalise product, service, financial and, above all, labour markets. By 1996, the Kohl government had adopted this agenda, but many key measures were blocked by the SPD majority in the *Bundesrat* as 'unsocial'. As new party leader, Lafontaine sought to redefine globalisation as an ideology of global and European macro-economic co-ordination to promote growth and employment. This too involved benchmarking the USA, but with respect to the 'accommodative' monetary policies of the Federal Reserve, and to neo-Keynesian ideas within US academia. Lafontaine's attempt to define globalisation – and Europeanisation – as a problem of deflation rather than competitiveness proved abortive when he abruptly resigned as Federal Finance Minister in early 1999. The dominant discourse was about the success of flexible US labour markets. However, there was also a strong undercurrent of resistance to importing US 'hire and fire' policies, notably when both Schröder and his rival Edmund Stoiber rejected these policies in the 2002 federal election campaign. The favoured word in both main 'catch-all' parties remained flexibilisation rather than liberalisation.

More directly relevant to the agenda of economic policy was the phenomenon of Europeanisation because it involved direct German institutional participation through the complex machinery of the EU in a wide range of policies about completing both the European single market and Economic and Monetary Union (EMU). Both these major projects were powerfully endorsed by the German political establishment, but – as we see below – involved major domestic adjustment problems (see Dyson 2004). The European single market and EMU were again predominantly catalysts for a domestic discourse of competitiveness.

The single market strengthened EU oversight of competition policy through a supranational regime. This development was by no means warmly welcomed by ordo-liberals to the extent that EU policy on mergers and acquisitions was more discretion based and evolutionary in approach than their favoured rule-based and depoliticised approach. However, in other respects EU state-aid policies that aimed at a level playing field of market competition represented a major challenge to the traditional interventionist, especially subsidy policies practised by the federal government and, in particular, by *Länder* governments. The result was new conflicts between these governments and the European Commission. In 2002, Schröder took up the theme of defending German industrial interests against excessive Commission intervention, underlining the new degree of contest in relations. Nevertheless, in this changed context, defence of the privileges of the German public savings banks became unsustainable. In addition, EU liberalisation of telecommunications and, later, energy markets threatened traditional patterns of state control. This process was eased in the case of telecommunications by the way in which the Deutsche Post and Siemens redefined their corporate interests as global players. It also offered the Federal Finance Ministry important new sources of revenue through privatisation and auctioning of a new generation of mobile phone licences in 2000. In essence, domestic telecommunication liberalisation paralleled EU liberalisation. However, in energy liberalisation there was strong political resistance, especially from *Länder* and local governments that feared the loss of revenues. The German federal government worked with the French government to lengthen the period of energy liberalisation.

EMU was an additional catalyst for the discourse of competitiveness. This effect took two forms. Competitive pressures were sharpened by the elimination of exchange-rate risk, and by price and cost transparency with a single currency. In addition, EMU involved the loss of both monetary policy and exchange-rate policy as well as tight restrictions on fiscal policy so that only investment and wages remained as domestic instruments of macro-economic adjustment. This represented a major change in economic policy. By the time of the Schröder government – which coincided with stage three of EMU – the agenda had shifted to strengthening competitiveness through improved investment conditions, greater wage moderation and flexibility, and labour-market flexibility. Neither investment (other than public, which had to meet the EU's tough fiscal-policy rules) nor wages were under the direct control of the federal government. The government's main policy instruments to improve investment conditions included business-friendly taxation (where the Schröder government has, on the whole, delivered), lighter-touch regulation (where business saw it as failing), and a reduction in social-security contributions by employers (where revenues raised from the new ecological tax were helpful, but where, overall, little progress has been made). As we shall see, wages and labour-market policies were far more contentious, especially with the trade unions and the SPD's left wing.

Despite its encouragement to trade and investment, EMU has had negative economic effects for German growth and employment. First, Germany entered into the single currency at a high rate of exchange. This disadvantage vis-à-vis other euro-zone economies was initially offset by the depreciation of the euro against the US dollar between 1998 and 2002. This depreciation acted as a stimulus for export-led growth, but, by 2003, had lost its dynamic. Second, other euro-zone economies benefited more in that before the single monetary policy Germany had enjoyed lower nominal interest rates because of its role as the anchor currency of the Exchange Rate Mechanism (ERM). With the euro, falling nominal interest rates outside Germany acted as a stimulus to growth. Germany lacked this stimulus. Third, with identical nominal interest rates linked to the single monetary policy, and an inflation rate lower in Germany than the euro-zone average, Germany had higher real interest rates (nominal rates minus inflation) than in other member states. The result was higher costs of investment. Finally, falling interest rates outside Germany eased the fiscal problems of other states in meeting the rules of the Stability and Growth Pact. Germany lacked this benefit. As we shall see below, the Stability and Growth Pact evolved from a German-inspired creation in 1995–7 to a straitjacket that threatened a deflationary pro-cyclical fiscal policy on Germany by 2002–3.

Germany's economic problems of growth and unemployment were compounded by the sudden shock of unification in 1990 and its aftermath. German unification was defined as a crisis, but essentially and crucially one requiring intervention both to stem the rapid and large migration of GDR citizens to the Federal Republic by extending social and economic benefits to the GDR, and to incorporate the GDR into the tried-and-tested institutional and policy arrangements of the Federal Republic. Neither in 1990 nor thereafter was it defined as a crisis requiring a transformation of the (West) German political economy. The result was a series of policy decisions that ignored the implications of the sizeable productivity differentials between the two systems, had negative effects on German growth and employment, and delayed the process of economic convergence between east and west for decades. The exchange rate between the GDR Mark and the Deutschmark was set too high, against the advice of the *Bundesbank* which forecast a large-scale loss of output and jobs in eastern Germany. The process of wage convergence between east and west moved much faster than productivity convergence, again penalising output and jobs. The effects of these policy failures were felt directly in the real economy. By 2000, the unemployment rate in the new *Länder* was over 17 per cent, twice as high as the figure in the west, at just under 8 per cent. Less than 5 per cent of German exports derived from the east, despite the fact that eastern Germans made up at least 15 per cent of the population. These effects were to some extent offset by huge transfer payments from west to east. However, the scale of these transfers had serious negative effects on fiscal deficits and public debt so that by 2003 Germany was in breach of both the deficit rule (maximum 3 per cent of GDP) and the debt rule (maximum 60 per cent of GDP) of the EU. The interest rate-to-tax revenue ratio of the German federal budget grew from 12.4 per cent in 1990 to 21.4 per cent in 1999. In addition, state subsidies in the east encouraged a construction boom, followed by years of consolidation. According to the European Commission in 2003, one-third of the difference in growth between Germany and the rest of the euro-zone was attributable to the deep crisis in the construction sector.

To the above four factors is to be added the prospect of rapid population decline over the next decade at a time when the United States and France are expected to experience growth. Its effects are to be found not just in the mounting financial problems of social policies, especially pensions and health care, but in an associated fall in innovation and with a lower trend rate of economic growth (Société Générale 2002). With fewer in employment, growth can only be maintained either by higher productivity (which slowed in the 1990s), by increasing the proportion of the population – especially women – in work, by increasing the birth rate or by immigration (see chapter 9 in this volume). In consequence, German economic policy is inextricably bound up with difficult and painful choices not just about social policy reform, but also about immigration and participation rates in employment if a fall in potential growth rates is to be avoided.

Together, post-Fordism, globalisation, Europeanisation, German unification and population decline have highlighted the rigidity of the German labour-market as a central policy problem. According to the Annual Report of the Council of Economic Advisers for 2002–3, the absorption of the shock of German unification would have been easier and faster with flexible labour markets (Sachverständigenrat zur Begutachtung der gesamtwirtschaftlichen Entwicklung 2002). In this area more than any other the slow, tentative and reluctant pace of policy change suggested a 'catastrophic equilibrium'. The reduction of sick pay by the Kohl government in 1996 proved hugely controversial and was reversed by the Schröder government, a symbol of the hostility to ordo-liberal-inspired reform. There was some evidence of change in wage policy, led by the IG Bergbau, Chemie und Energie (the Miners', Chemical and Energy Workers' Union), with more scope for firms in financial trouble to set aside the *Land*-wide wage agreements for their sector, and greater discretion to works councils to vary pay. In addition, there was strong east German opposition to the transfer of *Land*-based sectoral wage bargaining. To be fair, with the Alliance for Jobs, the Schröder government had some success in 2000–1 in encouraging biennial, productivity-oriented wage bargaining, spearheaded by IG Bergbau, Chemie und Energie. However, faced with rising unemployment and rank-and-file militancy, the trade unions – led by IG Metall and Ver.di (the largest union whose membership is drawn from the service sectors including, most importantly, the public sector) – opted for a more confrontational approach in 2002–3, arguing that they had made sacrifices but that employers had failed to respond by creating jobs. This confrontational approach heralded the demise of the Alliance for Jobs as an instrument of reform.

Together, the progressively deteriorating unemployment rate in 2002–3, electoral setbacks in *Land* and local elections, combined with the determination of the new Federal Minister for Economics and Labour, Wolfgang Clement, to tackle obstacles to job creation, especially protection against redundancy in small businesses, turned out to be catalysts for labour-market reform. But the 'tipping point' was the failure of the Alliance for Jobs meeting that Schröder convened on 3 March 2003. This failure was rapidly followed by a government statement of the chancellor on 14 March 2003 outlining measures to reduce the employment costs on smaller businesses by relaxing redundancy provisions, reducing the length of unemployment benefit and tying it more tightly to willingness to work, and encouraging plant-level wage bargaining. Though small steps in the direction advocated by ordo-liberals, they reflected the 'tipping point' of the failure of the Alliance for Jobs, an unintentionally decisive event with long-term transformational consequences.

Process: Europeanisation and the Erosion of 'Soft' Power

An account of the process of German economic policy management in 2003 necessarily differs from that in 1987 because of the major changes in the context of European integration. The single-market project and EMU meant that the internal constraints on economic policy that were stressed in Katzenstein's account are now complemented by powerful external constraints. German federal governments are caught up in an increasingly difficult political dynamics of negotiating their way around both external and internal constraints, especially in fiscal policy. The structural consistency that Katzenstein (1997c, p. 33) later noted between domestic semisovereignty and increasing 'associated' sovereignty based on pooling sovereignty at EU level has meant that their interaction in economic policy has been generally supportive. However, ideationally, the interaction has been more problematic, consequent on the greater success in 'uploading' ordo-liberal than managed capitalism policy preferences and institutional arrangements to the EU level. In consequence, managed capitalism has been on the defensive. Also, structurally, Europeanisation of economic policy is complex in its forms and differentiated in its domestic effects. Despite these qualifications, and indeed to help strengthen domestic ordo-liberalism through external disciplines, the Federal Finance Ministry has used Europeanisation of economic policy as a means to embed and enforce the logic of reform. This strategic orientation was first apparent in the Annual Economic Report for 2000 (Bundesministerium der Finanzen 2000).

EMU rests on three pillars, each embodying different types of external constraints. First, the monetary pillar represents supranational integration around the European Central Bank (ECB), in whose governing council the *Bundesbank* is but one voice and vote amongst many. With the demise of the old ERM the hegemony of the Deutschmark is gone, along with the *Bundesbank*'s monetary-policy leadership in Europe. Having lost monetary policy to the ECB, the *Bundesbank* is no longer as significant a parapublic institution in economic policy as it was before 1999. Instead, it has been reformed to make it a more effective contributor in the ECB by centralising its management. The combination of the loss of monetary policy with internal centralisation has undermined an important element of co-operative federalism.

In two senses, an important continuity remains in the new monetary pillar. The ECB's mandate as an independent central bank dedicated exclusively to price stability,[1] and able to decide on its definition of price stability and its monetary-policy strategy, represents the 'uploading' to the European level of German ordo-liberal ideas and the *Bundesbank* model. Also, the situation of asymmetric power in economic policy co-ordination consequent on this authoritative role of the ECB is reminiscent of the *Bundesbank* (cf. Iversen et al. 2000). By making clear that its monetary policy will be a non-accommodating one, the ECB, like the *Bundesbank* before it, is able to signal what is intolerable in fiscal and wage policy, and bring sanctions to bear. This external threat and discipline raised doubts about the credibility of Lafontaine's policy of reflation as a means of reducing unemployment. The risk was that such a policy would not be accommodated by the ECB and that consequent higher interest rates would drive growth down and unemployment up. Similarly, in 2002 the ECB signalled what it was prepared to tolerate in the German wage round and the risks in breaching the rules of the Stability and Growth Pact.

[1] That is, the ECB's goal is to maintain price stability, not growth; the ECB has, however, been criticised for using data on both price changes and changes in the money supply to achieve this goal, and, hence, determine monetary policy.

Different in character is the fiscal pillar of 'hard' co-ordination, represented by the EU's Stability and Growth Pact. This pact again represented German ordo-liberal policy arguments 'uploaded' to the EU. It involved the commitment to remain within a budget deficit rule of 3 per cent of GDP (backed by sanctions), and a fiscal stance of 'close to balance' over the economic cycle. The process of co-ordination was 'hard' in that it included not just peer review of national convergence programmes, but also early warnings and ultimately sanctions if the rules were breached. The threat of an early warning to Germany in February 2002 about breaching the 3 per cent rule was averted by intense and astute German negotiations designed to avert serious political embarrassment before the *Bundestag* election that September. But, following the election, the European Commission issued a formal warning to both Germany and Portugal, which came despite a major budget consolidation programme in 2000. In November 2003, the Commission's threat to impose the sanctions procedure against Germany prompted a major crisis of authority both for the Commission and for the Stability and Growth Pact. In collusion with France, the Schröder government averted sanctions, but at considerable cost to its own reputation and that of the EU.

The third pillar of economic co-ordination, employment and structural reform, exemplifies the rapid growth of 'soft' or 'open' co-ordination at the EU level. This process involves jointly agreed policy guidelines (notably the annual Broad Economic Policy Guidelines and the Employment Policy Guidelines), peer review of national plans and reports, monitoring of performance including recommendations, and 'benchmarking' and diffusing best practice. In particular, the Broad Economic Policy Guidelines identified policy issues in which there was a deficit of action in Germany, notably in structural reforms to the budget (a national stability pact, and pension and health reforms) and in labour-market reforms (including tax and benefit reforms to strengthen incentives to work, reduction of wage-related costs especially for those on low wages, and greater flexibility in employment contracts and working conditions).

These processes of 'soft' co-ordination brought a widening range of ministries into the framework of economic policy management, notably *Land* education ministries, and those dealing with labour-market and social-policy issues. It also revealed a German problem of domestic policy co-ordination, in particular related to the so-called Lisbon process that sought to effect a broad range of measures to strengthen the productive and employment performance of the European economy. Because of the need to co-ordinate a range of federal ministries with *Land* ministries, the Federal Finance Ministry had difficulty in making specific and detailed commitments. This difficulty stemmed from a lack of conviction that it could deliver.

EMU can be seen as part of the process of 'taming' the German state, and, hence, as consistent with the semisovereignty argument; Germany was being asked to abandon the strongest EU currency and the dominant monetary-policy role in Europe. But a paradox was at work. EMU – notably the Maastricht Treaty (1991) and the Stability and Growth Pact (1997) – was also a case of Germany 'projecting' its own power to the European level. In post-war Germany, economic policy has been central to the projection of 'soft', ideational power. EMU was a notable example of German institutional power through exporting its ideas, preferences and practices. It reflected a strong rather than weak state identity that can be traced from the assertive behaviour of Karl Schiller during the 1969 revaluation crisis, and during the first discussions about EMU in the context of the Werner Report of 1970, through to the design of EMU between 1988 and 1997 (see Dyson and Featherstone 1999). This built on the foundations for a strong state identity around economic policy laid by Ludwig Erhard's espousal of ordo-liberalism (Nicholls 1994). Germany punched closer to its weight in economic policy than in other fields, a capacity symbolised by tough-minded negotiators like Schiller, Hans Tietmeyer and Helmut Schlesinger. It was always possible to discern a clear sense of German interests underpinning economic policy management, and a willingness to articulate those interests. Economic policy was bound up with re-establishing Germany as a respected international actor as well as with securing domestic social and political stability. Evidence of this sense of distinctive interest and its self-confident projection is provided by the singularity of German ordo-liberal ideas at a time of ascendant Keynesianism at the international level in the 1950s. Taming and projecting were two sides of the same coin of German economic policy. In effect, elements of weak and strong state identity were fused in EMU.

Hence, German economic policy was distinctive in that it was not an instance of a more general 'leadership-avoidance reflex' (Bulmer et al. 2000). Within the Federal Economics and Finance ministries, as well as the *Bundesbank*, there was a stronger inclination than in the Federal Chancellery or the Foreign Ministry to define the terms under which multilateral engagement could take place and the Franco-German relationship make progress on economic policy co-ordination. However, with the emerging and accumulating effects of post-Fordism, globalisation, Europeanisation and German unification, Germany experienced a shift from a strong state identity in economic policy (tamed to meet political requirements of European unification) to a weaker identity. This loss of confidence and credibility was bound up with mounting problems of policy failure in growth and employment and in fiscal stability and sustainability. Hence – contrary to early expectations – economic policy was not a simple case of German unification and retrieved external sovereignty leading to a stronger state identity. A loss of confidence and credibility translated into diminished 'soft power', including a diminished capability to make 'side-payments' by 'cheque book' diplomacy to facilitate EU deals on its own terms.

EMU has been part of a wider range of factors that have weakened German state identity in economic policy. Its particular contribution has been to subject the semisovereign state to increased pressures for adjustment because of a monetary policy that is less clearly focused on German needs (too restrictive because of inflationary pressures elsewhere in the euro-zone, and because of Germany's output and growth problems) and because of a fiscal policy that requires tough budget consolidation at a time of economic stagnation. In addition, benchmarking German performance in employment and structural reforms has shown Germany in a poor light. The result is a paradox. German success in 'uploading' policy ideas, preferences and practices to the EU level was followed by the erosion of the very foundations of soft power that had made this 'uploading' originally possible. This suggested that Germany depended on whether economic policy change at the EU level remained 'path dependent', locked into a trajectory of institutionally shaped change originally set by Germany that disadvantaged Germany, or whether the erosion of its soft power triggered a change of trajectory that – paradoxically – would benefit Germany.

Process: Reconfigured Relationships, Changing Nodal Points and Problems of Policy Leadership

Post-Fordism, globalisation, Europeanisation and German unification were also important in reconfiguring relationships within, and between, state and society. The result was manifested in changing nodal points and new problems of policy leadership. These effects on policy process were particularly clear with stage three of EMU on 1 January 1999 because it marked a clear turning point in the organisation of economic policy. Stage three put on to the agenda the issue of how German economic policy was to be organised to match the capability of the British and the French finance ministries both to project clear, coherent positions in EU negotiations, and to be credible negotiating partners by effectively delivering on commitments. The same issue arose with respect to the *Bundesbank*: how to strengthen its role within the ECB in terms of both functions and ability to speak with one voice on monetary policy. The answers seemed to be a more effective Federal Finance Ministry, in the first case, and in the second, a more centralised *Bundesbank* with new functions. Europeanisation was in effect acting as a catalyst for a reorganisation of semisovereignty in economic policy management.

Strikingly, this issue did not arise with respect to strengthening the role of the Federal Chancellor in economic policy management. Helmut Schmidt, and Erhard earlier, were really the only chancellors who identified themselves strongly with economic policy before Schröder and his self-identification as the chancellor of economic reform. There are, however, important differences. Schmidt and Erhard had been more comfortable with economic policy arguments, and had sought to shape and lead debate. In contrast, Schröder relied more exclusively on personal contacts to key figures in banking and industry to influence economic policy. In this respect his governing style was more akin to that of Helmut Kohl, though he was more preoccupied with economic policy than Kohl had been. But he was less disciplined and less macro-economic in approach than Schmidt. Notable was the continuing weak position of the economic policy division in the Federal Chancellery under Schröder: its role and power was not elevated. The Chancellery was not turned into a powerful instrument for economic policy reform. Schröder chaired summit meetings of the Alliance for Jobs, which was organised from the Chancellery, but these were presentational rather than problem-solving working sessions. In the Alliance he was unwilling to lead debate by setting his own agenda and settled for a brokerage role rather than a role as 'motor' of reforms, using the threat of government intervention to force the pace of change. In practice, the economic-reform process under Schröder was highly individualistic in relation to each issue. The Alliance for Jobs was either sidelined (for instance, over the works constitution law) or reduced to 'accompanying' a reform process whose motor was elsewhere (as in pensions reform). Schröder was happier with loose deals on reform outside the Alliance (compensating trade unions for pension reform by works constitution law reform). Other key areas in the work of Alliance for Jobs, notably labour-market reforms, were kept off the agenda by Schröder, despite pressure from his economic policy division. This approach was motivated by electoral considerations (not offending the trade unions before the 2002 election) but came back to haunt him with rising unemployment, and scandal in the organisation of job placement.

The key structural change in the balance of ministerial power over economic policy came elsewhere. Central to economic policy management at the federal level had been the complementarity and competition between the Federal Economics Ministry and the Federal Finance Ministry. Until 1972, the Economics Ministry remained in the driving seat, reflecting the political weight of Erhard and then Schiller. The relative decline of the Economics Ministry can be dated from 1972 as it came under successive FDP ministers. This decline began when Schmidt secured the move of the division for money and credit as a condition of his moving to the Finance Ministry in 1972. Hans Tietmeyer crossed over as State Secretary to Finance in 1982 (a 'big beast' in economic policy). Then, crucially, in 1998 European policy co-ordination and macro-economic policy was assigned to the Finance Ministry, leaving the Economics Ministry under a non-party figure as, effectively, a trade and industry ministry. Lafontaine's personal and political ambitions as new Finance Minister informed the changes in 1998. But they were already part of the agenda of the Finance Ministry – namely, to establish a stronger co-ordination role in economic policy management and, not least, in relation to its European dimension. The Finance Ministry's talk of the Europeanisation of economic policy in the Annual Economic Report of 2000 reflected more than the policy logic for concentrating authority over economic policy (Bundesministerium der Finanzen 2000). It expressed the ambition of the Finance Ministry to gain greater domestic leverage over economic policy.

However, this ambition came into conflict with the *Länder*, and highlighted the limitations of co-operative federalism and the potential conflicts consequent on the Federal Finance Ministry having to play a stronger role as nodal point between the EU and the *Länder*. As early as 1996–7 the Finance Minister, Theo Waigel, proposed a national stability pact agreed between the federal government and the *Länder* with a clear distribution of budgetary ceilings and sanctions. In essence, it was designed to emulate the EU's Stability and Growth Pact both to give Germany credibility in proposing it, and to ensure that Germany did not lose reputation and negotiating power by failing to deliver on its own promises. But the proposal failed, in part because the *Länder* could not agree on a formula for this purpose, but largely because they rejected the loss of sovereignty entailed in agreeing to such a pact. Eventually, Hans Eichel as Finance Minister agreed guidelines with the *Länder* in 2001, but they deferred the commitment to have budgets 'close to balance' till after 2004. The threat of an early warning from the EU in February 2002 hastened the agreement of a national stability pact that brought forward this commitment. But the absence of clear budgetary ceilings and sanctions meant that Germany still failed to match internally what it required of the EU. The fiscal conditions attached to 'associated' sovereignty at the EU level were a good deal more stringent than those attached to semisovereignty in Germany itself. Here was a potentially unstable misfit between the two levels and an exposed position for the Federal Finance Ministry.

To this problem of the Federal Finance Ministry as nodal point between the EU and *Länder* was added the problems within co-operative federalism consequent on German unification. As chapters 2 and 4 have shown, the system of horizontal and vertical fiscal transfers had to be redesigned to cope with the addition of the new and poorer eastern *Länder*. The result of unification was a new and larger category of losers in the transfer system, and a debate about fiscal equity that led to a ruling of the Federal Constitutional Court. Along with fiscal changes in the budget consolidation package and in the tax reform of the Schröder government, the effect was to exacerbate seriously the budgetary positions of the *Länder* governments and of local authorities. Federalism was in consequence beset by new tensions and conflicts that undermined the effective functioning of semisovereignty and the interface with 'associated' sovereignty at the EU level. Further significant changes, which have been discussed in greater detail in chapter 5 in this volume, have also occurred in the *Bundesanstalt für Arbeit* and the *Bundesbank*, two major parapublic institutions in the area of economic management.

The structures and functioning of managed capitalism are crucially dependent on the nodal role of the 'peak' employer, business and trade union bodies in organising relations between their members and the state. Here growing problems of leadership have emerged as a result of the rapid decline in trade union membership and the threat of exit by firms from business and employer organisations. The leaders of these organisations have been tempted to respond by seeking to mobilise their memberships around clear and tough positions. This behaviour has made consensus difficult to maintain and dialogue hard to sustain. A key casualty was the Alliance for Jobs. Falling membership support and decentralising tendencies, for instance in wage bargaining, also make it more difficult for trade union, employer and business organisations to claim legitimacy as 'encompassing' organisations that can credibly negotiate with the state.

In particular, the continuing role of '*Land*-wide' sectoral collective bargaining (*Flächentarifverträge*) is in question. Firms threaten to exit from these agreements and the employer organisations that negotiate them in order to gain sufficient flexibility to relate wages to economic conditions that vary over time and across regions and localities. In the new eastern *Länder*, there has been a notable unwillingness to support the development of employer organisations and trade unions for this purpose and a preference for flexibility. The Federation of German Industry (BDI) under Hans-Olaf Henkel developed a radical critique of *Land*-wide sectoral collective bargaining, to the irritation not just of the trade unions, but also of the Federation of German Employers (BDA) whose members are responsible for collective bargaining. Some trade unions, led by IG Bergbau, Chemie und Energie, sought to counteract the exit threat from firms by negotiating more flexible *Land*-wide agreements, and by being innovative about their contents. But this flexibility was offset by the effects on trade union leadership of falling membership, and the view, notably in IG Metall and in Ver.di, that potential members must be mobilised by more radical efforts to achieve real advances for them. The result was further strains in the system of industrial relations as this behaviour was seized on to claim that the traditional structures of managed capitalism favoured insiders over outsiders and that the costs were borne by the unemployed.

These developments in the interface between state and society were bound to affect the capacity of the party system to provide the level of consensus required for a smoothly functioning semisovereignty in economic policy. By April 2003, Guido Westerwelle, the leader of the FDP, was calling for a German Thatcherism and – along with the finance spokesperson for the CDU/CSU parliamentary party, Friedrich Merz – talking of disempowering the trade unions. As party leader, Angela Merkel gave the CDU a sharper cutting edge on economic reform in 2004, promoting new ideas for financing the welfare state that aimed at reducing non-wage labour costs. The Greens were torn between a modernising discourse and a desire to come to the protection of the beleaguered trade unions. But most problematic of all was the position inside the SPD which – especially after Schröder's Agenda 2010 proposals – was being forced with great reluctance to accept flexibility in redundancy and in collective bargaining, along with cuts in the size and length of unemployment benefit. Overall, the federal government was led by a party that was deeply committed to managed capitalism policy arguments, but that was dealing with a policy agenda increasingly set by ordo-liberalism. Increasingly, the SPD-Green coalition seemed the vital node for brokering consensus between ordo-liberalism and managed capitalism but in circumstances that were less favourable.

Conclusions: Tipping Points, Contest and Paradoxes

This chapter has suggested some modifications in our understanding of German economic policy, especially by sharpening our analytical tools for dealing with policy consensus, contest and change. First, reference to the incremental bias of the semisovereign state fails to offer a sufficiently sharp analytical tool for understanding processes of economic policy change in Germany. More useful is an analytical framework that distinguishes between catastrophic equilibrium, tipping points and crisis interventions. Contemporary discussions of the German political economy favour a rather 'doom-and-gloom' view of *Reformstau* and gridlock (though cf. Holtmann and Voelzkow 2000). This seems the logical outcome of the juxtaposition of a slow-moving incremental bias with economic problems that are mounting in scale and urgency. For both historical and institutional reasons, there is a greater political reluctance than, for instance, in Britain or France to act as a reform 'motor', developing and using a crisis narrative to mobilise political energy around a clear and decisive shift in the direction and pace of change. Heroic leadership evokes unwelcome historical images and associations. However, policy change is not locked into the either/or of catastrophic equilibrium or crisis intervention. Incremental change can itself be associated with a shift in the trajectory of institutional and policy change, in the unintended form of tipping points. The failure of the Alliance for Jobs to provide clear answers to mounting economic problems is potentially such a tipping point. It creates the space for the capture of the agenda by ordo-liberal policy arguments.

Secondly, reference to political consensus about the social market economy fails to offer a sufficiently sharp analytical tool for examining patterns of consensus and conflict about economic policy. It is important to distinguish between systemic consensus about the deep core beliefs of the social market economy, which have become bound up with the very identity of the post-war political order, and debate within the economic policy subsystem. Within this policy subsystem there is a contest for power over policy between different advocacy coalitions, each held together by shared core policy beliefs that define the nature of economic problems, and how to deal with them. It is possible to identify three advocacy coalitions: the ordo-liberal, the managed economy and the neo-Keynesian. External developments like post-Fordism, globalisation, Europeanisation and German unification have been vitally important in empowering ordo-liberalism and disempowering managed capitalism. Not least, two variables have been critical in this process: the threat of exit by, and increasing voice from, large firms, and the erosion of managed capitalism's capability to use social policy as side-payments for economic adjustment.

Finally, the German political economy is caught up in two paradoxes. The first paradox stems from the domestic misfit between, on the one hand, an ordo-liberalism that is made increasingly powerful by an ascendant discourse of competitiveness, and, on the other, the key characteristics of a political system that shares and diffuses power. In short, the underlying political theory of ordo-liberalism fits less closely with the semisovereign state than that of managed capitalism. A key part of the explanation is that, historically, ordo-liberalism's image of a strong state enforcing market principles and economic stability pre-dates the political construction of the Federal Republic (see Labrousse and Weisz 2001). In contrast, the political theory of managed capitalism rests on an image of an 'enabling' state whose role is to organise co-operation both by legislation that encourages social partnership, and by social policy side-payments to cushion the effects of economic change. This role has, however, been made more difficult by developments that have undermined the legitimacy and co-operative behaviour of the social partners, and that have weakened the capacity of the state to use social policy as side-payments. The German state is less capable of playing an enabling role in sustaining co-operative behaviour.

This disequilibrium between the interdependent economic and political orders suggests a high and continuing risk that the German political economy will be stuck in a catastrophic equilibrium. The risk of entrapment in catastrophic equilibrium arises for two reasons. There is a structural inconsistency between an ascendant ordo-liberalism and a semisovereign state (revealed in a failure to push through the policy prescriptions of ordo-liberalism); and there is a structural consistency between managed capitalism and the semisovereign state (exhibited in an unwillingness to embrace reform). These two scenarios seem to approximate respectively to the Kohl government's reform programme between 1996 and 1998 and the Schröder government's approach to reform between 1998 and 2003. Both can be seen as examples of catastrophic equilibrium.

However, as this chapter stresses, seemingly small events – like the collapse of the Alliance for Jobs or the enduring labour-market crisis – can lead to large-scale and unintended effects, shifting the trajectory and pace of change. Alternatively, policy effects may also take the form of ordo-liberalism propelling to the centre of the political agenda the issue of the structural transformation of the German state and how it relates to the economy. Such a reform agenda might embrace the federal system, electoral timetables, and forms of corporate and labour-market governance, all designed to expedite policy change. Such radical change would require a crisis narrative that post-war political elites have hesitated to adopt for historical reasons. It should not, however, be assumed that they would never embrace such a narrative. In the context of the agenda-setting forces identified in this chapter, a dominant crisis narrative is likely to be ordo-liberal in inspiration and in its definition both of the causes of policy failure that need to be urgently tackled and of the direction of structural transformation of the German state.

The second paradox is reflected in the way in which German success in uploading its domestic economic policy beliefs, institutional arrangements and practices into European economic governance has translated into German weakness. The very soft power that enabled Germany to achieve this success has been undermined by this accomplishment, leaving Germany embarrassed by the constraints of inappropriate monetary and fiscal policies and, as in November 2003, subverting the Stability and Growth Pact that had its origins only eight years before in a German initiative. German economic interests are deeply bound up with how European economic governance evolves, but its agenda-setting and negotiating powers over this evolution have declined rapidly. If the evolution of European economic governance shows itself to be locked into the path-dependence it has set, Germany will be under even greater pressure to reform its product, service and labour markets radically. These pressures would favour ordo-liberal policy arguments and the prospects of a discursive construction of a crisis of the German state requiring its structural transformation.

7 Industrial Relations: From State Weakness as Strength to State Weakness as Weakness. Welfare Corporatism and the Private Use of the Public Interest

Wolfgang Streeck

Can being governed by a state that is not fully sovereign be anything other than a crippling disadvantage for a country?[1] In his seminal analysis of post-war West Germany, Peter Katzenstein suggests it can. Indeed he argues that precisely *not* having command of full state capacities afforded West Germany more effective governance than comparable countries. This was because semisovereignty, according to Katzenstein, protected the West German state from counterproductive illusions of omnipotence other states at the time still held, and forced it to cultivate means of public policy other than direct state control – means much better matched than traditional state intervention to the evolving problems of governance in a changing world.

Successful semisovereign governance, in Katzenstein's sense, rests on two pillars. First, a fragmented, decentralised state whose capacities for direct intervention are limited must learn to make deals with independent actors in civil society which command their own sort of sovereignty which cannot be ignored or circumvented. A state of this sort must, therefore, be a 'co-operative state' (Wilke 1983), one that governs more by negotiation and co-optation than by legal command (Scharpf 1993). Where this works – in a political system that has learned to build a culture and develop techniques of indirect control – independent social organisations and institutions with their guaranteed autonomy and power turn into agents of publicly licensed self-government, under the roof of a negotiated public order of which the state is just one element among others, although a pivotal one (Streeck and Schmitter 1984).

---

[1] This chapter is based on a first review of information collected in the context of joint research with Christine Trampusch on the origins and the effects of the Alliance for Jobs of the Schröder government, and more generally on the changing relations between organised interests and the state in Germany since the 1980s. I am grateful to Christine Trampusch, Anke Hassel and Britta Rehder for constructive criticism and valuable suggestions.

Social autonomy is, thus, transformed into delegated public responsibility, and organised private groups become quasi-public agencies of societal governance much more competent and legitimate in dealing with the problems of their constituents than state bureaucracies could ever be.

Second, the social groups that are to become partners in governance of a co-operative state must be organised in a way that makes them suitable for the purpose. In Katzenstein's language, the deficiencies of the decentralised semisovereign German state were compensated by a society capable of governing itself through centralised intermediary organisations. Competition between different organisations for the allegiance of the same group does not normally give rise to responsible behaviour; nor does organisational instability of any other sort. Social groups included in semisovereign governance should, therefore, as Olson (1982) puts it, be represented by large encompassing organisations, externally inclusive to make it impossible for them to impose the costs of their policies on outsiders, and internally heterogeneous to force them to integrate divergent special interests and learn to align them behind a broad, centrist compromise. Civil society, in other words, must be represented by a small number of organisations that can legitimately and effectively speak for their constituents, together covering the society as a whole and not excluding any significant social category. Such organisations, described as 'corporatist' by the literature of the 1970s (Schmitter 1979; Lehmbruch 1979; Katzenstein 1984), can be expected to identify their interests, both substantive and organisational, with those of the society as a whole, or at least define them in such a way that they take the public interest sufficiently into account to enable a semisovereign state to avoid disruptive conflict.

One of the showpieces of Katzenstein's theory of benevolent semisovereignty was industrial relations. Here the German configuration of a weak and decentralised state and a centralised society connected by a variety of parapublic institutions was almost ideal-typically present. Under *Tarifautonomie*, the government was barred from direct intervention in wage setting. The void was filled by encompassing trade unions and employers' associations safe in their positions, and disciplined precisely by their power, which they were both allowed and obliged to exercise, and which could be exercised best only in co-operation with one another and with the state. Protected by the system of semisovereignty from radical change – for example, in the form of a statutory incomes policy – unions and employers negotiated incremental change, and took responsibility for its implementation, if only because nobody else could have done this for them. Unions in particular were held responsible by their deep involvement in a peculiar parapublic institution at the workplace level, co-determination (or *Mitbestimmung*) of workers, which had been extended in the 1970s, and to which Katzenstein devoted much attention. The result, according to Katzenstein, was a level of 'social peace' unique among large countries at the time, in turn supporting exceptional industrial competitiveness and enviable macro-economic performance.

This chapter deals with what became of German industrial relations after Katzenstein. It argues that as far as Germany is concerned, the days are gone when it was an advantage for the governance of industrial relations to have a weak state. Katzenstein's successful politics of private–public co-ordination required economic and political conditions that it could not by itself reproduce. With hindsight, it can be seen that, first, the capacity of the German state for effective concertation of capital and labour as well as, second, the social and economic benevolence of German-style free collective bargaining depended on a historical background that was taken for granted even when it was already dissolving. Among the variables that were for too long treated as constants were high and stable export-driven economic growth making full employment a normal condition, and the willingness and ability of trade unions to put their political and institutional loyalties above the articulated interests of their members. While the latter ended with the wave of worker militancy in 1969, the former finally disappeared with the first oil crisis in 1973.

In the mid-1980s when Katzenstein was writing his thesis on semi-sovereignty, the specifically West German configuration in industrial relations of a weak state and strong organised interests was already in crisis. The combination of institutionalised monetarism, as imposed by the *Bundesbank* from 1974 onwards, with an unchanged collective-bargaining regime – and especially a metalworkers' union that had sworn never to forget the 'lessons of 1969' (see below) – was generating rising unemployment that presented increasingly intractable political problems to the government. For a while, the West German political economy managed to respond to its institutionally imposed condition of low inflation and high wages with structural change towards an internationally highly competitive production pattern that came to be referred to as 'diversified quality production' (Streeck 1991). Moreover, between the first and the second oil crisis, fiscal reflation helped hide the trilemma between free collective bargaining, monetary stability and employment – a trilemma that, given the West German institutions, could only be resolved at the expense of the latter. However, when this had run its course, the very opportunity structure of semisovereignty and the same close intertwining of state and organised civil society that Katzenstein had celebrated, both constrained and enabled the social partners and the government, dependent as they were on social peace, to cover up the country's employment problem by diverting the welfare state to the purpose of a defensive management of the labour supply. In the process, the endemic pressures of a permanently unbalanced labour-market incrementally, but fundamentally, recast the relationship between labour, business and the state, and, in the end, placed the issue of state sovereignty – of the state's capacity to govern – firmly back on the economic agenda.

Context: The Rise of Welfare Corporatism

Katzenstein's semisovereignty thesis described a weak state successfully holding well-organised interest groups accountable to national economic objectives. But in Germany in the 1980s and 1990s, less encompassing, though still firmly entrenched, 'social partners' learned to use their privileged political status to take advantage of the condition of semi-sovereignty and utilise core public institutions for the purpose of subsidising an increasingly untenable labour-market regime. Step by step, the public use of private organised interests, as described by Katzenstein and others, *turned into a private use of the public interest.* By the late 1990s at the latest, in the *Bündnis für Arbeit,* or Alliance for Jobs, of the Schröder government, the decay of *Modell Deutschland* became visible in a lasting political deadlock over labour-market reform, as corporatism in the sense of responsible group self-government gave way to something like corporatism in the French or Italian meaning: the pursuit of special group interests in the public realm at public expense, first, in collusion with the government and, later, against its – reluctant – resistance.

How could this have happened? Economic semisovereignty – and in particular the lack of control of the federal government over the money supply, which was controlled by the *Bundesbank* – had protected both unions and the government from Keynesian temptations. As unions could not expect the state to underwrite excessive wage increases, they found it in their interest to moderate their wage demands in the light of their predictable macro-economic effects. This, however, changed to a significant degree in 1969 when, in particular, IG Metall attributed the unofficial strikes to its co-operation with the economic policy of the government, and with its *Konzertierte Aktion* specifically. In subsequent years, union wage policies became more responsive to the demands of a growing and more interest-conscious membership. In 1974, in the wake of the first oil shock, the Brandt government was forced to settle for a public-sector wage increase of above 10 per cent; a few months later it resigned. Having lost confidence that the government would ever be able to rein in the unions, the *Bundesbank* unilaterally switched to a monetarist policy that was non-negotiable for both unions and government. Immediately thereafter, mass unemployment became the critical problem of the (West) German political economy, which it has remained until the present day (Scharpf 1991).

The government of Helmut Schmidt, who became the chief propagandist of tripartite *Modell Deutschland,* depended on the political support of the unions, and could, therefore, not afford politically to intervene in collective bargaining.[2] Nor was it within its powers to adjust the money supply to what would have been required for a return to full employment. Indeed, faced with the unrelenting monetarism of the *Bundesbank,* the unions formally walked out of *Konzertierte Aktion* in 1978. In the same year, the government, trying desperately to find a way back to full employment, started an attempt at internationally concerted fiscal reflation. This failed when, in 1979, the United States, in violation of the Bonn summit agreements, unilaterally switched to a policy of tight money while almost simultaneously the world economy was hit by the second oil shock. With unions bent on defending the labour-market regime that provided both high wages and low wage dispersion, and that had served them and their members well, the result was an increasing public debt that coincided with rising unemployment, both of which, in turn, helped to cause the demise of the SPD-FDP coalition in 1982.

Already in the late 1970s, then, semisovereignty had begun to turn into a liability. While it continued to prevent the government from using monetary policies to shore up the labour-market, it also forced it under *Tarifautonomie* to leave the regulation of the labour-market to unions and employers. Early attempts by Chancellor Helmut Kohl to undercut union strength never got anywhere near what happened during the period in Britain; though this was probably also for lack of trying as Kohl understood only too well the political constraints of semisovereignty. Conflicts in industrial relations and between government and unions did rise. Soon, however, unions and employers learned to use the Bismarckian welfare state as a functional equivalent to Keynesianism – compensating for the adverse employment effects of free collective

---

[2] Katzenstein documents a memorable article by Helmut Schmidt, published in the *New York Times* in May 1976, where he pointed out that 'The entire process of setting wages and salaries is the exclusive responsibility of collective bargaining partners. The government and parliament would not even dream of changing this. In our experience, there exists no better solution' (quoted in Katzenstein 1987, p. 156).

bargaining, not by increasing aggregate demand, but by retiring excess labour and taking it out of the market (Streeck 2001c). As the government, given its limited powers, had nothing better to offer to contain the number of unemployed, it more or less willingly acquiesced.

In subsequent years, successive Kohl governments, under electoral pressure to do something about unemployment, but unable, effectively, to intervene in the labour market, were happy to allow the social partners to proceed with industrial restructuring under a high-wage and high-productivity labour market regime by having the social-security system absorb the victims. Indeed, this willingness to use the social-security system in such a way extended to a point where the costs of a defensive management of the labour supply themselves began to contribute to unemployment. This culminated in the period after unification when Kohl had to mend his fences with the unions to shore up national unity for a consensual *Institutionentransfer,* or institutional transfer, from west to east (Lehmbruch 1998), and to prevent 'radicalisation' in the east. In the process, the productivistic consensus that Katzenstein had described as characteristic of German industrial relations was gradually replaced with a *welfare-state consensus,* underpinned by the institutional entrenchment of unions and employers' associations in the self-government of the social-security system, until that consensus, too, began to crumble under its rising economic costs in the mid-1990s.

Agenda: Combating Unemployment

When Kohl became chancellor in 1982, the last attempt at fiscal Keynesianism had failed, unemployment continued to rise, and public debt was at a record high. Both government and unions were aware that, economically, *Bundesbank* monetarism had become the only game in town; more than Thatcher, however, Kohl had to fear the negative electoral consequences of high unemployment. And, while the unions were strong enough to resist government intervention in *Tarifautonomie,* they were also afraid of letting unemployment grow further. Their answer was a strategy of work redistribution in the form of a reduction in the amount of time worked.

How exactly work redistribution was to be accomplished became a matter of divisive contention among unions. For a time, the metalworkers' union, IG Metall, wavered between, on the one hand, early retirement at no loss of pension entitlements, and, on the other, cuts in weekly hours at no loss of pay, until, in early 1984, it settled for the latter, and started a campaign for a thirty-five-hour working week (*Wochenarbeitszeitverkürzung*). Five other unions, under the leadership of the chemical workers, instead opted for what came to be called a reduction of lifetime working hours (*Lebensarbeitszeitverkürzung*). In part, this reflected the traditional antagonism between 'left' and 'right' unions. But a different age structure may also have played a role: as IG Metall members at the time were younger on average, an equal reduction of hours for all may have been more popular with them. For their leadership, member support was central as they had concluded early on that working-time reduction was not to be had without a long strike.[3]

On the employers' side, preferences were clear. Employers expected cost increases and organisational rigidities to result from a thirty-five-hour working week; both of these they feared. They, therefore, strongly urged the new government to come to their help. This it did by trying to influence the debate among the unions in favour of the so-called 'Gang of Five', by passing legislation under which the social-security system would cover part of the costs of early retirement if a replacement was hired. Still, in the summer of 1984 the metal workers went on a six-week strike for a thirty-five-hour week. The strike ended in arbitration giving the union a reduction of weekly working time at full pay to 38.5 hours, with the prospect of a later reduction to thirty-five hours.[4]

As it turned out, if ever there was a Pyrrhic victory, it was that of IG Metall in 1984 (Streeck 2001c). To reach a settlement the union had to accept extensive provisions on working-time flexibility. Subsequently, these became the major productivity tool of German employers, who became adroit at uncovering the productivity reserves in working-time arrangements. As a result, unions and works councils lost control of the wage-effort bargain. This made it easy for employers, especially in large firms, to compensate high wage settlements with productivity improvements that made part of the workforce redundant. Consequently, the resistance of the large firms that dominate the employers' associations to wage increases declined as, unlike the losses in international market share resulting from industrial conflict, rising labour costs could easily be overcome by reorganising work within the company. The indirect effect was a crisis of solidarity within the employers' camp that began to undermine the organisational basis of tripartism.

---

[3] That the chemical workers looked for alternative ways to cut the labour supply had to do with their particular experience in the late 1960s and early 1970s, which was a lost strike. It convinced their leaders that, in their industry, successful industrial action was not possible (Schudlich 1982).

[4] This year, 1984, was the same year that the British Prime Minister, Margaret Thatcher, crushed the miners' strike, which gave rise to much comparative comment on the outstanding strength of West German unions and the extraordinary stability of the West German industrial-relations system.

Moreover, as the details of working-time flexibility have to be negotiated at the workplace between employers and works councils, the 1984 agreement set in motion a substantial decentralisation of industrial relations that is still continuing. Furthermore, growing work intensity as a result of productivity-enhancing reorganisation, first, dampened the enthusiasm of IG Metall members for further reductions in the amount of time worked, and, second, helps to explain why, in the 1990s, the leadership gradually switched their position to that of the dissenters of the early 1980s. This change in position eventually led IG Metall leaders to call, during Schröder's first term in office, for a general retirement age of sixty (*Rente mit Sechzig*). Finally, employers had agreed to the arbitration award only after Kohl had promised their leaders in a telephone conversation to pass a law prohibiting unemployment benefits being paid to workers laid off as a result of the indirect effects of an industrial dispute. The intended outcome was to make it less easy for a large union, such as IG Metall, to call a strike. Indeed, since 1984 there has not been any strike of national significance in the metal-working sector.[5]

In subsequent years, the political countermeasures taken by government and employers against working-time reductions, together with the long-term effects of the settlement of the 1984 strike, led to a joint reliance amongst unions, employers and the government on the welfare state to reduce the labour supply through a variety of forms of early retirement. Firms in the metal-working industry used the various legal opportunities available to them to thin out and rejuvenate their workforces – that is, to reduce the average age of their workforces – as extensively as firms in the chemical and other sectors, and with no less support from their works councils.[6] In the course of the 1980s, the public pension system developed into a safety valve for a labour-market regime that generated employment risks for ever larger segments of the workforce.

---

[5] The simultaneous growth in international competition and the shift to lean production made it more difficult for employers' associations to call a lock-out. In spite of the decline in union bargaining power caused by the legal changes after 1984, this may have reinforced the tendency of large employers to accept high wage settlements, and to deal with them by driving up productivity and trimming down workforces, thus adding to unemployment.

[6] It is important to note that apart from the one piece of legislation passed in 1984, there were several other instruments of defensive labour-supply management that had been around since the 1950s and 1960s; at that time, however, they had only been used to deal with individual sectoral crises, such as those in coal mining and steel. The same was true for labour-market policy which, in the 1990s, when early retirement through the pension system had reached its limits, turned into a 'holding pen' for the unemployed. The use of the welfare state in the 1980s and 1990s for removing excess labour from the labour-market was the result of incremental change that had not been originally intended. On early exit policies in Germany and elsewhere, see Ebbinghaus (2002b).

It also allowed firms to restructure in response to pressures for 'lean production' and 'downsizing', without having to face the resistance of works councils and local unions. By absorbing the surplus labour created by high wages, low wage dispersion and strong employment protection through publicly funded early retirement *inter alia*, the German welfare state of the 1980s slowly turned into a functional equivalent of the Keynesian reflation state.[7] The price of this development was twofold. First, there was a growing need for the government to subsidise the social-security funds. Second, in the German welfare state, based as it largely is on employer and employee contributions, statutory non-wage labour costs (i.e. these contributions) had to rise. Removing surplus labour from the market to fight unemployment, thus, made labour even more expensive, requiring the labour supply to be cut further – a downward spiral in which the method of choice to fight unemployment became another, potent contributor to it.

What was true for the pension system was also, roughly and in a narrow sense, true for labour-market policy in general, and, in particular, for short-term work, job-creation measures and further training. Conceived as temporary devices to protect and upgrade the skills of unemployed workers until the restoration of full employment, labour-market programmes became, over the years, permanent stopgaps for a low-employment labour-market regime. Especially after unification, labour-market policy came to support a giant 'second labour market' hiding away large numbers of unemployed in make-believe jobs before they were sent back to social assistance or unemployment benefit, or went into early retirement. The *Bundesanstalt für Arbeit*, which administers labour-market policy and, as chapter 5 in this volume has discussed, is governed on a tripartite basis by the state and the social partners, today collects a hefty 6.5 per cent of gross income, up to an indexed upper income limit, from all workers. In 2002, it had a staff of 90,000 and a budget of € 50 billion, around 40 per cent of which it spends on so-called 'active labour-market policies'.[8] By contrast, the entire public university system in Germany costs about € 27 billion per year.

---

[7] Giving an entirely new meaning to Helmut Schmidt's statement in 1976, also in the *New York Times* article quoted in note 2 above, that the 'social peace' for which West Germany was envied the world over was 'primarily an achievement of our well-developed system of social security, combined with the principle of autonomy under which the labor unions and employers' associations are allowed to pursue their interests and negotiate their differences' (quoted in Katzenstein 1978, p. 156).

[8] This compares with 3 per cent, 64,000 employees, and a budget of DM 33 billion (€ 16.9 billion) in 1985 when Katzenstein was developing his semisovereignty thesis (Katzenstein 1987, p. 69).

By the late 1980s, the economic burden of early retirement became so heavy that the Kohl government undertook the first attempts at retrenchment. Some measures, such as a slow increase in the legal age of retirement, even gained the support of the Social Democrats. But then unification arrested reform, and, indeed, turned back the clock. The tensions of the 1980s between the Kohl government and the unions receded as the challenge of unification pulled government, employers and unions closely together. In particular, to keep East Germans from migrating to West Germany, the West German welfare state, with the support of all parties, was, at an early stage, extended wholesale to the new *Länder,* together with the currency, the market economy, the legal, education and health-care systems and, of course, the collective-bargaining regime (cf. chapters 2 and 8 in this volume).

When economic disaster struck, in part predictably and in part following the unexpected breakdown of eastern European export markets, mass unemployment resulted in the tools of defensive labour-supply management that had been developed in the 1980s being used on an unprecedented scale. In effect, this amounted to western German workers and employers shouldering the lion's share of the costs of unification through rising social-security contributions. After the end of the short post-unification boom in 1993, high non-wage labour costs began to depress employment in the west. They also were perceived by employers as impairing their competitiveness at a time, in general, of economic internationalisation, and, in particular, of increased economic liberalisation in Europe following the push for a single market. This set the stage for the conflicts of the mid-1990s that contributed to the defeat of Kohl in 1998; this, in turn, led to the Schröder government's attempt to forge an 'Alliance for Jobs' with the unions.

Funding the unexpectedly high and growing costs of unification through the social-security system must have been convenient to Kohl's government, which had promised not to raise taxes while being constrained by the EU's approaching Economic and Monetary Union (EMU) to cut public deficits. That high social-security contributions themselves increased unemployment and eroded employer confidence in the governing coalition posed a political dilemma that the government eventually tried to address by attacking other, non-statutory non-wage labour costs, especially employer-paid sickness benefits. In the early summer of 1996, this caused the breakdown of the hitherto amicable relations between Kohl and the unions, which, from then on, bet their entire political capital on an SPD election victory in 1998. Among employers, high taxes on salaries drove a wedge between small and medium-sized employers, on the one hand, and large, increasingly multinational companies, on the other. While the former suffered from what was for them a crippling cost squeeze, the latter were able to use flexibility provisions in collective agreements to pay for high labour costs out of productivity improvements, in the same way as they had learned to respond to high wage settlements. Failing this, they could always, and with growing ease, relocate production abroad, buying the support of the works councils with generous supplements to the early-retirement pensions publicly provided.

For the unions, the matter was less straightforward. High social-security contributions meant losses in employment and in real wages for union members. On the other hand, however, there was the interest of an ageing membership in high and early pensions. Of particular importance here is that the Bismarckian German welfare state, organised on an 'insurance principle', not only emphasises cash transfers over services, but also tailors benefits to a worker's skill level and previous wage to protect his or her social status. Typically, the result has been long spells of benefit-supported unemployment. Amongst other things, numerous legal possibilities to reject job offers on the ground that they are unacceptable (*unzumutbar*), combined with lax enforcement of rules on the willingness to work by the employment office, have also contributed to this outcome.

In the 1990s, the *Bundesanstalt für Arbeit* in particular became the focal institution of welfare corporatism, a relationship between government, unions and employers different from the demand- and supply-side versions of neo-corporatism that prevailed in the 1970s and part of the 1980s. Welfare corporatism is a response to lasting unemployment which is untreatable, for economic or political reasons, by Keynesian demand-side management as well as neo-liberal and 'left' supply-side policies. Under welfare corporatism, industrial relations and social policy become densely intertwined, with the continued operation of the industrial-relations system depending on subsidisation by the social-security system. Jointly using the public social-security system to compensate core categories of the victims of an exclusive labour-market regime – so as to make reform of that regime less politically pressing – unions, employers and the government together sustain a 'low activity, high equality' employment system (Streeck 2001b) by obliging each other in complex ways; these complex ways include consensual co-management of economic change at the workplace, toleration of labour-market rigidities, a modicum of wage moderation, the use of social-security contributions to fund core government activities (Trampusch 2003b), and a strong role for unions and employers' associations in the government of the social-security system.

Process: Less Encompassing Organisation

The failed attempt by the unions to fight unemployment by redistributing work as well as the subsequent defence of existing labour-market institutions by using the social-security system undermined the encompassing organisation of business and labour and of the industrial-relations system as a whole. In particular, it gave rise to a progressive decentralisation of the regulation of employment conditions. Over time, the social partners of semisovereign governance increasingly corresponded less to Katzenstein's image of stable, centralised, publicly responsible private governments. Instead, forced to become more attentive to the demands of their members that they found difficult both to ignore and to change, they became resistant to government efforts to make them take the changing needs of public policy into account.

New divisions arose in the employers' camp; these were reinforced by the internationalisation of product markets and production systems. As pointed out above, small firms were less able to take advantage of the flexibility provisions of the 1984 settlement than large firms; for them, working-time reduction was simply an increase in costs. The same applied to early retirement and to the rise in social-security contributions that it required; while small firms had to pay the same contributions as large firms, they often could not afford to let their more experienced workers retire. Large multinational German firms, facing unprecedented price competition in domestic and international markets, responded to rising labour costs by asking their domestic suppliers for price reductions. Sometimes this directly followed wage rises conceded by the large firms which, in their capacity as leaders of the employers' associations, also, in effect, negotiated on behalf of their suppliers. The declining resistance of large firms to wage demands, owing to both foreign competition for market share and the new opportunities to compensate wage rises by productivity increases, convinced the *Mittelstand*, or small and medium-sized employers, that large companies were using their dominance of the employers' associations to secure labour peace for themselves, at their, the *Mittelstand*'s, expense.

By the mid-1990s, after the end of the unification boom, an unprecedented revolt was under way inside the system of business associations. In the 1970s, Hanns-Martin Schleyer, the then President of the BDA, or Confederation of German Employers' Associations, had also been elected, in personal union, President of the BDI, or Federal Association of German Industry. During his double presidency, which coincided with the Schmidt government, the corporatist centralisation of German business associations reached its peak, and so did the relative influence of employers' associations as compared with industry associations. A decade and a half later, the situation had almost been reversed. After the short interlude of national unity in the wake of unification, the more specialised and less encompassing industry associations came to serve as representatives of the interests of *Mittelstand* firms, and their most forceful and militant spokesman, Hans-Olaf Henkel, became the President of the BDI. Using neo-liberal rhetoric hitherto unheard from a German business leader, Henkel became highly visible by publicly confronting his counterparts at the BDA, first Klaus Murmann and then, after he had caused Murmann's resignation, Dieter Hundt.

Henkel's favourite themes, which were outside his formal jurisdiction as President of the BDI, were a reform of collective bargaining, especially its decentralisation, and a substantial reduction in social benefits and non-wage labour costs. While some leaders of German industry distanced themselves from his firebrand rhetoric, Henkel was re-elected several times as his public pronouncements reflected growing disenchantment among his constituents with the Kohl government's close relations with the unions in the early 1990s. After the introduction in 1995 of compulsory insurance to cover nursing care for the elderly (*Pflegeversicherung*), again to be paid for by a salary-based tax on workers and employers, a large segment of the German business class lost confidence in Kohl's ability and willingness to accomplish the social retrenchments they considered necessary in a period of economic internationalisation.

Discontent with Kohl expressed itself in the debate, initiated by business interests, over Germany's viability as a location for production (the *Standort Deutschland* debate). This emphasised the alleged economic disadvantages of Germany as a production site, and reached its peak after Kohl's re-election in 1994. Henkel's call for radical changes in industrial relations and for cutbacks in social costs took up the interests of smaller firms that could not easily relocate production abroad, and, thus, helped the BDI to shed its traditional image as a representative of large industry. Later, the new concerns of the *Mittelstand* were taken up not just by the leaders of various powerful industry associations, but also by politicians in the FDP, and by the leader of the CDU/CSU parliamentary party (*Fraktionsvorsitzender*), Wolfgang Schäuble, who aspired to succeed Kohl in 1998. As the cleavage between BDI and BDA deepened, many employers' associations began to lose members, especially after IG Metall had gained a high wage settlement in 1995 when the large and influential firms had, again, caved in to the union for fear of losing international market share (Schroeder and Ruppert 1996).

Pressures to decentralise collective bargaining were exacerbated by the situation in east Germany. Very few firms there had joined the employers' associations in the first place. Of those that were covered by industrial agreements, a large number paid less than the official wage, often with the consent of works councils desperate to protect employment in their workplace (Schroeder 2000). Paying *unter Tarif*, or below the official rate, soon spread to firms in distress in the west, and so, too, did the practice of more or less tacit concession bargaining between employers and works councils, even though these are charged by law to enforce adherence to industrial agreements (Bispinck 1997). Unions often looked the other way, in the hope that better times would return sometime and somehow. IG Metall, in particular, observed helplessly the growing de facto decentralisation of collective bargaining, sometimes trying to prevent it, though sometimes condoning it under pressure from the membership. With time, unions learned to insert clauses in industrial agreements that allowed individual employers, with the consent of either the works councils or the parties to the industrial agreement, to suspend wage increases, extend working hours or cut working time at reduced pay (so-called *Härteklauseln*, or hardship clauses; or *Öffnungsklauseln*, or opening clauses).

For the unions, redefining their role in collective bargaining to allow for greater local autonomy was difficult as the new challenge coincided with a rapid decline in their institutional position and organisational strength. Katzenstein had still been able to point to 'an increasing membership in a shrinking workforce', which he took as showing 'that in its organisational structure and political presence West German labour is a model of strength for the unions in all of the major industrial societies, except for Sweden' (1987, p. 28). But between the mid-1980s and the mid-1990s, coverage of private-sector employees by works councils fell from 51.4 to 41.6 per cent (Hassel 1999).[9] In addition and partly for the same reasons, union density declined dramatically. Hardly ten years after unification, the number of union members in (unified) Germany had returned to what it had been in West Germany in the late 1980s. Low union membership reflected low employment as much as high unemployment; this was especially true in eastern Germany. Low union membership has also been caused by the growth, first, of the informal economy and, second, of non-standard forms of employment; these two phenomena are caused, not least, by the high costs of labour. In addition, general demographic change and the reluctance of younger workers to join unions – caused by different

---

[9] More recent data on works-council coverage are not available as the German Federation of Unions (DGB) has failed to publish aggregate information on the works-council elections of 1998.

employment situations, experiences at work and career expectations – have resulted in a rapid increase in the average age of union members. Early retirement has further raised the proportion of pensioners among the membership. By the late 1990s, pensioners accounted for 19 per cent of those organised in unions affiliated to the *Deutscher Gewerkschaftsbund* (DGB), or German Federation of Unions. Disregarding the retired and the unemployed, overall union density in the private sector of the German economy fell from 27.3 per cent in 1980 to no more than 18.6 per cent in 1999 (Ebbinghaus 2002a).

While the decentralisation of collective bargaining and several moderate wage rounds in the second half of the 1990s[10] brought the membership losses of employers' associations to a halt, unions watched their own organisational crisis in helpless bewilderment. The transformation of the *Flächentarifvertrag*, or sectoral collective agreement – driven as it was by individual employers and works councils – proceeded against the passive resistance of unions; this transformation was, however, beyond the control of a union movement uncertain and divided over its response (Hassel and Rehder 2001). Several union mergers were accomplished, but the haemorrhage was not stemmed. Mergers also seem to have weakened the peak association, the DGB, which now represents a very small number of large and basically self-sufficient affiliates. Although the cleavage between the metal workers and the chemical workers in particular is not new, the DGB today seems to find it harder than ever to build a united front for tripartite national negotiations.

Welfare corporatism divided employers. It prevented neither the decentralisation of industrial relations nor the encapsulation of welfare corporatism in a shrinking segment of the German economy. But by the late 1990s, welfare corporatism had become one of the last strongholds of a union movement no longer able to gain for its members growing wages or secure employment. Today, involvement in the running of the social-security system, with its huge parafiscal budgets, assures industrial unions a national role at a time when wage setting is becoming more decentralised. Indeed, welfare corporatism seems like a strange travesty of the *gesamtwirtschaftliche Mitbestimmung*, or co-determination throughout the entire economy, that German unions had envisaged in the immediate post-war years. Workplace co-determination, to which Katzenstein rightly pays so much attention, was, by and large, accepted by employers during the 1980s (Kommission Mitbestimmung 1998), the more so as it became in practice increasingly

---

[10] Where wage moderation was partly caused by union concern for the cohesion of employers' associations, which is essential for industry-wide collective bargaining.

driven by the needs and concerns of individual firms. Very much in Katzenstein's sense, *Mitbestimmung*, or co-determination, continued to function as a parapublic infrastructure of co-operation between labour and capital, but in a way he could not have foreseen: by providing an institutional framework for the management and workforces of large companies within which they could negotiate the externalisation of the social costs of competitive restructuring to the public. In its 1979 ruling on co-determination, which is quoted by Katzenstein (1987, p. 162), the Constitutional Court still defended the presence of trade union representatives on the supervisory boards of large firms as a way of 'preventing or at least diluting the "enterprise egoism" expected in the wake of expanded co-determination'. Clearly this was expecting too much.

Already in the mid-1980s, Katzenstein had noted that German unions were 'on the defensive both politically and economically' (1987, p. 28). However, he failed to anticipate the looming disaster of the policy of work redistribution that unions adopted precisely to overcome that crisis. He also believed that somehow, expanded co-determination would spawn new union goals and activities, like 'qualitative growth and the deliberate steering of technological change', not to mention the 'humanisation of work', rivalling and pushing back more traditional trade union concerns (1987, p. 135). But as the years passed successive attempts at redefining the interests of the membership came to nothing. Unable to set new goals for themselves that would have given them a universalistic mission at a time when stable unemployment rendered the defence of high wages and social benefits increasingly particularistic, unions found themselves forced to operate as mere 'wage machines' whose claim, which Katzenstein found still to be widely accepted, to 'represent the interests of organised and unorganised workers' (1987, p. 28) was rapidly losing credibility.

Today, having lost much of their industrial power, German unions must rely on their political power – from electoral pressure to influence within the SPD – to secure for their members, if not employment, then an early exit from employment, and if not rising wages, then high pensions and unemployment benefits. Unlike its monetary policy, the social policy of post-war Germany's semisovereign state has turned out to be wide open to capture by safely established 'social partners'. During the 1990s, it was above all their hold on the welfare state that enabled German unions to defend the standard employment relationship, and to resist labour-market reform without having to worry much about the consequences. In fact, in light of the shrinking and ageing core membership of unions as well as in light of the failure of all alternative programmes, unions also had good organisational reasons for taking the side of the recipients of benefits against those paying for them, who are mostly young and not organised.[11]

Process: Even Less Sovereignty

By the mid-1990s, less centralised and encompassing organisations of business and labour faced a state whose sovereign capacity had further declined. In Katzenstein's time, semisovereignty had taught the West German state to make a virtue out of necessity, and become adept at co-operating with what once were well-organised interest groups. Now, not only had German society become less organised, but the ability of the state to align the interests of unions and employers with its political needs had further diminished.

As already shown by the fate of *Konzertierte Aktion,* or concerted action, the (West) German state has never been particularly good at formal tripartite negotiations with business and labour. Indeed, the same condition of semisovereignty that, according to Katzenstein, stands in the way of unilateral state action, also seems to obstruct hard bargaining with interest groups. Corporatist political exchange requires a unified position on the part of the government. But as Katzenstein has shown in impressive detail, the capacity of the Chancellery to control the ministries has always been low; coalition government further weakens the authority of the chancellor; federalism requires the government to seek the support of a majority of *Länder* governments for major legislation, which limits the concessions it can offer to organised groups; the budgets of *Bund, Länder* and local communities are so intertwined that even minor changes in the tax system cause enormous technical and political complications; independently scheduled elections at *Länder* level result in an almost permanent election campaign, especially as their outcome may change the composition of the *Bundesrat*; and a whole panoply of courts, most importantly the Constitutional Court, can be called upon to defend established groups' rights, such as *Tarifautonomie* or the

---

[11] An important, yet under-researched, aspect of welfare corporatism seems to be that involvement in the management of labour-market policy offers unions, and to an extent employers' associations, indirect access to financial resources enabling them, among other things, to maintain their organisations even where, in the east for instance, they only have relatively few members. A central role in this seems to have been played by the *Bundesanstalt für Arbeit* which, until its reorganisation after the 2002 election, was basically controlled by the 'social partners'. The *Bundesanstalt* spends billions every year on retraining and further training; some of these monies go to organisations controlled by unions and employers' associations.

social-insurance principle. All of this can offer disaffected interest groups or rival and competing parties and party factions ample opportunity to prevent or undo tripartite agreements.

While this had been so for some time, in the 1990s the capacity of the German federal government to impose its will on organised interests further declined. With unification, not only has the heterogeneity of interests in the federal system increased, but so, too, has the number of *Länder* elections during a federal government's period in office. Moreover, European integration and, especially, budget consolidation under the Stability and Growth Pact have ruled out rewarding trade union co-operation with increases in public spending of whatever sort. Other concessions, such as extended rights to workplace representation or further increases in employment protection, have become difficult to make for other reasons, in particular resistance from smaller firms that employers' associations can no longer ignore. European integration also made the government more dependent on union wage moderation, both because budget consolidation requires public-sector wages to remain under control, and because wage moderation represents the main short-term protection for the government against even higher unemployment, with all the fiscal and electoral risks that involves.

Moreover, as Roland Czada (2003) has pointed out, party competition in the German political system has intensified, voting has become more volatile, and the electoral majorities of governments have shrunk. International comparison shows that political agreement between the major parties, as well as stable, broadly based national governments, may neutralise institutional veto points; indeed, these factors may make for effective governance even where organised interests have numerous opportunities to intervene. Germany, however, according to Czada, is not only the OECD country with the greatest number of veto points, but it is also the least likely to produce electoral/parliamentary majorities broad enough to override group interests. As declining majorities in a more volatile electorate lead to intensified party competition, governments become more vulnerable to interest-group pressures.

The entrenched centrism of the two big parties that Katzenstein praised as a pillar of political stability has not helped. Regardless of whether the Christian Democrats or the Social Democrats are in power, cuts in social entitlements are always likely to be challenged by the opposition in the next election, be that election at the federal or *Länder* level; this makes it impossible for the SPD, when in government, to corner the unions on social-policy reform. Also, the declining ideological coherence of the large parties seems to have reinforced the factionalism bred by a federal system that gives regional party organisations their own electoral base supporting independent leaders with a national role and, often, national ambitions. Similar reasons account for the growing independence of the parliamentary groups of governing parties from their party leaders in government, making it likely that tripartite agreements are reopened by the *Bundestag*; this also gives interest groups that were forced to make concessions in corporatist negotiations a chance to have them 'undone' in parliament.

Perhaps most importantly, there were irresistible temptations for the federal government to make its peace with welfare corporatism, regardless of the spiral of high non-wage labour costs and unemployment that it entailed (Trampusch 2002). In the 1990s, a tacit deal had evolved under which the social partners tolerated the government drawing on the social-security system to cover part of the unexpectedly high costs of unification, enabling it to avoid raising taxes or further increasing the public debt. In return for being allowed to collect what, in effect, was a hidden tax, the state confirmed its commitment to both the extension of the exclusionary West German labour-market regime to East Germany and its public subsidisation. It also continued to acquiesce in the 'colonisation' of its social policy by unions and employers. However, whilst public–private co-operation of this sort undoubtedly contributed to 'social peace', it also appears to have compromised government authority and the state's residual sovereignty to an extent that these were even less effective when the skeleton of low employment in the joint welfare-corporatist closet could no longer be ignored. When tax competition in an internationalising economy required cutting corporate taxes while EMU demanded, at the same time, budget consolidation, the funding of the welfare state by social-security contributions became more safely enshrined than ever, even disregarding the intricacies of the German *Finanzverfassung*, or financial constitution, and the indispensability of the welfare state for social peace and government political support in the east.

From the Kohl Failure to the Schröder Deadlock

In the mid-1990s, growing discontent among business interests with declining economic conditions forced the Kohl government to address the issue of high non-wage labour costs. Since incremental change in line with the logic of semisovereignty had caused the problem – and would in any case no longer satisfy business and key political allies – Kohl tried to obtain from the unions, in tripartite negotiations, an agreement on a comprehensive reform package. Although IG Metall and DGB in late 1995 came to his assistance with their offer of a national *Bündnis für*

Arbeit, and although an understanding was reached in principle to cut aggregate non-wage labour costs to less than 40 per cent of pre-tax wages paid to workers, Kohl's consensual approach failed and the government in the end resorted to unilateral legislation. This, too, failed when the CDU/CSU lost the 1998 election.

Why did the Kohl *Bündnis* fall apart? Within the realm of business, *Mittelstand* pressure undermined the position of the traditional leadership. In particular, Hans-Olaf Henkel, the chief of the BDI and self-appointed representative of all those dissatisfied with German corporatism, demanded that the government act on its own to reverse the trend of the past decade. With business divided, Henkel and his followers managed to win the support of the FDP, the small liberal party that formed part of the coalition government that was led by Kohl, which was still chafing from its defeat on several social-policy issues in the Kohl era. Three *Länder* elections in the spring of 1996, in which the FDP was unexpectedly successful and in which the opposition parties (SPD, Greens, PDS) gained no ground, seemed to suggest that the electoral risks of unilateral reform were smaller than had been thought. Within the CDU, Schäuble, distancing himself from Kohl's policy of habitual compromise, began to champion a platform of painful social-policy reforms. In the end, Kohl was forced to include demands in the government position for the *Bündnis* that the unions could not but reject if they wanted to avoid political humiliation. As was to be expected, they walked out, and the *Bündnis* never materialised.

Once the tripartite negotiations had failed, the government embarked on unilateral measures for labour-market flexibility and lower non-wage labour costs. More important than its content, the proposed legislation signalled a departure from Germany's normal politics of consensus, and might have opened a political space for further government unilateralism. In addition to a first step towards pension reform and several changes in social benefits, the government catered to *Mittelstand* sentiments by cutting sick pay, which is paid by employers directly and outside the public social-insurance system, for six weeks at one hundred per cent of a worker's wage. Sick pay, however, may be regulated not just by law but also by collective agreement. Legislative intervention was therefore bound to cause a conflict of principle over the right of unions to collective bargaining and the proper role of the state. Moreover, as the high level of sick pay was the result of a historical strike victory of the metalworkers in the 1950s, it was of symbolic significance for the unions and considered non-negotiable by them.

In June 1996, immediately after the breakdown of the Alliance, the unions organised the largest protest rally in the history of post-war

Germany. Unfazed, the *Bundestag* passed the reform package. Shortly thereafter the conflict over sick pay escalated. In October, large firms in the metal industry, such as Siemens and Daimler-Chrysler, came under pressure from their works councils; they broke ranks with their associations, and refused to implement the cuts. The event left employers' associations in disarray, intensified conflict in the business camp, and caused bitter mutual recrimination between government and business.

It is today widely accepted that Kohl's unilaterally enacted social-policy and labour-market reforms contributed to the outcome of the 1998 election. During the campaign, in which it received unprecedented political and financial support from the unions, the SPD promised to rescind the reform legislation. Moreover, Schröder committed himself to a revival of tripartism, and to creating the *Bündnis für Arbeit* that Kohl had not been able to bring about. For the unions this meant that any future changes in social policy or in the labour-market regime were to be conditional on their agreement, although for Schröder it may not have been much more than a convenient device to avoid questions for the details of his unemployment strategy. Once the SPD had won, its left wing under the then party leader and Federal Finance Minister, Oskar Lafontaine, insisted that it kept its election promises, and, as a result, scrapped the Kohl reforms immediately. While a *Bündnis für Arbeit* was established in December 1998, the legislative changes were never discussed there, and were delivered to the unions without anything in exchange.

During Schröder's entire first term, the *Bündnis für Arbeit*, which started with tremendous publicity, remained deadlocked. Hard bargaining on employment-enhancing labour-market and social-insurance reforms never happened, perhaps because the government could not agree on its own strategy, perhaps because it had nothing much to offer in exchange. While the government hung on to the Alliance for the photo opportunities it offered an embattled chancellor, both business and labour seem to have kept it alive basically to be able to threaten the government and each other with their exit. On pension reform, the CDU, retaliating for the SPD election campaign of 1998, opposed the government's proposals, sided with pensioners, and won several *Länder* elections in 1999. At the end of that year, Schröder and the SPD were pronounced dead and were rescued only by the Kohl party-finance scandal. After the experience, unilateralism was out of the question for Schröder and, even more so, for the SPD and its parliamentary party. To mend fences with the unions, which continued to refuse to co-operate on institutional reform, they were handed various improvements in co-determination, outside the *Bündnis* and again without explicit concessions in return.

The only major success the Schröder government achieved in the context of the Alliance was the two-year moderate wage settlement of early 2000, after a period of slack demand and the Keynesian rhetoric of Lafontaine as Finance Minister had produced a high wage rise immediately after the change of government in early 1999. Indeed, during its entire first term, the government spent most of its political capital with the unions on wage moderation – an issue that formally never came on the Alliance agenda because of union insistence on *Tarifautonomie*, or collective bargaining free from government interference – not least because the employers and the public expected it. Wage moderation being important as it was to the government for domestic as well as European reasons, the unions seem to have extracted in return a promise from the chancellor to forgo unilateral labour-market or social-security reform. Given the logic of electoral competition and the strong position of the SPD parliamentary party, that promise may not have been difficult to make.

By the middle of Schröder's first term at the latest, the *Bündnis für Arbeit* was mired in deadlock. Schröder knew that Kohl's attempt to achieve non-incremental change by tripartite agreement had failed, because of unbridgeable differences between what the government felt was necessary and what the unions were willing to accept. But having himself brought upon Kohl the punishment by the voters for his subsequent turn to unilateral reform, Schröder saw no alternative but to try again for a consensual solution. Unfortunately for him, what the unions had learned from the events was that they had no rational reason to co-operate. If corporatist concertation, as has often been pointed out, depends on the government being credibly able to threaten unilateral action, then it was even less likely to happen in Germany after 1998 than before. A state that is unable to overcome resistance is also very likely to be one that is unable to make divergent interests pull together. Consensus politics, if it is to accomplish more than the sort of change that would happen anyway, requires not a weak but a strong state. This was interestingly reflected in the frequent German debates at the time of the 'Dutch Model', which moved from the notion of a solidaristic '*Polder* society' to the position that, unlike in Germany, there is no *Tarifautonomie* in the Netherlands; this 'deficit' enables the government to take wage-setting out of the hands of unions and employers if they are unwilling to take government policy into account.

As far as the unions were concerned, Schröder did not know what to offer them to entice them into co-operation; nor, indeed, did the unions know what to ask for except that everything should, basically, remain the way it was. By the 1990s, German governments could no longer count on the gentle push and pull of parapublic institutions bringing organised social interests into line with public interests, as in Katzenstein's world. Instead major parapublic institutions had turned into bridgeheads inside the state of increasingly particularistic interest groups; the government needed to regain these bridgeheads if it was to re-establish its freedom of manoeuvre. Growing economic and societal dualism, a tendency that Katzenstein had already observed (1987, p. 147), was not a major concern for a union movement safely entrenched in its encapsulated domain and catering to the interests of an ageing core membership. Nor was it as such a problem for a government that had been more than willing to absorb the external costs of social peace at public expense. It was only when the costs of mutual exploitation for the state exceeded its benefits that governments began to make half-hearted attempts to extricate themselves from welfare corporatism, reasserting as public interest their own institutional interest in stopping the downward spiral of high social expenditures and low employment. At that stage, however, the congenital weakness of the semisovereign German state made it difficult if not impossible for any government to move unions out of their passive and active resistance that had given up any political ambition beyond the hard-headed defence of their *Besitzstand*, or existing property and privileges; a defence, moreover, based on 'cost-benefit' calculations. Nor could the employers' associations, forced to take into account the concerns of small and medium-sized firms, be relied upon any more to help the government buy time. Having never really got going, German tripartism had run its course.

Now a Strong State?

Tight interdependence between the state and organised social groups in Germany, according to Katzenstein, makes 'large-scale departure from established policies an improbable occurrence' (1987, p. 35). Unable to accomplish radical change, West German politics learned to cultivate consensual incremental adjustment, which for a time served the country well as it protected political trust and provided stable conditions for investment and consumption.

Nowhere was it written, however, that incrementalism would always proceed in the direction of economic and political sustainability. Social dysfunctions, especially those that are deeply rooted in stable institutional structures, may take time to accumulate before they become acute. Incrementalism continued in the 1980s in the face of persistent unemployment and growing social dualism, responding to the evolving structural problems with a series of stopgaps that only added to the drift. Imperceptibly, but nevertheless fundamentally, the underlying logic of interdependence changed, while the economic foundations of the social peace that incrementalism was dedicated to preserving dwindled away.

By the second half of the 1990s, the radical changes that had one last time been delayed by the *Institutionentransfer* to East Germany had become imperative for any government interested in its capacity to govern. But turning around a long-term evolutionary trend exceeded the capacities of a semisovereign state whose principal achievement had been smooth co-operation with organised civil society in the very incremental adjustment that had now become obviously insufficient. Both Kohl and Schröder had to learn that not only was there no incremental solution to the economic and political problems facing their governments, but there also was no prospect of consensual radical change. There was some incremental change, even during Schröder's first term. Labour-market policy was cut back somewhat; part of the cost of early retirement was internalised in collective agreements; changes in the practice of collective bargaining allowed individual firms more space for customised workplace agreements; and a funded supplementary pension scheme was introduced to alleviate the pressure on the public pension system. But none of this did anything significant to break the spiral of high social insurance contribution, and low employment. At best, it prevented the economic burden of the welfare state on the labour-market from growing even faster.

When incrementalism was no longer capable of aligning the interests of state, unions and employers – not to mention attacking the root causes of endemic under-employment – state weakness in the 1990s became exactly that: a weakness that spelt stagnation and decline. The semisovereign German state had fitted in well with the managed capitalism after 1945, when the task was to embed a liberal market economy in the post-war settlement. When semisovereignty worked, an organised and disciplined society kept a weak state in check while compensating for its disabilities; to discipline interest groups that use their political privileges to provide for their members at public expense, however, a weak state is not strong enough.

Today the favourite means of governments trying to rein in rent-seeking interest groups is liberalisation. But paradoxically, liberalisation seems to require a strong state, particularly in a well-organised civil society. In this respect semisovereignty is both too much and too little. It is too much in that it implies deep public intervention, by the state in co-operation with organised social groups, in the functioning of the market economy. But it is also too little in that a liberal economy requires a state that is capable of overriding organised interests that refuse to internalise the costs of their behaviour and have ceased to be responsive to public interests. If the taming of organised interests requires less state sovereignty over the economy, it also seems to require more state sovereignty over society.

In early 2002, with defeat in the upcoming election almost a certainty, Schröder exploited a minor scandal in the giant patronage machine of the *Bundesanstalt für Arbeit* to dislodge its self-government, and call for fundamental labour-market policy reforms. In a striking departure from the tripartism of the by then defunct *Bündnis*, he appointed a commission under the leadership of Volkswagen personnel director, Peter Hartz, to devise a plan for cutting unemployment by half within two years. Only two of the fifteen members of the so-called Hartz Commission were representatives of trade unions, and only one represented the established organisations of business. Under the pressure of the election campaign, with the CDU ridiculing the commission as Schröder's last chance, both the unions and the SPD were blackmailed by the Federal Chancellery into supporting the conclusions that Hartz, under public prodding from Chancellor Schröder, put forward about six weeks before the election.

When, against all expectations, Schröder won a second term, many expected the brief exercise in state unilateralism to be over. For a while this was exactly what seemed to be coming, and once again, as in 1998, the unions readied themselves to collect the rewards for their campaign support. But then, all of a sudden, Schröder dissolved the once so powerful Federal Ministry of Labour – the union stronghold inside the government machinery[12] – and merged its largest part into the Federal Ministry of Economic Affairs. To head this new 'super ministry', he appointed a political heavyweight from the right wing of the SPD, Wolfgang Clement. Shortly thereafter, a series of incremental emergency measures that had become necessary to balance the state and social-security budgets – measures that had been put off so as not to disturb the collective amnesia and the good feelings that had turned around the election, but which were otherwise considered, rightly, by the political class to be business as usual – caused an unprecedented loss of confidence in the government. In part, this was because nothing of this sort had been hinted at during the election campaign. But it was also

---

[12] Throughout Helmut Kohl's chancellorship from 1982 to 1998, the Federal Ministry of Labour and Social Affairs was headed by Norbert Blüm, who came from the social catholic wing of the CDU and was also a member of IG Metall. Following the 1998 federal election, he was succeeded by Walter Riester, who had previously served as deputy leader of IG Metall.

because somehow it suddenly dawned on the public that no end to this sort of business as usual was anywhere in sight.

Apparently terrified by the prospect of an unending series of similarly unpopular incremental changes consuming his entire second term, Schröder – and Clement – pushed a good part of the Hartz Commission's recommendations through *Bundestag* and *Bundesrat* by the end of 2002; legislation included the first significant measures ever taken to improve the employment prospects of the low skilled. Simultaneously, the federal government appointed another commission, along lines similar to those of the Hartz Commission and over the head of the minister in charge, to propose fundamental reforms of the social-security system. As a round of crucial regional elections was approaching, Schröder announced in his 2003 New Year address that all groups in society would have to make sacrifices. Meanwhile reorganisation of the *Bundesanstalt*, under its new, government-appointed leadership, was proceeding rapidly while the unions, with a new and untested DGB leader, were watching in disbelief.

As chapter 6 in this volume has argued, the first months of 2003 represent a decisive turning point in the history, not just of the Schröder government or the SPD, but of the semisovereign German state. After a humiliating defeat in the Lower Saxony *Land* election, the chancellor called a final meeting of the Alliance for Jobs on 3 March 2003, only to declare its failure once and for all and advise the assembled representatives of unions and business that from now on the government would legislate the necessary reforms on its own. On 14 March 2003, in a much-heralded statement of policy before the *Bundestag*, Schröder announced his now famous 'Agenda 2010', in which he embraced most of the economic and social policy reforms proposed by the opposition during the 2002 campaign. All attempts having failed to make the 'social partners' generate consensus policies that could have been enacted with bipartisan support, by early 2003 the only way to obtain that support, essential under German federalism, was with policies devised against rather than with the unions. These were the main losers of the new turn of events, together with the traditionalists in the SPD. Schröder's first term had shown that an SPD chancellor cannot govern against the unions and the opposition at the same time. Since the unions had proved unable or unwilling to co-operate, they were now pushed aside in pursuit of a new state unilateralism based on nothing less than a de facto grand coalition.

Success of state unilateralism in German conditions is far from assured, in terms of both economic policy and party politics. In 2003 and 2004, the CDU/CSU did its best to expose the SPD-Green government's many breaking-points. One year after Agenda 2010 was announced Schröder had to give up the party leadership, in the face of another series of successive election defeats. As discussed in chapter 4 in this volume, in mid-2003 the SPD and CDU/CSU agreed on a joint effort to reform the federal system, so as to allow future governments more constitutional space to pursue their own policies independent from the opposition. While any attempt to extricate the state from the constraints of semisovereignty is, in path-dependent fashion, itself subject to these, there seems to be no alternative to it.[13]

---

[13] Semisovereignty, as Katzenstein often reminds us, was created not to support German prosperity, but to tame German power. For the outside world, its main benefit was not its economic success, but that there was no longer a strong German state. That today Germany lacks the state capacities it would require in a changed world to recover its economic strength need at first glance not be of concern to other countries, especially those that in the past were at the receiving end of Germany's extraordinary economic competitiveness. But *Schadenfreude* may be expensive as the size of the German economy is such that its decline inevitably drags down its neighbours as well. Ending the domestic semisovereignty of the German state may be not just in the German interest.

8   Social Policy: Crisis and Transformation

Roland Czada

Peter Katzenstein (1987, pp. 168–92) portrayed the West German welfare state as a highly segmented polity governed by consensual politics and providing generous social benefits. In fact, at first sight, not much has changed during the past two decades: compulsory insurance for all wage earners (*sozialversicherungspflichtige Beschäftigung*) is still provided by separate funds for pensions, health, unemployment, occupational accidents and – since 1995 – nursing care for the elderly (*Pflegeversicherung*). The system is still highly fragmented, and is administered according to a person's region of residence as well as that person's occupation. Thus, several regional funds are in charge of pensions for blue-collar workers (*Arbeiter*), whereas pensions for white-collar employees (*Angestellte*) are funded on a national basis. Civil servants (*Beamte*) receive their old-age benefits from current state budgets, while other public-sector employees are covered by the national white-collar workers' insurance scheme, supplemented by a complementary insurance which puts them on a par with civil servants. There is an entirely separate pension scheme altogether for miners, and finally, self-employed persons (*Selbstständige*) are allowed to opt out of the system altogether, which they normally do, since private pension and medical providers normally offer better levels of cover at lower costs than the statutory schemes.

Health insurance too still rests on a multitude of local, regional and national institutions. Although employees have been free to choose their health insurance fund since 1996, which has inevitably weakened the linkage to occupational status, the federal government has introduced a portfolio balance system to support those funds with bad risks. These are usually the old established local blue-collar workers' general health funds (*Ortskrankenkassen*), which were founded in the 1880s as part of Bismarck's welfare initiative to attract workers away from trade union-led health funds (Katzenstein 1987, p. 172). None of these insurance schemes is capital-based; instead they all rely on current inflows of social-security contributions to meet their commitments (the so-called 'pay-as-you-go' system). Inevitably this makes the system particularly vulnerable to economic downturns, which immediately open up a revenue-outlay gap.

Both employees and employers still share most of the costs of social security by each paying an equal proportion of the employee's salary as a compulsory social-insurance levy. Apart from work-related compulsory insurance schemes, a number of additional tax-financed social programmes are run by state, federal and local governments. These are meant to provide for social needs that fall outside the remit of the compulsory insurance funds, such as child benefit (*Kindergeld*), home construction grants (*Eigenheimzulage*) and grants for higher education (BAFöG). In consequence, welfare allowances are available in some form to almost everyone resident in Germany (cf. Katzenstein 1987, p. 186). However, in recent years public welfare spending has steadily increased. The total share of general government contributions (that is, tax-financed contributions) to social-security programmes rose from 26.9 per cent in 1991 to 32.5 per cent in 2000. In 1999, an eco-tax was introduced to generate extra resources for the ailing old-age pensions system (cf. chapter 10 in this volume). During the 1990s, total employee contributions to social-security programmes remained constant at around 28 per cent of the total income for these programmes, whereas the total employers' contributions decreased from 42.5 per cent to 36.9 per cent (Eurostat 2003, p. 7). Yet despite the increase in state (i.e. tax-based) funding for these programmes, statutory social-insurance contributions have exceeded 40 per cent of the average gross salary since the mid-1990s (Hagen and Strauch 2001, p. 24). Not surprisingly, the subject of social-security contributions has become a hotly debated topic, especially as Germany is the only country that still levies such contributions at such a high level on employers. It has been argued that these non-wage labour costs have both exacerbated Germany's unemployment problem, by making it prohibitively expensive to employ new staff, and compromised the international competitiveness of German companies. Politically, therefore, one of the major goals of welfare-state reform policies since the mid-1990s has been to reduce the very high level of non-wage labour costs (in other words, the social-security contributions levied on employees and employers).

During the 1990s, the German welfare state ran into deep trouble. However, remedial action has been limited to incremental reductions in the costs and benefits of welfare programmes, and, in particular, to a shift towards a greater degree of tax funding for such programmes. Yet, despite its persisting institutional structure, the welfare state has changed considerably in terms of its financial flows, political-power structures, scope of services and general policy concepts. When compared with Peter Katzenstein's portrayal of 1987, the situation in 2004, with acute political conflicts and considerable benefit cuts, indicates a welfare state in transition. Traditional features of social corporatism, such as party consensus and work-related paternalism, have been superseded by new forms of decision-making, including corporatist technical advisory commissions, issue-specific (and hence volatile) party alliances, the emergent use of market principles and a more universalistic approach to the funding and delivery of welfare benefits. Although this transition has by no means been completed, its driving forces, which will be addressed in the next section, are clearly visible.

Context: the 'German Model' and the Challenge of Unification

Two distinct factors make up the context of these recent policy challenges to the German welfare state. The first can be traced back to the so-called 'German Model' of forced industrial modernisation policies; the second stems from the unification of the economically weak socialist German Democratic Republic with the still prosperous Federal Republic of Germany. Of course, the German welfare state has not been insulated from broader pressures of globalisation and demographic changes; however, because of their general character, these will be discussed separately later in this chapter.

As chapter 7 has shown compellingly, Germany's social-security funds were used from the 1970s onwards to compensate generously those large segments of the workforce who fell victim to the gradual process of industrial modernisation and restructuring. Faced with rising unemployment from the mid-1970s onwards, Germany simply transferred its least-productive sections of the workforce into the welfare system, in stark contrast to both the American and British social workfare policies and the Scandinavian active reintegration programmes. A corporatist productivity coalition of unions, employers and the state agreed to exploit the then buoyant social-insurance funds to finance early retirement for older workers and to facilitate companies' efforts to rationalise the least-qualified and least-productive elements of their workforces. An Early Retirement Act (*Vorruhestandsgesetz*) was passed in 1984, and a Law on Part-Time Work for the Elderly (*Altersteilzeitgesetz*) followed in 1988. In a collaborative effort, employers and works councils (*Betriebsräte*) helped to implement these laws, which overall were very effective (Table 8.1). The Federal Labour Office (*Bundesanstalt für Arbeit*, BA) was given the task of financing both measures from its unemployment insurance funds, supplemented by some additional federal grants.

Table 8.1. *Growth of early retirement, 1975–99*

	Average age of new pensioners retiring due to unemployability		New pensions for formerly unemployed persons (% of all new pensions)				Unemployable early retirees (% of all pensioners)	
			Western Germany		Eastern Germany			
Year	Male	Female	Male	Female	Male	Female	West	East
1975	56.3	59.2	3.7	0.7			3.5	
1980	54.7	57.7	8.4	1.6			4.8	
1985	54.8	54.3	11.9	1.1			7.9	
1990	53.9	52.6	13.7	1.8			10.7	
1995	53.5	51.4	24.2	3.4	60.2	6.4	8.7	10.2
1999	52.9	50.8	26.9	2.1	54.5	1.8	14.4	31.4

Source: Hagen and Strauch 2001, p. 17.

However, because the BA's financial responsibility was from the outset limited until 1988, the pension schemes were faced with a double challenge in the early 1990s, when they had to absorb not only large numbers of pensioners in western Germany who had retired early, but also – following unification – all pensioners in eastern Germany.

Self-evidently, a German-style pay-as-you-go system, under which wage earners' contributions are almost immediately transferred to pensioners as cash benefits, is particularly sensitive to a relative decline in regular employment. For 2003, the Federal Statistical Office (*Statistisches Bundesamt*) reported 26.955 million wage earners compared with 30.984 million persons living on social-security income (Figure 8.1; Bundesministerium für Gesundheit und Soziale Sicherung 2004). By comparison, the respective numbers for 1985 were 20.378 million wage earners contributing social-insurance fees, against 16.876 million persons living on welfare. As a result, the ratio of wage earners to welfare recipients has fallen from 1.2:1 in 1985 to 1:1 in 1997, and in 2003 stood at below 0.9:1.

Figure 8.1 shows that the number of wage earners paying social-security contributions has declined steadily since unification. Although this has principally been caused by large-scale job losses, mainly in eastern Germany, from 1992 onwards, the peculiarities of the welfare state have themselves also been responsible. Until recently, employment policies were focused entirely on measures to create a skilled workforce

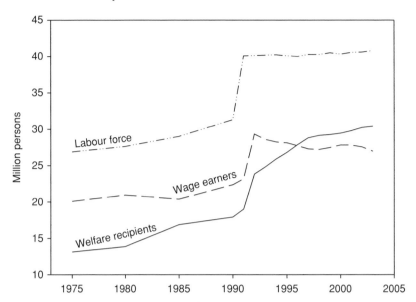

Figure 8.1. Labour force, wage earners and welfare recipients, 1975–2003

Note: The *labour force* includes all persons engaged in economic activity working regular weekly hours (paid civilian and military employment, self-employment and unpaid family workers) plus all those unemployed but seeking work. *Wage earners* pay compulsory social insurance fees (*sozialversicherungspflichtige Beschäftigung*). *Welfare recipients* are defined as persons living solely from social security income, including old age pensioners (who receive *Arbeiter-, Angestellten und Knappschaftsrenten*), recipients of un-employment support (*Arbeitslosengeld und hilfe*), recipients of income support (*Sozialhilfeempfänger*) and asylum seekers (*Asylbewerber*). Not included are welfare recipients living on accident annuities (*Unfallrenten*) and students' grants as well as workers in training and job creation schemes.

Source: Bundesministerium für Gesundheit und Soziale Sicherung 2004.

and to enhance productivity, rather than on job creation in low-skill (and low-income) areas. Although tax cuts for low-income groups had been introduced in 1996 following a ruling by the Constitutional Court, this did not create any new incentives for recipients of income support to find work. Until the end of 2004, for an average-sized family, employment of any sort meant a withdrawal of benefits, meaning that overall net income often either stayed the same or was even lower than the level of benefits.

Nonetheless, despite a declining number of wage earners who are subject to social-insurance contributions, Figure 8.1 also shows that the

total labour force, which measures the number of people who are economically active or seeking work, has grown considerably between 1975
and 2003. In the aftermath of unification, this was a result of the growth
of Germany's population. However, because of continued high unemployment, much of the economic potential created by this increase
has lain idle in post-unification Germany. But at the same time, millions
of workers have also taken on so-called 'mini-jobs', or become 'pro-
forma self-employed'.

Since the mid-1990s, part-time jobs of less than fifteen hours work per
week, which are not paid above DM 620 (€ 318) per month (€ 400 since
April 2003), are tax-free and also partly free of social-security contributions and entitlements. The number of such 'mini-jobbers' has increased
steadily, rising from 2.8 million in 1987 to over 4.4 million in 1992 and
to 6.5 million in 1999 (ISG 1999, p. 2). In 2002, more than 50 per cent
of 'mini-jobbers' were either younger than twenty-five or older than fifty-
five; 70 per cent were women (mainly housewives). In this way, mini-
jobs act as stabilisers of the continental Bismarckian social-insurance
state that focuses on skilled, highly paid male breadwinners, and
which thereby results in a comparatively low female employment rate
(M. Schmidt 1993).

Meanwhile, the incidence of 'pro-forma self-employment' (*Schein-
selbstständigkeit*) also increased dramatically during the 1990s. Under
this rubric, employees of companies reclassify themselves as self-
employed sub-contractors, thereby avoiding the payment of social-
security contributions altogether. For instance, haulage drivers can
become formal owners of a truck financed and operated by a freight
company or carrier. Of course, most of these self-employed persons still
depend on an 'employer', but despite government restrictions, pro-
forma self-employment is growing in a number of service industries, with
estimates ranging between 1 million and 1.4 million *Scheinselbstständige*
in 2001. Clearly, the overall number of 7 million mini-jobs and pro-
forma self-employed persons has to be seen as a consequence of steeply
rising non-wage labour costs in the aftermath of German unification.

The disproportionate rise in welfare recipients and, as a result, in non-
wage labour costs first became apparent in 1992. Figure 8.1 shows that
this was an effect of the so-called 'unification shock' (Sinn and Sinn 1992;
Schluchter and Quint 2001), which saw Germany's GDP per capita drop
by DM 6,000 (€ 3,077) to DM 34,990 (€ 17,943) as a result of the
number of inhabitants growing more than economic output. In addition,
while eastern Germany experienced massive job losses in the aftermath of
a historically unique de-industrialisation process (cf. chapter 2 in this
volume), the western German economy, which remained strong, had to

shoulder the resulting social costs. Initially, total net financial transfers to the new *Länder* (consisting of special federal grants, EU grants, fiscal equalisation schemes, federal supplement grants and social-security contributions, minus taxes and social-security contributions collected in the east) amounted to almost 10 per cent of GDP in the early years, and only fell to 4 per cent towards the end of the 1990s. Sinn and Westermann (2001) note that the current account deficit of the eastern *Länder* amounts to 50 per cent of their GDP. Eastern Germany's dependency on resource imports is therefore much greater than even that of the south Italian *Mezzogiorno*, which is often referred to as the classic example of an essentially parasitic economy (Sinn and Westermann 2001, pp. 36–7). Two-thirds of the current account deficit in the new *Länder* has been financed by public transfers; the remaining one-third has been met by private capital flows. Crucially, more than half of the public transfers have been spent on social security and only 12 per cent on public infrastructure investments (Sinn 2000).

Accordingly, the social expenditure ratio, which expresses state welfare expenditure as a share of GDP, has risen sharply after unification (Figure 8.2). Before 1990, the social-security funds were, generally speaking, in good financial health, and therefore seemed to be well prepared for shouldering the immediate social costs of unification. However, by 2003, the reserve had shrunk to a historic low of just half of one month's expenditure, thereby reaching a critical limit for a pay-as-you-go system. This 'shrinkage' occurred despite the fact that Germany had increased social-security contributions on several occasions, whereas its competitors had generally managed to reduce them.

Because of the costs of welfare, there is a considerable difference between salaries and take-home pay. In 1999, the 'average' production worker took home less than half of what it costs to employ him or her, defined as net income plus employer's and employee's social-security contributions plus taxes, compared with about 70 per cent in Britain or the USA (OECD 2000). Growing welfare expenses and rising labour costs not only reduced the demand for labour, but also slowed disposable income growth. During the 1990s, even though gross real wages per capita increased by 2 per cent, net real wages per capita rose by just 0.3 per cent annually. Consequently, the trade unions' moderate wage claims in the second half of the 1990s did not translate into increasing levels of employment figures, but instead only reduced the rate of increase of disposable income. In other words, Germany's high welfare burden has squeezed private consumption, which grew by just 1.5 per cent annually between 1991 and 2001, well below the level achieved in other industrialised countries.

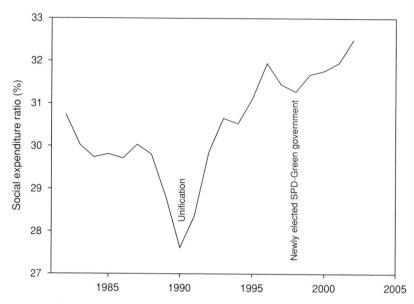

Figure 8.2. Social expenditure ratio, 1980–2002
Source: Bundesministerium für Gesundheit und Soziale Sicherung 2004; Czada 2002, p. 160.

Agenda: the Quest for a New Welfare Consensus

Before unification, a reform of the welfare state had never seriously been on the political agenda. Although the CDU/CSU-FDP government under Chancellor Helmut Kohl was in favour of a more flexible labour market, and implemented moderate cutbacks in social-security spending (cf. Figure 8.2), only minor changes were made. Just before the fall of the Berlin Wall in November 1989, the *Bundestag* passed a pension reform bill to compensate for future imbalances created by West Germany's adverse demographic developments (cf. chapter 9 in this volume, pp. 197–8). The law was backed by a broad coalition of parties, trade unions and employers, and thus followed the traditional consensual model of welfare politics.

In fact, and in a major change in policy, the government planned to cut both taxes and social-security contributions from 1990. Despite slow GDP growth rates and still moderate unemployment figures, public-sector deficits had shrunk during the preceding decade. There had also been a sharp rise in corporate profits. In 1989, the compulsory pension funds noted that their cash reserves were at their highest since the introduction of the pay-as-you-go scheme. The 1989 report of the government's Council of Economic Advisers (*Sachverständigenrat*) – published just a few weeks before the fall of the Berlin Wall – actually encouraged trade unions to switch the emphasis in their work-related demands away from issues of quality to issues of quantity, such as wage levels. The rationale behind this was to boost private consumption by improving employees' share of the expansion in corporate profits that had developed hitherto (Sachverständigenrat zur Begutachtung der gesamtwirtschaftlichen Entwicklung 1989, p. 166). In return for a deregulation of the labour market, the unions were offered a growth and employment strategy based on lower taxes, lower social-security contributions and higher wages. In essence, the federal government pursued a corporatist strategy similar to that of the Netherlands, which eventually led to the widely praised 'Dutch Model'.

However, following unification, this strategy failed for two reasons. On the one hand, the reconstruction of the eastern German economy called for a massive increase in public spending and private investment. There was no longer any leeway for wages to increase and – even more importantly – the *Bundesbank* had to raise interest rates to a historic high in order to curb the inflationary pressures unleashed in the post-unification boom. Moreover, Germany, once among the world's major net exporters of capital, had to redirect capital outflows to the tune of DM 200 billion (€ 103 billion) per year in order to finance the reconstruction effort in the east. Interest rates remained high, and, as noted in chapter 1, total public-sector debt doubled within a decade. This meant that the demand-led growth strategy of the late 1980s was no longer viable for simple economic reasons.

On the other hand, there was a political impediment to welfare-state reforms. Unification policies started from the general assumption that West Germany's structures of governance did not need to be reformed in the process of their transfer to the new *Länder* (Schäuble 1991, pp. 115–16). Based on the principle of 'institutional transfer' (Lehmbruch 1992, p. 41; see also chapter 2 in this volume, pp. 26–9), the whole legal and organisational system of the west had been transferred to the new *Länder*. Unfortunately, a number of West German institutions revealed themselves to be ill-suited to dealing with the task of transforming a socialist command economy into a capitalist market economy. In response, the federal government initiated a series of legislative amendments that were soon dubbed 'repair laws' (*Reparaturgesetze*). Remarkably, despite their far-reaching redistributive character, all these laws and consecutive amendments were passed with broad parliamentary majorities.

Throughout the 1990s, before the political class recognised the need for a more coherent reform of the country's redistributive policies, welfare policy was characterised by more-or-less permanent agenda shifts. Before the crisis of unification, few had considered the inter-regional redistributive effects of social-security funds and their consequences. Yet Mackscheidt (1993) has shown that these have long had a greater impact than even the federal system's financial equalisation schemes. Whereas the latter had always been politically highly controversial, the manner in which social-security funds were channelled from prosperous regions to poorer ones was akin to a hidden agenda. Inter-regional redistributions had, since the mid-1970s, functioned as an informal way of supporting the restructuring of old industrial regions. Massive resource transfers to the new *Länder*, however, threatened to overburden this widely, if tacitly, accepted system. As a result, the top priority for fiscal and welfare policy shifted to increasing public revenues and social-security contributions, whilst simultaneously cutting benefits.

But instead of cutting taxes and social-security expenditure, the federal government delayed and, eventually, reversed its plans. Moreover, it became clear that a much more fundamental reform of the welfare state would be needed if its collapse was to be avoided in the long run. Even though the West German pension reform of the late 1980s had already made some provision for population decline after 2015, unification drastically changed this forecast. As a result of high rates of unemployment and early retirement in the east, a stagnating portion of economically active persons had to pay for a rapidly growing number of pensioners at a much earlier stage than had originally been predicted.

From the mid-1990s onwards, therefore, the federal government tried to forge alliances within the party system and with trade unions, business groups and employers' associations in favour of far-reaching welfare-state and labour-market reforms, most of which, as will be discussed below, met with failure. It was not until the new millennium that all the main political parties, as well as the trade unions and employers' associations, agreed that high labour costs (in terms of taxes and social-insurance contributions) had been hampering employment and economic growth. Consequently, welfare-state reforms have now become a top political priority not only for the federal government, but also for employers' and business associations and the unions. On 14 March 2003, Chancellor Schröder announced his 'Agenda 2010' package of comprehensive social-policy reforms, designed to solve the long-term problems of the German welfare state.

In light of the decline in individual welfare entitlements and social expenditure ratios prior to 1990, one could be forgiven for assuming that retrenchment policies framed a hidden agenda for welfare policies ever since the mid-1970s, and that it was only the unification crisis after 1992 which stretched the system to breaking point. In fact, as Seeleib-Kaiser notes in a lucid analysis (2002), the post-unification changes must be seen in the context of this long-term development, the cumulated effect of which has been a retreat from the public guarantee of living standards. This principle of *Lebensstandardsicherung* had been 'the major achievement and *leitmotiv* of post-war policy ever since the historic 1957 pension reform' (Seeleib-Kaiser 2002, pp. 31–2). At the same time, family support programmes have expanded considerably, including increased child allowances and tax credits for families, a rising number of childcare facilities (albeit from a very low level in the west) and other entitlements such as parental leave.

Process: Decline of Party Accommodation and Corporatist Concertation

In the West German polity, policy-making proved to be slow and incremental due to high consensus thresholds based on the legislative veto of the *Bundesrat* and macro-corporatist concertation (Katzenstein 1987; Lehmbruch et al. 1988). In addition, ever since the foundation of the Federal Republic, social policies have been characterised by numerous bipartite (union, employers), tripartite (state, unions, employers) and multipartite (insurance schemes, service providers, expert councils, professional associations) sectoral bodies. In this system, major changes could effectively only be undertaken in the context of a grand coalition (Katzenstein 1987; Lehmbruch 2000). However, as this section shows, the policy-making process in the areas of employment, health and pensions during the past decade reveals a rapid decline in party accommodation and corporatist concertation.

Employment Policies

Notwithstanding some successive minor changes to labour-market legislation (*Arbeitsmarktförderungsgesetz*, AFG), the general direction of employment policies remained stable throughout the 1980s. However, in 1993, the AFG was amended to allow contributions to the unemployment insurance fund to be channelled into huge work-creation schemes (*Arbeitsbeschaffungsmaßnahmen*) in the east. As a result, the level of contributions to the unemployment insurance fund had to be raised several times during the 1990s; simultaneously, the corporatist Federal Labour Office (BA), which administered the funds and the work-creation schemes, was able to increase its power considerably in the field of labour-market policies. In 2002, however, a scandal surrounding rigged employment statistics prompted a full-scale reorganisation of the BA, and the Federal Employment Agency which emerged from its ruins is based on a managerial approach which includes much lower levels of corporatism and bureaucracy (cf. chapter 5 in this volume, pp. 109–10).

During the sixteen years of the Kohl era, 'labour-market reforms remained a process of incremental coping mostly with imminent financial problems' (Schmid and Blancke 2003, p. 217). It was not until 1998 that the newly elected SPD-Green government tried to introduce a more comprehensive reform programme. To this end, it initially followed the traditional macro-corporatist concertation approach, via the 'Alliance for Jobs, Vocational Training, and Competitiveness' (*Bündnis für Arbeit, Ausbildung und Wettbewerbsfähigkeit*) – a permanent tripartite body composed of the government, employers' and business associations, and trade unions. However, as chapter 7 in this volume has shown, the Alliance was largely a failure (cf. also chapter 6). In addition to some irreconcilable differences between the employers and unions, the resolution of which was not helped by the attempt to deal with very different policy issues within just one, top-level forum, the federal government had unexpectedly lost its *Bundesrat* majority soon after the Alliance for Jobs had been established. Thus the Alliance suffered not only from a broad policy brief which was simply incompatible with an institutionally segmented polity (Lehmbruch 2000, p. 98), but also from inadequate capacity of the federal government to act as a third-party guarantor of corporatist agreements (Czada 2003).

Shortly before the final failure of the Alliance for Jobs, the government appointed a new circle of leading unionists and employers to examine proposals on a more specific topic. Under the chairmanship of Peter Hartz, director of personnel at Volkswagen and a long-standing member of IG Metall, the so-called 'Commission on Modern Labour-Market Services' (or, more popularly, the Hartz Commission) was set up in 2002 to develop proposals for a new employment exchange service and for employment programmes geared towards competition and entrepreneurship. To this end, the Hartz Commission made thirteen separate proposals (Hartz et al. 2002). Among the most important was the so-called Personal Service Agency, which has now been introduced in all of Germany's 181 unemployment offices (*Arbeitsämter*). Under the proposal, unemployment offices or private temporary job agencies will employ anyone unable to find new work within six months, with the aim of neutralising the traditionally high levels of protection against dismissal. In addition, the commission proposed the merger of un-employment and local authorities' social welfare offices (*Sozialämter*) into so-called 'job centres', including the combination of long-term unemployment assistance and general income-support payments (*Sozialhilfe*). The latter has become the most controversial element of the Agenda 2010 reform package and was finally passed in the *Bundesrat* only on 9 July 2004 (cf. chapter 4 in this volume, p. 85).

An additional proposal by the Hartz Commission aimed to facilitate self-employment, by means of the so-called '*Ich AG*', which sees a fixed tax rate of between 10 and 15 per cent levied on those self-employed persons with an annual income of between € 15,000 and € 20,000. Many of the proposals contained in the commission's report came from reform-oriented trade unionists. Walter Riester, a former deputy leader of IG Metall and Federal Labour Minister from 1998 to 2002, established the commission and appointed Hartz, a former colleague from his union days, as its head. The largest German trade union, Ver.di, was also represented while commission members from industry included representatives from Daimler-Chrysler, BASF, Deutsche Bank and the consultancy firms Roland Berger and McKinsey. Other members of the commission were Peter Gasse, regional head of IG Metall in North Rhine-Westphalia, and his predecessor Harald Schartau, who went on to become Minister for Labour in that state.

What is striking is the way in which corporatist negotiations at the peak level of labour-market associations and the state were replaced by a newly established policy network based on SPD-affiliation, reformist orientation, personal reputation, experience and expertise. Simultaneously, the focus on a rather more closely defined set of problems replaced the broad scope of issues which had characterised the corporatist emphasis of the Alliance for Jobs. In any case, the SPD-Green government has stuck to an open style of consensus mobilisation focused on 'friendly' experts who are loosely associated with the incumbent parties. By contrast, Chancellor Kohl used his personal networks as well as 'fireside' talks with high-ranking business and union representatives. Initially, Chancellor Schröder seemed to favour a similar style, but following the breakdown of the Alliance for Jobs and the defection of the business elite to support his challenger Edmund Stoiber (CSU) in the run-up to the 2002 federal election, Schröder refocused his attention on experts from within the SPD or academia.

In terms of results, the new approach of 'government by commission' has had a limited impact. In addition to the reduction of unemployment benefit (*Arbeitslosengeld*), which is funded from insurance contributions, unemployment assistance for the long-term unemployed

(*Arbeitslosenhilfe*) and general income-support payments (*Sozialhilfe*) were merged with effect from 2005. As these two schemes had been run separately by the Federal Labour Office and local authorities, a new interface between labour-market institutions and municipal poverty-relief programmes seems to be emerging. However, this will probably necessitate further reforms, not least a comprehensive reform of municipal finances and the complex federal system (cf. chapter 4 in this volume).

Pension Politics

Pension issues have often served as a test case for consensus-building capacities across party lines and on both sides of the corporatist divide. In West Germany, party concordance and corporatist agreements prevailed throughout the post-war era. However, as noted above, the recurring financial crises caused by a decline in the number of contributors and a disproportionately growing number of recipients in eastern Germany meant that pension politics became highly controversial after the mid-1990s. Table 8.2 clearly illustrates the impact of unification, as a result of which huge surpluses in the west will have to compensate for huge deficits in the new eastern states until well beyond 2016. In 2003, an estimated € 13 billion deficit in the east contrasts with a surplus of € 14 billion in the west. These reserves in the west would have sufficed to stabilise the pension contributions of wage earners well below the current level of 20 per cent of gross income in 2004. Apart from unification-related problems, demographic changes call for major modifications of the old established Bismarckian model. Starting with the 1992 reform, subsequent pension law amendments of 1997, 1998, 1999, 2001 and 2003 have cut future pension entitlements considerably, thereby paving the way for a new system of compulsory insurance combined with private retirement provisions.

The pension reform of 1989, which came into effect in 1992, was backed by a broad coalition of parties, unions and employers, and, thus, followed the established consensual model. Initiated before the fall of the Berlin Wall, the reform was intended to correct future imbalances caused by demographic changes in West Germany. Most importantly, from 1993 onwards, pensions were to be adjusted in line with increases in annual net income and not, as had been the case previously, with increases in earnings. This measure was to prevent pensions in the future from exceeding 70 per cent of the average net income of active wage earners (the net replacement rate).

Table 8.2. *Net balances of the compulsory pension fund financed equally by employees and employers, 1999–2016 (€ billion)*[a]

Year	Net balance (revenues minus expenditures)		
	Western *Länder*	Eastern *Länder*	All Germany
1999	9.3	−4.4	4.9
2000	6.5	−5.9	0.6
2001	6.5	−6.5	0.0
2002	9.7	−13.4	−3.8
2003	14.5	−13.2	1.3
2004	15.4	−13.6	1.8
2005	15.2	−14.0	1.3
2006	15.1	−14.2	0.9
2007	15.1	−14.2	0.9
2008	15.6	−14.5	1.1
2009	16.0	−14.9	1.0
2010	16.7	−15.3	1.4
2011	16.6	−16.0	0.6
2012	15.8	−16.7	−0.9
2013	17.4	−17.1	0.3
2014	18.8	−17.7	1.1
2015	19.4	−18.4	1.0
2016	20.9	−19.1	1.8

Note: [a]2002–16 forecast.
Source: Bundestagsdrucksache 15/110, pp. 62, 111–12.

However, the combined effects of unification, mass unemployment and early retirement meant that further reforms soon became necessary,[1] and in June 1996, a Commission on the Further Development of the Pension System was established. Following its recommendations, the CDU/CSU-FDP government legislated for a further gradual reduction in the net replacement rate for standard pensions from 70 to 64 per cent between 1999 and 2030. This time, the SPD opposition, backed by the

---

[1] With an additional 800,000 persons taking early retirement, pension funds have had to pay out an extra DM 20 billion (€ 10.3 billion) since 1992. The pension payments for 4 million pensioners in the new *Länder* amounted to DM 75 billion (€ 38.5 billion) between 1992 and 1997. Therefore, additional costs of DM 37 billion (€ 19 billion) per annum, which had not been anticipated in the preceding reform, have had to be borne by wage earners, pensioners and the state.

unions, put up fierce resistance – not least because of the federal elections that were just ten months away at the time of the bill's passage through parliament. On 11 December 1997, the first piece of pensions legislation since the foundation of the Federal Republic not to be agreed by a broad cross-party majority passed the *Bundestag*. After its election victory in 1998, one of the first acts of the SPD-Green government was to suspend the 1997 pension reform. Here was another novelty in postwar welfare politics which casts doubt on whether Katzenstein's portrait of 'policy stability even after changes of government' is still valid (1987, pp. 4, 35).

The politics surrounding pension reform in 1997 and 1998 only foreshadowed future party dissent and programmatic volatility. Indeed, the 'Jekyll and Hyde' years in the politics of pensions were still to come: in 1999, fiscal problems forced the SPD-led government to revert to the austerity measures of its conservative predecessors. Reneging on its election promises, the SPD planned to replace the wage indexation of pensions by price indexation for a certain period to lower the replacement ratio from 70 to between 67 and 68 per cent. In 2000, the government published yet another reform proposal, which not only exceeded the planned cuts of the previous CDU/CSU government, but was also likely to change the system's basic operating principles. Apart from a radical reduction in benefit levels, it introduced a private statutory pension scheme that would in the long run have gradually transformed the corporatist Bismarckian pay-as-you-go system into a fully capital-based pension. The so-called *Riester-Rente*, or Riester pension, named after the then Federal Minister for Labour and Social Affairs, Walter Riester, met with a barrage of criticism from the CDU/CSU and the trade unions. Again, the unions' wholehearted support for a CDU/CSU position in a highly controversial area of welfare policy was quite a novel experience. The unions were particularly opposed to the fact that the shift towards a private mandatory pension fund signalled a departure from the traditional joint financing of pensions by employees and employers. The CDU/CSU opposition initially even rejected those parts of the government bill which were in line with their own former plans and pre-election statements. As a consequence, the SPD-Green government had to trim the reform package so that it was no longer subject to *Bundesrat* approval. What is more, the SPD was forced into making substantial concessions to its own left-wingers just in order to secure the government's *Bundestag* majority.

The pension reform in 2000 and 2001 was, therefore, an example of semisovereignty without consensus, which made the parties in government vulnerable to all kinds of pressure from within their own ranks.

Nonetheless, the reform initiated a mixed pension system, composed of a reformed pay-as-you-go compulsory pension scheme and a new private, but non-mandatory, pension. The private component gives employees the option of contributing up to 4 per cent of their earnings by 2008 into company or other private schemes. Employees can invest in a range of schemes offered by private insurers, including private-pension insurance organisations, investment funds, life insurance funds, and savings banks. All private pensions must meet certain criteria before employees are eligible for state subsidies and tax exemptions, and – contrary to the Bismarckian tradition – all benefits will be taxable. The incentives and subsidies for making contributions to private accounts are targeted at lower-income individuals and families. Pension credits earned during a marriage can be shared equally by both spouses through a new pension-splitting option. The government also introduced reforms to improve old-age security for women, including compensation for reduced earnings during child-raising years, and granting pension credits to mothers who could not pursue part-time employment.

Despite its departure from the established model, the 2000 pension reform was still ultimately incremental in its impact and failed to address the long-term financial problems caused by demographic change. In November 2002, a new Commission for Sustainability in the Financing of the Social Security System under Professor Bert Rürup (the so-called Rürup Commission) was set up in order to address yet again the long-term financial aspects of the pensions and health-care crisis. Its recommendations included a gradual increase in the retirement age between 2011 and 2035 from the current level of sixty-five to sixty-seven, penalties for early retirement and a reduction in the annual increases in pension payments. A majority of the twenty-six commission members, consisting of experts who were generally close to the SPD-Green government, backed the final report's recommendations to safeguard intergenerational justice and limit future pressures on the social-insurance systems. Only commission members affiliated to the trade unions opposed the proposals.

In August 2003, the Rürup Commission calculated that the combined effect of the 1989 and 1992 reforms was already to reduce the real value of pensions by 30 per cent in 2030. On top of that, the Riester reform of 2000 imposed a further cut of 7 per cent, while an increase in the general retirement age will mean another 3 per cent reduction. In other words, from the viewpoint of 2003, the average pension benefits in 2030 will be 40 per cent lower than they would have been under the pre-1989 rules (*Berliner Zeitung*, 9 August 2003). This means that supplementary private pension provision has become indispensable for anyone below the age of fifty. The reduction in benefits combined with an increase in funding from general taxation has also meant that the premiums for the compulsory pension insurance could be cut from 20.3 per cent of gross income in 1999 to 19.5 per cent in 2003. This saving, along with state bonuses, is meant to be invested into private or company pension plans. In summary, the era of the all-embracing, Bismarckian work-related compulsory insurance schemes aimed at status security is over. So far, however, the public has not yet shown a great awareness of this new mix of compulsory and private provisions, since this will only fully affect those generations of pensioners who are still to come.

Health Care

The German health-care sector still constitutes a classic example of semisovereignty. Because federal and state governments share legislative authority, the *Bundesrat* has been involved in all fields of general health legislation. In addition, a large number of other actors dominate the field, such as various organisations of insurers, service providers (doctors and hospitals), pharmaceutical producers, consumers and their respective peak associations (cf. Döhler and Manow 1967). The process of formulating health policy has always been guided by networks of experts, many of them linked to the main peak associations. A host of advisory bodies, commissions and consultative meetings are part of the decision-making process. As a result, the incremental 'muddling through' approach which has befallen most health-care reforms can be traced to an early stage in the policy cycle, and not usually to the constitutional vetoes embedded in the federal structure. In fact, most health-care legislation during the past decades did not implement any restructuring of the institutional relationship between health insurers, providers and the insured. Modest co-payments for medications, dental treatment, hospitalisation and other items were introduced in 1982. These payments were further increased by the Health Care Reform Act of 1989 and again by the Health Care Structural Reform Act passed in 1992. The latter introduced new regulatory instruments, which included the reorganisation of the governance of health insurers and a cap on medication costs and prospective hospital payments. In addition, it proposed measures to overcome the separation between out-patient medical care and hospital care that prevailed in the old Federal Republic, and it introduced a free choice of health funds for the insured (Blanke and Perschke-Hartmann 1994).

Politically, the law rested on the famous 1992 Lahnstein compromise between the CDU/CSU and the SPD. This excluded the liberal FDP, even though the latter was in government with the CDU/CSU. The reform was a partially successful attempt to reduce the institutionalised power of the medical profession and the pharmaceutical industry, both of which have traditionally been protected by the FDP. The Lahnstein compromise was part of a stream of informal consensual policy-making that was characteristic of the immediate post-unification period (Manow 1996). However, this was followed by a period of intensified party conflict, conceptual volatility and political stalemate.

Most of the reforms passed between the mid-1980s and 2000 attempted to redistribute the increasing cost burdens between the various stakeholders. There was no intention, as in old-age pension policies, to alter the balance between public and private insurance schemes. Though the health sector is characterised by fierce competition between hospitals, doctors and pharmaceutical companies, and though a number of new competitive elements have been introduced, a health-care market based on privately financed products and services has never developed. Moral hazard, information asymmetries and cherry-picking became even worse after the strict corporatist order had been loosened, and once the insured were able to exercise some degree of freedom in their choice of insurance fund.

Most stakeholders agree that the severe inefficiencies in the health-care system are caused by fragmentation, duplication and overlap, and accordingly, recent health-care reform acts have tried to integrate the different levels and sectors of care. For instance, free contracts between insurance providers and rehabilitation clinics have been allowed and even encouraged in order to overcome the division between funding agencies and care providers. The health-care system still rests on the basic assumption that everybody should be entitled to receive all the necessary services, and that the doctors should decide what is necessary for their specific patients. It is only recently that the issue of prioritisation has arisen. The long-established 'Federal Committee of Panel Doctors and Sickness Funds' is now expected to provide authoritative definitions for measures of quality assurance, as well as developing criteria for whether certain diagnostic and therapeutic services are appropriate. However, its attempts to impose a ceiling on expenditure for drugs and medication fell foul of European cartel laws, and were declared unlawful following a case brought by Germany's powerful pharmaceutical industry. In 2003, plans to establish a National Centre for Medical Quality again met with fierce resistance from physicians and the pharmaceutical industry, who decried the proposals as leading straight back to GDR socialism.

Traditionally, quality assurance issues have been in the domain of individual physicians and organisations and recent debates on such issues have to be seen in the context of a renewed increase in health-care expenditure – mainly as a result of the abolition of spending caps for medicines. The corresponding rise in contribution rates from 13.5 per cent to 14 per cent of pre-tax income brought cost containment back onto the agenda in 2002.

In 2003, a new informal 'grand coalition' on health emerged between the governing SPD and the opposition CDU/CSU, with the aim of cutting health benefits again and further limiting the sector's regulatory autonomy. In a rare show of unity, the unions and employers' associations even called for the abolition of the statutory regional associations of accredited physicians (*Ärztekammern*), which act as clearing houses between individual doctors and the statutory health funds, thereby removing care providers from the scrutiny of the insurance funds. As the 1992 Lahnstein compromise had illustrated, a grand coalition in health policy can overcome the bicameral legislative veto and also withstand pressures from well-organised groups, such as insurance funds, physicians and pharmaceutical firms. Once again, however, the new inter-party consensus agreed in 2003 led neither to institutional reform nor to the prioritisation of certain treatments and medicines. Instead, new market-like incentives were introduced, including the removal of sick pay from the bipartite-financed compulsory schemes. Patients are now expected to pay € 10 for each quarter in which they visit the general practitioner (GP) (the so-called *Praxisgebühr*). Indeed, the 'gatekeeper' function of GPs will be strengthened, as specialists must collect another € 10 if patients cannot present a referral letter. Other plans include additional co-payments for dentures, reductions in maternity benefits and death grants, and cuts in benefits for parents nursing sick children. Even though this has meant at least a temporary improvement in the financial position of the health-insurance funds, such measures, and especially the *Praxisgebühr*, remain deeply unpopular among the population (*Die Welt*, 31 July 2004).

In health policy, governments have continued to rely on benefit cuts and incremental measures like budgeting, co-payment and competitive incentives for the various stakeholders. Only recently have prominent politicians of all parties called for a more fundamental reform in order to address the permanent crisis in health policy, with a universal compulsory health-insurance scheme for all citizens supplemented by voluntary private insurance contracts (*Bürgerversicherung*) being the preferred model. Inevitably, the chances for a fundamental systemic change are still small, not despite, but because of, recurring grand coalitions in health politics.

Consequences: Erosion of Self-Governance and New Forms of Intermediation

The institutional segmentation of the West German political system has been emphasised, in particular, by Gerhard Lehmbruch and Fritz Scharpf. Lehmbruch pointed to incompatibilities of party competition and co-operative federalism (Lehmbruch 2002), whereas Scharpf's research on 'policy interlocking' and the 'joint decision trap' offered a key explanation of failed policy reform initiatives in different sectors (cf. Scharpf 1988). Peter Katzenstein's (1987) seminal work on 'semisovereignty' struck a similar chord; however, in contrast to Lehmbruch and Scharpf, he praised as a virtue what they had both considered to be a design fault.

Yet it is doubtful whether either of these models can adequately account for the overall stable course of welfare policies during the 1980s. Throughout this decade, the CDU/CSU–FDP government commanded a comfortable majority in the *Bundesrat*, and from 1982 to 1990, this arguably made the Kohl government the most sovereign compared with all its predecessors and successors in office. Even during the 1950s, the Adenauer government lost its *Bundesrat* majority for a few months (March 1956–January 1957). The political issue of divergent majorities in the bicameral legislature did not emerge until after the 1972 federal election (cf. Figure 3.2 in this volume, p. 64). By contrast, the CDU/CSU–FDP coalition after 1982 held a majority of five to thirteen votes in the *Bundesrat* throughout the 1980s; it was not until the Lower Saxony election in 1990 that things changed. Thus, with a solid *Bundestag* majority and markedly weakened labour unions (after unemployment figures exceeded one million in 1981), Kohl was presumably the most powerful chancellor since Adenauer.

To explain why policy remained so stable during the 1980s, one therefore has to focus on a range of factors outside the domain of the constitutional veto structures. By stressing the deep fears within the Kohl government that welfare cuts could adversely affect its electoral performance, Zohlnhöfer (2001b) has cast some doubt on the exclusive validity of the institutional explanation provided by Scharpf and Lehmbruch. A second important factor was the strength of the CDU's social-catholic wing, which was led by Norbert Blüm, a self-confessed defendant of the welfare-state consensus. As Federal Minister for Labour and Social Affairs in every single Kohl cabinet (and therefore in charge of the largest spending ministry), he was able to make full use of the principle of ministerial autonomy (*Ressortprinzip*) to act as a powerful stalwart of the Bismarckian welfare state from 1982 until the advent of the Schröder government in 1998.

The anatomy of neo-liberal strategic policy changes in the UK, Sweden and the Netherlands shows that problem load is an important predictor of policy change. The 'pain threshold' above which parties and governments in those countries felt forced to act, irrespective of their ideological backgrounds, had not been reached, by any stretch of the imagination, in West Germany before 1990. Bearing all that in mind – the solid majority of the Kohl government in both chambers, prevailing electoral considerations against benefit cuts, a powerful unionist pro-welfare wing in the CDU, and the moderate problem load of the time – constitutional veto potentials cannot explain the course of welfare-state reform during the 1980s. This becomes even more apparent when the welfare policies of the 1980s are compared with those of the following, post-unification decade.

But here too, an explanation focusing on formal veto powers fails to account for the delay in cutting social-security contributions and income taxes which the federal government had planned in 1989. On the contrary, the early 1990s have been characterised as the last triumph of corporatism, party concordance and co-operative federalism (Sally and Webber 1994; Lehmbruch 2000). Even though the Kohl government had grown stronger as a consequence of its electoral dominance in the new (eastern) *Länder*, and even though the *Länder* had temporarily suspended their constitutional rights in order to approach unification problems in a united and flexible manner, the federal government actively sought to include key representatives of business, unions, the *Länder* and the SPD opposition in a range of fora. In particular, the SPD had been incorporated into the newly established unification policy network with the *Treuhandanstalt* (THA) as its focal point (see chapter 5 in this volume). Prominent SPD figures such as Klaus von Dohnanyi and Detlef Karsten Rohwedder, as well as union leaders such as Franz Steinkühler and Dieter Schulte, had been appointed to high-ranking positions within the THA's executive, supervisory and operative structure.

As a result, the early 1990s witnessed something of a temporary revival of large-scale inter-party consensus and corporatist politics. The usual segmented policy-making had been bypassed for a while, at least until 1992, when the first signs of the severe economic crisis caused by unification prompted an examination of the original concept of a market-led transformation process and institutional transfer.

The 1990s were, undoubtedly, an active period in terms of agenda shifts and health reform in particular (Kania and Blanke 2000). After decades of corporatist policy-making and its last triumph in the immediate post-unification period, the following years brought a crisis of consensus politics and corporatist self-government. To draw a conclusion from a political-science perspective, the German welfare state of 2003 was characterised by more state intervention and more market elements than the one Katzenstein described in 1987. State regulation and tax-financed state subsidies increased, as did co-payments of the insured and the share of private insurance contracts, while the share of the Bismarckian wage-related compulsory insurance contributions decreased. Most remarkable, however, is the rapid loss of 'self-governability' and its requisite associational capacities. Germany is no longer 'a good example of how government can enact the rules and then leave the doctors and sick funds to carry out the programme with little intervention' (Glaser, quoted in Katzenstein 1987, p. 184). The same is true for other fields of social policy because of increased conflicts among stakeholders over their share of a shrinking pie.

But even so, Katzenstein's assertion (1987, p. 192) that 'a closely knit institutional web limits the exercise of unilateral political initiatives by any one actor' continues to hold true. Whether this continues to encourage incremental policy changes, as it did in times of affluence, has become a moot point. The 1990s were characterised by sequences of political stalemate and a deepening of state involvement rather than corporatist incrementalism. The latter depends not only on consensual policy-making. Making semisovereignty work requires strong commitments among and within organisational actors participating in sectoral self-governance. Without the peak associations being able to commit their organisational substructure and their individual members to make their resources available in support of corporatist arrangements, consensus is almost irrelevant since it cannot translate into viable policies. The creeping decentralisation of the industrial-relations system, both in terms of lower membership density and adherence to the principles of collective bargaining, seems to be one of the main problems in this respect (Ebbinghaus 2002a; see also chapters 2 and 7 in this volume).

These far-reaching changes within the industrial-relations system suggest that the German combination of a 'decentralised state' and a 'centralised society' emphasised by Katzenstein (1987) is no longer valid. German organised capitalism has decentralised very rapidly, at least in regard to labour-market associations, because of the industrial-relations crisis in the east and because of a generational change in business and union elites. The argument that such a development towards 'social disorganisation' has been sparked off by a combination of post-modernism, individualisation and the effects of globalisation (Beck

1996) may constitute part of the explanation, but it cannot account for some specificities of the German case. First, this argument neglects the reform plans of the pre-unification Kohl government, which resembled the Dutch and Swedish concepts and could not be realised in the post-unification period. Germany's political economy and welfare state would quite simply look entirely different if unification had not occurred. Second, global market pressures did not normally weaken, but rather sustained corporatist capacities in Germany and other European countries (Katzenstein 1985). Third, the industrial-relations crisis did not emanate from big global firms, but from the small and medium-sized industries of eastern Germany in particular. The export industry is still interested in industry-wide collective bargaining which protects it against excessive wage demands. In contrast small firms often cannot afford wages paid in the big export industries, and, therefore, prefer decentralised bargaining structures. It is for this reason that industry-wide bargaining has persisted in big firms, and therefore still covers a majority of employees. When it comes to political representation, however, small and medium-sized enterprises are stronger, a result principally of their privileged access to the *Land* level of government and via the statutory chambers of trade and industry (*Industrie- und Handelskammern*).

In contrast to its centralised Swedish, Dutch or Austrian counterparts, the German federal government failed to forge a corporatist deal with the industrial peak organisations, because it was unable to guarantee that such an arrangement would be implemented appropriately (Czada 2003). Towards the end of the 1990s, unions and employers became increasingly aware that reform packages agreed in the corporatist arena would have been jeopardised in the legislative process. The *Bundestag* opposition, through its *Bundesrat* majority, could jointly govern the country alongside the elected government. Indeed, it tried to do so in the pre-election year 1997, and again, in particular, after 1998. It must be remembered that it was much easier to bypass such institutional gridlock in the era of the 'two-and-a-half' party system, which generated only three possible coalition strategies. After 1990, in a system with five relevant parties, sixteen *Länder* and a state of perpetual election campaigning, this all became much harder to achieve.

Since the mid-1990s, then, corporatist incrementalism has suffered from institutional segmentation, as well as from the decreasing capacity of the peak associations to commit their members to a particular course of action. In addition, the main parties have found it much harder to bypass these obstacles via a cross-party consensus. In consequence, Chancellor Schröder has adopted new strategies to circumvent potential legislative vetoes as well as gridlocks in the corporatist arena. In particular, the SPD-Green government has attempted to short-circuit the established policy communities in health, pensions, the labour market and social assistance through the deliberate use of special commissions. True, their role as advisory bodies in the German political system is in no way new and all major welfare reforms have, so far, been accompanied by special commissions. The Schröder government, however, used them as a device to channel the political debate, to test public opinion, and to exert pressure on the opposition and *Länder* governments as well as on interest associations. The replacement of classic corporatism by expert and stakeholder committees appointed by the federal government might be considered to be an appropriate way to strengthen its authority in times of institutional and conceptual uncertainty. Given the implementation of the Hartz proposals and the influence of both the Hartz and Rürup Commissions on the Agenda 2010 reform debate, the shift to government by commission has had a substantial impact. Like parapublic institutions, the commissions serve as 'political shock absorbers'. Moreover, the government's authority to set up, recruit and dissolve them opens up much more direct mechanisms of control than corporatist negotiations allowed for.

Studies on the 'new politics' of the welfare state (e.g. Pierson 1996) have emphasised the constraints in dealing with policy change, structural reform and retrenchment issues. Institutional path dependencies and the popularity of welfare programmes are said to result in the need for policy-makers to take small steps, and to follow 'blame-avoidance' strategies. Semisovereignty, party concordance and corporatist intermediation as described by Katzenstein (1987) have long been best suited to that kind of incremental adjustment: indeed, the 'Bonn Republic' was quite successful in that respect. The new 'Berlin Republic', however, has experienced a decline in social partnership, shrinking capacities of associational self-governance, and intensified party conflicts. Potential blockades and uncertainties of the policy-making process have resulted from changes in the party system, fluctuations in industrial governance, and the transformation of the structure of the state. The latter has included a reinvigoration of the regulatory state and governmental initiatives to be found not only in social policy, but in many other policy fields as well (cf. Czada 2002).

9 Immigration and Integration Policy: Between Incrementalism and Non-decisions

Simon Green

Introduction

In the context of immigration policy, Peter Katzenstein's (1987, pp. 209–53) original analysis of the recruitment and management of 'migrant workers' reflected the political priorities of the time. During the mid-1980s, West Germany was still struggling to come to terms with the immediate effects of the so-called 'guestworkers' immigration (*Gastarbeiter*), under which millions of young, mainly male workers from Mediterranean countries (principally Turkey, Yugoslavia, Italy, Spain, Greece and Portugal) had been recruited between 1955 and 1973 for work in West Germany. Although the recruitment ban (*Anwerbestopp*) of 23 November 1973 did prevent further new arrivals of labour migrants, most of the 4 million or so workers who remained in the country at that time began to make West Germany their home for good (Castles 1985).

This abrupt change in policy had a number of effects, which together helped to transform the issue of migrant labour into a much broader policy area by the time of unification in 1990. First, the perspectives of the remaining guestworkers in 1973 changed. Even though few members of this first generation of immigrants had initially envisaged spending the rest of their lives in West Germany, the practical likelihood of return to their countries of origin diminished with every year that passed (Bischoff and Teubner 1992, pp. 114–17). Second, the prospect of settling in Germany for either the medium or even the long term encouraged the development of new, secondary migration to West Germany in the form of dependants, otherwise known as family reunification (*Familiennachzug*). It was precisely this kind of migration which caused the total numbers of non-nationals in West Germany to stabilise at around 4 million during the mid-1970s, indeed rising to 4.7 million by 1982.[1] Many of these new migrants were economically inactive, and the

---

[1] For these and other data used in this chapter, see Beauftragte der Bundesregierung 2002, 2004; also via http://www.destatis.de, http://www.bamf.de, http://www.unhcr.ch, http://www.bva.bund.de.

proportion of foreigners paying into employment-related insurance schemes (i.e. excluding those who were self-employed and those on low tax-free incomes) practically halved from almost two-thirds in 1972 to just over one-third in 1982. Such secondary migration continued to take place throughout the 1980s and 1990s.

Third, the establishment of a new, stable minority of immigrants in West Germany created, in turn, 'pull' factors for new migration, especially in the form of asylum seekers during the 1980s and 1990s, many of whom came from Turkey and later from eastern Europe. Already in 1980, the number of new asylum seekers had exceeded 100,000 for the first time. Rapid tightening of procedures did lead to a subsequent reduction, but numbers soon rose again to once more exceed 100,000 by 1988.

Fourth, the establishment of new family units in West Germany during the 1970s and 1980s, both via the former guestworkers and, later, via recognised refugees, resulted in an increase in the number of children born to non-German parents in West Germany. This was important because, until 2000, German citizenship law made no provision for territorial ascription of citizenship at birth (*ius soli*). Crucially, the exclusive reliance on the principle of descent (*ius sanguinis*) before 2000 meant that children born in Germany of non-German parentage were designated foreigners rather than German nationals at birth, with significant effects for their symbolic and practical inclusion into German society. Even after a new citizenship law came into force in 2000, the limited form of *ius soli* that was introduced meant that only around half of these children actually became German at birth (cf. Green 2000, pp. 113–14). Consequently, there is a third generation of 'foreigners' (in legal terms only) growing up in Germany today. In addition, naturalisation has traditionally been a difficult, lengthy and often costly bureaucratic exercise, which relatively few foreigners, even if they fulfilled the stringent conditions, actually chose to apply for. It is for these reasons that it is usual to speak of foreigners or non-nationals (*Ausländer*) in the German context, as opposed to immigrants or ethnic minorities.

The issue has, therefore, evolved considerably since the mid-1980s. No longer purely a question of economics and labour-market management, immigration policy can now be broken down into two main areas. First, immigration itself is governed by a patchwork of different regulations dealing with asylum, family reunification and, most recently, labour-migration policy again. Parallel to these, there are also special entry and citizenship provisions for ethnic Germans (*Spätaussiedler*) from eastern Europe and the former Soviet Union (cf. Rock and Wolff 2002), for whom West Germany operated a 'right to return' policy from the early 1950s onwards. Second, the focus has been increasingly on inclusion (or more popularly, integration), not only in social, linguistic, cultural and legal terms, but also in the form of the acquisition of German citizenship.

Yet politically, none of the three main parties, the CDU/CSU, the SPD and the FDP, had made much progress towards adapting their policies to the realities of the ethnically and culturally diverse society that had established itself by the mid-1980s. In fact, the then dominant political maxim that Germany was not 'a country of immigration' (*Deutschland ist kein Einwanderungsland*) continued to be repeated in government position papers until the late 1990s. What is more, the overall goal of the government's *Ausländerpolitik* (or 'foreigners' policy') was limited to a somewhat nebulous framework first defined in 1977 by a joint federation–*Länder* commission (see Katzenstein 1987, p. 239). This established three policy aims: the prevention of further labour migration, the encouragement of return migration and the integration of remaining foreigners into German society. These parameters (*Eckwerte*) were confirmed by a second federation–*Länder* commission in 1983, which had been established under the new Kohl government when it came to office in October 1982.

In effect, the choice of parameters meant that policy, as Katzenstein himself notes, 'was based on contradictory premises and advocated inconsistent objectives' (Katzenstein 1987, p. 219), especially in terms of the second and third aim. Formally speaking, the 1977 framework had been agreed by a cross-party consensus between the federal government and the *Länder*. Yet this superficial consensus hid the very different party approaches to integration that lay just below the surface, and which had already started to emerge in 1979, when the first Commissioner for Foreigners' Affairs, Heinz Kühn (SPD), published his now famous memorandum on the future of *Ausländerpolitik* in West Germany (see Katzenstein 1987, pp. 240–2). In it, he urged his party to adopt more proactive integration measures, and the Schmidt government's attempt to introduce what at the time would have constituted a radical reform of citizenship policy in early 1982 was a direct consequence of Kühn's ideas. However, the CDU/CSU did not share Kühn's vision, and the bill was vetoed in the *Bundesrat*. Katzenstein was, therefore, right to conclude that 'West German policymakers advocated a vaguely defined policy of social integration that permitted a broad spectrum of interpretations by all the relevant political actors' (Katzenstein 1987, p. 219).

The political differences between the parties, especially over integration, increased considerably after the Kohl government came to power.

Its originally polarising rhetoric and (admittedly ineffective) attempts in 1983–4 to promote voluntary repatriation, combined with the entry into parliament of the aggressively pro-immigration Greens in 1983, encouraged the SPD to diverge ever further from the CDU/CSU's conceptual position on integration, and hence to end the cross-party consensus that had existed in the 1960s and 1970s (cf. Green 2004; Murray 1994). With the liberal FDP in the 1980s also harbouring grave misgivings over some of its senior coalition partner's policies, notably over family reunification, an effective policy stalemate ensued, under which non-decisions followed by periodic incremental policy change became the normal pattern of development (Green 2004).

This in itself would not have been a problem had Germany's rate of evolution into a multiethnic, culturally diverse society kept pace with policy developments. But in reality, the rate of changes brought about by immigration far outstripped the shifts in policy. Thus, by the end of 2003, some 7.3 million non-nationals lived in Germany, representing 8.9 per cent of the population; a level that had, moreover, remained more or less constant since the mid-1990s (Table 9.1). This total included almost 2 million Turkish citizens and 1 million citizens from former Yugoslavia; in 2003, 20 per cent of all non-nationals, a total of 1.5 million persons, had been born in Germany. In cities such as Frankfurt am Main and Stuttgart, non-Germans constituted, in 1995, 30 per cent and 24 per cent of the population respectively. In 2003, the average residence period for *Ausländer* stood at no less than sixteen years, compared with nine years in 1980 (Katzenstein 1987, p. 230). Yet right until its departure from office in 1998, the Kohl government stubbornly refused to acknowledge that Germany had, in fact, become a country of immigration. Far from being merely symbolic, this denial meant that, by 2004, Germany had adopted few of the policies that are common in countries with a similar immigration dimension, such as integrated labour-market access and residence policies, an inclusive citizenship regime and anti-discrimination legislation (cf. Green 2003).

This chapter discusses the changing relationship between the semi-sovereign mode of governance and policy outcomes in this controversial and important policy area for Germany. It asks both to what extent semisovereign structures and outcomes are still in evidence in this field, and whether these outcomes are still able to provide solutions to the policy challenges of the new millennium. It shows that the evolution of the policy area since the 1980s to include a whole range of new issues has resulted in a reconfiguration of the actors in this field, with political parties in government now adopting a far more activist role. Yet despite these structural changes, outcomes in both immigration and integration

Table 9.1. *Immigration and the non-national population in Germany, 1990–2003*

	1990[a]	1991	1992	1993	1994	1995	1996	1997	1998	1999	2000	2001	2002	2003
Total non-national population (millions)	5.343	5.882	6.496	6.878	6.991	7.174	7.314	7.366	7.320	7.344	7.297	7.319	7.336	7.335
As per cent of total population	8.4	7.3	8.0	8.5	8.6	8.8	8.9	9.0	8.9	8.9	8.9	8.9	8.9	8.9
New asylum applications (000s)	193	256	438	323	127	128	116	104	99	95	79	88	71	51
Ethnic German immigrants (000s)	397	222	231	219	223	218	178	134	103	105	96	98	91	73
Naturalisations (000s)	20	27	37	45	62	72	86	83	107	143	187	178	155	141

Note: [a]Western Germany only.
Source: http://www.destatis.de; http://www.bva.bund.de; http://www.bafl.de; Beauftragte der Bundesregierung (2004).

policy have remained stable, albeit each for different reasons. In immigration, there has been a general consensus, especially over the prevention of new labour migration. By contrast, disputes in integration policy have been more ideological in their nature, both between and within the main parties, which have utilised Germany's numerous political veto points to produce nothing more than infrequent and incremental policy changes throughout the 1990s and into the new millennium. Furthermore, the analysis presented here illustrates that when changes were made, they were frequently the result of institutional machinations between the parties in the lower and upper houses of parliament, the *Bundestag* and *Bundesrat*, rather than the process of traditional consensual negotiation across party and state–society boundaries typically associated with German politics.

Context

The context of Germany's immigration and integration policy cannot be separated from unification, which was accompanied by massive new influxes in the form of asylum seekers and ethnic Germans from the former Soviet Union. These soon forced Germany to amend its traditionally generous entry policies for these two groups (Green 2001, pp. 91–5). Table 9.1 shows that over 1.2 million persons claimed asylum in Germany between 1990 and 1993, prompting a cross-party deal on immigration, to include asylum seekers, ethnic Germans and citizenship, in December 1992. The changes were enacted in July 1993, and their centrepiece was an amendment of the constitutional guarantee of asylum in Article 16 of the Basic Law. Henceforth, asylum applicants from 'safe countries of origin', or who had passed through 'safe third countries' (such as other EU states) to reach Germany, could be rejected more-or-less out of hand. The changes, which followed a bitter political dispute between the parties (cf. Bade 1994), helped to produce a real reduction in the numbers of new applicants, which by 2003 had fallen to 51,000, their lowest level for almost twenty years (Table 9.1). By contrast, even after their right to unlimited immigration was effectively removed in 1993, ethnic German immigrants, who still numbered 73,000 in 2003, retained an enormously privileged position vis-à-vis other groups of immigrants (Münz and Ohliger 1998). Not only did they receive automatic German citizenship, but they were given language classes and social assistance that was otherwise only available to recognised refugees.

In addition, the collapse of the GDR meant that the Federal Republic of Germany could finally consider reforming its citizenship law. Throughout the period from 1949 to 1990, successive West German governments had deliberately maintained a broad, pre-war definition of citizenship that included the population of the GDR in order both to undermine the smaller state's legitimacy and to reinforce its own claim to be the only true representative of Germans (*Alleinvertretungsanspruch*). Any reform of this explicitly all-German definition of citizenship was, therefore, impossible as long as the GDR existed (Green 2001).

Despite unification fundamentally changing the external and internal environment in which immigration policy was formulated, the second policy goal – integration – remains as elusive in Germany as in other member states of the EU. In many of the issues and deficits identified by Katzenstein (1987, pp. 224, 229–32), little progress has been made over the past twenty years, especially in relation to German nationals. Thus, even though foreigners' average wages and housing conditions have improved, the gap between their standards and those enjoyed by Germans remains wide (Beauftragte der Bundesregierung 2002, pp. 315–24). As the OECD's PISA study in 2001 showed, it is this lower socio-economic status, as opposed simply to nationality, which impacts on the low levels of educational attainment of non-national children (Beauftragte der Bundesregierung 2002, pp. 182–3). In 1999, almost 20 per cent of foreign school children failed to obtain even the lowest kind of school qualification (*Hauptschulabschluss*), compared with just 8 per cent of Germans. Naturally, this, in turn, affects non-nationals' ability to secure places in vocational-training schemes (*Ausbildung*): whereas two-thirds of German teenagers were in such schemes in 1999, the equivalent share for non-nationals was less than 40 per cent. In consequence, the unemployment situation among foreigners in western Germany (where over 95 per cent of foreigners live) has been steadily worsening. In 1983, the unemployment rate among *Ausländer* was around 1.5 times that of Germans (Katzenstein 1987, p. 229); by 2000, that multiplier had increased to 2.1.

This marginalisation has persisted in legal terms, too, despite some modest recent improvements. On the one hand, the proportion of non-nationals holding the most secure form of residence status (*Aufenthalts-berechtigung*) provided for in the main piece of legislation governing this area until 2005, the *Ausländergesetz*, has increased to around 10 per cent from the mere 0.2 per cent in Hesse in 1977 cited by Katzenstein (1987, p. 224). On the other hand, this higher figure still pales into insignificance considering that two-thirds of non-nationals have been resident for longer than the eight years required for this permit.[2] Likewise,

---

[2] Of course, it may be that individual non-nationals have not fulfilled the other criteria for this residence permit, such as five years' pension contributions. In addition, EU citizens,

naturalisations (excluding ethnic Germans) have been steadily increasing, due to a number of reforms during the 1990s leading up to the new citizenship law in 2000 (Green 2000, pp. 110–12). Since the 1980s, when the number of naturalisations in any given year rarely exceeded 0.3 per cent of the total foreign population, rates have risen to peak at 2.6 per cent in 2000, the year the new citizenship law came into force. However, since then, the rate has actually fallen for three years in a row, to the extent that the total number of naturalisations in 2003 (141,000) was lower than before the new law, which at the time was hailed as a historic liberalisation. Indeed, despite this improvement, Germany's naturalisation rates remain among the lowest in the EU (cf. Waldrauch and Çinar 2003, p. 271). Moreover, despite the overall increases in naturalisations, once new net immigration and live births of non-nationals in Germany are factored in, it is still likely to take decades before the share of non-nationals in the total population is reduced from its 2003 level of 8.9 per cent to the EU average of around 5 per cent. Here, too, it is easy to underestimate the barrier to inclusion in Germany represented by naturalisation: as well as granting the right to vote, most key public sector positions are only open to German or EU nationals.

Taken as a whole, therefore, non-national residents represent a structurally socio-economically disadvantaged section in German society. This persistent marginalisation, combined with heavy concentration of immigrants in specific areas of Germany's major cities, has caused alarm among politicians and commentators alike. In March 2002, the news magazine *Der Spiegel* published a typically polemic, but nonetheless powerful critique of integration policies so far, describing the emergence of 'parallel worlds' under the headline 'The Underbelly of the Republic' (*Der Spiegel*, 4 March 2002; see also Luft 2003). Significantly, ethnic Germans are experiencing similar problems in their integration, despite that group's preferential legal position (cf. *Der Spiegel*, 24 February 2003).

At the same time, the prospect of new labour immigration has reappeared in recent years, as a result of the emergence of skills shortages in key sectors of the German economy, as well as the demographic effects of increasing life expectancy and of falling fertility rates, which in Germany, at around 1.3 children per woman, are among the lowest in the EU. The combination of the two latter factors has potentially seismic

---

who make up 25 per cent of all non-nationals in Germany, are effectively excluded from immigration and residence restrictions. But even allowing for these, the difference between residence periods and residence status of non-nationals in 2003 was stark.

implications for Germany's publicly financed health and pensions systems, which both rely on current transfers between contributors (those in work and employers) and beneficiaries (mainly older people) (cf. chapter 8 in this volume). As in so many other aspects of German politics, the problem was, of course, already evident in the mid-1980s (Katzenstein 1987, pp. 191–2); however, it was not until new UN and German-government reports in 2000, which calculated that Germany required some 500,000 new migrants annually just in order to keep the size of its working population constant, that a new urgency was injected into the issue (cf. Schmid 2001, p. 21). The challenge of demography is further complicated by the fact that, despite some 4.5 million un-employed in mid-2004, the German economy is short of both skilled and unskilled labour (Green 2002). In response, Otto Schily, the SPD Federal Interior Minister, in 2000 set up a cross-party commission on immigration headed by Rita Süssmuth, a CDU politician and a former speaker of the *Bundestag*. In its report of summer 2001, it recommended that up to 40,000 new labour migrants should be granted entry to Germany each year (*Migration und Bevölkerung* 4/2001). Thereafter, the commission's proposals formed the basis for the federal govern-ment's December 2001 bill for Germany's first full immigration law (*Zuwanderungsgesetz*), although it took no less than three years for this bill finally to become law.[3]

Agenda

It is against this complex, and often contradictory, background that the main political parties have been wrestling with the various policy chal-lenges of immigration and integration. This task has been further complicated by the fact that the electorate has rarely shown much enthusiasm for either more liberal immigration or more inclusive inte-gration policies such as citizenship, and populist right-wing parties have periodically been able to capitalise on this concern at local, *Land* or European elections. When combined with the almost constant cycle of electioneering that has characterised post-unification German politics, the two main parties have been understandably cautious in putting

---

[3] The first version of the *Zuwanderungsgesetz* was introduced into parliament in December 2001 and passed the *Bundesrat* in controversial formal circumstances in March 2002, as a result of which it was struck down by the Constitutional Court in December 2002. The bill was reintroduced in 2003 and referred by the opposition-controlled *Bundesrat* to the conciliation committee between both chambers of parliament (*Vermittlungsausschuss*) in the summer of that year. It took a further year's negotiations, and a personal intervention by Chancellor Schröder in May 2004, to complete the bill's legislative passage in July 2004. The new law finally came into effect on 1 January 2005.

forward potentially unpopular proposals in this field. The policy agenda itself can be divided into four main areas: promotion of integration, prevention of further labour migration, reduction in the number of asylum seekers, and protection from threats to internal security.

The first, and probably most controversial, aspect of the agenda is the area of integration policy, despite the fact that the CDU/CSU, SPD, FDP, Greens and PDS have all repeatedly emphasised in policy statements the need to improve the integration of non-nationals. While this degree of consensus clearly sets the main parties apart from the more extreme fringes, some of which, not unlike the CDU/CSU in the mid-1980s, advocate forms of repatriation policy, the devil, of course, lies in the detail. Accordingly, the definition of integration has provided fertile ground for party conflict, which has carried over into some, but by no means all, aspects of policy. For instance, while citizenship has been a highly politicised area of policy over the past twenty years, all main parties now agree that formal and mandatory integration courses for foreigners are necessary in Germany.

Essentially, the political debate on concepts of integration has revolved around the extent to which non-nationals should be expected to assimilate (i.e. take on the majority culture), and how the norms to be accepted by all immigrants or non-nationals, irrespective of their religious or cultural affiliation, should be defined (cf. Joppke and Morawska 2003). Here, the ideas of the various parties vary considerably: whereas the conservative CDU/CSU has generally emphasised the need to maintain Germany's Christian-occidental tradition and culture in the light of large-scale, non-European and Muslim immigration, the SPD, Greens and PDS have usually argued for a more pluralist, humanist and secular interpretation of integration. However, the distinction between the parties has not always been clear-cut: thus Interior Minister Schily notoriously declared in 2002 that 'the best form of integration is assimilation' (*Süddeutsche Zeitung*, 27 June 2002).

Nonetheless, the basic party differences over conceptualisations of integration are reflected in citizenship policy, and, in particular, the question of dual citizenship. A reform of citizenship had already been promised in the 1992 immigration compromise that paved the way for the asylum reform, but in a *prima facie* case of non-decision-making, internal differences within the CDU/CSU-FDP coalition prevented such a reform in the period from 1994 to 1998 (Green 2004). When the SPD-Green government came to power in 1998, it immediately resolved to tackle this issue head-on, and its original proposal for a new citizenship law of early 1999 envisaged a general (as opposed to exceptional) tolerance of dual and multiple citizenships, both when the children of non-nationals gained German citizenship via *ius soli*, and in naturalisations. Germany's rejection of dual citizenship has in practice been a major disincentive to naturalisation, as obtaining release from one's previous citizenship in practice is time consuming, complicated and expensive (see poll data in Hagedorn 2001, p. 159).

However, this proposal was utterly rejected by the CDU and especially the CSU. Both parties argued that the requirement for naturalisation applicants to be released from their previous citizenship was the only significant guarantor that immigrants were fully integrated into German society. For the same reason, the CDU/CSU opposed even the limited form of territorial ascription (*ius soli*) which the law aimed to introduce, as this, too, in combination with *ius sanguinis* via the parents, would have created dual citizens at birth. This position reflected the CDU/CSU's fundamentally different approach to citizenship, which holds that natur-alisation should represent the end of the integrative process, rather than, as argued by the SPD and Greens, constituting a stage towards it. Crucially, in the question of dual citizenship, the public agreed, and the CDU/CSU was able to force this provision to be dropped by mobil-ising an unprecedented petition campaign in early 1999, which, in turn, helped to swing the outcome of the Hesse state election in February of that year in favour of the CDU. The results of this opposition for policy outcomes will be returned to in the final section of this chapter.

The second defining aspect of the agenda is the prevention of new labour migration. Ever since 'guestworkers' recruitment was stopped in 1973, no permanent labour migration has been permitted, although since 1990 there has been a range of opportunities for temporary workers (mainly in agriculture) to come to Germany. More recently, as noted above, this agenda has somewhat been overtaken by events, with skills shortages and demographic developments requiring a reassessment of existing policies. Again, the parties have adopted a range of positions, ranging from broadly liberal proposals on the left (especially regarding the right of asylum seekers to work) to inherently restrictive responses from the right, with the CSU leader, and chancellor candidate in 2002, Edmund Stoiber, preferring a more proactive family policy and retrain-ing programmes to new labour migration. But here too, the boundaries can easily be blurred: it was the SPD-Green government which, under pressure from the CDU/CSU, delayed by seven years the introduction of free movement of labour from the ten new accession states to the EU in 2004.

But in general (and ironically), this has meant that business interests in labour migration have recently been more closely aligned to the SPD than to their more natural Christian Democratic allies. This was graphically illustrated in early 2000, when Chancellor Schröder announced the introduction of the so-called 'Green Card' programme, under which up to 20,000 highly qualified IT specialists were to be recruited to work in Germany for up to five years. While industry broadly welcomed this initiative, despite its limited scope (cf. *Der Spiegel*, 2 September 2002), it met with howls of protest from the CDU/CSU, for whom this represented the thin edge of the wedge for general new labour migration.

All the same, the policy differences between the SPD and CDU/CSU in this area, although significant, have been less ideological than over integration. Both parties accept that highly skilled migrants must be allowed entry to Germany to fill specific labour shortages; equally, both parties are clear in their desire to prevent new unskilled migration, despite labour shortages in less highly skilled areas such as the hotel trade and catering. Consequently, these two principles underpin the final content of the *Zuwanderungsgesetz* on labour migration, and much of the to-and-fro that accompanied its parliamentary progress between 2001 and 2004 may be considered to have been largely cosmetic.

The third agenda concerns the on-going desire to reduce the number of asylum seekers in Germany. Ever since 1980, asylum has been an ever-present issue in German politics as a whole, and it even dominated the agenda in late 1992 and early 1993, as numbers of applicants shot up after unification. In particular, the origins of Germany's constitutional asylum provisions as a reaction to persecution in Nazi Germany have imbued this issue with especial emotional significance. As a result, Germany's treatment of asylum seekers has been seen not only as a reflection of its own international humanitarian obligations, but also as confirmation that the lessons of Nazi Germany have been learned.

Initially, the small numbers of applicants permitted Germany to be quite generous with its provision (Green 2001, p. 89). But as numbers increased during the 1980s and 1990s, governments attempted to make Germany progressively less attractive as a destination (Münch 1992). This process culminated in the 1993 amendment of Article 16 of the Basic Law, and was backed up by a series of procedural laws which reduced formal processing times. In addition, welfare benefits that were once relatively generous have been gradually eroded. Furthermore, by excluding persecution by non-state actors, Germany has traditionally adopted a comparatively narrow definition of refugee status under the 1951 Geneva Convention. Its initial recognition rates have, thus, been among the lowest in the EU, rarely rising above 10 per cent annually, and indeed falling to just 5 per cent in 2003.

To a greater or lesser degree, the CDU/CSU, SPD and FDP (but not the Greens) have all supported this relentless restriction of policy, not least for financial reasons: the costs for housing, feeding and clothing asylum seekers are borne either at *Land* or at local level. After the rapid increases in the number of claimants during the early 1990s, regional governments of every political colour became desperate to limit expenditure. For this reason, the Europeanisation agenda and burden-sharing between EU member states in the area of asylum has attracted broad support from the parties. However, this enthusiasm waned somewhat between 1999 and 2004, when it became clear that a harmonised European asylum regime would (and did) actually result in the liberalisation of some aspects of Germany's policy.

The fourth principal issue on the policy agenda in this area concerns internal security, which has played a pivotal role in policy debates, especially in recent years. As an agenda item, it in fact encompasses both the immigration and integration policy dimensions. In terms of immigration, governments of all persuasions have been keen to appear tough on crime and criminal behaviour by non-nationals. For instance, tough new conditions for deportation were introduced in 1996, prompted in part by violent demonstrations by Germany's Kurdish population in support of Kurdish independence in the early 1990s. Inevitably, this agenda was given a whole new dimension of importance by the terrorist attacks on the United States on 11 September 2001, and by the subsequent revelation that some of the perpetrators had previously lived, quite legally, in Germany. With this in mind, the SPD-Green government rushed through two security packages in 2001 and 2002. Internal security also dominated the final stages of the negotiations over the *Zuwanderungsgesetz* in 2004, when one of the sticking-points was whether detention without trial (*Sicherungshaft*) for suspected foreign terrorists should (and indeed even could) be introduced.

Such events have, of course, simultaneously reinforced the profile of the integration agenda. The fear that radical Muslims will establish parallel societies, or that they might even act as 'fifth columnists' to establish an Islamic state in Germany, has been a powerful political mobiliser, especially among conservative political elements. For instance, following a 2003 ruling by the Constitutional Court, several *Länder* have passed laws explicitly forbidding female Muslim teachers (but not students) from wearing headscarves, while simultaneously permitting the display of Christian and Jewish religious symbols, such as crucifixes, in the classroom. In 2000, Friedrich Merz, a key figure in the CDU/CSU, polarised public opinion by speaking of the need for non-nationals to adopt Germany's prevailing culture (*Leitkultur*)

(Klusmeyer 2001). Similarly, and in explicit response to the internal security agenda, the 1999 Citizenship Law introduced the requirement for applicants for naturalisation to sign a declaration of loyalty to the German constitution. From 2005, the *Länder* are referring all applications for citizenship to the internal security service (*Verfassungsschutz*) for cross-checking against its files.

Parallel to these two aspects of internal security is the question of racist violence, which remained at a worryingly constant level during the 1990s. This has been a particular problem in the new eastern *Länder*, where, in 1999, there were up to four times as many racist attacks per capita as in the west (*Der Spiegel*, 11 September 2000). Following anti-foreigner riots in Hoyerswerda and Rostock in 1991 and 1992 respectively, as well as the murder of ten Turks by Germans in two arson attacks in 1992 and 1993, racist violence subsided, but without ever going away. High-profile cases of asylum seekers being attacked in the east occur with depressing regularity and the federal government's attempt to ban the extremist National Democratic Party of Germany (NPD), which was rejected by the Constitutional Court in March 2003, is indicative of this issue.

While all four agendas have been characterised by lively party political competition and disagreement over policy proposals, the real differences between CDU/CSU and SPD policies have frequently been surprisingly modest (cf. Hailbronner 2001). Indeed, the disputes have often been of an ideological rather than a concrete nature. Nowhere has this been more evident than in the discussion in early 1999, when the CDU/CSU argued that permitting dual citizenship would actually be counter-productive to the integration of non-Germans living in Germany. Yet as noted above, the evidence suggests that it was the long processing times and high costs involved in securing release from one's previous citizenship, rather than a putative lack of commitment to Germany, that discouraged many foreigners from applying for German citizenship.

A second issue which is characterised by a high degree of ideology has itself been a subsidiary item on the policy agenda for the past twenty-five years: the age limit for non-EU children to immigrate with their parents (*Kindernachzug*). In 1981, this was set at sixteen by the SPD-FDP federal government (Green 2004, pp. 43–7). However, and despite being enshrined in law in 1990, this limit has constantly been criticised as being too high by the CDU/CSU, who have maintained that, in order to maximise a child's chances for integration into German society as an adult, this limit should be set at the school-starting age, namely six. By contrast, the Greens have long argued in favour of raising this age limit to the standard EU level of eighteen. In the course of the negotiations for the *Zuwanderungsgesetz*, the issue again returned to the agenda, but the federal government and the CDU/CSU opposition simply could not agree on whether the new age limit should be fourteen, twelve or ten, even though these reductions would have affected only a very small number of persons (*Die Zeit*, 4 April 2002). In 2003, Interior Minister Schily even pushed through an amendment to the EU's Family Reunification Directive in order to accommodate the ongoing debates over the *Zuwanderungsgesetz*. It was therefore particularly ironic when it suddenly transpired during the final negotiation rounds for the *Zuwanderungsgesetz* in spring 2004 that the CDU/CSU had in fact agreed to retain an age limit of sixteen for *Kindernachzug*. Without detracting from the saliency of these issues for the individuals affected, it has sometimes appeared as if party protagonists have deliberately chosen not to see the larger picture for fear of being branded as 'weak' on immigration and non-nationals.

Process and Institutional Configuration

Although the current political goals of immigration and integration policy remain similar, at least in name, to those of the 1970s and 1980s, the institutional configuration of the policy field has evolved considerably since then. This has reflected the shift of the policy focus away from labour-market issues to residence and citizenship policy, and is symbolised by the transfer, by the early 1980s, of overall responsibility for *Ausländerpolitik* from the Federal Labour to the Federal Interior Ministry. Indeed, the dominance of the Interior Ministry in this sector was cemented by the new forms of immigration that emerged from 1980 onwards, in particular asylum seekers and ethnic Germans. Its structures have adapted to reflect this change in priorities, and, by 1992, *Ausländerpolitik* had been accorded its own division (*Abteilung*). Like many other federal ministries, the Interior Ministry is principally concerned with the formulation of legislation; implementation is a matter for the *Länder*.

In terms of policy outcome, the identity of the incumbent minister has played an important role. Two ministers, Friedrich Zimmermann (CSU) and Manfred Kanther (CDU), both of whom pursued an uncompromisingly tough approach to *Ausländerpolitik* in 1982–9 and 1993–8 respectively, were ultimately frustrated by their failure to win enough allies within the governing coalition for their hardline policies (Green 2004). By contrast, Wolfgang Schäuble (CDU) and Rudolf Seiters (CDU), who headed the Interior Ministry in, respectively, 1989–91 and 1991–3, as well as Otto Schily (SPD), who took office in

1998, have all taken more pragmatic approaches, thereby ensuring that major pieces of legislation were enacted under their stewardship.

Prior to the 2002 *Bundestag* election, the Federal Labour Ministry was the second key actor in this field. Until then, it retained responsibility for the integration of foreigners (a remnant from the guestworkers era, which was afterwards transferred to the Interior Ministry), as well as hosting the principal independent office in this field, the Federal Commissioner for Foreigners' Affairs (*Beauftragte der Bundesregierung für Ausländerfragen*) (Geiß 2001), which was created by the SPD-FDP government in 1978. Its second incumbent, Liselotte Funcke (FDP) (1981–91), endeavoured to provide a liberal voice in the policy-making process. Indeed, at critical junctures she was able to muster enough support from within her party to be able to avert some of Interior Minister Zimmermann's more draconian measures. However, the office's effectiveness in policy formulation over the years has been limited by its consultative status. Ms Funcke's two successors, Cornelia Schmalz-Jacobsen (1991–8) and Marieluise Beck (appointed after the 1998 election), have had to rely on informal mechanisms and the office's public profile as their main source of influence.

Crucially, the general shift in responsibility towards the Federal Interior Ministry has been accompanied by a reduction in the role of the dominant parapublic institution, the Federal Labour Office (*Bundesanstalt für Arbeit*, BA), which, until 1973, had acted as co-ordinating agency between government, unions and employers in a corporatist setting (Katzenstein 1987). Its withdrawal from the arena has meant that parapublic institutions are practically absent from this entire field, with the Federal Office for the Recognition of Refugees (*Bundesamt für die Anerkennung ausländischer Flüchtlinge*, BAFl), the other main body in this area, acting as an implementing rather than a formulating institution.

Nonetheless, the future may hold more of a role for both the commissioner and parapublic institutions in this area. Like the welfare reforms outlined in chapter 8 of this volume, the government's 2001 proposals for the *Zuwanderungsgesetz* were based substantially on the recommendations of a specialist commission (the so-called Süssmuth Commission). Even though its members were carefully chosen by Schily for their proximity to his own positions, its cross-party and corporatist nature did serve to depoliticise the issues in a similar way to parapublic institutions. In addition, the *Zuwanderungsgesetz* has upgraded the BAFl (now the BAMF) into a new parapublic general regulatory office for migration, including responsibility for integration courses and the co-ordination of new labour migration. Likewise, the Commissioner for Foreigners' Affairs was renamed, promoted and relocated after the 2002 election.

As the Commissioner for Migration, Refugees and Integration, as she is now known, Ms Beck was reappointed as a parliamentary state secretary (*parlamentarische Staatssekretärin*) within the Family Ministry. Although the office continues to be located at the ministerial periphery, and is viewed with mistrust by the dominant Federal Interior Ministry, Ms Beck's new position gives her a much higher profile, both formally and informally, in the co-ordination of government policy.

Societal organisations such as churches, welfare organisations and unions have also seen their role and impact diminish, as the policy agenda has shifted away from practical labour-market integration to more abstract issues such as citizenship and naturalisation. In any case, interest representation in this field is structurally weaker than in other policy areas, for four reasons. First, foreigners themselves are poorly organised into a myriad of local organisations, often structured by nationality, and their formal involvement in policy-making is restricted to the local level, where most towns in Germany now operate consultative councils (*Ausländerbeiräte*). Second, neither unions, churches or welfare organisations have foreigners as their primary clientele. Third, the bargaining power of non-nationals and interest groups vis-à-vis the state is low because, in contrast to other sectors, they are not central to policy implementation. Fourth, as foreigners cannot vote in *Land* or federal elections, the political incentive to heed their wishes is correspondingly low.

The gap created in *Ausländerpolitik* by this reduction in the role of societal groups and parapublic institutions has not been left unfilled, with the profile of parties themselves increasing correspondingly since the early 1980s. This coincided with the increasing politicisation of *Ausländerpolitik* from the late 1970s onwards, as the government grappled with the implications of the 1973 recruitment ban and the increasing numbers of asylum seekers. With the political stakes now higher, the parties began to take a much more active interest in *Ausländerpolitik*. In fact, in the absence of effective societal input and of the depoliticising effect of parapublic institutions, the coalition parties became the primary control mechanism over ministerial autonomy in policy-making. Thus in 1988, Interior Minister Zimmermann, who had drafted proposals for a draconian tightening of residence policies for non-nationals, was principally thwarted in his plans by the CDU's moderate social-Catholic wing and the FDP, which refused to support them. When a revision of the 1965 *Ausländergesetz* came before parliament in 1989, it was the parliamentary spokesmen of the coalition partners and not the Interior Ministry who had a major hand in formulating the all-important parameters of the new law (*Eckwerte*). The Interior Affairs Committee of the *Bundestag* also made some vital changes to some of the bill's naturalisation provisions (Green 2004, p. 71).

This comparatively intrusive role of the coalition parties' own experts in the domain of the Interior Ministry, namely the direct formulation of policy, has continued into the 1990s. A series of amendments to the *Ausländergesetz* in 1996 were organised not by the Interior Ministry, but by the parliamentary parties. When Interior Minister Manfred Kanther failed to produce a citizenship bill (as had been laid down in the coalition agreement) by half way through the 1994–8 *Bundestag*, it was the more liberal elements from within the CDU parliamentary party who publicly proposed an alternative solution. Most obviously, the referral of the *Zuwanderungsgesetz* to the conciliation committee between *Bundestag* and *Bundesrat* in 2003 inevitably shifted the focus away from technical norms and onto political horse-trading.

One of the main arenas in which this higher profile for political parties has manifested itself is in the *Bundesrat*, not necessarily in terms of content, but certainly in terms of decision-making and timing. Already in 1982, the CDU/CSU had used its majority in the *Bundesrat* to veto a bill by the SPD-FDP government which would have liberalised naturalisation for second-generation immigrants. This pattern of instrumentalising the *Bundesrat* for (national) party-political purposes continued throughout the 1980s and 1990s, as the genesis of three major decisions in this policy area since 1990 shows (Green 2004). In May 1990, the CDU/CSU-FDP government pushed the new *Ausländergesetz* through the *Bundesrat* just days before it lost its majority in that chamber following the *Land* election in Lower Saxony. In 1999, the SPD-Green government's proposals for dual citizenship had to be amended in order to regain a *Bundesrat* majority following the loss of Hesse to the CDU as a result of the petition campaign in February 1999. In order to secure the votes of the SPD-FDP coalition in Rhineland-Palatinate to re-establish its majority in the *Bundesrat*, the government was prepared to bring the FDP on board in a new compromise solution. As a result, the bill's most controversial and radical provision (the general acceptance of dual citizenship) was dropped altogether, while dual citizenships created by *ius soli* in Germany would only be valid until the child reaches the age of 23 (Green 2000, pp. 115–21). Lastly, in 2002, the fate of the *Zuwanderungsgesetz* depended on the voting decision of the state of Brandenburg in the *Bundesrat*, which itself was mired in controversy and ultimately ended up being overruled by the Constitutional Court. The important point is that the *Bundesrat* once again acted as the major locus of decision-making against the background of disagreement between the governing and opposition parties in the *Bundestag*.

Essentially, the combination of an increased role for political parties and a greater focus on ideological areas of political difference is no surprise, nor indeed a coincidence. Katzenstein's case study of labour migration showed how this controversial policy area could be depoliticised in its content (albeit not in its presentation) through the central role of the BA and societal groups in policy-making. However, with their retreat from the policy-making centrestage in the early 1980s, and against a background of continued public unease over immigration, there has been no check on the SPD's and CDU/CSU's populist instincts to politicise a restrictive agenda for electoral reasons, irrespective of whether or not such an agenda is currently in Germany's best interests.

Lastly, it is worth noting briefly the role of the Constitutional Court. As in other policy areas, its interventions have been infrequent, but no less significant for that (Joppke 1999). For instance, in 1990, 1996 and 2002, the court respectively ruled against voting rights for foreigners, in favour of the asylum compromise, and against the *Zuwanderungsgesetz* on formal grounds. When it does rule, its decisions, therefore, tend to have a major impact in circumscribing the limits within which policy outcomes can be negotiated. With new issues now arising out of the integration agenda, such as the balance between an individual's religious freedom and the secular role of the state, or between the rules on deportation and the individual's right to due process, its role shows no sign of abating.

Consequences and Conclusions

The changing emphasis of *Ausländerpolitik* away from its labour-market focus to broader issues of immigration, asylum and citizenship has meant that policy formulation no longer 'occurs in a network in which state institutions are tied closely to the major interest groups' (Katzenstein 1987, p. 219). But that has not meant that the sovereignty of the state has increased, as the role of political parties, either through their membership of the governing federal coalition or their ability to exercise a veto in the *Bundesrat*, has compensated for the absence of parapublic institutions and the lower profile for societal interests.

Yet crucially, formal outcomes have remained broadly incremental. The 1990 *Ausländergesetz*, although constituting a significant change from its 1965 predecessor, remained incremental in its essence because it merely formalised what had more or less become accepted administrative practice in the twenty-five year life-span of the old law. The 1993 amendment of asylum policy was arguably also incremental. The basic nature of the constitutional provision remained untouched (as was in any case constitutionally prescribed), and despite numbers of new asylum seekers falling sharply in the following two years, it is only since 1999 that they have fallen below the sensitive 100,000 per annum mark. The constitutional amendment of asylum was accompanied by two other measures: first, a temporary entitlement to simplified naturalisation for certain groups was changed into a permanent one and second, ethnic German immigration from the former Soviet Union was to be gradually phased out over the coming decades. By their very nature, both these measures were highly incremental too.

Similarly, the 1999 Citizenship Law had its most radical elements pruned after the success of the CDU/CSU's petition campaign against dual citizenship. Even though a number of significant changes remain, as a result of which for instance the proportion of naturalisations tolerating dual citizenship under the new law has actually doubled, the overall effect of the law remains incremental, as its disappointing impact on numbers naturalised in Germany illustrates (Table 9.1 above). More recently, the federal government's 'Green Card' programme has not fulfilled even its rather modest aspirations of recruiting 20,000 IT specialists, with only two-thirds of the quota filled by the end of 2002.

In particular, the 2004 *Zuwanderungsgesetz*, which is undoubtedly the most significant and comprehensive piece of legislation ever to have been passed in Germany in this area, represents less of a 'great leap forward' than the federal government and the Süssmuth Commission originally intended (details in Bundesministerium des Innern 2004). Thus, the possibilities for new labour migration are limited to individual highly skilled migrants. The law's extension of Germany's grounds for asylum to include non-state persecution and gender grounds in fact stems from the EU's 2004 Asylum Qualification Directive, and in any case will not affect a large number of applicants.[4] New integration courses are primarily limited to new arrivals: the existing 'stock' of non-nationals (so-called *Bestandsausländer*) are allowed to attend the courses if there is spare capacity. In the area of internal security, which threatened to engulf the very diverse elements of the negotiations in the conciliation committee in April and May 2004, non-nationals can now be deported based on an 'evidence-based threat assessment' (*tatsachengestützte Gefahrenprognose*), in other words without being first convicted of a criminal offence. Yet not only is the number of affected persons small,

---

[4] It is worth noting that between 25 and 30 per cent of all applications for asylum in Germany are dismissed on formal grounds, such as an incomplete written application or a failure to keep to strict deadlines. This high proportion will of course not be directly affected by the changes.

but this provision is certain to end up before the Constitutional Court before long. Perhaps the most important exception to the rule of incrementalism in the *Zuwanderungsgesetz* is the reduction of the complex residence titles in the *Ausländergesetz* from five to just two (temporary and permanent residence).

In conclusion, the case of immigration and integration policy clearly confirms the overall elements of the semisovereignty model. Significantly, this case study shows that even if the institutional configuration or the relative status of these institutions changes, then outcomes are still likely to be incremental. During the Kohl era, the parties within the governing coalition played a major role both in formulating policy and in providing a counterbalance to what has on occasions been a hardline ministerial agenda. By contrast, under the SPD-Green government, party and ministerial agendas have not diverged as much, and it has been the opposition via its dominance of the *Bundesrat* that has had a major impact on ensuring the continued incremental nature of policy outcomes.

Finally, where does this leave the question of the effectiveness of semisovereignty? Can this mode of governance deliver the policy outputs necessary to enable Germany to meet its challenges in the areas of immigration and integration? On this question, the notion of semisovereignty as an asset appears to score badly. As this chapter has argued, the past twenty years have seen long periods of inactivity combined with occasional, tentative policy reforms; together these can scarcely be considered to have been sufficient to address the reality of immigration in most German cities. It is worth noting that the federal government first pledged in 1984 to naturalise those non-nationals permanently resident in Germany. Twenty years on, this goal remains as distant as ever, with little prospect of significant progress in the medium term.

More significantly, the deleterious long-term impact of demographics on support ratios between those in work and those not has been known for decades. Even though immigration is no panacea to such structural problems (Green 2002), it is difficult to see how Germany will cope without at least some more new labour migration than the *Zuwanderungsgesetz* envisages. But more importantly, even if such restrictions are relaxed, can Germany really hold its own in a global competition for skills? So far, the experience of 'Green Card' holders has been far from positive: having uprooted themselves to go to Germany, many have been left 'high and dry' following the downturn of the 'new economy', with inflexible bureaucracies often granting just three months' grace to find a new position before serving deportation papers (*Der Spiegel*, 2 September 2002). Such deeply ingrained restrictive implementation of policy, especially when combined with nagging problems of racist violence, make it very difficult to see how Germany will be able to compete with other countries in the global race to recruit the brightest and best.

But the sometimes painfully slow progress of policy cannot solely be attributed to institutional constraints and veto points, although these are clearly important. Much is also a result of the ideological nature of party-political conflict in this area. In turn, this means that the political price of compromise in the short term can be discouragingly high. In an era when centripetal politics have blurred the political differences in many liberal democracies, especially in the areas of economic policy, it cannot be that surprising if political parties choose instead to politicise immigration and integration, with its high potential for polarisation and hence voter mobilisation. It also has one other critical advantage over other policy areas: those who are directly affected are usually unable to express their disapproval at the ballot box.

10   Environmental Policy: the Law of Diminishing Returns?

Charles Lees

Introduction

It is interesting to note that Katzenstein's original work on the semi-sovereign state did not include environmental policy as one of its specific domains for analysis (Katzenstein 1987). To a certain extent this is a curious omission, given that it was precisely at that point in the late 1980s that Germany's reputation as an 'environmental leader' (Weale 1992a, 1992b) was at its highest and that, in this policy domain at least, the German semisovereign state's capability to manage change appeared the most pronounced. Indeed, compared with other large European states, Germany in the 1980s was highly responsive to both the real environmental challenges associated with complex industrial societies and the higher levels of public unease about the trajectory of such societies, as manifested by the discourse of the 'new politics' and the emergence of Green parties (Lees 2000a, 2000b). As noted in chapter 1, some of those states, such as the United Kingdom, were characterised by unitary structures. Thus, the fact that the semisovereign Federal Republic outperformed states that were assumed to possess superior steering capacities was in itself worthy of note.

In defence of the original decision to omit environmental policy, however, one might also point out that it is when one is in the midst of change that it is hardest to define its overall parameters, trajectory and long-term consequences. Almost two decades later we are better placed to enjoy the benefit of hindsight and to take the long view.

This chapter's account of environmental policy-making in the Federal Republic explicitly takes that long view and is framed within a 'historical institutionalist' narrative (Krasner 1988; Hall 1989; Skocpol 1992; King 1995). It argues that German environmental policy has developed through a pattern of 'punctuated equilibria' in which 'rapid bursts of change [are] followed by long periods of stasis' (Krasner 1988, p. 242). In other words, the policy choices made at the time of institutional formation have a persistent and determinate impact over environmental

212

policy-making in the long run. In addition, 'standard operating procedures' (SOPs) have developed which routinise activities, and inhibit anything more than incremental change. Over time, the persistence of
established policy choices and SOPs can lead to sub-optimal institutional
performance and policy failure. In turn this leads to episodic junctures,
in which the ideas that underpin policy-making, the policy choices these
ideas generate, as well as the structures of governance that frame policy
processes undergo rapid change. More often than not these junctures are
prompted by changes in the external environment in which institutions
operate. As is discussed elsewhere in this volume, one such change
obviously has been German unification, which has had a profound
impact across the board. The other change, more limited in its scope
but absolutely crucial to the development of environmental policy, was
the deleterious impact of the German 'economic miracle' in the 1950s
and 1960s on Germany's environmental resources. It will become apparent to the reader that, in this policy domain, the response of Germany's semisovereign state to environmental degradation from the
1960s and 1970s onwards was an effective one. This contrasts somewhat
with the Federal Republic's subsequent response to the challenge of
unification. Thus, environmental policy-making remains one of the Federal Republic's success stories, but the upward curve of innovation that
began in the 1960s and 1970s has now flattened out. Germany conducts
environmental policy from a position of strength, but the success of
the recent past now threatens to hamper future improvement. In short,
German environmental policy may be suffering from the law of
diminishing returns.

Context

Environmental Context

Environmental degradation is no respecter of national borders and the
parameters of policy problems and solutions are often of a 'trans-
boundary' nature. Thus there is an inherent tension between this
trans-boundary nature of environmental problems and the state-centred
framework within which solutions are often defined. It is perhaps not
surprising, therefore, that the Federal Republic has been relatively proactive in the formulation, and advocacy beyond its borders, of environmental rules and norms. Germany's position at the centre of the
European landmass means that it encounters strong economic and
environmental interdependencies. It shares a border with nine other
European countries, and has a relatively long coastline, stretching from

the North Sea coast of East Friesland on the Dutch border, through to the Baltic coast west of the Polish city of Szczecin. Of the surface area of the old Federal Republic, 53.7 per cent is given over to agriculture along with 56.9 per cent of what was the German Democratic Republic (GDR); 29.8 (27.6) per cent is forested; 1.8 (2.9) per cent is covered by water; and 12.2 (7.9) per cent is given over to traffic, housing and other forms of development. Germany is also relatively densely populated, with densities of 256 people per square kilometre in the old *Länder*, and 148 per square kilometre in the new (Pehle and Jansen 1998, p. 82).

Germany has long been a north–south transit country and, with the opening up of central and eastern Europe, it has now become the focus of east–west transit as well. This has aggravated problems associated with German economic development – such as high levels of industrialisation and reliance on the manufacturing sector (industrial production accounts for 38.3 per cent of Gross National Product (GNP) in the old *Länder*, and 34.9 in the new) (OECD 1993). The number of automobiles owned in West Germany rose from 17.8 million in 1975 to 30.6 million in 1990. Moreover, car journeys account for more than four-fifths of all passenger services (Pehle and Jansen 1998). Germany is the largest consumer of energy in Europe, half of which is imported. In the old *Länder*, 40 per cent of energy needs are met by oil, whilst coal accounts for 27 per cent, gas 17 per cent and nuclear energy 14 per cent.

The Federal Republic as a whole suffers from two further problems. First, although it generates no more than average levels of waste per head of population, high levels of population density make waste disposal a problem. There are practical problems associated with finding new landfill sites, whilst public hostility has constrained policy-makers' use of high-temperature incineration (Lees 1998) and public enthusiasm for recycling has not been matched by Germany's capacity to do so (Pehle and Jansen 1998). Second, Germany's reliance on energy imports led to a strategic decision in the early 1950s to build up its nuclear energy capacity. However, public hostility to nuclear power combined with resistance from many of the *Länder* forced Germany to strike deals with COGEMA in France and BNFL in the United Kingdom to reprocess its nuclear waste (Rüdig 2000, p. 51).

Moving away from the Federal Republic's longstanding environmental problems, the specific environmental impact of unification has been immense – both in terms of the scale of environmental degradation that now needs to be tackled and also in terms of the ability of the Federal Republic both to tackle these problems and to maintain its position as an environmental leader internationally. As far as the scale of problems presented by unification is concerned, audits of environmental resource damage in the new federal states make for sobering reading. In the GDR, 69 per cent of energy needs were met by burning lignite, with oil accounting for only 14 per cent of production. The reliance on lignite has now gone, but the pollution problems associated with the Communist regime's neglect of environmental concerns persist, with an estimated 42 per cent of rivers and 24 per cent of lakes contaminated beyond the capacity of water purification plants to clean them up. Only 3 per cent of rivers and 1 per cent of lakes are still considered healthy. On top of this, the new *Länder* have to clean up the legacy of badly managed waste sites (*Altlasten*). All in all, the total cost of bringing environmental standards in the new *Länder* up to those of the old was, in the early 1990s, estimated at between DM 82 billion and DM 321 billion (€ 42 billion and € 164.6 billion) (OECD 1993).

In terms of the Federal Republic's reduced capacity to tackle such problems, three factors are of note. First, the lack of environmental expertise in the new *Länder* persisted into the 1990s and hampered the efforts of state governments in the former GDR to address their environmental problems. Second, the new *Länder*'s profound economic difficulties – a *leitmotif* throughout this volume – have led many state governments to adopt a policy stance that is often hostile to environmental measures that they regard as being in conflict with the more pressing need to revive local economies through reduced costs and greater competitiveness. Moreover, the *Länder* collectively constitute a powerful set of veto players (see Tsebelis 2002; Schmidt 2000b) within the semisovereign state, so the impact of such recalcitrance is felt not just at the state level but at the federal level as well. Finally, there is a knock-on effect at the international level and especially in terms of Germany's reputation as an environmental leader within the EU. There are three reasons for this. First, a greater number of potential veto players *per se*, as well as a more diverse set of preferences between them, make the process of national preference formation harder. Second, even where this process of preference formation is successful, the outcome is one that is (a) less progressive in environmental terms than tended to be the case before 1990 and (b) reflects the recognition of all domestic players that Germany will struggle to meet enhanced environmental standards for the foreseeable future. Finally, a need to secure derogations for the new *Länder* and a reduced capacity to supply side-payments during interstate bargaining means that Germany has expended a great deal of political capital at the EU level and is no longer as able to shape policy in the way that it was able to do in the past.

To sum up, Germany's geographical position and political economy make it both vulnerable to environmental degradation and aware of its economic and environmental interdependence with its neighbours. In particular, the combination of the old Federal Republic's economic success and the legacy of command economics in the new *Länder* adds to Germany's environmental burden. Nevertheless, as is discussed below, the combination of Germany's federal structure, rules and norms of governance, plus the pressure of the Greens, environmental campaigners and public opinion have served to provide a benign 'political opportunity structure' (Kitschelt 1986; Tarrow 1994) for the emergence of environmental policy activism. As touched upon above, the outcome of this has been a body of regulatory legislation that led, in the late 1980s and early 1990s, to Germany being branded an environmental leader. Nevertheless, as also discussed above, the impact of unification has (a) aggravated existing environmental problems associated with high levels of industrialisation; (b) introduced new problems associated with the command economy of the former GDR; and (c) reduced the Federal Republic's capacity to respond to either set of problems.

Historical Context

The origins of German environmental policy-making go back in one form or another to the nineteenth century. Prior to 1871, environmental regulation was carried out by the individual *Länder*, through local ordinances which were embedded in private and public law, such as building regulations, public health and police laws. These laws placed restrictions upon production methods if they were considered to cause an air-pollution problem but the authorities' interpretation of what constituted a problem was tempered by the 'duty of toleration' (*Duldungspflicht*) set out in the Civil Code of 1873, which allowed for a certain degree of hardship in order to promote social welfare. Wilhelmine Germany was a rapidly industrialising state in which the governing alliance of 'iron and rye' deemed industrial growth and wider social welfare to be one and the same (Wey 1982, p. 109; Weidner 1995, p. 1). In such a utilitarian climate, early legislation was of limited scope – concentrating on the immediate vicinity of the emitting premises. Although technical change and democratisation increased the amount and ambit of legislation, the tendency to focus upon individual emissions remained a key element of German environmental policy.

Up until the First World War, it was the *Länder* that remained the main innovators in environmental policy. In the case of air pollution, individual pollution-control authorities could issue 'technical instructions' (*Technische Anleitungen*, or TAs) to emitters, forcing them to take measures commensurate with the *Stand der Technik* ('best available technology', or BAT) – a norm that is still in use today. Water pollution took longer to be regulated because it was so often of a 'trans-boundary' nature – involving spillover across *Länder* through rivers and other waterways. This increased the difficulty in establishing responsibility for individual acts of pollution, and in enforcing subsequent measures against emitters. Such technical obstacles were aggravated by a reluctance to 'nationalise' environmental policy (Wey 1982, p. 38).

In 1912, Prussia called for negotiations to begin in order to establish centralised legislation to control water pollution (Skou Andersen 1994, p. 124), but these did not take place because of the Great War, and trans-boundary co-operation remained limited to partnership agreements (*Genossenschaften*) established between contiguous *Länder* in order to manage individual river resources (Weale 1992a, p. 162).

Following the abolition of the *Länder* by the Nazis in 1934, a National Water Law was drawn up, but, again, the outbreak of war prevented its enactment. Thus, by the end of the 1950s, there was still no federal legislation in West Germany, and most of the regulatory devices used by the *Länder* to control both air and water pollution had been in place since 1914 (Skou Andersen 1994, p. 124).

It was clear that such a decentralised and piecemeal approach to environmental legislation was unsustainable. For instance, in 1949, water resources were regulated by over 119 laws, 70 of which applied to the Rhine alone. Having resisted federal regulation in the past, industry now pressed the federal government to harmonise legislation. Thus in the 1950s, the first (albeit fairly toothless) items of federal legislation, the Water Household Act of 1957 and the Clean Air Maintenance Law of 1959, were enacted.

By the early 1960s, it was clear that West Germany's 'economic miracle' had inflicted massive damage on water and air resources in the Federal Republic. This damage was at its most apparent in the highly industrialised Ruhr region, where, for instance, it has been estimated that over 600,000 tons of dust were discharged annually into the air during the 1950s (Weale 1992a, p. 163). In the early 1960s the SPD-led state of North Rhine-Westphalia responded to this by enacting a raft of measures, focusing on air pollution, that were to become the models for future federal legislation (Dreyhaupt et al. 1979). However, the emergence of popular environmental awareness in Germany was not confined to the so-called (SPD-run) 'A-*Länder*'. Significant elements within the new environmental movements mobilised around a bourgeois or 'value-conservative' (*wertekonservativ*) agenda and it was very much the cross-class, cross-party nature of popular protests that was also able to exert leverage over Christian Democratic 'B-*Länder*' such as Bavaria and

Baden-Württemberg. The common pressures on both 'A' and 'B' *Länder* at that time meant that the states had little or no incentive to exercise their potential veto power once the federal level began to encroach on a policy area that was still regarded as the prerogative of the *Länder*.

Nevertheless, in the early 1960s this encroachment was still a few years away and German environmental policy conformed to the historical institutionalist paradigm, in which SOPs established in the nineteenth century remained broadly in place and the *Land* level retained primary responsibility for the formulation and implementation of environmental measures. The first real punctuation in this equilibrium, however, did take place in 1964, when the federal government issued its first effective TAs, specifying licensing procedures for emitting facilities and setting out air quality standards for five major pollutants (dust, chlorine, sulphur dioxide, nitrogen dioxide and hydrogen sulphide). As was discussed in the introduction to this chapter, historical institutionalist accounts argue that such episodic junctures only take place when an institution's performance is sufficiently sub-optimal as to make such changes unavoidable. In this case it was the recognition, by the mid-1960s, of the extent of environmental degradation associated with the West German economic miracle. Nevertheless, the persistence of routinised SOPs must also be noted and, in keeping with the long-established norms of *Länder* legislation, facilities were required to tackle their emissions along the lines of BAT (Weale 1992a, p. 163).

Environmental policy at the federal level received an added impetus with the establishment of the SPD-FDP coalition in 1969. Policy-makers looked for inspiration to the USA, where the federal government had recently established the Environmental Protection Agency and the Council on Environmental Quality, as well as enacting the Environmental Protection Act.[1]

The Brandt chancellorship was relatively innovative by the standards of the time, and established three principles that have become the normative benchmark of environmental policy in the Federal Republic and beyond: the prevention principle, the 'polluter pays' principle, and the co-operation principle (Paterson 1989, p. 273). Although many countries stressed the latter two principles, the emphasis on prevention was unusual in the early 1970s (Skou Andersen 1994, p. 125). But despite this early phase of innovation under Brandt, the period from

---

[1] It should be noted that the words *Umweltschutz* (environmental protection) and *Umwelt-politik* (environmental policy/politics) are translations of the North American usage (Weidner 1995, p. 3). In a similar vein, the Council of Experts on Environmental Questions (*Sachverständigenrat für Umweltfragen*), which published its first paper in 1972, was directly modelled on the US Council of Environmental Experts.

1971 to 1974 was to prove a false dawn in terms of environmental policy. The establishment of the Federal Agency for the Environment (*Umweltbundesamt*, or UBA) in 1974 was to prove the high-water mark, and the combination of a world recession following the oil-price rises in 1974 and 1975 and the replacement of Brandt with Schmidt as chancellor led to a period of stagnation. Nevertheless, the Brandt period left a legacy of environmental legislation, such as the Air Traffic Noise Act (1971), the Leaded Petrol Act (1972), the Waste Disposal Act (1972), the DDT Act (1972), the Federal Air Quality Protection Act (1974), as well as administrative directives such as the Technical Instruction for the Maintenance of Air Purity of 1974 (Weidner 1995, p. 7).

Despite the retrenchment of the Schmidt years, the genie was out of the bottle. The late 1970s saw the environmental baton taken up by the 'citizens' initiative' groups and the, now well-documented, formation of the proto-Green parties at the sub-national level (see Scharf 1994; Markovits and Gorski 1993; Kleinert 1992; Hülsberg 1988; Bickerich 1985; Müller 1989; Mettke 1982). During this period, significant societal interests were well ahead of political and administrative elites on environmental matters (Weidner 1995, p. 13). In time, and after much civil conflict, the agenda of such interest groups began to permeate through the wider polity.

Eventually, the political classes responded to what had become a wave of popular environmental awareness. In 1980, the SPD-FDP coalition declared its intention to join the '30 per cent club', and to reduce the Federal Republic's sulphur-dioxide emissions to 30 per cent of their 1980 level by 1993. The CDU/CSU-dominated *Bundesrat*, under the leadership of the then minister-president of Bavaria, Franz Josef Strauss, backed the declaration. Two years later, in the last months of the Schmidt government, German environmental policy took another step forward with the agreement between the SPD and FDP on the Ordinance on Large Combustion Plants (*Großfeurungsanlagenverordnung*, or GFAVO). The GFAVO set out to reduce sulphur-dioxide and nitrogen-dioxide emissions by 50 per cent over the course of the decade (Pehle and Jansen 1998, p. 96). The GFAVO is interesting for three reasons. First, although it was only an 'end of pipe' solution, the legislation had a real impact, and had been bitterly opposed by the FDP-run Federal Economics Ministry on the grounds that it reduced the competitiveness of German industry. Second, despite the opposition of the Economics Ministry, the FDP did eventually agree to the measures – even though the party was repositioning itself (and re-emphasising its economic liberalism) in preparation for bringing about the demise of the Schmidt-led coalition by transferring its allegiance to the CDU/CSU.

Third, rather than abandoning the legislation, the incoming CDU/CSU-FDP coalition took over the GFAVO, and even tightened up some of its provisions. As Pehle and Jansen have noted, this was a change in the dynamics of party competition over environmental policy. Whereas, in the past, the CDU/CSU might have been expected to oppose such measures, and to repeal them when in government, there now appeared to be no real partisan opposition to such measures in principle (Pehle and Jansen 1998, p. 88).

If anything, the CDU/CSU temporarily outflanked the SPD in the early 1980s. In addition to tightening up the GFAVO and introducing additional US-style vehicle-emission limits, the then Federal Minister of the Interior, Friedrich Zimmermann (CSU), oversaw the introduction of a new Air Pollution Control Law in July 1983 that became the model for the subsequent European Directive on Large Combustion Plants. Around this time, Zimmermann also pushed for a strong Directive on Vehicle Emissions (vetoed by the UK), and positioned the Interior Ministry behind elements within the West German scientific community who were beginning to shape the international debate on global warming and carbon-dioxide emissions. At the same time, the SPD began to review its environmental-policy positions, mainly in order to counter the electoral challenge from the Greens. Over time the SPD adopted much of the Greens' environmental programme, including the commitment to phase out nuclear power over a ten-year period. Scientific opinion was divided as to whether tackling global warming required less or more reliance on nuclear power, but the political argument was clear: no political party could now allow itself to be outflanked along the newly salient dimension of environmental politics. The Kohl government's creation of the Federal Ministry for Environment, Nature Protection and Reactor Safety (*Bundesministerium für Umwelt, Naturschutz und Reaktorsicherheit*, or BMU) in 1986, although directly the result of shortcomings in the administrative response to the Chernobyl disaster, was also symbolic of the emerging new consensus on environmental matters in the Federal Republic.

In the following year, 1987, the *Bundestag* reacted to the debate on nuclear power, carbon-dioxide emissions and global warming by setting up a Commission of Enquiry on Preventative Measures to Protect the Earth's Atmosphere (*Enquete-Kommission Vorsorge zum Schutz der Erdatmosphäre*). The commission was made up of eleven members of the *Bundestag* and eleven scientists, and held a remit to fund research projects and to hold hearings on the topic. The commission's third annual report, released in late 1990, recommended the reduction of carbon-dioxide emissions to 30 per cent below 1987 levels by 2005. In

December 1990 the federal government adopted a modified form of this target of 25–30 per cent.

By the early 1990s, therefore, Germany was the acknowledged leader of environmental policy in Europe. At the same time, Germany tried to offset the anti-competitive effects of domestic legislation by trying to impose similar costs on other EU member states through EU legislation. It is not clear how much this was a genuine attempt to mould EU policy, or more a means of placating domestic opposition – particularly from one of the German employers' umbrella groups, the BDI. What is clear is that German proposals for the EU to adopt a common carbon-dioxide and energy tax fell foul of EU-level lobbying. Despite an attempt by Federal Environment Minister Klaus Töpfer to use Germany's presidency of the EU to ensure the adoption of such a tax, the European Commission made its introduction conditional on similar measures being adopted by other OECD countries, and the Council would go no further than encouraging member states to adopt their own measures. At the EU level, the 'soft law' approach to environmental policy (see Flynn 1997) had become dominant, whilst, domestically, the tightened economic circumstances of the mid-1990s shifted the focus of politics away from environmental issues and back towards that of Germany's competitiveness (the *Standort Deutschland* debate). Once again, partisan divisions over environmental policy began to emerge. On the one hand, the ruling CDU/CSU-FDP coalition was unwilling to compromise German competitiveness through further legislation on the issue of a carbon-dioxide/energy tax. On the other hand, the SPD and Greens argued that existing legislation did not go far enough, and that nuclear power had to be included in any future legislation. With the *Bundesrat* controlled by the SPD, legislative gridlock meant that environmental policy was temporarily becalmed. It would take the election of the SPD-Green coalition, under Chancellor Gerhard Schröder, on 27 September 1998 to break the impasse.

Agenda

In broad terms, environmental policy responses fall into three categories. First, policy-makers can rely on voluntary means. These can range from informal/normative methods – such as encouraging citizens to recycle their waste, and to adopt consumption patterns that encourage producers to cut down on packaging – to more formal devices, such as the International Standards Organisation ISO 14001, which benchmarks standards for environmental management systems (EMS). A second response is to opt for a more coercive regulatory framework. Finally, policy-makers can opt for economic instruments. These can be divided into a further two categories – rights-based mechanisms (such as tradable permits and quotas), and 'green' or eco-taxes.

The Federal Republic remains particularly reliant on regulatory instruments and voluntary agreements (VAs) (see Helby 2001; Busch and Jörgens 2001). Regulation is based on the long-established BAT principle, as well as the more recent 'precautionary' and 'polluter pays' principles. This 'command and control' approach – framed within a set of abstract principles – is evident in the majority of (West) German environmental legislation, which tend to set out policy principles in the abstract, and to enforce those principles through regulation and the setting of targets. Moving on to VAs, Germany – along with the Netherlands – remains the EU member state that has adopted the highest number of these agreements. But in the Netherlands such agreements have been replaced by more legally binding covenants (Wurzel et al. 2003, p. 116) whilst in Germany most remain legally non-binding, albeit 'within the shadow of the law'. Paterson has described these SOPs as a form of 'regulated self-regulation' (Paterson 1989, p. 284).

Since the election of the SPD-Green coalition in 1998, the Federal Republic's routinised reliance on regulatory instruments and VAs has been augmented by a greater emphasis on economic instruments. The 1998 coalition agreement included, *inter alia*, initiatives to convert 10 per cent of Germany's surface into an integrated 'biotope' (*Biotopverbundsystem*), extend 'protected areas', sanitise the production cycle and reduce industrial waste (SPD-Greens 1998, pp. 13–20). However, the new policy mix can best be seen in the two main planks of the SPD-Green coalition's first term in office: the phasing out of nuclear power and the introduction of the so-called 'eco-tax'.

The SPD-Green coalition's policy on nuclear power was driven by preliminary work carried out by the Greens whilst in opposition, particularly in collaboration with the Öko-Institut in Darmstadt (Rüdig 2000, p. 55). The planned withdrawal from the use of nuclear power entailed two steps – first, a revision of the Federal Energy Law establishing a legal framework for withdrawal from nuclear power and, second, a programme of 'consensus talks' with the nuclear industry in order to reach a timetable for the closing down of reactors. This latter measure is consistent with the established German norm of self-regulation and the routinised practice of establishing VAs. Again, this demonstrates the persistence of SOPs, not just in German environmental policy-making *per se*, but also in terms of the specific mix of instruments used by the coalition once in power at the federal level of government. During the 1980s and 1990s, SPD-Green coalitions at the *Land* level used VAs and it is consistent with a historical institutionalist account that these practices were uploaded to the federal level. The best example of such a *Land*-level antecedent, not least because of the personnel involved, is the setting up of the Advisory Council for Questions of Withdrawal from Nuclear Power (*Beirat zu Fragen des Kernenergieausstiegs*, or BfK) in Lower Saxony during the 1990–4 SPD-Green coalition in that state. Ultimately the BfK's rather modest record of success was to become a source of political conflict between the SPD and Greens in Lower Saxony (see Lees 1998, 2000a).

Given these difficulties in Lower Saxony, why did Gerhard Schröder (who was minister-president of Lower Saxony at the time) or Jürgen Trittin (who was the leader of the Lower Saxony Greens) resort once again to the same type of voluntary agreement once in power at the federal level later in the decade? In fact, lessons had been learned from the Lower Saxony experience and it had originally been envisaged that the BfK arrangement would not be repeated and that the decision to phase out nuclear power would be decided by a simple parliamentary majority. However, two factors were at play that prevented this. The first was that ever since the 1980s there had been a de facto moratorium on the construction of new nuclear power plants in the Federal Republic. This was because *Länder* governments, which implement the federal nuclear programme, became increasingly unwilling to confront anti-nuclear protestors following the popular unrest associated with the planned power plant at Whyl in Baden-Württemberg in 1975 (Paterson 1989, p. 278) and later at the reprocessing plant at Wackersdorf in Bavaria (Rüdig 2000). This leads us to the second factor. Given that the incoming SPD-Green government was effectively pushing at an open door in terms of the phasing out of nuclear power, the benefits of relying on the coalition's parliamentary majority to drive legislation through were outweighed by the potential costs of overtly politicising the issue and leaving the federal government open to challenge in the courts by other societal actors.

Both of the factors described above are symptomatic of the constraints placed upon political action in Germany's semisovereign state and will be returned to in more detail in the following section of this chapter. Nevertheless, the cumulative effect of such factors has been that, despite its dependence on nuclear power, Germany has still to find a politically acceptable outlet for nuclear waste. In the 1970s, the federal government designated a site at Gorleben in Lower Saxony as its preferred location for the storage of nuclear waste. But in 1979, following consultation with the *Länder*, the proposed site was moved to the Wackersdorf plant mentioned above. In addition, the government placated the growing anti-nuclear movement by ordering that no nuclear plant would be allowed to operate without securing adequate means for the disposal of nuclear fuel. Unfortunately, the TAs relating to nuclear waste management stipulated that the only adequate means of disposal of such waste was reprocessing. Given that this was not possible in the Federal Republic, German energy producers signed reprocessing contracts with France's COGEMA and the UK's BNFL (Rüdig 2000, p. 50).

When the SPD-Green coalition came to power, the Federal Environment Minister Jürgen Trittin proposed to move quickly to end the reprocessing of nuclear fuel. This prompted a low-level inter-governmental row with France and Britain, both of which argued that the decision to cancel the reprocessing contracts was illegal. In itself, this would not have been too damaging; however, the disagreement came early in Schröder's chancellorship and on the eve of the Federal Republic's presidency of the EU. Moreover, BNFL threatened to respond to Trittin's action by returning unprocessed fuel rods to the Federal Republic. This in turn brought Trittin into conflict with the then minister-presidents of North Rhine-Westphalia and Lower Saxony, Wolfgang Clement and Gerhard Glogowski. Clement and Glogowski were concerned that the transportation of returned waste to the so-called 'interim' storage sites of Ahaus and Gorleben would reignite the anti-nuclear protests associated with the CASTOR transports of the 1980s and that it would be their states that would have to meet the costs of policing them.

Thus, in one fell swoop, Trittin had mobilised against him an array of stakeholders drawn from both the domestic and international arenas. In particular, the nuclear industry, supported by German industrialists worried about higher energy costs, kept up a steady PR offensive against Trittin's proposals, linking them to the *Standort* issue. Eventually Trittin backed off and in 2001 the federal government resumed the shipment of nuclear waste to British and French reprocessing facilities. Inevitably, this decision brought the Greens political leadership into direct conflict with the anti-nuclear movement from which it emerged (Hunold 2001).

The coalition's troubles with nuclear energy were aggravated by unease within the coalition with the final VA on the withdrawal from nuclear power. This was agreed in June 2000, and stipulated a thirty-two-year life-span for nuclear reactors based on estimated levels of energy output. This fell far short of the ten-year time-span put forward by the Greens and accepted by the SPD back in the 1980s. This long withdrawal period was combined with a concession that production allowances would be allowed to be shifted between plants, meaning that energy producers are able to 'cherry pick' the most efficient plants. Given that these are generally the newest plants, this means that some reactors will remain in operation for a very long time to come. Bearing in mind the experience of the BfK in Lower Saxony it is perhaps not surprising that the federal VA on phasing out nuclear power has failed to live up to the expectations of many Green activists.

The other key plank in the SPD-Green coalition's environmental programme was the eco-tax (*Ökosteuer*). In historical institutionalist terms the eco-tax really does represent a break with the established SOPs of German environmental policy. Eco-taxes have been used in the Federal Republic since the 1970s (Wurzel et al. 2003, p. 116) but the real forerunners in their use were the Scandinavian countries and, to a lesser extent, the Netherlands. By the late 1990s Britain, France and Italy had also introduced substantial forms of eco-taxation (Luckin and Lightfoot 1999, p. 243). By contrast, Germany has lagged behind in this respect.

Proponents of eco-taxes draw on neo-classical economics for their arguments (see Pigou 1920; Pearce et al. 1989), the gist of which is that a carefully constructed eco-tax reflects the marginal social costs of production, including marginal environmental costs, and taxes the externalities of production and resource use. Moreover, such taxes encourage firms to continue to improve their environmental practice over time – above and beyond the kind of arbitrary limits set out in regulatory frameworks. Furthermore a revenue-neutral eco-tax can produce a 'double dividend' that not only improves environmental practices, but – by shifting the burden of taxation from labour to emissions and resource use – also lowers non-wage labour costs. Thus, in theory, the double dividend is, first, an improved environment and second, lower unemployment (Strübin 1997, pp. 170–1).[2]

Not surprisingly the 'double dividend' argument gained considerable political leverage with the Greens and elements within the SPD. Of the latter, the most vociferous exponent was Oskar Lafontaine. Lafontaine's short period in office gave momentum to the SPD-Green government's plans to shift the burden of taxation towards energy use and consumption through both an increase in the duty on fuel and energy, and a reform of Germany's system of corporate taxation. It was originally envisaged that the law would be introduced in three stages, but practical politics (and a worsening economic situation after 2000) have led the coalition to favour a more piecemeal approach. Nevertheless, annual tax increases on energy (DM 0.005 or € 0.0025 per kWh) and road

---

[2] The downside of eco-taxes are that they can (a) be socially regressive, and punish the poorest members of society, who spend a greater proportion of their household income on energy use; (b) disrupt the workings of the market; (c) carry substantial implementation, administrative, monitoring and transaction costs; and (d) lead to lower revenues as agents adjust their behaviour over time (see Strübin 1997, pp. 170–1).

use (DM 0.06 or € 0.03 tax increase on petrol) are not universally popular, and there have been disagreements on the shape and scale of opt-outs for gas-fired power stations (Lightfoot and Luckin 2000). As with all such measures, the eco-tax 'front-loads' the political costs onto the coalition, whilst the environmental benefits take longer to become apparent.

There is one other aspect of the environmental agenda in the Federal Republic – that which is imposed upon it through agreement at the inter-governmental or supranational level of governance. Many of these agreements, such as the 1997 Kyoto climate change protocol, bear the distinct footprint of the German policy-making style – in particular the setting of clear targets for reductions in emissions over specified timescales. Others, and in particular those emanating from the EU, are more problematic, not least because of the challenge that much EU environmental legislation presents to the established SOPs of German environmental policy. In the early phase of EU environmental policy-making Germany was quite successful in uploading its own SOPs and norms to the European level (Weale 1992a; Wurzel 2004). However, as discussed earlier, Germany is now less able to shape policy at the EU level. Thus, in the last decade the EU has moved away from the kind of command-and-control instruments favoured by the German environmental policy community and towards a more diverse mix of Environmental Quality Objectives (EQOs), framework directives, procedural measures and soft law policy instruments (Wurzel 2004; Flynn 1997).

This shift in policy style and content at the EU level has had two effects at the national level in the Federal Republic. On the one hand, German policy-makers have responded to the EU's more flexible approach by adapting legislation in order to make it more compatible with existing SOPs. On the other, the Federal Republic has come under pressure from the EU to introduce a wider mix of policy instruments. For instance, EU Directive 2003/87/EU has forced Germany to introduce legislation to allow the rights-based mechanism of emissions trading across the EU by the beginning of 2005. By summer 2004, the Emissions Trading Act (passed by the *Bundestag* in March 2004) only applied to carbon-dioxide emissions and the small print of the act has brought Trittin's Environment Ministry into conflict with German industry and caused intra-coalition conflict with (SPD) Economics Minister Clement. Rights-based mechanisms remain unpopular with German environmental policy-makers and this and other EU directives demonstrate a degree of 'misfit' between German SOPs and those at the EU level, leading to significant adaptational pressures being brought to bear on the Federal Republic (Wurzel 2004, p. 291).

Given the constraints upon it, it is perhaps inevitable that the SPD-Green coalition has enjoyed a mixed level of success in pursuing its environmental agenda. In its first term, the timetable for the planned withdrawal from nuclear power disappointed Green activists but was popular with the electorate, whilst the eco-tax was popular with activists but not popular with the voters. Moreover, as in the early 1990s the world economic crisis of 2000–2 once again shifted the emphasis of public debate away from 'quality of life' issues such as the environment towards 'bread and butter' issues like unemployment. Only in the last weeks of the 1998–2002 parliament did the environment return to the top of the agenda, following the floods in eastern Germany of August 2002.

The Greens' relative success in the 2002 federal elections strengthened the party's hand vis-à-vis the SPD and, as a result, it managed to bargain more power for the Environment Ministry in the new government (SPD-Greens 2002, p. 87). Nevertheless, midway through its second term, the SPD-Green coalition has a number of ambitious medium- and long-term targets that it must work towards. As of July 2004, these include:

1 the inherited national target (set in 1995) of reduction of carbon-dioxide levels to 25 per cent below 1990 levels by 2005;
2 implementing the National Climate Protection Programme (introduced in 2000 in order to help meet the 1995 carbon-dioxide target) through the consolidation of the eco-tax, promotion of renewable energy and fuel switching and energy-efficiency improvements;
3 phasing out lignite coal production in the new German states of the former GDR;
4 ensuring that the decision to phase out nuclear power by 2025 remains on track;
5 extending the rights-based system of emissions certificate trading, as laid out in EU Directive 2003/87/EU, beyond carbon-dioxide to encompass other gasses identified in the Kyoto Agreement such as CFCs, methane and nitrous oxide.

Process

The SPD-Green coalition's room for manoeuvre in working towards the goals noted above will continue to be constrained by the routinised SOPs associated with the process of policy-making in Germany's semi-sovereign state. As already noted elsewhere in this volume, Katzenstein's original analysis of the policy process in the Federal Republic identifies an ideal-type of policy network, conceptualised as three 'nodes'. These nodes consist of: (1) the consensual party system; (2) co-operative federalism, consisting of the division and co-ordination of competences between federal, *Länder* and, to a lesser extent, local levels; and (3) the diverse public and private interests that influence the policy-making process, in other words parapublic institutions and non-governmental organisations (NGOs) (Katzenstein 1987, pp. 35–60). Katzenstein regards these as potential blocks to innovation, as the existing structures constitute 'such a tightly integrated policy network that major changes in policy stand little chance of success' (1987, p. 35). Later in the book, Katzenstein goes on to moderate his earlier pessimism, arguing that 'it is easy to mistake incremental change for incapacity to change' (1987, p. 350). This chapter follows Katzenstein's schematic before assessing whether such a mistake has taken place in the section on 'Outcomes'.

Node One: the Consensual Party System

As already noted above, the consensual party system had been able to generate some innovations in environmental policy during the 1960s and 1970s, but these fell short of expectations in many quarters. The rise of the Greens was a direct result of this failure of the established parties to address popular unease about the environment. But whilst the popular environmental movements of the 1970s were characterised by their cross-class, cross-party nature, the Greens were quickly to assume a clear position on the left of the party system. Following an initial period of struggle between its 'new left' and conservative wings, the party assumed its familiar left-libertarian and/or post-materialist character by the end of the decade (Markovits and Gorski 1993, pp. 192–7). Potentially at least, this crystallisation of Green politics on the left of the party system raised the likelihood for partisan conflict over environmental issues and thus the emergence of veto players mobilising to block future policy change.

The initial impact of the emergence of the Greens was felt at the *Land* level but this spread to the federal level in 1983 when the Greens entered the *Bundestag* for the first time, having won 5.6 per cent of the vote in the federal election (Padgett 1993, p. 28). Over time, much of the agenda around which the party mobilised was adopted by the other parties – especially the SPD – in the process of so-called *Themenklau* (issue theft). The established parties were alive to the electoral appeal of much of the Greens' agenda – which included significant changes in the way that the environment was managed. As a result, the Greens soon became a party of the mainstream, a position that was confirmed in 1998 when the party entered into a coalition with the SPD to form the federal government.

At both the *Land* and federal levels, the Greens, as a new arrival to the party system, have had to overcome an initial lack of administrative expertise. Unlike the SPD, which was already deeply embedded in the administrative structures and norms of the Federal Republic, the Greens were relative outsiders to the well-established interplay between politics and the administration which characterises Germany's 'party state' (*Parteienstaat*). The SPD was 'expertise rich', which meant that when the party came to power at either the *Land* or federal level, existing ministerial positions could be filled with in-house staff if so desired. This reduced the start-up costs to the SPD when taking office, leading to continuity of policy-making and the retention of institutional knowledge. It had the effect of a 'virtuous circle' in that such expertise filtered back into the party networks, informing their policy-making discourse, and educating future cadres. By contrast, the Greens were 'expertise poor', with very few in-house resources to call upon when taking over ministries, and precious little experience to draw on from within the party networks. However, over time, the Greens have been able to overcome these obstacles (Lees 2000a, p. 22) and, as a result, the party is now an established player in the environmental policy network.

A brief mention should also be made at this point of the one significant party to emerge as a result of unification – the PDS (the successor party to the ruling party in the GDR, the communist SED). Much has been written of the PDS's regional concentration in the new federal states and of its ideological profile (see Hough 2001, 2002; Lees 1995). In so far as it is relevant to environmental policy, the PDS is not noted for its environmental activism and is more concerned with the redistributionist issues of the traditional left. In July 2004, the PDS was no longer a significant player within the *Bundestag* but its persistence at the *Land* level in the new federal states means that it continues to possess veto player potential in the manner discussed earlier in this chapter.

Taken in the round, the consensual party system in the Federal Republic has to some extent depoliticised many aspects of the environmental policy debate. In doing so it has also served to integrate the Greens into the political mainstream and distance the party from the extra-parliamentary anti-nuclear movement from which it emerged. Thus, as already noted in the previous section, Trittin's decision to resume transports of nuclear waste to reprocessing plants in Britain and France led to the Greens' leadership coming into conflict with anti-nuclear groups. This led to activists within these groups accusing the Greens of co-optation into what they regarded as a 'nonsense' consensus around the issue of nuclear power (Hunold 2001, pp. 130–1).

However, it would be a mistake to overstate the level of consensus within the party system and areas of partisan conflict remain, for three reasons. First, the federal dimension of party competition and, in particular, the tendency for opposition parties over time to gain control of the second parliamentary chamber, the *Bundesrat*, allows such parties to act as veto players and thus constrain the potential for significant changes in policy direction (Lehmbruch 1976). Second, even in the *Bundestag* itself, there remains the potential for party-political conflict over the scope and direction of environmental policy – such as in 2000 when the CDU/CSU tabled a parliamentary initiative in the *Bundestag* for the withdrawal of the eco-tax (Wurzel et al. 2003, p. 125). Finally, the debate over speed limits for motor vehicles on Germany's motorways is characterised by high levels of polarisation along party-political lines, with the bourgeois parties tending to mobilise against any such speed limits in quite a populist manner. For instance, the 1989–90 SPD-Green coalition in West Berlin found itself up against the powerful motorists lobby, following the decision by the (SPD) Transport Minister to impose a 100 km/h speed limit on West Berlin's single stretch of motorway, the AVUS. Although justifiable on environmental grounds, the AVUS decision was not successful in terms of practical politics. Overnight, the opposition CDU – in co-operation with the motorists' association ADAC – was gifted with an issue around which to mobilise opposition to the coalition (Lees 1998).

Node Two: State Structures

Given the origins of environmental policy in the Federal Republic, it is not surprising that Germany's regulatory structure is highly sectorised. This sectorisation exists between ministries at the national level, and between the federal level and the *Länder*. Moreover, additional sectorisation between competing ministries occurs at the *Länder* level, although the precise nature of this sectorisation varies from case to case.

Following the reactor catastrophe at Chernobyl in 1986, the federal government created a new Federal Environment Ministry, the BMU, which served to reduce considerably the extent of horizontal sectorisation of environmental policy in the Federal Republic. Prior to the creation of the BMU, the structure of policy-making was more fragmented. Unlike the analogous US institution, the existing *Umweltbundesamt* (UBA), or Federal Environment Agency, had no power to create policy, but was rather restricted to research and policy advice. Actual policy-making competencies were mainly shared between the Federal Ministry of Health (*Bundesministerium für Gesundheitswesen*) and the Federal Interior Ministry (*Bundesministerium des Innern*), which took over responsibility for air noise, and water cleanliness from the Health Ministry with the advent of the Brandt administration in 1969 (Weale 1992b, pp. 165–6). The environmental competencies of the two ministries were ceded to the BMU in 1986, along with responsibility for climate change (ceded from the Ministry of Transport) and nature protection (from the Agriculture Ministry). These changes were not just the result of public pressure; they also occurred because the environmental protection measures in place at the time failed to cope adequately with the consequences of the Chernobyl disaster (Weale et al. 1991, pp. 122–35).

The BMU quickly developed into a major ministry of state, and, by 1993, had a staff of 850 and a budget of DM 1.262 billion (€ 650 million) (Weidner 1995, p. 29). Along with the tasks of developing TAs, co-ordinating the clean-up in the new *Länder*, and the promotion of international and supranational co-operation and policy-making, the BMU is also charged with the dissemination to the general public of information on environmental issues. This public relations function was one area where the previous structures failed miserably. During the Chernobyl disaster, for instance, the task of passing on information to the public was divided between the Health and Interior ministries, as well as the individual *Länder*. As a result, the public were supplied with partial and often contradictory information, no doubt contributing to the levels of public unease seen in Germany during this crisis.

Other BMU policy competencies include the protection of bodies of water and the sea, protection of ground water, wastewater treatment, nature conservation, and the disposal of nuclear waste. However, enforcement functions are carried out by three separate federal agencies. These are:

1 the Berlin-based Federal Environment Agency (*Umweltbundesamt*), which, amongst other aspects of its work, has the task of preparing technical standards, providing public information, monitoring the North Sea, and enforcing legislation relating to chemicals, detergents, pesticides and genetic engineering;
2 the Bonn-based Federal Agency for Nature Protection (*Bundesamt für Naturschutz*), which, promotes and co-ordinates the technical aspects of national and international nature protection, and enforces the Federal Nature Conservation Act; and
3 the Salzgitter-based Federal Agency for Radiological Protection (*Bundesamt für Strahlenschutz*), which implements the Federal Atomic Energy and the Radiological Protection Act.

Despite devolving enforcement functions to these three agencies, some policy-making competencies still remain with other federal ministries. For instance, the research and development policy on energy and the environment is the task of the Federal Ministry of Research and Technology, whilst energy policy itself lies within the ambit of the Federal Ministry of Economics and Labour. Other tasks remain with, amongst others, the Federal Ministries of Agriculture, Transport and Health.

The creation of the BMU has brought about one highly paradoxical change in the dynamics of the policy-making process. Before its creation, where the interests of the environment and other policy areas clashed, this manifested itself as intra-departmental conflict; the creation of the BMU has, however, turned this dynamic into an inter-departmental one. Moreover, given the Federal Republic's tendency to produce coalition government and the principle of ministerial autonomy (*Ressortprinzip*), such intra-departmental conflicts have often had a party-political dimension to them. This has led to tactical behaviour that was often detrimental to the furthering of environmental legislation. For instance, civil servants transferred across to the new ministry claimed that they were no longer as much 'in the loop' as they had been in their old ministries, and that the BMU was usually not informed about relevant policy initiatives from other ministries until a late stage of development. Inter-departmental tension has, in the recent past, been most pronounced with the Federal Ministry of Economics, which clashed with the BMU over, for instance, the 1994 Comprehensive Waste Management Act (*Kreislaufswirtschaftsgesetz*), the setting of targets for the reduction of carbon-dioxide emissions (Pehle and Jansen 1998, p. 96), and the recent EU-driven legislation on emissions trading discussed above. For its part, the BMU has tried to shift the parameters of political debate in its favour by way of public relations, such as briefing against Economics Ministry proposals.

In terms of co-ordination problems between the federal level and the *Länder*, the picture is mixed. On the one hand, some aspects of public law strengthen the hand of the federal government. For instance, Article 73 of the Basic Law grants exclusive jurisdiction (*ausschließlichen Gesetzgebung*) to the federal government in fields that are tangential to environmental protection (such as federal railways, air traffic, international affairs, etc.), whilst Article 74 grants the federal level concurrent jurisdiction (*konkurrierende Gesetzgebung*) which in effect allows the federal government to assume control of domains previously regulated by the *Länder* (in areas such as the control of noise and air pollution, nuclear energy and coastal protection). In addition, in the areas of nature protection and hunting, regional land use and planning, Article 75 grants the federal government framework jurisdiction (*Rahmenvorschriften*) and the overall position of the federal level was further strengthened in 1994, when the Basic Law was amended to make environmental enhancement a 'state aim' (*Staatszielbestimmung*) (Pehle and Jansen 1998). On the other hand, Articles 83–5 of the Basic Law – which deal with the execution of federal legislation by the *Länder* – present the federal level with problems of oversight and do provide the potential for co-ordination problems between the different tiers of government. In particular, Article 85 of the Basic Law provides for the tasking of the administration of federal legislation to the *Länder* (*Bundesauftragsverwaltung*) and provides opportunities for *Land* governments to obstruct the *Bund* at the implementation stage. For instance, during the 1990–4 SPD-Green coalition in Lower Saxony, Environment Minister Monika Griefahn (SPD) responded to concerns within the coalition about procedures for the storage of nuclear waste by contesting and slowing down their implementation in the state – despite the relatively close oversight of nuclear policy exercised by the federal government (Lees 1998).

Moving on to the *Länder* level, it is impossible to construct a general model of environmental regulation because of the heterogeneous nature of the actual structures in place, involving both horizontal and vertical sectorisation. All *Länder* have some form of Environment Ministry, but the actual competencies vary from state to state. One of the reasons for this is that the process of coalition formation in individual states often involves trade-offs between parties that affect the structure of ministries. For example, the need to accommodate the Greens' demand in Hesse for the Ministry of Justice meant that from 1995 to 1998, the environment portfolio was melded together with those of energy, health, youth and the family (Lees 2000a); whilst in Berlin, in 1989, the local *Alternative Liste* insisted upon the inclusion of competencies relating to city development and traffic in their Environment Ministry, rather than the SPD-staffed Ministry for Construction and Housing (Lees 1995, p. 16). Sectorisation also occurs because of the heterogeneous structure of *Länder* administration (two- or three-tiered, depending on the state), and because the level of administration where environmental responsibilities lie varies as well. To counter co-ordination problems, most *Länder* have established special units for dealing with environmental policy (Weidner 1995, p. 33), such as the Lower Saxony State Office for Ecology (*Niedersächsiches Landesamt für Ökologie*) (Lees 1998).

Finally, in the Federal Republic the role of the courts is central to the governance of environmental policy, both in terms of arbitration between the different tiers of administration and also as a political resource to which private citizens, interest groups and political parties can turn in order to challenge the scope and direction of policy. An example of arbitration between the different tiers of government was the Federal Constitutional Court's ruling in 2002 on a case brought by the state of Hesse, which claimed that the federal government had acted unconstitutionally in negotiating directly with the energy firm RWE over the minutiae of safety measures at the firm's Biblis plant. On this occasion, the Constitutional Court sided with the federal government, arguing that the agreement was part of the federal-level voluntary agreement on withdrawal from nuclear power, rather than a matter of routine regulation, which would have fallen under the jurisdiction of the *Länder*. Needless to say, the potential damage that would have been done to the federal government's co-ordination capacity if the decision had gone the other way was considerable.

In terms of individuals, interest groups and political parties, the antinuclear movement has been quite successful in blocking key elements of the Federal Republic's nuclear programme. For instance, as has already been noted, there had been a de facto moratorium on the building of nuclear reactors since the 1980s owing to the difficulties experienced by pro-nuclear *Länder* in implementing the aims of federal legislation. Thus, as Paterson notes, by the end of the 1970s 'three out of eleven plants under construction had lost their permits and four more had been halted because of actual or threatened suits' (Paterson 1989, p. 281). Over the years, cases have been brought under laws relating, *inter alia*, to personal damage, common fault liability, strict liability according to the Federal Act on Environmental Liability, damage to private environmental property, neighbourhood nuisance laws, and the acts on standard contracts and fair competition. Again, the resources provided by such laws demonstrate the potential co-ordination problems inherent in Germany's semisovereign state.

Node Three: Parapublic Institutions and NGOs

Although the traditional social partners, the employers' organisations (BDI and BDA) and the unions (DGB), have an active interest in the parameters and development of environmental policy, much of the input into the policy-making process takes place at the sectoral level of, for instance, energy policy or waste disposal. This is consistent with the established SOPs of policy-making in the Federal Republic. Over time, traditional sectoral interests – such as the Industrial Energy and Power Generation Association (*Verband der Industriellen Energie- und*

Kraftwirtschaft e. V.), the German Association of Gas and Water Experts, the German Association for Water Resources and Land Improvements, and the Association for Waste Water Technology – have been joined by relatively new organisations associated with the wider environmental movement, such as BUND and the Öko-Institut, as well as academic research institutes such as the Berlin-based Research Unit for Environmental Policy (*Forschungsstelle für Umweltpolitik*).

The inclusion of these newer organisations has been used by some *Land* ministries to break the monopoly on expertise enjoyed by the established parapublic institutions and to end what many regarded as the cosy pro-industry consensus within established policy networks. Writing in the early 1990s, Czada describes how the Hesse government eventually resorted to court proceedings in order to install the Öko-Institut on the state's oversight committee for atomic energy, against the wishes of powerful industry players such as Siemens (Czada 1993b, p. 79). Much of the impetus for this and similar efforts has come from the Greens, who have tried to open up the existing environmental policy network to 'their' client groups (such as NGOs, lobbyists, academics and practitioners). In doing so, the Greens not only provided patronage and privileged access for their client groups, but also provided existing policy networks with new sources of expertise (Lees 1998, 2000b).

At the *Länder* level, a key arena for input into the policy-making process has been through the use of sectorally based advisory councils, such as the Berlin Energy Advisory Council (*Energiebeirat*), and the Lower Saxony BfK and Second Government Commission on the Avoidance and Use of Waste (*Zweite Regierungskommission Vermeidung, Verwertung*). This is consistent with the pattern at the federal level with the Council of Experts for Environmental Questions (*Sachverständigenrat für Umweltfragen*) and the Scientific Advisory Council 'Global Environmental Change' (*Wissenschaftlicher Beirat der Bundesregierung 'Globale Umweltveränderung'*) advising the government on environmental matters.

Advisory councils issue reports on the sectoral issues within their remits, recommend best practice to *Bund* and *Länder* governments, and assist in the drawing-up of appropriate legislation to address environmental problems. Given the mix of 'traditional' sectoral interests and new environmental groups, there is a potential for conflict within the councils. However, notwithstanding instances such as the legal action in Hesse described above, the dominant norm in such networks remains broadly consensual, and the focus on scientific expertise tends to take the heat out of debate (Lees 1998).

Consequences

Up until the mid-1990s, there was a common perception that German environmental expertise was second to none. This impression of environmental competence was partly the result of the ease with which the discourse of environmentalism has permeated the polity of the Federal Republic over the past two decades. The reasons for this were both normative and structural. In terms of norms, there had been a long tradition of 'romantic' environmentalism in Germany, dating back to the nineteenth century (Lees 1995, p. 8), as well as the high levels of 'post-materialist' value orientation amongst the younger generational cohorts of the electorate (Inglehart 1990, p. 163; see also Padgett 1993; Paterson and Southern 1991; Dalton et al. 1984).

With regard to structure, the nature of institutional rules (such as the state financing of parties, electoral laws, and those rules that reinforce interaction between government and interest groups) in the Federal Republic was favourable to environmental mobilisation (Kitschelt 1986, pp. 57–68). As Weale (1992a, p. 74) has observed in comparing the records of environmental regulation in (West) Germany and Britain:

For a complex variety of historical reasons there are elaborate mechanisms of political accountability built into the German system of government . . . As a result of these historical pressures there is in Germany a striking (to the outsider at least) amount of institutional attention devoted to the detailing and elaboration of policy principles and programmes, and there are firm institutional safeguards to ensure that administrative and political action is underpinned by an account of its rationale.

Weale's assertion is that the combination of norms and structure inherent in the German administrative culture has been conducive to effective environmental policy. The norms of expertise and accountability, combined with the sectorised structure of German administration, enabled the efficient dissemination of environmental information, expertise and practice.

The empirical evidence still supports this contention. Germany has more low-emission cars than any other European country, has the highest proportional use of lead-free petrol, and has some of the most stringent emission limits. In a world-wide context, Germany is at the forefront of sewage-purification technology (in the old *Länder*, over 90 per cent of the inhabitants live in homes that are connected to the sewage mains, and 90 per cent of sewage is purified biologically), as well as the setting of limits on dioxin emissions from incineration. Germany also ranks alongside the USA and Japan in renewable-energy research and development. Politically, Germany has assumed a leadership role in international environmental policy, such as at the 1992 UNCED Conference in Rio, the Helsinki and Sofia protocols on long-range air pollution, the Vienna Agreement and Montreal Protocol on protecting the ozone layer, and collaborative measures to protect the North Sea and Baltic (Weidner 1995, pp. 49–50). Germany also hosted the common secretariat of the European Environment Advisory Councils network from 1999 until 2002.

Nevertheless, one is struck by what is still a relatively technocratic and restricted policy network, with high vertical interdependence (sharing service/policy-delivery responsibilities) and a degree of isolation from the wider polity. Moreover, the outcome of such a configuration is the persistence of SOPs such as an over-reliance on regulatory measures and VAs. Between 1972 and 1994, the federal government enacted eight major pieces of environmental legislation. These were the Waste Disposal Act (1972), the Federal Air Quality Protection Act (1974), the Waste Water Charges Act (1976), the GFAVO (1982–3), the Waste Avoidance Act (1986), the Environmental Impact Assessment Act (1991), the Environmental Liability Act (1991) and the Waste Management Act (1994); however, as Pehle and Jansen have pointed out, all of these pieces of legislation are heavily reliant on traditional 'command and control' measures or, in the case of the water, waste and transport sectors, a mixture of command and control plus VAs (Pehle and Jansen 1998, p. 96). This mix remains dominant within the current SPD-Green coalition's environmental policy toolkit, despite the introduction of the eco-tax in 1999 or the limited introduction of rights-based measures to regulate emissions trading in 2004.

The almost breathless phase of policy innovation of the 1980s and early 1990s is now a thing of the past, and, in light of Germany's high environmental standards, further improvements are likely to be harder to achieve. This was recognised as early as 1993, when an OECD report on Germany praised what it called Germany's 'remarkable progress' over the previous two decades, but warned that the Federal Republic would have to embrace economic instruments if it was to tackle the 'rising marginal costs of pollution abatement as environmental quality improves' (OECD 1993, pp. 208–9). German environmental experts have not been blind to this and, indeed, the government's own Council of Experts (*Sachverständigenrat*) on Environmental Questions recommended introducing an eco-tax during the Brandt chancellorship (Sachverständigenrat für Umweltfragen 1974). More, however, needs to be achieved in this respect.

Germany's reliance on regulatory instruments is consistent with the historical-institutionalist perspective outlined in the preamble to this chapter. It is clear that German environmental policy has now regained a state of equilibrium, following the 'punctuation' of the past twenty years. The institutions of policy-making are firmly in place, SOPs have re-established themselves, and change is once more incremental rather than rapid. Nevertheless, it should be remembered that some degree of change – such as the introduction of the eco-tax – continues to take place and again this is consistent with Katzenstein's original observations about the capacity of German policy-making apparatus to adapt over time. To conclude, given the constraints upon them, incremental change continues to be the 'politically logical choice' (Katzenstein 1987, p. 351) for German environmental policy-makers and, *ceteris paribus*, policy outcomes remain acceptable both in real terms and in terms of public perceptions within Germany of the Federal Republic's performance to date. Thus, at present Germany's semisovereign state is not obviously a liability in responding to the environmental challenges the Federal Republic currently faces and in the popular imagination environmental policy-making remains one of the Federal Republic's success stories. But when looking to the future, policy-makers must ponder whether, as the OECD has warned, the legacy of that success story means that Germany is now inevitably suffering from the law of diminishing returns.

11 Administrative Reform: Is Public Bureaucracy Still an Obstacle?

Klaus H. Goetz

Public administration and public policies aimed at its reform occupy a central position in Peter Katzenstein's (1987) analysis of the semisovereign state. They appear in four distinct ways. First, a decentralised bureaucracy is the third of four defining features of the 'decentralised state' that Katzenstein contrasts with 'centralised society'. The fourth feature, the constrained power of the chancellor, is also closely connected to the administrative organisation of the German state, since the constitutional right of ministers to run their departments without interference from the chancellor 'reinforces the bureaucratic fragmentation (*Ressortprinzip*) inherent in the federal bureaucracy' (1987, p. 23). Second, two of the three 'nodes' of the policy network – co-operative federalism and parapublic institutions – are directly associated with public administration. Co-operative federalism is, to a large extent, about co-operation between the administrations at local, *Land* and federal levels, and many parapublic institutions – such as the Federal Labour Office (*Bundesanstalt für Arbeit*) – are public authorities in all but name. Third, public administration is key to explaining patterns of policy development, for 'West German bureaucracy presents structural obstacles to large-scale changes no less formidable than the interaction of coalition governments, co-operative federalism, and parapublic institutions' (1987, p. 255). Finally, administrative reform serves as an illustrative case study for the 'analysis of the organization and political capacities of the West German state' (1987, pp. 254–5).

It is not difficult to see why public administration and administrative policy should be at the heart of the debate about the semisovereign state. Public administration forms the institutional backbone of the state and is its most tangible manifestation. The evolution from the sovereign state to semisovereignty should, therefore, show itself in the organisation and operation of public authorities. The ideational foundations of the professional civil service, the *Berufsbeamtentum*, in particular, are intimately tied up with the notion of a state that is imbued with internal sovereignty (*Hoheitlichkeit*) vis-à-vis its citizens,

239

and has a monopoly over the means of legitimate coercion. German administrative law has long maintained that sovereign state tasks involving the exercise of the state's coercive powers must regularly be carried out only by civil servants (*Beamte*) rather than ordinary state employees.

Administrative change in Germany since the publication of Katzenstein's book has confirmed the intimate connection between evolving notions of statehood and administrative policy. Both the measures pursued by the last Kohl government under the label of the *schlanke Staat* ('lean state') and the programme subsequently launched by the Schröder government under the banner of the *aktivierende Staat* ('enabling state') were, in essence, about the organisation of public administration and the manner in which it interacts with the public. The story of administrative development over the past two decades or so can, in many respects, be told as one of an accelerated decline of the classical *hoheitliche* administration. There are at least three aspects to this: a selective 'pushing back' of the borders of the state, notably through privatisation; internal administrative reorganisation inspired by the idea of turning public authorities into *Dienstleistungsunternehmen* ('service enterprises'); and a 'de-hierarchisation' of the relations between public authorities and citizens, fostered through a 'co-operative administration' and 'direct democracy'.

Taken together, these three dimensions of administrative change signal a major recomposition of the administrative state; indeed, for some, public administration is gradually being replaced by public management and public–private partnerships. In the 1980s, Katzenstein (1987, p. 19) noted that 'even a casual visitor riding West Germany's trains or buying some stamps in the local post office cannot help discovering that she is dealing with the personification of concentrated rather than diluted state power'. By now, the post office, along with the state telecommunications operator, has been registered on the stock market, and the German railways have been transformed from an administrative authority into a company ('corporatisation'), with a view to its eventual flotation on the stock market. The effects of corporatisation and privatisation (i.e. ownership transfer to the private sector) on public-sector employment have been far-reaching. Thus, in the early 1990s, before corporatisation and privatisation took full effect, a total of one million staff were employed by the federal railways and the postal and telecommunications services, of whom roughly half were civil servants. Whilst special arrangements have been put in place to protect the status of the latter – they are, in effect, 'loaned' to the private-law companies, whilst remaining officials – public employees in these companies have been removed from the public sector, and civil servants, once they leave the service, are not replaced (Goetz 2000b).

Corporatisation and privatisation are the most obvious ways in which the market is used to deliver services that were hitherto the preserve of public authorities. But 'marketisation' and the introduction of private-business practices have also played a big role in the internal reorganisation of public administration and in moves towards a more 'co-operative' administration. As far as internal reorganisation is concerned, many administrative branches at all levels – federal, *Land* and local – have been subject to reforms inspired by the principles of the New Public Management (NPM), which in Germany is often discussed with reference to the *Neue Steuerungsmodell* ('new steering model'). Its key features include an emphasis on 'steering by outcomes', decentralised responsibility for results, performance monitoring, and 'flexible organisational structures and budgeting practices' (Reichard 2001, p. 548). Internal reorganisation along – real or imagined – business lines implies that public authorities increasingly take on characteristics traditionally associated with the private sector. One needs to add to this the growing reliance on administrative institutions established under private law rather than public law (sometimes referred to as 'organisational privatisation'), including cases where the exercise of sovereign state powers is involved. Finally, one should take note of the growth of the 'co-operative state' (Benz 1996) – associated with administration through negotiations, understandings, arrangements, informal agreements and private-law treaties – and of a raft of initiatives designed to achieve greater citizen involvement in public policy-making through 'direct democracy'.

If judged by the standards of the traditional understanding of internal sovereignty, the thrust of the public-sector changes just outlined is unambiguous. However, as noted above, in relation to public administration, the semisovereignty argument has at least four facets, and, if considered in those terms, the record of the past twenty years or so is less clear-cut. It is easiest to draw a conclusion as regards administrative change as a test case for reform capacity. Unlike the period surveyed by Katzenstein, major structural reforms have occurred during the years under review here, even though they have not been guided by an overall public-sector reform programme. Clearly, it is no longer possible to speak of the 'impossibility of effecting major changes in policy' (Katzenstein 1987, p. 243). This finding echoes Manfred Schmidt's recent, more broadly based 're-visiting' of the semisovereignty thesis. He finds 'a political system that, despite its complex architecture and the numerous veto players and co-governing forces, is endowed with a reasonable level of elasticity and adaptiveness, provided that the challenge is large enough and the major political actors broadly agree in their perception of the issues at stake and are willing and capable to cooperate' (2003, p. 240).

By implication, this also suggests that the capacity of public administration to block change has declined. Thus, the 'resistance of state institutions to externally defined or imposed changes' (Katzenstein 1987, p. 273), likened by Katzenstein to the 'shackling of power through the system of coalition politics, co-operative federalism, and parapublic institutions' (1987, p. 273), appears to have weakened. The following analysis documents, in part, this progressive weakening.

In terms of the administrative dimensions of federalism and parapublic institutions, developments over the past two decades are broadly in line with Katzenstein's analysis. As the next section will make clear, the administrative architecture of federalism has not been altered in any fundamental way (see also chapter 4 in this volume), and although the 'buffer' function of parapublic institutions may have been challenged (see chapter 5 in this volume), they remain central to the administrative organisation of the German state.

Finally, how have the third and fourth features of the 'decentralised state' – a 'decentralised bureaucracy' and organisational restrictions on the power of the chancellor – fared over time? Recent work on the German federal ministerial executive suggests a dual centralisation (Goetz 1999, 2000b): the powers of the Federal Chancellery have grown vis-à-vis the ministries, as the *Ressortprinzip* has been increasingly undermined; and, within the ministries, the powers of political co-ordination units that are directly subordinate to the political leadership have grown vis-à-vis the line units, thus calling into the question the traditional image of 'bottom-up' federal policy-making largely driven by a highly specialised bureaucracy (Mayntz and Scharpf 1975). There are indications that this is part of a wider trend in German public administration that points to the reassertion of political authority, with a concomitant loss of bureaucratic autonomy. For example, several *Länder* have in recent years adopted the traditional 'South German' model of a directly elected mayor heading the local council and the council administration; they have, thereby, done away with appointed chief executives. It is increasingly difficult to conceive of the bureaucracy (a term that in political discourse has now wholly negative connotations) and the civil service as a 'balancing factor (*ausgleichenden Faktor*) vis-à-vis the political forces that shape the life of the state', as the Federal Constitutional Court still did in the 1950s (Bundesverfassungsgericht, p. 162).

After a brief outline of the system of public administration, which stresses the themes of decentralisation and standardisation, the remainder of this chapter examines in greater detail some of the developments noted above that call for a revision, or at least a modified restatement, of the semisovereignty thesis in so far as it relates to public administration. The choice of empirical examples is, thus, biased towards change and discontinuity. Of the three cases that formed the core of the 1987 analysis – the evolution of planning and co-ordination mechanisms in the Federal Chancellery, and, as subsidiary themes, territorial reform and the politics of the 1972 Radicals' Decree – only the first has continued to preoccupy practitioners and, albeit to a lesser extent, academic analysts. This topic is, once again, considered in some depth, to be followed by a discussion of the implications of privatisation, internal administrative reorganisation, and a 'co-operative' administration and 'direct democracy'.

Context

The German administrative system comprises three main tiers – the federal administration, the administrations of the sixteen *Länder*, and the local government level – each of which enjoys institutional autonomy under the Basic Law.[1] Each tier, in turn, comprises several organisational layers. In the case of the federation (*Bund*), they include, in particular, the supreme federal authorities (notably the federal ministries) and a range of subordinate federal administrations, such as the Foreign Service, the Federal Finance and Tax Administration, the Federal Administration of Waterways, the Federal Border Police, the Criminal Police Office, the three federal intelligence services, the federal armed forces and the defence administration (Busse 2001b). In the *Länder* (with the exception of the city-states of Berlin, Bremen and Hamburg), the basic administrative organisation comprises three levels, including the supreme *Land* authorities (of which, again, the *Land* ministries are the most prominent), an intermediate tier, and a host of lower-level specialist agencies (Frank 2001). Local authorities, which typically comprise counties and municipalities, enjoy constitutional protection under the constitution, but, in terms of their functions and

---

[1] There is a vast literature on German public administration and administrative reform, much of it in German and written from a legal perspective. With the exception of classical accounts only available in the German language, preference is given to English-language sources and more recent publications. For broader surveys in English see Benz and Goetz (1996); Derlien et al. (1998); König and Siedentopf (2001); Muramatsu and Naschold (1996); Wollmann and Schröter (2000).

financing, they are closely interwoven with *Länder* administrations (Gunlicks 1986).

Territorial decentralisation is combined with organisational variety. Thus, one finds a proliferation of functionally specialised administrations, for example, for public security, law and order, education, science, research and culture, social services, public health, taxation, economic and agricultural promotion and regulation, and environmental protection, to name but the major branches. There are no standard territorial subdivisions, so that different administrative authorities serve different geographical units. Public administration takes on many institutional guises whether in public-law or in private-law form, or as direct or indirect authorities.[2] The legal sources regulating administrative procedures are almost as diverse as the administrative matters dealt with. And public administration relies on a rich repertoire of instruments, including, for example, formal administrative acts, plans, contracts or informal acts, such as the provision of information.

The emphasis on institutional autonomy of the three main tiers and on fragmentation (Aberbach et al. 1994) is, however, in need of qualification, as there is a very dense network of inter-administrative linkages (Benz 2001b). For example, there are cases of joint administration, where federal and *Länder* authorities share responsibility for fulfilling a task; and the *Länder*, in addition to performing their own tasks, also carry out administrative responsibilities on behalf of the federation (*Bundesauftragsverwaltung*), in which case the federation enjoys rights of supervision and may, under certain conditions, issue instructions to the *Länder* authorities. Most importantly, federal legislation has over the years established a detailed set of legal norms regulating administrative requirements and standards at *Land* level. Similarly, the *Länder*'s responsibility for local government legislation allows them to mould local administration in considerable detail, and the tasks of local authorities are comprehensively determined by federal and, in particular, *Länder* laws.

Institutional autonomy in principle, combined with upper-level legal regulation in practice, is also evident when it comes to the organisation of public employment. The German public employment system distinguishes between two main staff categories: civil servants (*Beamte*)[3] and

---

[2] Indirect public administration comprises institutions 'with special tasks constituted under public law which are not incorporated into the direct state or local authority administration . . . These are largely the social insurance funds' (Bundesministerium des Innern 2003, p. 18).

[3] In the following, the terms civil servant and official are used interchangeably. The term public employee is used for all staff who are not civil servants.

public employees (salaried employees and wage earners) (Bundesministerium des Innern 2003). The ideational foundations of the civil service are intimately tied up with the notion of the sovereign rather than the semisovereign state. They can briefly be characterised as follows. First, as already noted, the state is imbued with internal sovereignty (*Hoheitlichkeit*) vis-à-vis its citizens, and has a monopoly over the means of legitimate coercion. Sovereign state tasks involving the exercise of the state's coercive powers must, in most instances, be carried out only by civil servants. Second, as an institution, the civil service acts as promoter and defender of the public good (*Gemeinwohlverpflichtung*). Third, the civil service is to be organised in a manner that ensures that officials are able to act as guardians of the public good in the exercise of sovereign state tasks by helping to ensure impartiality, objectivity and regularity. The constitutionally safeguarded 'traditional principles of the civil service' (*hergebrachten Grundsätze des Berufsbeamtentums*) are supposed to guarantee an impartial, objective and regular administration. These principles include, in particular, a requirement that administrative tasks that regularly involve the exercise of sovereign authority must, as a rule, be entrusted to officials; an emphasis on formal educational qualifications, professionalism, seniority and political neutrality (although officials may be active members of political parties and stand for elected office without losing their status); recruitment into one of the four main civil service categories (basic, intermediate, executive and higher civil services), which civil servants usually enter at the lowest level of the respective category; life-long tenure; full-time service; no right to strike; and a special bond between civil servants and the state. By contrast, public employees are employed on the basis of ordinary employment law in combination with collective agreements negotiated between the public employers and the trade unions.

There is neither an integrated national civil service nor a national public-service system comprising salaried employees and wage earners. Rather, the services of the federation, of each *Land* and of local authorities are legally separate. This implies, for example, that the geographical mobility of staff is restricted, as there is no legal obligation on the part of one employer to accept an official or employee originally hired by another. Yet, the oft-invoked *Personalhoheit* – or sovereignty in personnel matters – of the *Länder* and of local authorities is subject to considerable legal constraints. As far as the civil service is concerned, federal statutory law establishes common parameters, in particular through the Federal Civil Service Framework Law (*Beamtenrechtsrahmengesetz*, BRRG) and the Federal Remuneration Law (*Bundesbesoldungsgesetz*, BSG). Despite its characterisation as a 'framework' law under Article 75 of the Basic

Law, the BRRG stipulates in detail the internal organisation of the civil service. The civil service laws adopted by the individual *Länder* largely replicate the BRRG. Similarly, the Federal Remuneration Law, adopted under the federation's concurrent legislative powers, establishes a common pay structure for all civil servants, although changes in legislation adopted in 2003 allow the *Länder* a modest degree of discretion in determining certain pay elements, notably holiday pay and Christmas bonuses (*Frankfurter Allgemeine Zeitung*, 30 July 2003).

Standardisation across the civil service also holds for the Federal Civil Service Pension Law (*Bundesversorgungsgesetz*). This national uniformity is mirrored in the case of public employees. For salaried employees, top-level collective agreements cover all employees irrespective of their employer, and for wage earners there are common agreements for the *Bund* and *Länder*, and a separate agreement for local authorities. In the annual collective negotiations on public servants' wages, representatives of the federation lead the employers' negotiating team. But here, too, there have been moves towards greater differentiation, with Berlin, in the face of an acute budgetary crisis, in 2003 leaving the *Länder* association that negotiated collective agreements for all *Länder*. Several other *Länder* have threatened to follow Berlin's example. Finally, it is worth noting that, over the years, the terms and conditions of employment for officials and public employees have converged to a large extent.

Although the main legal and institutional outlines of the public employment system have not changed greatly over recent decades, there have been very significant qualitative and quantitative shifts. The qualitative shift can be described in terms of the progressive extension of the *Leistungsstaat*. As Benz (2001a, p. 97) argues, this 'providing state' fulfils not only the classical core sovereign functions of external defence and the maintenance of domestic law and order, but a wide range of additional economic, social and cultural functions, such as the provision of a property order, social rights, public education for all citizens, or the promotion of basic research. The exercise of many of these functions contains elements of *Hoheitlichkeit*, but the state's economic, social and cultural functions are not primarily defined through the exercise of legitimate coercion. For example, the legal requirement to attend school is an expression of the state's coercive power, but the provision of education is not defined through coercion (though some pupils may see it differently!). The post-war expansion of the *Leistungsstaat* finds its expression in the rapid growth of public employment between the 1950s and the early 1980s. Thus, between 1950 and 1980, the total number of personnel in direct public administration at the federal, *Länder* and local levels rose from 1.3 million to 3.5 million. To these figures must be added, in particular, the personnel of the federal postal services and the federal railways.

During the 1980s, expansion slowed, but unification then led to a further massive expansion of public-sector employment by some 40 per cent in 1990 and 1991. Most of this growth was accounted for by the creation of *Länder* authorities and the reorganisation of local government. But the federal administration, too, expanded noticeably – from a total staff of 579,000 in June 1989 to 652,000 in June 1991, as federal field administration was extended to the new *Länder*, federal ministries established offices in Berlin, and the ministerial administration in Bonn successfully clamoured for additional permanent staff. Yet, as the huge costs of unification and its aftermath became apparent, a reversal set in. Between 1991 and 1997, overall public-sector employment, including direct public administration, the federal railways and post service, and indirect public administration, declined from 6,737,800 to 5,163,800, i.e. by 23.4 per cent. Six years after unification, it was, thus, less than 11 per cent higher for the unified Germany than for West Germany in 1989. The unification-related 'boom and bust' in employment was particularly pronounced in the case of the federal administration. Already by 1992, federal employment had begun to fall again noticeably, and by 1994, pre-unification levels were reached. By 1997, federal staff numbers were already 10 per cent lower than in 1989, and, by 2000, the federation employed some 500,000 staff, approximately 80,000 fewer than a decade previously in West Germany.

In spite of privatisation (see below), service provision remains at the heart of contemporary public administration. Thus, of *Länder* employees, 12 per cent work for the police service, 8.3 per cent for the judicial service, and 6.8 per cent for the fiscal and financial administration. By contrast, 36 per cent are employed in schools and 10.5 per cent in the higher education sector (as of June 2002). The concentration on service provision is even more pronounced at the local government level, where only 7.3 per cent of staff are employed in public safety, law and order, but 8.2 per cent in the school sector, 17.9 per cent in social services, 17.7 per cent in hospitals, and 5.4 per cent in science, research and cultural establishments (Bundesministerium des Innern 2003, p. 18).

Agenda

The decentralised nature of German public administration, organisational diversity and the dispersal of responsibilities for administrative policy have meant that – as during the 1970s and 1980s – administrative reform over the past two decades cannot be reduced to a coherent set of initiatives. However, whilst approaches to, and the outcomes of, administrative change have varied greatly, several key drivers of administrative policy can be identified. Two – the growing reliance on market-based and business-type solutions for public service provision, branded by critics as the 'economisation' and 'managerialisation' of public administration (König 2000), and co-operation and direct democracy – have already been mentioned. They will be discussed in greater detail below, since they relate directly to the changing nature of semisovereignty. Two others – unification and European integration – should at least be noted in brief.

The main administrative challenges arising from unification included the creation of the new *Länder*, with the full panoply of authorities that is typical of *Länder* administrations; the establishment of an independent sphere of local government; the introduction of a career civil service; the creation of a comprehensive legal framework for administrative action in the form of *Länder* administrative law; and the establishment of federal administrative offices in the east (Goetz 1993; for an evaluation see Derlien 2001b). Administrative reconstruction in the east relied overwhelmingly on tried-and-tested institutional templates imported from the west. This could be seen not least in the case of territorial reform, one of Katzenstein's three original themes. The local government map in eastern Germany closely resembled that of the Federal Republic before the territorial reforms of the 1970s in that it was highly fragmented, with a large number of small municipalities and counties (*Landkreise*). Thus, the new *Länder* inherited 189 counties (compared with 237 in the old *Länder*) and a total of 7,564 municipalities (compared with 8,509 in the west). In Brandenburg, for example, 67 per cent of its 1,775 municipalities had fewer than 500 inhabitants. The establishment of an independent sphere of local government was a central element in overcoming the legacy of Communism, which had stressed the unity of state power. Local government reform in the new *Länder* first focused on functional reform, i.e. changes in the tasks and organisation of local government, with territorial reform coming second. Although the amalgamation of municipalities and counties in the new *Länder* sometimes caused fierce controversy, it progressed in all the new *Länder*, partly because reform intentions were less ambitious and reformers more ready to compromise than tended to be the case during the 1970s, but also because the western experience served to legitimise the approach to, and outcomes of, territorial reform.

Institutional transfer had a strongly conservative effect. In the main, it reproduced West German administrative traditions in the east, with few innovative exceptions; moreover, it served to validate the western traditions, and, thus, reduce political pressure for reform, at a time when Germany appeared increasingly isolated from the international reform debate.

Since the mid-1990s, the Europeanisation of public administration has emerged as a key theme in comparative administrative analysis (Goetz 2000a). Europeanisation is mainly used as shorthand for effects of European integration on the administrative systems of the EU member states. Recent comparative research suggests that European integration is not associated with pronounced convergence in administrative practices amongst the member states (Page 2003). National administrative traditions appear to possess a remarkable capacity for accommodating, if not neutralising, adaptive pressures associated with the integration process. Also, whilst the EU may, in some policy areas, rival domestic actors in shaping public-policy trajectories, administrative policy has remained a domain in which national actors predominate. Thus, the EU does not constitute a major 'node' in the policy network. Yet, co-operation amongst national governments in administrative developments is undoubtedly growing in importance, as EU member states intensify the regularised exchange of information on administrative performance and increase the use of benchmarking techniques.

For all their transformative potential, neither unification nor Europeanisation can be linked to systemic change in German public administration. By contrast, privatisation, reorganisation inspired by new public management, and a policy of co-operation and citizen involvement challenge the fundamental tenets of the bureaucratic state. In its most radical form – privatisation – this agenda amounts to the abolition of public administration; however, the creation of markets within the public sector, the practice of contracting out, and attempts to make administrative authorities operate in a more entrepreneurial fashion are also informed by the assumption that classical bureaucracy is a hindrance to efficient and efficacious service provision rather than the guarantor of the 'public good'. At least from the mid-1990s, the Kohl government came to proclaim its support for a remodelling of public authorities in the image of 'service enterprises' (*Dienstleistungsunternehmen*) to be 'managed' rather than administered. The new SPD-Green government professed its intention to give a novel political orientation to the modernisation of state and public administration. In its programme 'Modern State – Modern Administration', adopted by the cabinet on 1 December 1999, the federal government rejected the previous concept of the 'lean state', since 'it was too restricted to the reduction of public tasks, and, thus, only offered a negative definition of objectives'

(Bundesregierung 1999, p. 1).[4] Borrowing heavily from the international reform discussion, the new guiding conception of public-sector modernisation has been the 'activating state' that takes account of the new 'division of responsibilities between state and society' (Bundesregierung 1999, p. 2). The activating state is 'not so much a decision-maker and producer, but rather the moderator and activator of societal developments, which it cannot and should not determine alone' (Bundesregierung 1999, p. 2). The federal government, it is noted, has a particular responsibility for creating the legal framework 'for a citizen-oriented and co-operative state with an efficient public administration' (Bundesregierung 1999, p. 2). In its 2002 assessment of the reform programme, the Federal Ministry of the Interior (Bundesministerium des Innern 2002, p. 71) argued that the modernisation process had reached a dynamic which had made it 'irreversible', as an 'unprecedented climate of reform had been achieved in the federal administration'.

Co-operation and direct democracy have been a fourth major theme on the administrative reform agenda. Co-operation takes many forms, all of which stress public–private 'partnership' rather than subordination. Direct democracy is principally linked to attempts to strengthen citizens vis-à-vis the administration through political means. This has been most pronounced at the local level, where, since unification, the use of plebiscitary instruments has become much more widespread. At the same time, most *Länder* have introduced the direct popular election of mayors who serve as heads of the local administration. Taken together, local government has been 'seized by a strikingly strong current towards strengthening its direct democratic potential' (Wollmann 2000, p. 49).

Process

Policy Co-ordination in the Federal Core Executive

As Katzenstein's analysis highlights, policy co-ordination in the federal executive has been a perennial problem. In discussions on the subject, two perspectives dominate. The first understands executive co-ordination as a means of resolving conflicts over political preferences and priorities both within the executive and between the executive and the political forces and institutions on whose continued support it depends. In this account, co-ordination requirements are mostly politically generated. They result, in particular, from the dynamics of coalition

---

[4] All translations into English are my own.

government, tensions between the executive and parliament, electoral competition, and inter-governmental conflicts.

The second perspective focuses on administrative-bureaucratic aspects of co-ordination. In this account, the need for co-ordination reflects the division of labour within modern bureaucracies, which mixes functional, institutional and territorial principles. Here, co-ordination is the attempt to cope with the tensions between the organisational principles of deconcentration, decentralisation, departmentalism and hierarchy, on the one hand, and the real-life interdependence of policy issues, on the other. Co-ordination is, thus, the attempt to ensure that 'organisationally necessary and desirable specialisation does not become dysfunctional' (Ellwein 1990, p. 167).

Whilst the distinction between political and administrative rationalities is, of course, analytically helpful, the ministerial executive is, by definition, of a dual character. It is both *Regierung* (government) and *Verwaltung* (administration) and the two dimensions cannot, empirically, be neatly separated from each other, either in functional terms or in terms of personnel (König 2002; Goetz 2004). Co-ordination arrangements reflect this political and administrative duality. Political co-ordination relies primarily on arrangements in which politicians dominate. Examples of such arrangements include coalition rounds, which are attended by key figures of the government and leading party representatives; written coalition agreements, which are negotiated by politicians prior to the formation of a government; and coalition working groups, which are set up for the preparation of major bills prior to their formal adoption by the federal government and consist of both members of the political executive and members of the ruling *Bundestag* parties. By contrast, administrative co-ordination devices are centred on officials, such as inter-ministerial co-ordination meetings at the level of heads of section or division. Typically, co-ordination at the political level tends to be less institutionalised and more fluid than at the administrative level, where there appears to be greater scope for, and, perhaps, need for, an explicit normative basis, for example in the form of the Standing Orders of the Federal Government or the Common Standing Orders of the Federal Ministries.

The Federal Chancellery occupies a central co-ordination role (Busse 2001a; Mertes 2000; Müller-Rommel 1994). Its organisation reflects its dual character as an eminently political body and an administrative authority. The Chancellery provides support and advice both for the chancellor and for the cabinet. In British terminology, it combines the tasks of the Prime Minister's Office and of the Cabinet Office. In its internal organisation, no distinction is made between the two responsibilities. The political leadership within the Chancellery consists of the chancellor, the head of the Chancellery and the ministers of state. Whilst the latter have a clearly circumscribed remit (although the chancellor may entrust them with special tasks), the head of the Chancellery covers, in principle, the full breadth of federal policies. A short examination of the evolution of this office during the Kohl chancellorship underlines both the blurring of political and administrative functions and the pivotal contribution of the Federal Chancellery to interministerial and executive–external co-ordination. The need to combine these dimensions in a single office was acknowledged with the appointment of Wolfgang Schäuble as Chief of the Chancellery in November 1984; he followed Waldemar Schreckenberger, widely seen as having failed in this office. Before coming to this post, Schäuble had been the chief whip of the CDU/CSU parliamentary party (*Erster Parlamentarischer Geschäftsführer*), and, thus, knew the parliamentary party extremely well. He was appointed as a minister without portfolio. As such, he was a full member of cabinet, and also remained a member of parliament. The reasoning behind Schäuble's appointment was revealed by Chancellor Kohl in a statement to the media:

Experience so far has shown that the political co-ordination between the government and the coalition parties and parliamentary parties, but also co-ordination within the government play an especially important role. In my experience, this task can be most effectively performed by a Federal Cabinet Minister who is a member of parliament . . . To ensure the closest possible link between administrative activity, the preparation of decisions and political co-ordination, I shall appoint Dr Schäuble to the official position of Chief of the Federal Chancellery . . . I am convinced that this new organisation of the Chancellery will make a significant contribution to the effective shaping of the policies of the federal government. (Bulletin der Bundesregierung, 16 November 1984)

With Schäuble's appointment, the Federal Chancellery began to metamorphose into the undisputed powerhouse of the federal government, the centre of co-ordination between the coalition partners, ministerial departments, government and parliament and also the *Bund* and the *Länder*. Working in tandem with the chancellor, Schäuble redefined the office, and his successors, Rudolf Seiters (April 1989 to November 1991) and Friedrich Bohl (November 1991 to 1998), built on the foundations he had laid. Gradually, the position of Chief of the Chancellery began to acquire the characteristics of a 'super minister'. As *Der Spiegel* (21 August 1995) said of Bohl, he acted as 'the man with the oil can', the chancellor's 'messenger and adviser, servant and executor', a 'sort of prime minister' serving directly under Kohl and 'thus considerably more equal than his cabinet colleagues'.

Following its election in the autumn of 1998, the SPD-Green coalition led by Chancellor Schröder brought about far-reaching changes in executive personnel. In the short time-span between taking office on 27 October and 18 November 1998, the new government sent fifty-one 'political civil servants', mostly administrative state secretaries and heads of division, into (temporary) early retirement (*Frankfurter Allgemeine Zeitung*, 19 November 1998); by the early summer of 1999, the two top tiers of the federal ministerial civil service had been comprehensively recast (Derlien 2001a). In the Chancellery, turnover was especially pronounced, as most sympathisers of the old government were replaced by officials with better links to the new governing parties.

Changes in staffing were accompanied by organisational alterations. In the Chancellery, a dual leadership was installed beneath Chancellor Schröder, consisting of Bodo Hombach, as Chief of the Chancellery and Minister without Portfolio, and Frank Walter Steinmeier, with the rank of an administrative state secretary. Hombach was to focus on political planning, advise the chancellor and deal with politically sensitive special tasks, such as guiding the talks on the government's 'Alliance for Jobs' or the international negotiations on the compensation for Jewish slave labour under the Nazi regime. By contrast, Steinmeier was to have prime responsibility for co-ordinating tasks, and took over most of the routine responsibilities that had previously been carried out by Kohl's last Chief of the Chancellery, Bohl, such as chairing the weekly Monday meetings of the administrative state secretaries from all ministries.

The importance of smooth co-ordination for executive effectiveness and the obstacles to attaining this elusive goal were all too evident during the first few months of the new government. Co-ordination deficits quickly became apparent at both the political and administrative levels. The SPD-Green coalition agreement had envisaged that no permanent forum would be set up for co-ordination between the two parties, thus discontinuing the practice of weekly coalition meetings under the Kohl government. Instead, a coalition committee, consisting of eight members of each party, would be convened only if and when one of the coalition partners so requested. Co-ordination was to be achieved through 'permanent and comprehensive consultations' rather than the creation of special institutions. Very soon, however, it became clear that co-ordination would need to take a more institutionalised form than was initially envisaged. Following a number of highly public disagreements during the first few weeks of the new government, a regular coalition committee was set up, consisting initially of Chancellor Schröder, the then leader of the SPD, Oskar Lafontaine (who, following his resignation, was to be replaced by the leader of the SPD parliamentary party, Peter Struck), and the two Green ministers, Joschka Fischer (Foreign Minister) and Jürgen Trittin (Federal Minister for the Environment) (*Frankfurter Allgemeine Zeitung*, 24 February 1999). In addition, permanent coalition working groups were set up, covering central areas of the government's reform agenda.

Co-ordination deficits within the coalition were exacerbated, and partly caused by, the lack of co-ordination within the governing parties. This was especially evident in the SPD, where the pact between Schröder and Lafontaine, which had done much to bring the party back to power, did not last beyond election night. This highly visible conflict was resolved in early March 1999, when Lafontaine resigned as SPD party leader and Federal Finance Minister, and Schröder was subsequently elected SPD leader. The struggle for dominance between Schröder and Lafontaine had made co-ordination efforts by the Chancellery difficult, not least because both Hombach and Steinmeier were seen as Schröder's men. Hombach, in particular, was mistrusted as an ideological ally of the chancellor; he was also viewed with suspicion by the SPD parliamentary party. The fact that he had no direct previous experience of politics at the federal level and did not belong to the *Bundestag* further reduced his effectiveness as a link to the parliamentary party. To the ill-concealed relief of many within his own party, Hombach resigned at the end of July 1999, to take on the role of the EU's co-ordinator for assistance to the Balkans. Within the Federal Chancellery, most of his tasks were taken over by Steinmeier, who succeeded Hombach as its Chief, but retained the rank of administrative state secretary rather than minister, a return to the practice of the chancellorship of Schmidt as well as that of the first few years of Kohl's chancellorship. A new minister of state, Hans-Martin Bury, was also appointed, to lead political co-ordination with the parliamentary party and the *Länder*. He joined two other state ministers, Rolf Schwanitz, who was responsible for co-ordinating federal policy for the new *Länder*, and Michael Naumann, who led federal cultural policy, following the concentration of administrative responsibilities for cultural policy in the Chancellery after the elections. With the exception of Naumann, who left office in 2001 and was replaced by Julian Nida Rümelin, this team led the Chancellery until the federal election of September 2002.

Several points are worth highlighting about the co-ordination arrangements created by the Schröder government. First, there is a striking similarity between the complaints about effective political and policy management during the new government's early period in office and the criticisms levelled at the first Kohl government, when the press spoke of an 'unending series of blunders' at the centre of government (*Die Zeit*, 16 November 1984). Like Kohl's, the Schröder government found that the management of the coalition and the harmonisation of political and administrative planning were more difficult than expected.

Second, having experimented with institutional innovations such as the installation of both a minister and a secretary of state in the Chancellery with a primarily political and administrative co-ordination remit respectively, the new government quickly returned to arrangements that emulated those of its predecessor, both in terms of formal organisation and informal practices. Despite the close identification between office and office holder at the level of the political executive, the political and institutional conditions under which successive governments have had to operate have been sufficiently powerful to compel very similar forms of institutionalisation.

Third, the arrangements that took shape enabled Chancellor Schröder to exercise a degree of control over his government that compared favourably to Kohl's heyday. Schröder's success in taking control over both the Social Democratic parliamentary and the national parties (Korte 2002) has been mirrored in his control over his cabinet. As under Kohl, key policy decisions are taken in the Chancellery, with the ministries often being relegated to the status of 'executive agencies' for decisions taken elsewhere. The reliance on expert commissions – established outside the executive – for the preparation of major policy reforms, a practice well-established under Kohl, but reinforced by Schröder, further weakens both ministerial agenda setting and policy formulation (Sturm 2003). This is part of a broader trend in which the scope for bureaucratic policy-making, driven by specialised officials, is increasingly restricted. 'Bottom-up' policy-making is challenged by 'top-down' initiatives.

Privatisation, Reorganisation, Co-operation, Democracy

If the changes in the federal core executive and, in particular, in the Chancellery are driven by power politics, administrative reform in the shape of privatisation, reorganisation, co-operation and direct democracy are typically justified in terms of increased efficiency and effectiveness, greater economy, improved services for citizens (or clients) and greater accountability. But these measures also have profound implications for the relationship between politics and administration. Briefly, both the bureaucratic character of German public administration and its relative autonomy – emphasised in Katzenstein's account – have declined, as has its capacity to withstand external reform pressures.

Privatisation

During the past two decades, Germany has undergone two very different kinds of privatisation. The first, post-Communist privatisation, was one of the key challenges facing German policy-makers in the wake of unification. The GDR had one of the largest state sectors amongst the Communist countries of central and eastern Europe. Privatisation in the east was, accordingly, a central plank in the creation of a market economy. By contrast, privatisation of partly or wholly state-owned companies in the west – industrial privatisation – has taken place in the context of a fully fledged 'social' market economy, in which private enterprise dominates economic activity.[5]

The policy of privatising industries in the west since the early 1980s has, in many ways, closely resembled privatisation efforts in other western European countries. In the main, it has focused on the full or partial disposal of federal stakes in industrial enterprises and financial institutions; and the transformation of administrative authorities into commercial enterprises under private law and their subsequent full or partial transfer into private ownership. Privatisation in the west has been characterised by a case-by-case approach, and the forms that privatisation has taken have been diverse. They have included, for example, the sale of subsidiaries belonging to public-sector industries and banks; the creation of private-law subsidiaries within a public group; the re-capitalisation of public companies with private-investor participation, with the result that the quota held by the federation has been reduced; the sale of minority or majority stakes in companies totally or partially controlled by the federation; and the outright sale of firms to private investors with or without prior tender. Between 1990 and 1999, the federal government collected some DM 32.6 billion (€ 16.7 billion) from privatisation; the Schröder government hoped to raise a further DM 52 billion (€ 26.7 billion) between 2000 and 2004.[6]

In the context of a discussion of administrative change, the main consequence of privatisation and corporatisation, which regularly precedes it, has been the removal of the staff of the affected firms from the public service, which, as a result, has seen a major contraction in the number of public employees, as noted above. Of course, many of the firms that have been privatised, such as Deutsche Lufthansa or Autobahn Tank&Rast, had long been organised as commercial enterprises,

---

[5] Privatisation in the east was primarily the task of the *Treuhandanstalt* and its successor organisations. See chapter 5 in this volume.

[6] For details of the enterprises privatised see Bundestagsdrucksache 14/4696.

even if they were publicly owned; their staff were not, therefore, officials or public employees. But in the case of railways, postal and telecommunications services and also the air-traffic control service, all of which used to be part of the federal administration with a total staff of some one million in the early 1990s, corporatisation and (partial) privatisation, respectively, have meant that the federal public service has undergone a severe contraction.

Internal Reorganisation[7]

The reorganisation of the structures and procedures of public administration broadly in line with the precepts of new public management (NPM) has been one of the most widely debated developments in the comparative study of public administration over the past decade (Pollitt and Bouckaert 2000). Until the early 1990s, Germany was largely unaffected by the NPM debate; and the federal administration, in particular, seemed immune to the kind of reform measures that are typically associated with NPM (Benz and Goetz 1996). By the mid-1990s, however, pressures for change had intensified sufficiently for the government to establish an Expert Commission 'Lean State' (*Sachverständigenrat 'Schlanker Staat'*), whose final recommendations were published in the autumn of 1997 (Sachverständigenrat 'Schlanker Staat' 1997a, 1997b). From the commission's recommendations and also from statements by the government of the day, the following main outlines of ministerial reorganisation emerged: a reduction in personnel (between 1994 and 1998, in addition to posts that had already been earmarked for abolition, ministries had to reduce their personnel by 1.5 per cent annually); a greater concentration on ministerial tasks, with non-core tasks to be transferred to other institutions; a flattening of organisational hierarchies, 'in particular since this allows the more direct exercise of leadership' (Sachverständigenrat 1997a, p. 117); and the unburdening of the political executive through the strengthening of political co-ordination units (*Leitungsstäbe*) designed to give the political leadership 'more scope to set objectives, develop strategies, take and implement political decisions' (Sachverständigenrat 1997b, p. 119).

For the most part, the modernisation efforts launched by the Kohl government from the mid-1990s were budget driven. Cutbacks in

---

[7] This section focuses on the federal administration. For a first survey of NPM-inspired reforms at *Land* level see Naschold and Bogumil (2000), with further references. The influence of the *Neue Steuerungsmodell* on local government is highlighted in many of the contributions to Wollmann and Roth (1999); see also Bogumil (2001), which contains further references to the copious literature on this subject.

ministerial staffing were announced before action was taken to reconsider the scope of ministerial activity and organisational structures and procedures. As the government pointed out, 'the pressure for rationalisation that results from scarce budgetary resources and global staff cuts must be used for far-reaching improvements of the internal organisation of authorities' (Bundestagsdrucksache 13/3923, p. 1). But the commission borrowed extensively from NPM rhetoric, and the government followed suit. For example, the government's 'Programme for Further Advances in Federal Administrative Effectiveness and Economy' of July 1997 noted that 'The administrative office as the mirror image of a hierarchical state . . . belongs to the past. The understanding of public administration must more and more be that of a *service enterprise*' (Bundesministerium des Innern 1997, p. 427; emphasis in the original).[8]

The Schröder government, from 1998, reinforced the use of NPM-inspired language, and referred explicitly to the international reform discussion in justifying its priorities. The 1999 programme 'Modern State – Modern Administration' (Bundesregierung 1999) was guided by the notion of the 'activating state', restricted to core state tasks. The 2002 report on the implementation of the modernisation programme (Bundesministerium des Innern 2002) underscores the shift towards market-type solutions and business practices as guidelines for the organisation of the federal administration. Thus, 'the federation as a moderniser' refers, amongst other things, to initiatives for a 'modern management', based on 'guiding visions', 'controlling', 'target setting', 'cost accrual accounting', 'ideas management' and 'gender mainstreaming'; 'performance-enhancing competition'; 'efficient administrative structures'; 'motivated personnel'; and 'modern technology'. 'More service – less bureaucracy' are to be achieved, in particular, through the use of advanced IT and internet-based technologies (Bundesministerium des Innern 2002).

Against the backdrop of decades of modest change in the federal administration, what is striking about the current modernisation programme is not just the extent to which the federation has caught up with the international reform discourse; even more noteworthy is the degree to which, by implication, traditional notions of public bureaucracy have been discarded. Just how radically the federal administration has really changed is, of course, a moot point, but the ideational foundations of the

---

[8] For an official summary of the Kohl government's reform measures see Lenkungsausschuss Verwaltungsorganisation (1998).

classical public bureaucracy have been eroded to an extent where even the traditional principles of the civil service appear increasingly obsolete. Thus, traditional justifications for the existence of a civil service that is distinguished by its functions, organisational principles, its special bond of loyalty to the state, and a legitimation grounded in its role as a guardian and guarantor of the public good are more and more difficult to reconcile with the reality of modern governance. Even if its formal abolition seems unlikely, an internal hollowing out of the civil service would appear inevitable.

Co-operative Administration and Direct Democracy

A third development challenging bureaucratic autonomy is initiatives aimed at the strengthening of public–private co-operation in administrative action and of direct democracy. Neither is a new idea; however, political and administrative reforms over the past decade or so have increasingly turned them into practice. Their influence has, perhaps, been most apparent at the local government level. Observers have noted that the use of the basic instruments of a non-hierarchical co-ordination and co-operation between public administration and private actors – including negotiated regulation, co-production, and exchange and contracting (Benz 1996) – has become increasingly widespread in local government (Bogumil 2002). They are accompanied by 'a reduction of competences of both local councils and the administrative leadership' (Bogumil 2001, p. 247). The scope for administrative policy-making is further restricted through the remarkable growth in the use of binding referenda at local level and the – by now – common practice of directly elected mayors who serve as heads of the council administration (Schiller and Mittendorf 2002). One of the most respected scholars of German local government argues that both developments have

significantly remoulded the institutional and power relations in the local-administrative arena. It lends itself to further sharpening and, as it were, further '*politicising*' the *political* profile and the *political* 'frame of reference' of local government by giving the citizens direct access to local decision-making and by strengthening the political accountability of the mayor as politico-administrative leader. (Wollmann 2002, p. 82; emphasis in the original)

The increase in stature of the mayor goes hand in hand with growing political direction and control of the administration; in fact, 'the main reason for shifting towards the directly elected "strong" executive mayor was the wish to strengthen the "governing" capacity of the mayor' (Wollmann 2002, p. 80).

Consequences

The changes in the organisation of the German state over the past two decades or so have several consequences for the semisovereignty thesis. First, it should have emerged from the above that although administrative change may typically be piecemeal rather than the result of grand reform designs, administrative development has been characterised by considerable dynamism, affecting all levels and most branches of the administrative system. Administrative policy does not, therefore, confirm arguments about a generalised resistance to change in the German political system. Second, it is difficult to argue that public administration itself acts as a major obstacle to reform. Rather, it is increasingly squeezed 'in the middle' between the market and the private sector, on the one hand, and politics, on the other. The former have been strengthened through privatisation, corporatisation, and a remoulding of public administration in the image of markets and private enterprises. Political authority over public administration has grown not just in the federal ministries, but also at the local level through the use of referenda and directly elected heads of the council administration. Bureaucratic autonomy vis-à-vis both politics and society has declined markedly. Most importantly, 'contemporary administration can no longer be adequately captured with the notion of bureaucracy. In the new administrative reality, the hierarchical steering structures that dominated in this model are complemented by structures of competition and co-operation' (Benz 2001a, p. 275). The demise of public bureaucracy means that the buffer between politics, state and society is rapidly disappearing. Modern public administration, especially if modelled on NPM precepts, will no longer be an obstacle to reform; however, nor is it likely to be able to act as a balancing force between politics, state and markets.

12   European Policy-making: Between Associated Sovereignty and Semisovereignty

William E. Paterson

> Conceptions of sovereignty are linked so closely to domestic structures that it is difficult to untangle the role of ideas from that of political organisation and practice.
>
> (Keohane 2003, p. 322)

It falls to very few social scientists to coin a term that defines a polity but this is precisely what Peter Katzenstein achieved with the concept of semisovereignty (Katzenstein 1987), which forged an indissoluble association between the old Federal Republic and semisovereignty. Moreover, this term is not just a convenient label, but a carefully worked-out explanation of the politics and policy style of the old Federal Republic. Many who have not read the book but who have encountered the term also assume that it refers to West Germany's sovereignty deficit in the international arena.

In Katzenstein's 1987 work, however, the emphasis is almost exclusively on internal constraints, many of them self-imposed, that limited the sovereignty of the West German state and by which, in Katzenstein's words, 'The West German state has been tamed rather than broken' (p. 10). These internal constraints included the system of co-operative federalism and the role of parapublic institutions, most notably the *Bundesbank*. It is, of course, Katzenstein's internally grounded conception of semisovereignty that most obviously suggests a continuing relevance to the post-unity polity.

Context: the Pre-Sovereign Years

The external dimension remained very largely unexplored, though Katzenstein enumerated, but did not analyse, a series of factors which informed his argument that 'Semisovereignty is an external condition of West German Politics' (Katzenstein 1987, p. 9). The description of the Federal Republic as externally semisovereign scarcely applies to the founding years, however, when the original Bonn institutions were created and from which a marked path dependency has flowed. West

Germany was regarded as the successor state to the German Reich, which had surrendered unconditionally in May 1945, but it occupied only something over half of its territory, and possessed no armed forces. Its capacity as an international actor was further constrained by a web of discriminatory institutions and provisions in the area of trade and production designed to prevent the re-emergence of a German threat. It was also, until 1955, an occupied state, where the three western powers possessed considerable reserve powers, especially in the area of external relations, and Berlin was still under a Four Power status. It is best described in these years as pre-sovereign rather than non-sovereign; pre-sovereign implies the condition towards which the Federal Republic was aspiring to move and does not exclude leverage and influence.

It is this point of departure that explains much of the content and style of German European policy. The Federal Republic had a notably weak state character. 'State identities are primarily external; they describe the actions of governments, in a society of states' (Katzenstein 1987, p. 20). Whilst this weak state could rely on the power of the United States and to a lesser extent the United Kingdom (France was at this time only in Germany as a result of its *honoris causa* status as an allied power), its urgent need to lift these provisions and to secure markets gave it an elemental interest in the creation of frameworks at a European level that would allow other European states, especially France, to lift these provisions. The imperatives of bipolarity had, of course, already impelled the United States along this line of thinking. The situational logic of these founding years is analysed in *The Federal Republic of Germany and the European Community* (Bulmer and Paterson 1987) where a distinction is made between the political importance of European integration as an arena of co-operation and its economic importance as an area of competition. 'Without European integration as a political arena of co-operation West German economic performance would have been perceived as a threat' (Bulmer and Paterson 1987, p. 7).

The Attainment of Semisovereignty

The conclusion of the Paris Treaties including the *Deutschlandvertrag* in autumn 1954 and their entry into force on 5 May 1955 brought to an end the Occupation Statute; its ending was not, however, co-extensive with the recovery of full sovereignty, and a great deal of singularity remained. West Berlin remained extremely vulnerable, and its status was to be tested, almost to destruction, in the Berlin crisis of 1958–62, and whilst it successfully resisted Soviet pressure, the corollary was a unilateral dependence of the Federal Republic on the western allies. The

Paris Treaties incorporated the Federal Republic into NATO but it was expressly denied any independent strategic planning capacity, the ability to engage in the development of ABC (atomic, biological and chemical) weapons or possession of any national units not assigned to NATO.

The entry of West Germany into NATO reflected and deepened further changes in the international context. Both Germanies were now cemented firmly into their respective alliance structures, and the alternative of western integration or pursuit of the unity imperative was no longer posed in such a sharp form. European integration, which had appeared checked by the rejection of the European Defence Community (EDC) in summer 1954, was relaunched with EURATOM and the European Economic Community (EEC). The context of European policy-making in the next three and a half decades was to be set by the intense interactive relationship between a steadily more potent Federal Republic and the western multilateral institutions.

Semisovereignty in a Sovereign Germany

The breaching of the Berlin Wall and the final achievement of German unity on 3 October 1990 appeared to change the context of German European policy-making fundamentally. All of the remaining allied reserve powers disappeared, Berlin re-emerged from Four Power status to become a capital in waiting, and all Soviet forces were to be withdrawn from eastern Germany. At Stavropol it had also been agreed that the new Germany's membership of NATO would be unrestricted. At the wider geographical level the ending of the division of Europe closed an era in which Germany was uniquely affected through the position of Berlin by the climate of east–west relations, a situation that imposed an asymmetric dependence on Germany's western partners.

If the events of 1989–90 had removed the vulnerabilities associated with Germany's front-line position, it was not immediately apparent what the geopolitical impact of Germany's altered position would be. Its significance would depend on the shape of the emerging European order and how Germany's altered position would be perceived by German elites. Whereas the Federal Republic's geopolitical position after 1949 was one that was determined by structural and systemic variables, the geopolitical position of the new Germany was a test bed for constructivism. This contrast is reflected also in Katzenstein's explanations. The 1987 version stresses structure whilst *Tamed Power* (Katzenstein 1997a) assigns a key role to constructivist explanations. The falling away of the formal restrictions on German sovereignty was accompanied by an apparent augmentation of German power resources.

German unity brought with it a major expansion of the territorial area of the state, a significant increase in population and a growth in economic resources, though this last factor very quickly turned out to be potential, rather than immediate, and to be outweighed for the foreseeable future by the financial burdens that unity would bring. Certainly, externally there were many analysts who equated increased resources with increased power and who assumed that increased power would translate into power politics (most famously Mearsheimer 1990).

Agenda

West Germany's singular position in 1949 as the larger part of a divided and defeated nation without any marked power resources, save for its strategic geopolitical position in a bipolar system, could not be addressed by hand-me-down realist politics. What was required was a set of policies which would re-establish Germany as an international actor and create economic and political institutions that would furnish a framework for West German economic interests and stabilise the West German polity. Adenauer's Rhineland vision addressed these goals by its espousal of multilateral institutions and the creation of the Franco-German 'special relationship' (Paterson 1998).

Whilst much of the agenda and process of Germany's European policy can be explained in terms of impaired state identity, West Germany's internal stability was potentially threatened by the division of the German nation. Anti-Communism and economic prosperity were the central elements in West Germany's emerging stability (Paterson 1973), but the contribution of the European agenda was crucial. European integration was essential to the economic success that underpinned the growing attachment of the citizens to the Federal Republic, and the Europeanised identity adopted by the Federal Republic was one that went some way towards neutralising the collective insecurities associated with the German past while seeming to promise an acceptable future, and a strong affiliational dimension, even if, as seemed increasingly likely, Germany remained permanently divided.

In the semisovereign period, discriminatory provisions on German production and trade had all been lifted, but there was no very significant change in the policy agenda of federal governments. The imperative of balancing arenas of competition with arenas of co-operation remained central; indeed, in a sense this increased in importance as West Germany took an ever larger share of intra-European trade. Moreover, European integration offered a counterbalance to the security area where West Germany's semisovereignty was at its most singular. It was, in its transformative aspirations, West Germany's most ambitious policy. It sought not just to increase West Germany's 'actorness', but also, through the process of European integration, to tame European states more widely. A recent publication referred to 'a deep-seated elite consensus (itself relying on a supportive, "permissive" public opinion) that multilateral co-operation was not just a valuable means to peace, security and prosperity in Germany and Europe, but had also become an end in itself, a guiding value of West German politics' (Jeffery and Paterson 2001, p. 180).

Post-unity

For a realist, the major elements in the altered geopolitical context and Germany's increased power resources after 1989/90 might have been expected to move the new Germany towards a European policy close to the 'post-classical' nation-state model of the United Kingdom and France rather than a continuation of the more post-Westphalian mode hitherto characteristic of German European policy (Paterson 2003).

This was emphatically not the case under the chancellorship of Helmut Kohl. The end of the Cold War and the achievement of unity were unsurprisingly seen as a success for pre-existing politics. If Germany was to build on these achievements then the cultivation of trust rather than the assertion of increased opportunities to exercise state power would be seen as the greater strategic priority. In realising this option Kohl relied on an updated version of Adenauer's Rhineland vision as an external legitimator and internal mobiliser (Paterson 1998).

In this vision, Economic and Monetary Union (EMU), the central project of the post-unity Kohl chancellorship, was 'nested' in a vision of a politically unified Europe. EMU was to occupy most of the policy agenda, but enlargement, though never as central to the Kohlian vision, was also important. Priority was clearly given to EMU and Kohl was never able to work out a convincing balance between Germany's key roles as 'integration deepener' and 'integration widener' (Tewes 2001).

The SPD-Green Government

By the time of the victory of the SPD and Greens at the 1998 federal election, the move to the final stage of EMU was assured and the central European policy agenda has revolved around the timing, costs and conditions of eastern enlargement, with conditions referring not only to accession terms but to the institutional and policy reforms contingent on enlargement. The other major agenda has been the moves to develop a European Security and Defence Policy (see Miskimmon and Paterson 2004).

In actual policy terms, the emphasis has been largely on continuity. Enlargement has proceeded perhaps more cautiously. The absence of the fixed timetable that characterised EMU and that allowed the federal government to push through its policy vision has been associated with a degree of foot dragging by domestic interests including the *Länder*. The continuing crisis in the former Yugoslavia has also provided a context in which significant changes occurred in the development of a European Security and Defence Policy (ESDP) and the role Germany could play in it (Jeffery and Hyde-Price 2001). An emphasis on reducing Germany's net contribution was already a feature of the late Kohl period, and change so far has been modest. There is a new institutional discussion precipitated by Foreign Minister Joschka Fischer's Humboldt speech of May 2000, which was worked out in the European Convention (2002–3). Germany played a key role in the Convention but had to accept more inter-governmentalism than it wished in the proposals for a new Council President and in the arrangements for the ESDP.

If actual policy change has been limited, there has been some change at the rhetorical level, and, in the first months of his chancellorship, Schröder frequently invoked national interest.

My generation and those following are Europeans because we want to be, not because we have to be. That makes us freer in dealing with others . . . I am convinced that our European partners want to have a self-confident German partner, which is more calculable than a German partner with an inferiority complex. Germany standing up for its national interest will be just as natural as France or Britain standing up for theirs. (Quoted in *Financial Times*, 10 November 1998)

This post-classical nation-state discourse also resurfaced in a number of Schröder's speeches in the aftermath of 11 September 2001, and as chancellor, he has been much more prepared to defend specific, narrow government interests rather than, as would have been the case in the past, leaving it to the appropriate specialist minister (Paterson 2003). For most of his incumbency, however, Schröder has stuck to the established multilateral European discourse, and the SPD '*Leitantrag*' of November 2001 was firmly in this tradition. Joschka Fischer, by contrast, has consistently articulated an integrationist vision very much in line with the established post-Westphalian discourse of the Foreign Ministry. His major innovation has been in relation to the security dimension where his rhetoric legitimised a significant extension of German capacity for intervention. This rhetoric was, however, not a normalising discourse since it turned on the singularities of German historical memory (*Nie wieder Auschwitz*).

Process

Im Anfang war Adenauer. (Baring 1969, p. 1)

The urgency of increasing Germany's international 'actorness', the continued role of the allied powers, and the impact of Konrad Adenauer as first incumbent gave the chancellor a powerful shaping and strategic role in West Germany's European policy. Adenauer had quickly built up an external relations section in the Federal Chancellery (Paterson 1994).

Two further singularities in German European policy-making stand out, and, like the position of the chancellor, they reflect Germany's weak international status. In many other states the Foreign Ministry played the central role in this period. This was the key period of institutional creation, and the core competence of foreign ministries is treaty negotiation. In this early period, co-ordination of national cross-sectoral policy positions was also less crucial since the European Coal and Steel Community, the principal institution, covered only two sectors, and the High Authority under Jean Monnet attempted to make a reality of the considerable autonomy accorded to it in the Treaty of Paris. In the final analysis, the chancellor was given the competence in the First Common Standing Orders of the Federal Government to take a binding decision in the case of interdepartmental conflicts over the demarcation of competences. The German case presented a stark contrast with the Foreign Ministry only being established in 1951. Its singular status was reflected in its leadership. Adenauer acted as his own Foreign Minister until 1955 and Walter Hallstein, the Permanent Secretary in that period, had, until his move to the Foreign Ministry, been head of the external relations division of the Federal Chancellery.

The Role of the Federal Economics Ministry

The other striking singularity of European policy-making in the Federal Republic was the prominent role played by the Federal Economics Ministry. In these early years, the pecking order of ministries was rather fluid, and, in a chancellor-dominated system, tended to reflect the closeness of the individual minister to Adenauer since other ministers did not possess a significant independent party and public standing, nor had their ministries built up the clientelistic relationships that were later to underpin the *Ressortprinzip*.

There was, however, one very significant exception, that of the Economics Ministry under Ludwig Erhard. As a result of the currency reform in 1948, Erhard possessed considerable public standing. His policy positions, moreover, were not defined by Adenauer, but by what he perceived as 'the needs of German industry' (Hesse and Goetz 1992, p. 185). Erhard had also played the key role in the pre-Bonn institutions, and could mobilise German industry behind his policy positions. On the basis of Erhard's position and the support of German industry, the Economics Ministry insisted on building up a position in the area. This was seen as crucial for the effective operation of a decidedly export-oriented West German economy. The Chancellery had established a Schuman Plan Secretariat under Dr Sahm, but in January 1951 the Economics Ministry was given the responsibility for the external orientation of German industry and trade (Hesse and Goetz 1992, p. 187). On that basis it established a *Montanunterabteilung*, or Coal and Steel Sub-Division, in the Energy Department of the Economics Ministry, and the ECSC was seen as falling primarily under the competence of the Economics Ministry, an outcome also facilitated by its technocratic character. Erhard was also able to insist that an official from the Economics Ministry head the first Permanent Representation to the High Authority of the ECSC. The position of the Economics Ministry was much resented by the Foreign Ministry and the grandly titled, but much less important, Ministry for European Co-operation (created in 1952 from the former Marshall Plan Ministry), and there was no final settled agreement on the final delimitation of competences in the early years, with the Foreign Ministry successfully asserting the principle that no department could engage in foreign negotiations without its assent and approval.

The establishment of the EEC and its subsequent expansion into new policy sectors in the semisovereign years gave an urgency to the question of co-ordination and a definitive agreement on European policy responsibilities. The Ministry of Economics was entrusted with the task of co-ordinating day-to-day European policy, whilst the Foreign Office was left with responsibility for long-term-oriented integration policy with the chancellor retaining his right to set policy guidelines (*Richtlinien-kompetenz*) (Hesse and Goetz 1992).

A series of books and articles by Bulmer and Paterson portrayed German European policy in these years as being characterised by loose co-ordination, sectorisation and bureaucratisation. On this basis, some quite wide-ranging conclusions about the semisovereign German polity were drawn. The assumption was that European policy-making was an externalised reflection of the institutionally complex semisovereign domestic policy process that Katzenstein, in particular, had illuminated. Works written in this vein did not argue, though, that West Germany was multilateralist because of internal semisovereignty/institutional pluralism, but rather that it was not a realist state because of internal semisovereignty/institutional pluralism. West Germany was not a state internally structured in a way consistent with realism's assumptions; the constraints of coalition politics, federalism, departmental sectorisation, the role of 'parapublic' institutions – the *Bundesbank* at their forefront – and strong, centralised forms of interest representation undermined the realist assumption of a coherent state representing a clearly defined national interest.

Our views have been challenged recently in an extremely interesting chapter by Derlien (2000). One key problem with his chapter is that while he himself incorporates a great deal of discussion about the fully sovereign German state, the views he attributes to us all date from before 1989 and refer to a quite different Germany with another set of external opportunity structures. In a robust defence of the German mechanisms, Derlien distinguishes between *post hoc* (German) and *ex ante* (British).

My contention is that the German pattern of *ex post* co-ordination, a policy style resembling management by exception, is ultimately superior to a practice of *ex ante* co-ordination of all policy matters regardless of their salience. Such a strategy is counter-productive, for it leaves little room for the recurrent, multi-issue bargaining process at the European level and the informal norm of reciprocity. (Derlien 2000, p. 6)

Here the differences between Derlien and ourselves are less than he supposes. In his conceptualisation, he focuses on the advantages for the wider European policy process, and we would have no problem with this view. Our work looked more at the effect on the coherence of the national position. In that connection, we often referred to the absence of a ringmaster on day-to-day issues. This is the role played by the Cabinet Office in the UK. Derlien argues that the Federal Chancellery is equivalent to the office of the Prime Minister and the Cabinet Office, but this is not very convincing since the co-ordination referred to relates to the European Council, rather than to routine policy issues (Derlien 2000, p. 6). The role of the Chancellery in relation to the European Council is uncontested by us.

External Dimension

Semisovereignty as an external condition of West German politics was reflected in two external aspects of German European policy. The first, and the one that has attracted the most scholarly attention, was West Germany's attitude towards participation in multilateral institutions. Walter Hallstein, Adenauer's closest policy confidant and chief German negotiator in the Rome Treaty negotiations, became first President of the Commission. This was a key appointment. While the ECSC had given central competences to the High Authority, the EEC formally accorded a greater role to the Council of Ministers, and much of the Commission's power was potential. Adenauer's commitment to multilateral integration and his relationship with Hallstein was a key element in launching the Commission on an expansive trajectory. This alliance was the more important given that the Commission's early years coincided with the election of De Gaulle, a key proponent of intergovernmentalism, as President of the French Fifth Republic. The manner in which the Federal Republic conceived its relationship with the Commission was to be a defining element of this whole period though it never quite regained the intensity of the Adenauer/Hallstein period, and Helmut Schmidt was often unable to conceal his impatience with the Commission (or indeed US presidents and UK prime ministers!).

Somewhat paradoxically, given the emphasis laid on multilateral institutions, the level of German representation in the Commission has been notably weak. One possible explanation is that imperatives of staffing the institutions of a semisovereign polity (*Bundesbank* and *Länder* governments, etc.) overstretch the resources of the political class. This weakness at the level of commissioners is reflected also in senior positions in the Directorates-General where the weak co-ordination mechanisms of the federal government impede the pursuit of a personnel policy to ensure that these posts are occupied by sympathetic officials. Here France and, more recently, the UK provide a striking contrast.

In general terms, however, the relationship with the multilateral institutions was characterised by what is sometimes called 'exaggerated' and 'reflexive' multilateralism and, as Anderson and Goodman famously argued, 'In the eyes of German political elites institutional memberships were not merely instruments of policy but also normative frameworks for policy-making' (Anderson and Goodman 1993, pp. 23–4).

If reflexive multilateralism was one side of the coin of what I have called the 'leadership-avoidance reflex' (Paterson 1993, p. 10), then the other side was the close bilateral relationship with France. This relationship was the privileged partnership that brought enormous benefits to the two states, initially as a vehicle, primarily, for reconciliation, but thereafter also as an instrument for collective action where the two states acting together were normally able to achieve more than they could acting individually.

In pre-unity Germany, the Franco-German relationship had played a key role in German European policy-making. Its role reflected not only the reconciliation imperative, but also the perception that a unilateral assertion of German power resources was likely to be counterproductive. All member states require allies in multilateral institutions, but the Franco-German relationship reflected German singularity. The original perception of the pre-sovereign years that discriminations and constraints on Germany could only be lifted in alliance with France firmed into a core elite belief that a manifest strategic leadership role for Germany, however impressive Germany's power resources had become, would remain closed and that this role could only be played in tandem with France (Paterson 1998). This version of semisovereign behaviour did not rest on formal constraints, but was self-imposed. By 1989/90 the relationship was heavily institutionalised and very strongly underpinned normatively.

The institutionalisation of the Franco-German relationship also reinforces the marked sectorisation of Germany's European policy. The extensive bilateral discussions held at various levels between the two governments are essentially conducted on a specialist basis. There is no agency in Berlin with the task of checking the views expressed by one federal minister to his or her opposite number. The greater degree of centralisation in the French government ensures, by contrast, greater compatibility in the French case. Thus, to take the agricultural policy area, it would be possible for the German and French Agriculture Ministers to come to a close pre-understanding on the CAP – but without necessarily ensuring that this agreement was adequately compatible with the overall objectives of German European policy. This pre-understanding would then have a privileged status because of its Franco-German character.

Post-unity

Under Kohl, the Franco-German relationship retained its centrality and exclusivity, and EMU, the central project of his post-unity European policy, was 'nested' in the Franco-German relationship (Dyson 1998). There was, however, some alteration in the terms of the relationship, and the balance of adjustment shifted to some extent on to France. Under the SPD-Green government, the shift in the relationship has been much more manifest. It has lost some of its exclusivity. Whilst Chancellor Schröder was not able to carry through the 1999 Blair/Schröder paper, the key point was more that this was an initiative on a central area where the partner was a state other than France. Even in the institutional debate, Franco-German exclusivity initially weakened. Chancellor Schröder insisted on his own initiative at Nice on an intergovernmental conference (IGC) in 2004, and the adoption of the SPD '*Leitantrag*' on Europe was choreographed with a visit by Prime Minister Blair to the Party Conference at Nuremberg rather than being closely co-ordinated at any stage with France. Part of this erosion was, however, contingent. It was always much more difficult to operate the relationship during a cohabitation and when cohabitation came to an end in 2002, a newly empowered President Chirac was able to revive, to some degree, the Franco-German relationship. He was aided here by the weakness of the Schröder government in the wake of the federal election and the emphasis on the European Convention. Institutional issues empowered the Foreign Ministry and Joschka Fischer, and if Germany sought to achieve institutional reform, the United Kingdom was a very unlikely ally.

There are, however, grounds for thinking that, while the Franco-German relationship will persist as the alliance of first resort, the future shape of the European Union will tend to reduce an exclusive reliance on 'the privileged partnership'. The grounds for anticipating a German shift to multiple bilateralism alongside a continuing though weakened Franco-German relationship derive from the future shape of the European Union characterised by a shrinking core and an enlarging periphery. EMU could be carried by the Franco-German relationship since the EMU-based EU follows a logic of convergence. Enlargement up to twenty-seven members by 2007 and possibly even beyond that in the next decade entails institutionalising a logic of diversity. In this larger and more complex EU, gridlock is a danger, and there is a clear aggregation of preferences problem. In an enlarged Europe over a range of issues the Franco-German relationship is unlikely to be the optimal vehicle for collective action it once was. Even in the run-up to enlargement, Germany had to make a series of very unwelcome concessions to France on agricultural financing and on voting weights at the Nice IGC. Future German governments will have to devise more attractive incentives for other member states than simple prior Franco-German agreement. Continued public finance shortages in Germany suggest that side-payments as a means of securing support will be less available. Taken together, these factors suggest a widening of German bilateral relationships beyond the Franco-German case. An earlier re-invention of the Dutch–German relationship after German unity was not especially problematic since Dutch preferences on major issues were, by that time, close to German ones, and it did not, therefore, present a major challenge to the Franco-German relationship. Britain, Poland and Spain will be more difficult partners to accommodate, and the split in the European Union on how to respond to the Iraq crisis, where eight members publicly expressed support for a much more pro-Atlanticist line in contradiction to Franco-German preferences, underlined that the period when the EU simply followed a Franco-German lead is now at an end.

Still a Reflexive Multilateralist

The European Commission under Jacques Delors played a key enabling role in the German unity negotiations, and its centrality to Germany's policy-making continued for the remainder of Kohl's chancellorship; by contrast, there was a perceptible *froideur* at times in Germany's relationship with the European Court of Justice. The European Parliament, despite its helpful role in the unity negotiations and its increased powers post-Maastricht, became a less central reference point.

However, the European Commission has become marginalised under Chancellor Schröder, who had to deal with the fall-out of the collapse of the Santer Commission and failed to develop a harmonious working relationship with Romano Prodi. The attempt by Chancellor Schröder and President Chirac to secure the adoption of Guy Verhofstadt as Prodi's successor in June 2004 was humiliatingly rejected in the European Council. More crucially, however, there has been a drastic reduction in the role of the *Bundesbank*, the defining parapublic institution of Katzenstein's semisovereign state, and its replacement by the European Central Bank (see chapter 5). Henceforward, in an absolutely central area, it is a question no longer of a multilateral reflex but more of necessary compliance. For the first time the European level of 'associated sovereignty' (Katzenstein 1997c) is cutting deeply into Germany's policy space.

The Internal Dimension

The loosely co-ordinated European policy machinery of the old Federal Republic reflected a polycephalic and to some extent post-Westphalian polity. On a simple realist reading the events of 1989/90 would have triggered a fundamental shift in the institutional structure towards a more interest driven and centralised model. Neither development took place. German unity was unsurprisingly seen as legitimating the foreign and European policies of successive German governments. This suggested policy continuity, and a continued integrationist policy did not demand highly centralised machinery. There were, moreover, strong structural and ideational barriers. The German political system is characterised by power sharing between partners, the *Ressortprinzip* and a relatively weak norm of information sharing between ministries. Moreover, this was an area of very marked path dependency where the basic division of labour between co-ordinating ministries had been established in the 1950s. Perhaps even more crucially the deepening of European integration launched with the adoption of the Single European Act and expanded by the Maastricht Treaty engaged the European Union much more extensively with the German polity. At one level this made the task of co-ordination even more challenging by bringing in more ministries as serious players in European policy, most notably the Federal Interior Ministry. On the vertical axis, the intervention of the EU much more deeply into the internal polity precipitated a strong and continuing demand for the *Länder* to utilise the possibilities inherent in Article 23 of the Basic Law and be co-involved in the formulation of European policy (Jeffery 2004). In consequence, policy-making became more semisovereign.

On the external dimension of European policy-making, German unity made Germany less semisovereign by reducing its asymmetric dependence on its western allies. Internally, the increase in the competences of the EU made Germany's internal semisovereignty more crucial to German EU policy-making. The inclusion of the *Länder* as key players alongside the federal government necessarily meant that in the policy and institutional issues, perceived as vital by the *Länder*, European policy-making was even more strikingly than before an 'externalised reflection of the institutionally complex domestic policy process' (Jeffery and Paterson 2001, p. 186).

This interplay between the extension of 'associated sovereignty' at the European level and the persistence of 'semisovereignty' at the German domestic level was to have wider repercussions, which will be analysed below. The interaction between 'associated sovereignty' and 'semisovereignty' has generally been seen as mutually supportive: 'The product of material power, strategic bargaining and historical accident, the institutional practices of associated and semisovereignty in Germany and Europe have evolved in mutually supportive ways' (Katzenstein 1997c, p. 44).

There is, of course, more to the story of post-unity European policy-making than the persistence of internal semisovereignty and increasing Europeanisation. The already strong role of the chancellor reached an apogee under Kohl, who was particularly successful in centralising policy-making around himself and the Chancellery by managing ideas and acting as an animator in a way that transcended the constraints of semisovereignty (Dyson 1998).

The pattern of sectorisation and institutional pluralism qualified by a prominent role for the chancellor and the Chancellery has continued under the SPD-Green government. There has been some reshuffling of co-ordinator responsibilities with the Foreign and Finance ministries gaining at the expense of the Economics Ministry, but sectorisation continues to dominate.

In sum, both the constitutional patterns and the evaluation of Germany's institutions dealing with European policy indicate an increasingly complex system which is characterised by an ongoing trend towards institutional and political pluralism. This process goes hand in hand with a segmentation of policy-making. (Maurer 2003, p. 138)

This sectorisation is, to some extent, compensated by a growing role for the chancellor. Schröder is unusual not only in his use of chancellorial power in relation to historic decisions, but also in his use of it to defend specific German interests like the car industry. In the first legislative period, he had to share the role with a strong Foreign Minister. Chancellor Schröder had intended to centralise European policy-making in the Chancellery after the 2002 federal election, but the Greens' success in that election allowed Joschka Fischer to fight off this proposal.

Implementation

While the overall pattern of decision-making in European policy remained constant, after unity there was, for a time, a sharp decline in the implementation of European legislation. Prior to unity, the Federal Republic had thought itself a *Musterknabe*, or model student, in terms of implementation. This enviable record was explained as a product of congruence, i.e. familiarity with multi-level systems of governance and the integrationist stance of the political and bureaucratic elite (Bulmer and Paterson 1987, pp. 174–5). Post-unity, semisovereignty appeared to be creaking, and Germany plunged in the implementation tables. This was partially the result of a not unexpected time-lag as the governmental systems in the new east German *Länder* got up to speed. The sheer volume of the single market legislation, its potential impact on hitherto sheltered German interests and the difficulty of reconciling environmental legislation with the parlous state of the new *Länder* were other contributory factors. It has not, however, ushered in a vicious circle of decline. Not for the first time the semisovereign system, aided by the ending of the main phase of the single market programme, demonstrated a marked capacity for reinvention, and moved from a relatively low implementation score of 68 per cent in 1991 to a consistent score in the mid-90s from 1996 (Maurer 2003, pp. 136–8).

If the *Länder* element of semisovereignty has not impeded Germany's return to a *Musterknabe* role in implementation, the role of the Federal Constitutional Court remains a singular complication in this area. Although German case law, like other jurisdictions, has accepted the European Court of Justice's doctrine of direct effect, the Constitutional Court continues to assert its right to review EC law against the basic rights set out in the *Grundgesetz* (Maurer 2003, p. 137). This claim introduces an element of doubt about the validity of even an EC law that has been correctly implemented in Germany.

Consequences

The pre-sovereign years of the Federal Republic were to have important and enduring consequences for German European policy-making. Arguably the most important was the adoption of a strategy of Europeanisation (Garton-Ash 1993). This strategy was not a substitute, as is sometimes argued, for the pursuit of state interests, but was the only route for the promotion of the nascent state interests of the Federal Republic that held out any prospect of achieving a level of international actorness for the new semi-state and for lifting the discriminatory provisions under which the economy still laboured. This point comes out clearly in Peter Katzenstein's *Tamed Power: Germany in Europe* (1997a).

'Germany is an ardent champion of a Europeanisation process through which it seeks to promote German state interests' (Katzenstein 1997c, p. 5). If the most striking feature of the founding period was the narrowness of the choices permitted by the international system, the way in which Adenauer was able to construct a legitimising narrative and encourage the emergence of a 'remarkably internationalised state identity' (Katzenstein 1997c, p. 5) was the *sine qua non* for the emergence of a stable polity. The weakness of the existing state identity and the elusiveness of the goal of national unity provided a context in which Adenauer was able to shape the identity of the nascent semi-state around the Rhineland vision.

This contribution has argued that German European policy has remained integrationist and directed towards the exercise of 'power only in multilateral, institutionally mediated systems in Germany, the EU, the Atlantic Community, and broader international fora that soften sovereign power' (Katzenstein 1997c, p. 4). The semisovereign mode of German internal European policy-making is in a Katzenstinian sense only the other face of 'taming power'. In terms of the choice that seemed to be opening up at the end of the 1980s as the power resources of the

Federal Republic grew between the post-classical nation-state and its existing more post-Westphalian mode, the argument has been that the German choice continues to be post-Westphalian where the preferred instruments of power are of the 'ideational' and 'soft power' variety (Bulmer et al. 2000). That a fully sovereign Germany would cleave to multilateralism and the extension of 'associated sovereignty' was, however, unknowable as the European debate developed in the late 1980s. At that time, Bulmer and Paterson emphasised the constraining and disabling effects of semisovereignty and perhaps underemphasised the manner in which this internal 'semisovereignty' strengthened rather than weakened the realisation of German policy goals. There was an assumption that Germany was in this area at a disadvantage in relation to France and the United Kingdom.

In the past decade the analysis has become much more differentiated. Behind the changed view of the impact of the policy-making machinery, there have perhaps been two crucial influences. First, despite its 'superior' co-ordination mechanisms, the failure of UK European policy in the 1990s stands in contrast to the influential role UK European policy had played in the mid-1980s, when Bulmer and Paterson (1987) was being completed. Second, the 1990s saw a reframing of the European Union, and our argument had always been that German institutions worked best in terms of long-term strategy and historic decisions where a powerful chancellor could transcend the constraints of semisovereignty. At the level of ideas the key influence was Bulmer's reconceptualisation of power in terms of four faces. First is deliberate, or realist power, a familiar conception which would see German power 'as a function of the forceful articulation of interests, combined with valuable power resources for articulating leverage'. Second is institutional power, which, as a notion of 'soft' power, is rather more subtle; it suggests that Germany's particular domestic institutional configurations – political, legal, economic – might present it with inherent advantages in pursuing its external goals. The third face is unintentional power, which is precisely that: power which 'arises from the unintended consequences of domestic economic and political power', which is 'dispositional rather than the product of deliberate action' (Bulmer 1997, p. 15). A classic example is the unintentional, but for other states extremely unwelcome, 'export' of deflation by the *Bundesbank* in 1992 as it went about its rightful business of managing the German domestic economy.

Finally, Bulmer points to the notion of systemic empowerment, the 'dyadic', 'reverse image' of the other faces, predicated on the assumption that 'German power is not just the product of forces emanating from Germany' (whether deliberate, unintentional or institutional), but may also be generated by particular features of the international system(s) with which Germany interacts (Bulmer 1997).

The general picture that emerges from this reconceptualisation is of a Germany which may still choose to avoid an explicit solo leadership role but which was uniquely well equipped to shape and realise wider milieu goals (Bulmer et al. 2000). At the level of co-ordination mechanisms the 'weaknesses' of the German co-ordination model were now seen to confer at least one important advantage:

> The syndrome of sectoral conflict, weak coordination and the arrival at a German position only at a late stage in the negotiation, does, however, bring one benefit, the likely avoidance of isolation and the last minute achievement of trade offs which are less open to those members like the UK which enter negotiations with a clear and well coordinated set of priorities that may entail less flexibility. (Bulmer et al. 2000, p. 28)

Institutional pluralism, our original version of internal semisovereignty, was now seen to confer important advantages. The strength of these institutions, hitherto perceived mainly as an impediment to co-ordination, was now emphasised. In much of the research carried out by Bulmer, Jeffery and Paterson the focus was on institutional power and institutional export (Bulmer et al. 2000) where Germany supplies the domestic institutional models which shape the solutions adapted at a European level. Here the list is extensive, running from the impact of the *Bundesbank* on the governance model for the European Central Bank (ECB), the *Länder* at the Maastricht and Amsterdam IGCs, German firms and the standard setting in the single market and the institutional elements of the European visions of Fischer and Schröder, as well as of the CSU leader and chancellor-candidate in 2002, Edmund Stoiber.

Two Conceptions of Semisovereignty

In its original form, semisovereignty captured West German singularity and the peculiar combination of externally imposed and self-imposed constraints under which it operated. There was, however, another wider view of semisovereignty which equates it with pooled or shared sovereignty framed by interdependence rather than post-bellum constraints. This view saw Europe as being transformed into a post-Westphalian society of states with the Federal Republic as a harbinger of a post-national future. This was the Germany associated with 'reflexive multilateralism'. In this conception of shared sovereignty all states are semisovereign and sovereignty becomes a bargaining resource. The post-bellum situation of the pre-sovereign years had compelled West

German elites to view sovereignty not in absolute terms but as interdependence strengthened; other major west European states found their more absolute conceptions eroded and they too were more prepared to see sovereignty as a bargaining resource.

The close relationship between shared sovereignty and semisovereignty was commented on by Peter Katzenstein in *Tamed Power* where he coined the term 'associated sovereignty' to capture the sharing of sovereignty at the European level.

The hard edges of power relations between Germany and Europe are also softened by the overlap of competences that characterise the institutionalisation of power relations within each. Although distinctive, the institutional practices that mark the European polity resemble Germany's on this score. The system of governance in the European polity is based on what one might call 'associated sovereignty', pooled competencies in over-lapping domains of power and interest, which is characteristic also of Germany's 'semisovereign' state. (Katzenstein 1997c, p. 33)

These two conceptions of semisovereignty co-existed in the first three decades of the Federal Republic but by the late 1980s, as German power resources increased and European integration also deepened after the advent of the Single European Act (1986), the question of whether German power resources were pushing it onwards from semisovereignty to the position of a 'post-classical nation-state', a position where Britain and France defined normality, or whether the future was to be post-Westphalian, in which the Federal Republic would define normality in a Europe of associated sovereignty, appeared to be on the table. In the decade immediately after unity Germany's institutional framework and the core values of the political elite inhibited moves towards a post-classical nation-state model and the balance of adjustment was largely made by other member states who, by adopting Economic and Monetary Union, embraced associated semisovereignty.

Beyond Congruence

Both Peter Katzenstein and Bulmer et al. focused on the advantages of congruence and the degree to which Germany's semisovereign institutions and associated sovereignty were 'mutually supportive'. Indeed in our work (Bulmer et al. 2000) we emphasised the way in which the reframing of the EU in the 1990s allowed German institutions to be uploaded on to the European level. We paid less attention at the time to the downloading associated with Europeanisation. These two processes are not mutually exclusive. The *Bundesbank* model is uploaded in the form and operating rules of the European Central Bank and then downloaded in terms of the replacement of the *Bundesbank* in a number of key functions by the European Central Bank.

The mutually supportive character of the European and German institutional system has now become more contested as European integration deepens. In particular the continued liberalisation impetus of the European Union now begins to hurt (Menz 2003).

> While the EU was earlier seen to be an overwhelming positive force when it opened up other states markets – one of the foundations of German post war recovery and consolidation – it is much less welcome when it acts to open up protected German markets to limit the scope of the state economic intervention. (Jeffery and Paterson 2004, p. 66)

In fostering the move to replace the *Bundesbank* by the European Central Bank Germany demonstrated that a semisovereign institutional system nevertheless disposed of considerable power. Once the European Central Bank was established, however, its capacity to exercise power was much more constrained. Whilst this makes the ECB model much more attractive to Germany's fellow member states, the one size fits all character of the *Bundesbank* has been much less comfortable for the federal government than the one bank (*Bundesbank*) fits all formula of the earlier period. Those tensions have been heightened by the recession and the poor state of German public finances, which leaves Germany open to sanctions under the Stability and Growth Pact it insisted on inserting into the EMU system.

The indications are that the interaction between the two levels is likely to become even more contested (Jeffery and Paterson 2004). The resource crunch engendered by the continuing costs of German unity means that Germany has few financial resources available to facilitate the uploading of German preferences. At the same time, the European Union on to which these preferences are projected is becoming increasingly complex with, as enlargement progresses, a shrinking core and a growing periphery. Meanwhile, downloading will continue. When this is considered to be of help in its own efforts, for instance in the area of liberalisation, it will undoubtedly be welcomed by the federal government; on the other hand, in a domestic system still characterised by semisovereignty, this is also likely to cause tensions with some prominent actors at both the federal and *Länder* levels.

Conclusion

This chapter has explored various conceptions of semisovereignty and its implications for European policy-making. It dissents from the view that external semisovereignty was present from the creation of the Federal Republic, but stresses the role of internal semisovereignty in the pre-sovereign period. In the semisovereign years from the ending of the Occupation Statute until German unity, the Federal Republic could be characterised as internally and externally semisovereign. In these senses of semisovereignty, Germany remained a singular case. In the wider sense of semisovereignty, as part of associated sovereignty, Germany by 1989 was arguably not wholly singular, but a harbinger of a future post-Westphalian European state order. Its singularity resided more in the way its domestic political system mirrored this emerging order than in its perceptions of a future European institutional order that were shared by a number of other member states.

In a fully sovereign Germany, formal external sovereignty is regained, but semisovereignty persists in three senses. First, in relation to its external environment, especially the Franco-German relationship and in its acceptance of external constraints, Germany continues to behave in a semisovereign manner, although this contribution has questioned the permanency of such a stance. Second, internal semisovereignty has arguably increased as the European Union interacts more profoundly with the German polity. At one level this fosters semisovereignty by impelling the *Länder* to participate more fully in the framing of European policy decisions. Third, this increasing semisovereignty is counterbalanced by the 'downloading' associated with Europeanisation. This is most visibly the case in relationship to the management of monetary policy but it is also a feature in a much weaker sense in the ESDP.

Hans-Peter Schwarz (1994) wrote of Germany as a new 'central power'. The argument of this chapter has been that in a Europe characterised by associated sovereignty this role has been played by a Germany (Bulmer et al. 2000) that continues to be characterised by internal semisovereignty and institutional pluralism. It is the prime example of what Chayes and Chayes (1995) refer to as the 'the new sovereignty' in operating effectively through international regimes, in this case the European Union.

There are, however, two major question marks against Germany's continuing ability to fill this role. In fulfilling this role analysts have typically stressed German 'soft power' and 'ideational power'. Germany's 'soft power' resources have been gravely weakened by the continuing crisis in public finances. It is very difficult to see where the resources are going to come from for side-payment and shaping purposes in the future. On ideational power the emphasis was typically on the way in which Germany was able to come up with ideas, which placed it at the centre of constitutive bargains. The preconditions for the successful performance of this role were elite and permissive consensus, which allowed German policy-makers sufficient latitude. The elite consensus is now frayed but still more or less intact. Elite and mass views on European integration continue to diverge but the prevailing elite consensus and the relatively low salience of European issues has allowed continued elite autonomy. The question is, for how long (Niedermayer 2003)?

13　Conclusion: Semisovereignty in United Germany

Peter J. Katzenstein

What has been the effect of unification on Germany? Was it negligible, as Tocqueville famously argued for the effect of the French Revolution on post-revolutionary France? Was it transformative, as British Prime Minister Margaret Thatcher feared at the time, as she watched what to her looked like a new German colossus poised once again at the apex of the European hierarchy of status and power? Or was it moderate, as I argue here, conforming to a pattern of change that typifies Germany well before 1989? The chapters in this volume provide an updated answer that gives me a welcome opportunity to revisit a book that I wrote almost two decades ago: *Policy and Politics in West Germany: the Growth of a Semisovereign State* (Katzenstein 1987).

I adapted the book's title from one of the classics of American political science, E. E. Schattschneider's (1960) *The Semisovereign People*. Schattschneider offers a sophisticated analysis of American political institutions and organisations as a mobilisation of class bias. 'The flaw in the pluralist heaven is that the heavenly chorus sings with a strong upper-class accent' (Schattschneider 1960, p. 35). Analogously, Germany's semisovereign state creates a bias for incremental action. What Stanley Hoffmann (1968) argued for the United States' foreign policy in world affairs, holds also for Germany's semisovereign state in domestic politics. A semisovereign state is not free to act as it pleases. Semisovereignty is a condition of politics affecting many states and many political issues, in Europe and world-wide, before 11 September 2001 and after. Specific to Germany though it may have been in the second half of the twentieth century, we find its core components in other countries. Britain's quangos (quasi non-governmental organisations), for example, have an uncanny similarity to Germany's parapublic organisations. Yet, quangos are embedded in a winner-take-all, majoritarian system that concentrates much more power in the hands of the prime minister than has been true for any of Germany's chancellors serving since 1949.

In the aftermath of German unification, Germany's semisovereign state has had more critics than admirers. In the interest of breaking the logjams of reform, especially on pressing economic and social issues, and in the hope of overcoming stalemate or inertia, some pin their hopes on the promise of a state that regains its freedom for taking decisive actions in domestic affairs. I find this surprising. We have much evidence, starting with, but not restricted to, German history, that shows sovereign states often leaving heavy footprints. They do not know how to step nimbly, and often back misguided approaches to policy, not smart ones. Alternatively, admirers of Germany's co-ordinated market economy and generous social-welfare system have focused on the intricate linkages of different policy sectors that fit together in a distinctive way. In this perspective, Germany is advantaged by avoiding the drawbacks of unco-ordinated Anglo-Saxon market systems and of political systems exercising strong hierarchical control (Hall and Soskice 2001).

The arguments of both critics and admirers point to the political relevance and importance of an inquiry into the politics of semi-sovereignty in united Germany. In this chapter, I place the original book briefly in the intellectual and political context in which I wrote it (section 1), examine the impact of unification on economic and social performance and on politics (sections 2 and 3), based on the preceding chapters review the effects of Germany's unification on its parapublic institutions and different policy sectors (sections 4 and 5), and conclude (section 6) with some brief reflections on the role united Germany plays in an integrating Europe.

Intellectual Context

Although I joined the Cornell faculty as a specialist in central Europe – defined in upstate New York in the early 1970s as anything 'between Narvik and Sicily' – this was my first book on Germany, published fourteen years after I had received my Ph.D. The reason for the delay was simple. Written after the resignation of Chancellor Brandt, and organised around the conceptual apparatus of 'the national' and 'the social question' – categories of German area studies at the time – my first attempt at an academic paper was hopelessly vacuous. I never sent the paper out for review by an academic journal. Only a comparative perspective, I thought, would do justice to the subject. I learned about comparisons in two different fields of scholarship: in comparative and international political economy, and in comparative public policy.

Work in the field of comparative political economy suggested the usefulness of the concepts of state and society for inquiring empirically into different state–society relations (Katzenstein 1978). The concept of 'policy network' was a useful device for the classification of political systems. How autonomous was the state? What was the degree of differentiation of state and society? And how centralised or decentralised were different states and societies? These questions propelled analysis beyond the meta-theoretical debates then engaging liberals, Marxists, and a small group of 'statists' who formed the nucleus for the eventual emergence of a historically informed institutional style of analysis.

Besides the classification of entire political systems, the concept of policy network offered the field of comparative public-policy analysis a tool for producing more fine-grained cross-national analyses of the policy process. Germany's semisovereign state, I argued, was defined by the three nodes of its policy network: political parties and the system of coalition government; an interlocking system of territorial politics that connects different levels of government; and parapublic institutions, conceived as both actors and arenas, which facilitate the process of policy implementation.

I learned a great deal about comparative public policy in a seminar that I co-taught in the 1980s with my Cornell colleagues Douglas Ashford and T. J. Pempel. Eventually we decided to write up our lectures in the form of a book series that we co-edited, and that eventually comprised seven volumes (Ashford 1981, 1982; Pempel 1982; Heclo and Madsen 1987; Katzenstein 1987; Kelly 1987; Tuohy 1992). The series was predicated on the view that public policy was the most promising way of watching states in action. This use of policy material made the state the subject not only of theoretical interpretation, but also of sustained empirical analysis. In sharp contrast to the field of international relations, in this research programme, unlike governments, states are conceived as structures not actors. Each book followed the same format. An initial chapter framed the country argument. Six case studies presented some of the policy material that we had accumulated while teaching the seminar under four similar headings (context, agenda, process and consequences). A concluding chapter broadened out the argument about the intersection of policy and politics.

The West German volume had its blemishes. Since I had dedicated the book to my two daughters, I decided to adjust the text, where appropriate, so that the gender of the chancellor was female. This did not endear me to at least one careful reviewer. And since this was the new and democratic (West) Germany, I had requested that the publisher avoid the colour brown for the book's cover. The publisher settled on a bronze metallic colour that, under the artificial light of the Cornell library, looks like a perfect brown; but as Ringo Starr, drummer of the Beatles, sang famously, 'you can't judge a book by looking at its cover'.

Poached from the field of international relations and German foreign policy, the title of the book hit a responsive chord among many readers. Though foreign to the two superpowers and uncomfortable for the main regional powers in Europe, West Germany's semisovereignty epitomised a condition familiar to most small states in world politics. Filtering data through this conceptual lens thus promised insights that might travel and could be applied to the analysis of domestic politics, not only in Germany but perhaps elsewhere. That was the bet I placed with the book's title and the argument that followed from it.

Unification and Economic Performance

German unification was a short-term boost for economic growth and a long-term drag on the fiscal capacities of the state. Once touted as an economic model (Markovits 1982), Germany has become the sick man of Europe, marked by low growth, persistently high unemployment, and advanced symptoms of economic and social stagnation. Or so the editorial writers of the business press have insisted for over a decade. These writers tend to forget, however, that Germany's economic miracle occurred in the 1950s and was due to the effects of economic reconstruction after the destruction wrought by the Second World War. Since the early 1960s, Germany has been a low-growth economy. It is, thus, a bit of a mistake to insist that *Wirtschaftswunder* has recently been replaced by *Wirtschaftsblunder*. It is true that Germany has developed labour markets which have been increasingly sclerotic in the 1990s. But this recent evolution has occurred under conditions of relatively low economic growth rates since the 1960s.

The conventional framing of German politics a decade after unification compares the drag induced by the cost of rebuilding East Germany, approaching almost € 1 trillion in 2003, with the dynamic growth of America's 'new' economy. In this view, economic and social stagnation in Germany offers a sharp contrast to an American economy that has gone from strength to strength. At the outset of the second Bush administration, in the year 2005, the conventional wisdom looks dated – at least to this American observer. Not since the presidency of Herbert Hoover has the American economy produced such a dismal record on employment during an economic recovery. Unemployment hovers around the 5–6 per cent mark, a deceptively low figure, because a sharp increase in long-term employment has made many of the unemployed drop out of the statistics the government collects. The bursting of the stock market bubble has eliminated trillions of dollars in financial assets. As a percentage of GDP, the American fiscal deficit in a time of recovery now exceeds the 3 per cent limit that the EU has defined as acceptable in Europe in times of recession. Japan and China are bankrolling, for the time being, the US budget deficit with a combined holding of about $ 1.4 trillion (equivalent to about € 1.2 trillion in mid-2004). With annual borrowing in excess of $ 600 billion (€ 492 billion) in 2004, financial markets are nervously anticipating a further erosion in the value of the dollar and a rise in American interest rates. The first Bush administration's policies have led to a more than $ 5 trillion (€ 4.1 trillion) turn-around in the government's fiscal future in four years, with more trillions to be added if the second Bush administration proceeds with its plan for a partial privatisation of social security. A colossal $ 500 billion (€ 410 billion) deficit in the American trade balance underlines the insatiable appetite of the USA for foreign capital. Time will tell whether the economic policies of the Bush administration will risk the economic future only of America, or also of the international financial system.

Not a friend of continental welfare states in general and of the German social market economy in particular, *The Economist* (10 April 1999) put together the data for the decade of 1989–98. GDP growth per head, 'the single best measure of economic performance', was just under 2 per cent for Germany, more than the 1.6 per cent rate for both Japan and the United States. Allowing for the economic boost unification brought about brings the German figure roughly in line with those for the USA and Japan. Since, however, the Japanese and American figures both reflect the positive economic effects of a brief speculative binge in the stock market, perhaps the original comparison is valid. The widely touted 'new economy' in the USA did not outperform the sclerotic German one in the 1990s: German productivity growth per worker increased three times faster than the US rate during the first half of the 1990s, while the US rate was leading the German one by a factor of two during the second half. However, in an era of global outsourcing the American economy appears to begin to imitate the European experience of weak job growth in periods of economic recovery, as has been true for the 2001–4 recovery. Economic pundits on both sides of the Atlantic may have to reconsider some of their overblown claims about the unquestioned superiority of the American economy.

Furthermore, often touted as an economic model to a moribund continent, the British economy grew in the 1990s at a lower rate than both Germany and France and has a higher GDP per capita largely because of the effects of unification. Only the unemployment figures support the conventional wisdom, with US rates well below German ones. But even here, the picture is less clear. The concept of the 'working poor' does not exist in Germany where, in contrast to the USA, gainful employment puts workers' earnings well above the poverty line. Overall, 'the notion that the American economy stands on top of the world is questionable', concludes *The Economist* in (10 April 1999), when America's economic fortunes were at their best. Five years later, that claim appears even more dubious, as US profit, productivity and industrial production numbers for the boom years 1999–2001 have been revised sharply downward (Norris 2001). Casual observation of everyday life in Germany supports the conclusion of *The Economist*. Germany's economic performance has declined, but apparently not to a level that makes the German social and political systems internationally uncompetitive, not to say unviable.

How do we square the analysis of *The Economist* with the arguments that Green and Paterson marshal in chapter 1 of this volume about Germany's weak economic performance? One contextual factor matters more than any other: national unification. A detailed study of the EU has been able to separate out the economic drag that unification imposed on the German economy between 1996 and 2000 (Directorate General for Economic and Financial Affairs 2002). One-third of the relative lag in German economic growth, or about 0.3 per cent, is a result of the 4 per cent of GDP, or about € 60 billion, that Germany transfers annually in the form of direct economic assistance to eastern Germany. These transfer payments have increased budget deficits, taxes and social-security contributions, thus dampening private investment and consumption. Another 0.3 per cent of foregone growth is owing to the rigidities in German labour markets, accentuated by the financing of the economic transfers to eastern Germany. The final 0.3 per cent of growth foregone is because of the initial overexpansion and subsequent sharp contraction in the eastern Germany construction industry in the wake of unification. *The Economist* (19 June 2004) argues that Germany's substandard economic performance is the main reason why, between 1994 and 2003, the Euro area's 1.8 per cent growth rate in GDP per capita lagged behind the USA by 0.3 per cent; without Germany, the two growth rates are identical. And with Germany the growth in labour productivity in the Euro area exceeds slightly that of the USA if proper indicators are chosen for comparison. Since 1997, even if we include Germany with its substandard employment record, more jobs have been created in the Euro area than in the USA; total employment has risen by 8 per cent compared with 6 per cent in the USA.

Demography and growth are closely intertwined. The sharp influx of foreigners into Germany came to an abrupt halt in the mid-1990s, slowing construction and consumption. Demography and migration, are issues of central importance to the long-term viability of the German welfare state and society. The rapid ageing of German society will make unsustainable the welfare programmes that Germany has legislated since the adoption of its 1957 pension reform, in a decade of large immigration from East Germany, which adjusted pensions to inflation and thus greatly reduced poverty among retired workers. Only a growing workforce of foreigners will be able to finance Germany's generous welfare state. As Simon Green notes in chapter 9 of this volume, one study by the United Nations estimates that Germany would need to bring in half a million migrant workers each year to maintain the size of its working population. In comparison, economic growth in the USA between 1980 and 2000 was a result substantially of a 50 per cent increase in its labour force. Between 1996 and 2001, foreign-born workers accounted for 89 per cent of the growth in the American workforce and 53 per cent of the growth of workers with doctoral or professional degrees. In the absence of any change in policy, declining fertility rates, a levelling of women's participation in the workforce, and increasing retirement rates of the baby boomers will in the next two decades cut one-third off the American rate of economic growth (Altman 2002). Germany is experiencing now what America may go through in a few decades. Unemployment, under-employment and the grey economy pose substantial problems that Germany's unification has accentuated. The necessity of importing foreign workers to compensate for the ageing of German society thus poses a central question: faced with the trade-off between welfare and identity, how will Germany choose?

Unification and Politics

The end of the Cold War and the disintegration of the Soviet Union dramatically reorganised European and international politics. Change led to the political implosion of Italy as one member of the erstwhile Axis. Italian domestic politics was intimately connected to the central ideological cleavage of the Cold War. When that cleavage vanished, the magistrates succeeded with their anti-corruption drive to bring down the entire political regime. In the second member of the old Axis, Japan, the 1990s brought about a less dramatic, but still far-reaching, reorganisation of the political system and great instabilities in Japan's financial markets. National unification showed that Germany was arguably more directly affected by the end of the Cold War than was either Italy or Japan. The German state regained full sovereignty in international affairs. Yet in its domestic politics, Germany continued to be marked by incremental change as the defining feature of semisovereignty (Schmidt 2003; Czada and Wollmann 2000).

Unification raises the interesting question of whether Germany's semisovereign state is at a basic level still the same it was two decades ago. How should we think about 'sameness' and difference over time? Germany experienced unification, not reunification, in the borders of 1937. It did not experience a restoration to a pre-existing self that had been divided during the Cold War. Yet, in the process of unification, Germany became larger in terms of land mass and population, raising fears among some foreign observers still thinking in the tradition of nineteenth-century *Realpolitik*. Yet Germany also became poorer, statistically, and, arguably, weaker in economic terms. How, then, do we think about self and other, strength and weakness at this juncture in German history?

Since the early 1980s, France and Poland, to name two of Germany's most important neighbours, have witnessed monumental political change. In the case of Poland, the collapse of Communism and European Union accession have had profound influences on every aspect of that country's political, social and economic life. And, as Vivien Schmidt (2002) argues, since the famous U-turn in its economic policy in the early 1980s, France has witnessed by far the greatest amount of change as compared to Britain and Germany. Yet on matters of political and social affairs, despite all the changes they have experienced, Poland and France are arguably still very similar to what they were before. In the language of general systems theory, this is called the super-additivity of parts. Systems are defined by the innumerable and complex interactions between their various components rather than by their sum. Put briefly, German unification has not made Germany any less German. While affecting the policy process in different sectors, it has not altered the general institutional make-up of Germany's semisovereign state. In the absence of a discernible, alternative pattern shaping politics and policy, as before 1989, semisovereignty continues to define the politics of policy in the new Germany.

This continuity is at first glance baffling. German unification should have affected German national politics more deeply than Italy's or Japan's. It did not, for reasons I tried to understand in a book published in 1989 with the subtitle *Toward the Third Republic* (Katzenstein 1989, pp. 307–9). Although that book's argument was informed by the thesis of Germany's semisovereign state, it focused especially on the issue of change. At the end of a decade marked by profound new currents in international politics, new social movements in national politics, and new production technologies in industrial plants, German politics was marked by a remarkable convergence between experimentation and continuity. Different sectors and firms in West Germany's economy were experimenting with new practices to respond to new challenges that confronted them both at home and abroad. And what I called West Germany's emerging Third Republic was tied to its predecessors by a remarkable degree of institutional and political continuity in national politics. The big change (*Die Wende*) that Chancellor Helmut Kohl had invoked at the beginning of his long tenure in the early 1980s never materialised. The main empirical finding of the 1989 book pointed to the convergence of flexibility with stability. Innumerable small changes were transforming politics, economy and society in a pattern that was tending towards increasing decentralisation in different industrial sectors. With change occurring within institutions rather than outside of them, and in small rather than large doses, it was easy then, as it is now, to overlook the cumulative impact that many unsynchronised small-scale changes have over time.

This is not to argue that small-scale change is the only pattern that Germany's semisovereign state has confronted and can master. The unification process, and the forceful exercise of the chancellor's leadership in a time of crisis, finds its analogue in the early years of the Bonn Republic when Konrad Adenauer monopolised foreign policy. In 1989–90, German politics resembled the chancellor-democracy of the early 1950s more than the semisovereign state that gradually evolved from it. In the unification process, Chancellor Kohl dictated the terms of policy. And those terms externalised for electoral reasons the costs of unity to the welfare state. Germans may have been ready for sweat, blood and tears, as Helmut Schmidt and the members of the *Aufbaugeneration*, or rebuilding generation, believed, and as Oskar Lafontaine, the SPD chancellor-candidate insisted in his unsuccessful electoral campaign in 1990. But the man who succeeded in making unification his greatest political triumph thought otherwise. He sensed that the Germany of 1990 was not the Germany of the early 1950s. Reconstruction after the Second World War occurred when Germans did not yet have a fully developed national consciousness of individual entitlement. Kohl was the last chancellor with an active memory of the Second World War; the last member of the *Bundestag* to have seen active service in the war retired in 1998. A generational break had been completed. A national sense of individual entitlement required, Chancellor Kohl was convinced, that a great national task be mastered without a great national effort requiring individual sacrifice. As was true of the United States after 9/11 and in the run-up to the Iraq war, spending and borrowing, not saving and sacrificing, became acts of patriotism. In the USA, patriotic practice was privatised as consumers went shopping in malls. In Germany, patriotic practice occurred in the public sector, most notably in the unflinching transfer of capital from west to east, under the auspices of a semisovereign state, totalling about 5 per cent of GDP year in and year out (V. Schmidt 2002, p. 239).

In a time of both opportunity and crisis, domestically unconstrained political leadership in the system of chancellor-democracy, not semisovereignty, dictated the course of unification – and most of the events that followed from it. A more cautious and incremental approach simply was not an option. Potential political instabilities in the Soviet Union made the acceleration of the unification process highly advisable, upsetting a ten-year timetable Kohl had envisaged as late as January 1990. The exercise of decisive political leadership and radical political change unfamiliar to Germany's semisovereign state had many costs. These costs were not paid in international politics, as, for example, Prime Minister Margaret Thatcher had feared. They were paid in domestic politics. At the time, many Germans were convinced that they would easily solve the follow-on problems to unification. My incredulity to the contrary notwithstanding, at the time of unification I was told by self-confident Germans more than once that the aftermath of unification would be child's play ('*das schaffen wir lässig, mit Links*'). Indeed the follow-on problems were mastered in a manner that solved the problem of the day without worrying about the problem it would create for the next week, month, year or decade. From the vantage point of American politics in 2005, we may call this a premature Americanisation of German politics. Germany's chancellor-democracy superseded semisovereignty only for a short time. But the pattern it established has persisted in important spheres of public life. Chancellor Kohl externalised the costs of unification to inflationary growth first, and the social-security budget and labour-market institutions later. Watching unconstrained power prevail, other actors followed suit. The consequence was to burden, and at times overburden, the capacities of Germany's semisovereign state.

The result of this process of externalisation, as Wade Jacoby argues in chapter 2 of this volume, has changed the balance of power between state and society in Germany. In Jacoby's words, the federal government has become a 'problem solver of last resort' (p. 22). The growing importance of the state was not the only development. Important interest groups have become more heterogeneous and relatively smaller when compared with the social sector they seek to organise or represent. This development has stopped far short of a wholesale reorganisation of Germany's system of federalism as some had advocated, or feared, in the early 1990s. And it did not lead to a dramatic transformation of the groups representing business and labour. But in a decade in which the deregulation and privatisation movement was weakening the state and strengthening society in many other countries, the effect of unification was to move Germany in a different direction.

Whether Germany's exceptional move has transformed a semisovereign state to a stalemate society may become more evident in the next decade. Political desperation of the government and political frustration of the opposition could easily generate policies, emanating either from the centre-left or the centre-right, that aim at re-establishing a new balance between state and society by strengthening state power, creating more economic and social spaces free from regulation, or refurbishing the institutional mechanisms of semisovereignty. Such a change would not be a singular event in European politics. It is easy to forget that only fifteen years separate the 'Dutch disease' of the early 1980s from the 'Dutch miracle' of the mid-1990s.

In the case of Europe's leading economic power, undue optimism is, however, unwarranted. The margin of error for small states is smaller than for large ones. Unification may have made Germany larger in some sense other than the 5 to 10 per cent increase in its economic potential or the 25 per cent increase in its territory and population. Compared with the *Reichstag* building, which is now home to the *Bundestag*, opposite it, the new Federal Chancellery in central Berlin looks oversized. At a cost of € 238 million, it is huge, five times the size of the White House, for example, and would look even more imposing if one added the two subterranean levels to the nine storeys of the central building. The political costs that accompany an increase in size, power and sense of self often remain unnoticed. They are considerable in a world where most countries are shrinking in relative size, and in the effect they have on the outcomes that affect them.

Federalism, Parapublic Institutions and Political Parties

Germany's semisovereign state is marked by a specific set of institutional arrangements: federalism, parapublic institutions and political parties. They provide for participation and expertise in a setting of relative political autonomy. These three nodes in Germany's semisovereign state act as political shock absorbers. They entangle deeply with one another all major political actors: federal institutional, social groups and party political. Mutual entanglement creates many veto points. And this makes incrementalism a normal policy choice and a natural policy outcome.

Federalism

Unification has affected, more or less deeply, all three nodes of the German policy network. In chapter 4 of this volume, Charlie Jeffery argues that, on the basis of Germany's federal system, unification has made the German state more centralised and German society less homogeneous. High unemployment rates and a collective sense of difference rooted in the GDR past have created a new space for a distinctive territorial politics in the five new states (*Bundesländer*). That space is more egalitarian in aspiration and more statist in form. Additionally, the costs of unification have put severe pressures on the politics of revenue sharing that have accentuated the political conflicts between donor and recipient states. Unification made Germany both bigger and poorer. The financial obligations of richer states like Bavaria increased, while solidarity with the poorer states in the east declined. As Wade Jacoby demonstrates in chapter 2 of this volume, after unification, without reform, transfer payments from the richer states in the west to the poorer states in the east would have increased by a factor of six, to about DM 20 billion (€ 10.2 billion) per year. This did not happen. Instead, in 1995 the federal government increased its annual contribution by a factor of five to about DM 25 billion (€ 12.8 billion). The renegotiation of this system for the years 2001–19 has made the annual costs for the federal government even more onerous.

A more heterogeneous Germany is a rupture with the recent history of the Federal Republic, not with the longer run of German history or with the territorial politics in other European states. Germany's federal system has been altered significantly by the growing financial burden that the federal government has assumed in the wake of unification; it has not been transformed. Arguments favouring solidarity, consensus and the desirability of common living standards throughout Germany are challenged by those favouring self-reliance, autonomy and a differentiation of living standards. Thus, co-operative federalism is challenged by competitive federalism. Lively debate and disagreements have not generated major institutional change in Germany's institution of federalism. But the dynamics of decision-making in existing federal institutions have evolved. The growing financial clout of the federal government gives it more political room to out-manoeuvre the opposition in the *Bundesrat*, illustrated for example by Chancellor Schröder's tactics to get his 2000 tax reform package adopted. Accompanied by an increase in the policy autonomy of the *Länder* in areas such as regional policy, such change, writes Charlie Jeffery in chapter 4 (p. 93), will 'unlock the federal system and rematch its operation to the now more decentralised society in which it is embedded . . . the new, post-unity federal system is gradually becoming more appropriate to the more decentralised society of post-unification Germany'.

Parapublic Institutions

Parapublic institutions are the second of the three institutional nodes of Germany's semisovereign state. In chapter 5 of this volume, Andreas Busch focuses attention on the history of three key institutions in the 1990s that appeared to rival the pre-eminence of the German state. The German *Bundesbank* had for decades been viewed by many as a shadow government (*Nebenregierung West*). And the German privatisation agency, the *Treuhandanstalt* (THA), was at the outset of the 1990s the shadow government in the east (*Nebenregierung Ost*). In the course of the 1990s, for different reasons, both institutions disappeared. One was transformed into a powerful European institution; the other was dissolved into the capitalist system that took hold in the former GDR. Finally, the Federal Employment Office (*Bundesanstalt für Arbeit*, BA) has become the institutional site where an important part of the German welfare state is managed and where the government has gone to fund a substantial portion of the costs of unification.

Before 1989, the *Bundesbank* had established a position of central importance in German and European politics. Unification set the stage for two momentous defeats of the *Bundesbank* at the hands of the federal government. In the year of unification, Chancellor Kohl followed political rather than economic imperatives. The offer of a currency union between East and West Germany in February 1990, and the parity conversion of the East German mark into the Deutschmark later that spring, were decisions taken against the express advice of *Bundesbank* president Karl-Otto Pöhl. Furthermore, the deep suspicions the *Bundesbank* harboured against a Economic and Monetary Union (EMU) did not stop the signing and ratification of the Maastricht Treaty in 1991 and the establishment of the European Central Bank (ECB) and EMU by the end of the decade. While the *Bundesbank*'s role in German politics has been diminished greatly, the imprint it has left on the European Central Bank, now also headquartered in Frankfurt am Main, is so great that one might well regard it as establishing at the European level a core ingredient of the institutional structure of the semisovereign German state.

In the GDR, the THA was widely perceived by East Germans to be the successor to the Socialist Unity Party (SED) and a manifestation of centralised state power. Yet centralisation proved to be no more than a façade that concealed another of Germany's parapublic institutions. In its institutional set-up, the THA was open to the representation of all of Germany's most important political actors on its supervisory and executive boards. Furthermore, in less than five years, it had sold or liquidated virtually all of East Germany's 270 *Kombinate* – about 12,000 firms employing, at one time, about half of the East German workforce – eliminating about 3 million jobs in the process and accumulating a deficit of about DM 275 billion (€ 140 billion). In a complicated process of land privatisation, the THA, with the assistance of the European Union (EU), created a distribution of land ownership far more concentrated and inegalitarian than the system that had prevailed in nineteenth-century Prussia. With a staff of less than 5,000, at the peak of its operation the THA was doing more mergers and acquisitions than had ever been done by any private investment bank in London or New York. As was true of the *Bundesbank*, the THA spanned the public and the private sectors, was largely autonomous, run by experts, and broadly representative of all the major actors in German politics. A quintessential parapublic institution, the *Treuhandanstalt* nonetheless created far-reaching structural rather than incremental policy change.

The transformation in the position of the *Bundesbank* and the liquidation of the THA have eliminated potential rivals that might have counteracted the increasing power of the federal government. The same is not true of a third parapublic institution. After unification, the federal government used the wage and salary earners' contributions to the BA to plug large holes in the federal budget and in the pension system rather than financing them through further increases in general taxes. After a major scandal about the falsification of labour-market statistics, the shake-up of the BA began in 2002. With its huge staff and budget, the BA has been an important target of the recommendations for reform by the Hartz Commission. As Andreas Busch and Wolfgang Streeck argue in chapters 5 and 7 of this volume respectively, it is conceivable that the federal government will eventually assume a permanently enhanced role in Germany's revamped labour-market institutions. For the time being, the hand of the federal government has arguably been strengthened in the ongoing process of institutional reform, as the influence of employers and unions has declined. But it is not clear how and whether a change of the rules at the top will change the way sectoral self-government will work at the local level.

The Party System

The party system is the third nodal point in Germany's system of para-public institutions. Building on V. O. Key's classical typology, Thomas Saalfeld in chapter 3 of this volume argues that the shock of unification and long-term social changes have altered parties-in-the-electorate and parties-as-organisations much more than parties-in-government. There is little evidence at the level of government that the party system has fractionalised significantly, despite the addition of the PDS as a significant electoral factor in the five eastern *Bundesländer*, and despite the broadening in the number of different political coalitions that are now possible in German politics. Significantly, the presence of the PDS in various coalition governments in the eastern states has had no noticeable effect either on political conflicts within the *Bundesrat* or on conflicts between *Bundesrat* and *Bundestag*. This is not to deny that unification has accelerated or reinforced some important political changes. Saalfeld's analysis underlines two of them: the increase in partisan dealignment and electoral volatility, especially in eastern Germany, creates a context for policy-making that is less predictable. And the lack of a mass membership basis for either CDU or SPD in the east has accelerated a Germany-wide trend towards the creation of party organisations as professionalised electoral machines. The number of partisan veto players and the distance between them has remained largely unchanged since the mid-1980s. And the declining cohesiveness of parties represented in the *Bundesrat* has given the federal government new instruments for getting its way, quite apart from its increased power in setting the country's political agenda. Saalfeld concludes that despite some notable changes in political context, the dynamics of electoral politics in united Germany largely continue to favour incremental political adjustments and a consensual style of policy-making.

Semisovereign politics does not preclude the possibility of large-scale institutional change and far-reaching political initiatives. Embedded as he is in a semisovereign state, the German chancellor can at times take dramatic action with far-reaching consequences in response to the pressures of the international system. Adenauer's decisive actions in the 1950s aimed at Germany's policy of western integration although it required a programme of rearmament deeply opposed by the majority of the population. Kohl's decision to heed the political imperatives of the policy of unification, despite its enormous economic costs, and his decision to relinquish national control over the Deutschmark, against the express wishes of the population, provide a second example of far-reaching political initiatives. And in domestic politics the possibility for grand coalitions, general as in the mid-1960s, or sectoralised for particularly urgent policy problems, such as in health, also can temporarily overrule what is the norm in the politics of Germany's foreign and domestic policy: incremental adjustment by a semisovereign state.

Policy Sectors

Public policies provide a mirror that permits us to analyse Germany's semisovereign state in action. Some core economic and social policy sectors have been affected greatly by unification and the process by which the costs of unification have been externalised: first by a chancellor in a moment of crisis politics, and subsequently by corporate actors who refused to internalise the costs of unilateral government action. This is not to deny the importance of other changes, both in the nature of German society and in the European context in which Germany operates. In other policy sectors, in contrast, policy-making in united Germany has changed less.

High-change Sectors

For historical reasons, economic policy is Germany's pre-eminent policy sector. The *Fourth and Richest Reich* (Hartrich 1980) was a spectre that haunted many, especially in Britain, who dreaded the prospect of a united, powerful Germany dominating Europe half a century after unconditional surrender in 1945. Some developments right after unification gave credence to this view. In response to the chancellor's inflationary electoral promises, for example, the *Bundesbank* externalised the costs of its counter-cyclical deflationary policy to the rest of Europe. Yet, as Kenneth Dyson argues in chapter 6, such fears were misplaced for one simple reason. They disregarded the decline in the relative success of the German economy, the rise of contesting discourse coalitions, and the importance of the European Union. The persistence of unemployment in particular opened a political space for domestic political debates about Germany's economic policies. Furthermore, the Europeanisation of Germany's monetary policy and a downgrading in the position of the *Bundesbank* have been of decisive importance for Germany and Europe in the 1990s. As a result, the *Bundesbank* has centralised its operation in Germany in a sharply reduced sphere of policy-making, eliminating the remaining vestiges of co-operative federalism in monetary policy.

The Europeanisation of Germany's economic policy-making has altered many facets of its economic policy: compliance, at times reluctant, with the policies of the European Central Bank (ECB); 'hard European co-ordination' in noisy negotiations over fiscal policy (particularly when Germany began to exceed, as it did in 2002, the limits it helped impose on budget deficits in the mid-1990s); and 'soft European co-ordination' and policy imitation of successful reforms in other states, such as the Netherlands and Denmark, on questions of employment policy and structural reform. All of these are part of a new, Europeanised pattern of economic policy-making. But there are other issues in which the gears of national and European economic policy-making mesh more noisily, such as Germany's competition policy, and the persistent closure of its banking and energy markets. The irony is that the EMU and the Stability and Growth Pact (1997) have both contributed substantially to the weakening of the German government's control over economic policy, a Europe-wide development that Germany, more than any other country, helped bring about. Erosion of national control over economic policy has thus gone hand in hand with domestic contestation over policy and an erosion in the self-confidence that Germany's approach to economic policy management is still a model for the rest of Europe.

The economic difficulties that followed unification, Wolfgang Streeck argues in chapter 7, are shown even more clearly in Germany's failing labour-market policies. In a game of political 'hot potato', all of the major interest groups refused to absorb the different kinds of costs that accrued to each of them as a result of unification. The government externalised the costs of unification to the social-security budget, which became the financial reserve for funding the growing costs of labour-market policies. The BA was permitted to fund very large job-creation schemes in eastern Germany with unemployment and social-security contributions. This policy helped contain the social consequences of mass unemployment in the east, brought about by the chancellor's politically common-sensical but economically non-sensical decisions on currency union and currency conversion rates, which resulted in an overnight four-fold increase in the value of the East German mark and the elimination of about three million jobs. Unions responded quickly. They externalised the cost of organising eastern Germany's workers to the public-sector by insisting, in the interest of organisational unity and union solidarity, on wage parity between west and east, despite persistent, sharp differences in productivity. Big business also externalised its costs to smaller firms and the German economy at large, by colluding with works councils at the plant level, thus exploiting hidden productivity reserves through early retirement and flexible working-time arrangements and, if needed, through shifting production out of Germany.

Small business was left with little else but trying to weaken the collective bargaining system, a core feature of Germany's institutional economy, since for small business it no longer held forth much promise. In eastern Germany, only about one-fifth of manufacturing firms are members of the employers' association engaged in collective bargaining. Unions lost, while works councils gained power, signalling a continuation of a decentralisation trend that had already been evident in the 1980s. The system of industry-wide bargaining eroded, as did the coverage of industry-wide wage contracts. Yet the system did not lose all of its stabilisers. In the late 1990s, the moderation of union demands in collective bargaining was motivated by the attempt to mollify smaller firms and to restabilise the entire collective bargaining system. And the collapse of a more aggressive union approach to collective bargaining in 2003 happened as the government and public opinion turned against the metal workers' union, IG Metall. A leadership struggle in the union ended in a victory for the more militant faction under Jürgen Peters. The consequences of these developments for Germany's system of industrial relations are likely to shift the balance from institutional to political elements.

Streeck's pessimistic account focuses attention on Chancellor Schröder's personalistic and opportunistic approach to labour-market reform issues after the 1998 election. Incrementalism, he argues, has led to deadlock. When he had the opportunity to do so during his first term, Chancellor Schröder did not address the institutional incapacities and blockages in labour-market policies. After a narrow election victory in 2002, the new government concentrated economic power in the hands of one economics and labour 'superministry' (formerly separate ministries), headed by Wolfgang Clement, a member of the reformist wing of the SPD. A rapid erosion of the public's confidence in the new government, prompted by tax increases that violated electoral promises, made Clement's job even more difficult. His task is to pressure Germany's powerful unions to accept more reforms, on questions of labour markets and pensions among others, than they have tolerated since 1997. Whatever the ultimate outcome of this economic reform initiative, the government is clearly seeking to escape from its labour-market and economic policy dilemmas through a centralisation of power, in anticipation of a looming fight pitting the SPD against some of the most powerful unions.

In his analysis of welfare-state policies in chapter 8 of this volume, Roland Czada concurs with this view. German unification and the rise in unemployment that came with it have greatly accelerated the inherent pressures that long-term demographic changes are putting on

Germany's welfare state. Long-term unemployment has been addressed through early retirement policies that have stretched the social-security system, yielding painful benefit cuts in the short term and a tentative move towards a partial reliance on market principles in the long term. By 2003, the adoption of a comprehensive social-policy reform package, Agenda 2010, illustrated that government, business and unions had agreed that welfare-state reform was a top priority if Germany's economy was to regain a more dynamic labour market and higher economic growth rates. But the policy process leading to reform has become less corporatist, less concerted and less consensual in the area of labour-market reform. In the face of benefit cutbacks, partisan conflict in pension policy has increased, together with a tendency towards policy stalemate, greater reliance on technocratic advisory commissions, issue-specific, volatile partisan coalitions, and more reliance on market principles. In sum, pressing political reforms of the welfare state have diminished its corporatist content while at the same time increasing elements of direct state intervention as well as market competition.

Low-change Sectors

The externalisation of costs that the government and the most important corporate actors adopted in response to unification has undermined and altered semisovereignty without eliminating it. These conditions do not, however, characterise all policy sectors. Health and environmental policies were included in the original analysis of Germany's semisovereign state (Katzenstein 1987, pp. 31–3) only as minor cases which illustrated the policy consequences of the interaction between a decentralised state and a centralised society. Both policy sectors continue to display important aspects of a semisovereign state. Immigration and administrative reform policies are a second pair of policy cases illustrating the different dynamics of Germany's semisovereign state, reflecting enormous social change on the one hand and adherence to the historical legacy of Germany's statist tradition on the other.

In chapter 8, Roland Czada writes that health policy 'still constitutes a classic example of semisovereignty' (p. 182). Since both federal and state governments have legislative authority, the *Bundesrat* is a central actor along with a large number of organisations representing health-care providers, the insured, the pharmaceutical sector, producers, consumers, and their respective peak associations. Policy is characterised by an incremental muddling-through process, combined with occasional inter-party compromises seeking to contain the explosion of health-care costs. Radical policy proposals are made, Czada concludes, yet 'the chances for a fundamental systemic change are still small' (p. 184).

After a burst of innovation in the 1970s and 1980s, argues Charles Lees in chapter 10, Germany's environmental policy may be suffering from the law of diminishing returns, thus showcasing incremental policy-making in a semisovereign state. In the 1970s and 1980s, grass-roots mobilisation, institutional innovations and legislative initiatives had made Germany Europe's environmental leader. Supported by technical expertise, the interaction between state and society created political conditions that favoured impressive policy innovation. Energised by party competition for a new constituency of the German electorate, policy innovation did not yield to inertia or gridlock. Yet, on this issue, as Germany's exit from the nuclear power industry and the contested issue of an eco-tax illustrate, the logic of semisovereignty and policy incrementalism were also evident in a policy network characterised by limited access and a technocratic mode of operation. And as the policy leadership of the government and citizen activism has receded over time, in the future policy change in this area is likely to be incremental rather than rapid.

Immigration is perhaps the most important long-term policy issue facing Germany. Simon Green argues in chapter 9 of this volume that the problems associated with this policy sector have broadened further to incorporate, beyond issues of economics and labour markets, asylum, social integration and political citizenship. A multi-ethnic and multi-cultural society poses profound problems to the self-conceptions of many Germans, in particular on the conservative side of the political spectrum. The CDU/CSU in particular continues to refuse to acknowledge publicly an undeniable social reality: Germany has become a country of immigration. Unification brought a large influx of ethnic Germans from the east who were automatically granted all the benefits of the social-welfare system. This illustrates the continuing powerful grip the concept of ethnic identity holds over Germany. German social policy thus finds itself between a rock and a hard place. Pressing are the requirements for a skilled labour force in an economy more open to international competition than that of any other industrial state of comparable size. And so are the requirements for a workforce sufficiently expansive to support an ageing society. One demographic estimate is that Germany will require about half a million migrants annually to keep the size of its population constant. Instead, a government commission in summer 2001 recommended a figure of just 40,000 new, highly skilled labour migrants per year, and ultimately this quota was scrapped altogether in the new immigration law. The requirements of funding the welfare state in the long term clash with short-term considerations of cost (in admitting political asylum seekers) and, since 9/11, of state security. Partisan conflict over the issue continues to be great and policy change has remained incremental, not because of the depoliticisation of a politics organised around parapublic institutions, but due to its opposite: partisan polarisation in the public sphere, reflecting a deeply divided polity over the concept and the content of Germany's collective identity.

Questions of administrative reform, argues Klaus Goetz in chapter 11, illustrate a change in the issues that are being addressed rather than in the political logic of the semisovereign state. The nature of state power continues to be central to any interpretation of German politics – from Chancellor Kohl's 'lean' to Chancellor Schröder's 'active' state. Furthermore, privatisation, internal reorganisations stressing the public 'service' rendered by the modern state, and moves to 'co-operative administration' engaging civil society have all tended to move Germany towards public management and public–private partnerships and away from a long-standing tradition that made the state appear to operate 'above' civil society. This is reflected in the increasing assertion of power by the Chancellery over the powers of the ministries, and in the rising power of the political co-ordination units subordinated to the ministries' political leadership at the expense of the ministries' line units. The state is less able than before to resist changes that originate from other parts of the polity or from Germany's international environment. Squeezed between civil society and the market and exposed more directly to democratic political forces, Germany's semisovereign state has been able to adapt to the enormous problems that national unification posed. Its essential characteristics survived a process of large-scale institutional transfer in which the state structure of the West German state was transplanted to the east (Lehmbruch 1998). In a new and more politicised environment, Germany's semisovereign state thus continues to function quite smoothly.

Summary

In his play *The Visit*, Swiss playwright Friedrich Dürrenmatt (1956) created the character of an old woman who, at the end of her life, returns, now very wealthy, to a poor village to exact revenge from a lover who had once spurned her in her youth. The old woman displays a remarkable combination of mechanical contraptions that substitute for the failing parts of her rotting body. What is unchanged is the authenticity of her memory and the white heat of her love-turned-hate that make the lady in old age the same person she was in her youth.

Dürrenmatt's literary vision extends to the German body politic. Each of the six policy case studies alerts us to numerous changes, some ephemeral and others consequential, in the contraptions of politics and policy. In the high-change policy sectors, the impact of national unification and a different European and global context have changed the character of incrementalism as semisovereignty has yielded significant ground to both more state intervention and greater market pressures. Partisan conflict, political stalemate and, more recently, major reform efforts – for example, on questions of labour markets, economic policy-making and social policy – for the time being leave open the question of whether we are witnessing a recalibration or a dismantling of the structure of Germany's semisovereign state. In contrast, in low-change sectors, the authenticity of the semisovereign state is readily confirmed. Viewed across both high-change and low-change sectors, 'the political institutions in present day Germany', writes Manfred Schmidt (2003, p. 238), 'allow for a moderately high level of elasticity and adaptiveness in the policy-making process, despite the indisputable existence of numerous veto players and co-governing forces'. Rather than over-generalise from severe blockages in some sectors or from incrementally smooth adjustment in others, it makes more sense to regard the politics of semisovereignty in Germany as holding continuing relevance across both high- and low-change policy sectors, balancing the requirements of change that Germany confronts with the requirements of order that it demands.

Conclusion: Germany in Europe

The secret of any legitimate polity is to make the requirements of its domestic political order compatible with those of its international environment. The history of the twentieth century records in its first half spectacular German failures and in its second half, for the most part, admirable German successes.

Semisovereign politics requires a double shift in analytical perspective (Katzenstein 1997c). We can no longer afford to adhere simply to the cross-national comparison of different national systems of politics. In Europe, open economies now go hand in hand with open polities. This is the result of decades of reconstruction (in the 1950s and 1960s) and readjustment (in the 1970s and 1980s) that prepared the ground for a regionalism that is opening national politics to the joint impact of Europeanisation and globalisation. At the same time, it will no longer do, as some students of international relations still insist, to analyse international or global politics without taking account of its domestic context. Political analysis that unravels the close connections between domestic and international affairs underlines the continued relevance of semisovereignty. Analysis should aim at highlighting the dynamic interconnectedness of empirical phenomena, combining a horizontal comparison across national systems with a vertical analysis of different political orders in a method that Philip McMichael (1990) has dubbed 'incorporated comparison'.

What is striking from this analytical perspective is the congruence between Germany's semisovereignty and Europe's 'associated sovereignty' (Katzenstein 1997c), as William Paterson points out in chapter 12 of this volume. It is no accident that a German political scientist teaching at Harvard laid the foundation for what soon became in international relations and, eventually, in comparative politics and sociology, a theory of transnational relations (Kaiser 1971a, 1971b); that an American specialist of German foreign policy wrote about Germany as a 'penetrated' political system (Hanrieder 1967, pp. 228–45); and that a group of researchers convened by the German Society for Foreign Policy focused on the centrality of the regional embeddedness of the Federal Republic (Deutsche Gesellschaft für Auswärtige Politik 1973). Since 1945, the interpenetration of domestic and foreign affairs has been constitutive of the Federal Republic: its state identity no less than the conduct of many of its policies.

Parcelling out much of Germany's internal sovereignty and pooling some of its external sovereignty is producing and reproducing power in Germany and in Europe, in a manner that defies the political analysis of realists and leaves incomplete the analysis that liberals offer. Realists expected a reassertion of German power, nineteenth-century style, in which power politics was defined solely in terms of the control over territory, population and material resources. The dogged defence, and indeed extension, of Germany's adherence to multilateral institutions and the eschewing of unilateral policy initiatives since 1990 has defied the expectations of realists who saw in Germany a new superpower (Bergner 1991) freshly poised at the dawn of a new cold peace (Garten 1992). German policies were one important reason why political realists have packed their bags and left Europe for Asian pastures they consider, probably mistakenly, 'ripe for rivalry' (Friedberg 1994; for a critique, see Suh et al. 2004). Liberal analysts (Moravcsik 1998) ground their analysis in a pluralist view of the aggregation of domestic interests as the determinants of state preferences. This flies in the face of both the critique that Schattschneider (1960) offered in his celebrated analysis of the semisovereign American democracy and of the politics of Germany's semisovereign state. Incorporated comparison points instead to the mutually conditioning effects of the purpose and the exercise of power in a multi-tiered polity that connects Germany's semisovereignty with Europe's associated sovereignty.

That congruence may not last forever. It could be ruptured by political developments in Germany, in Europe or in the world at large, compelling German and European politicians to reacquaint themselves with conceptions of power politics long forgotten. While fully grounded in the opportunism of democratic politics, Chancellor Schröder's occasional blustering about a 'German way' recalls, for the historically inclined, earlier and less happy periods of German and European politics. French misconceptions of using Europe, under French leadership, to balance against the USA remind us of President de Gaulle's world vision, already proved anachronistic in the 1960s. Neither German nor French politicians toying with political concepts of *Realpolitik* dating back to the nineteenth century are likely to succeed. Because of the enormous power the USA wields in world politics, the same cannot be said with similar confidence of the 'Wilsonianism with heavy boots' that typifies the unilateral brand of power politics the Bush administration has embraced since 9/11. The bad news is that the conditions that gave rise to Germany's semisovereign state and Europe's associated sovereignty are at risk. The good news is that this is not occurring at the hands of Germany or Europe. Chances are thus good that semisovereignty in Germany and associated sovereignty in Europe will be with us for a while longer.

References

Aberbach, J., H.-U. Derlien and B. Rockman 1994, 'Unity and Fragmentation –
Themes in German and American Public Administration', in R. Mayntz,
H.-U. Derlien, U. Gerhardt and F. Scharpf (eds.), *Systemrationalität und
Partialinteresse. Festschrift für Renate Mayntz*. Baden-Baden: Nomos.

Abromeit, H. 1996, 'Zwischen Reformbedarf und Reformunfähigkeit – Die
Alternativlosigkeit des kooperativen Föderalismus', in *Leistungen und Gren-
zen föderaler Ordnungsmodelle. Ettersburger Gespräche*. Weimar: Thüringer
Ministerin für Bundesangelegenheiten in der Staatskanzlei.

Adams, J. and P. Robinson (eds.) 2002, *Devolution in Practice: Public Policy
Differences within the UK*. London: IPPR.

Adelberger, K. 2001, 'The Consensus Puzzle: Decision Arenas and Economic
Policy in Germany, 1948–99'. Ph.D. thesis, University of California at
Berkeley.

Aldrich, J. 1995, *Why Parties? The Origin and Transformation of Political Parties in
America*. Chicago: University of Chicago Press.

Alemann, U. von 2000, *Das Parteiensystem der Bundesrepublik Deutschland*. Opladen: Leske+Budrich.

ALLBUS (Allgemeine Bevölkerungsumfrage der Sozialwissenschaften) 1996,
ALLBUSCompact 1996 (ZA-Nr. 3718). Cologne: Zentralarchiv für em-
pirische Sozialforschung, available via: http://www.gesis.org/datenservice/
ALLBUS (accessed 5 May 2003).

Altman, D. 2002 'Blunt Portrait Drawn of the US Work Force in 2020', *New
York Times*, 30 August 2002.

Anderson, J. and J. Goodman 1993, 'A United Germany in a Post Cold-War
Europe', in R. Keohane, J. Nye and S. Hoffman (eds.), *After the Cold
War: International Institutions and State Strategies in Europe, 1989–1991*.
Cambridge, MA: Harvard University Press.

Artus, I. 2001, *Krise des deutschen Tarifsystems: Die Erosion des Flächentarifvertrags
in Ost und West*. Wiesbaden: Westdeutscher Verlag.

Arzheimer, K. and J. Falter 2002, 'Ist der Osten wirklich rot? Das Wahlverhalten
bei der Bundestagswahl 2002 in Ost-West Perspektive', *Aus Politik und
Zeitgeschichte* B49-50/2002: 27–35.

Ashford, D. 1981, *Policy and Politics in Britain: the Limits of Consensus*. Philadelphia: Temple University Press.

1982, *Policy and Politics in France: Living with Uncertainty*. Philadelphia:
Temple University Press.

Bach, H.-U., D. Blaschke, U. Blien, C. Brinkmann, J. Fuchs, M. Gutsche, U. Möller, J. Kühl, E. Spitznagel, W. Steckel, E. Wiedemann and C. Wolfinger 1998, *Labour Market Trends and Active Labour Market Policy in the Eastern German Transformation Process 1990–1997*. Nuremberg: IAB.

Bach, H.-U., H. Gommlich and M. Otto 2001, 'Aktuelle Daten vom Arbeitsmarkt in Ostdeutschland', *IAB Werkstattbericht*, December 2001.

Bach, H.-U., S. Koch, H. Kohler, E. Magvas, L. Pusse and E. Spitznagel 2001, 'Der Arbeitsmarkt in der Bundesrepublik Deutschland in den Jahren 2000 und 2001', *Mitteilungen aus der Arbeitsmarkt- und Berufsforschung* 34/1: 5–27.

Bach, H.-U., S. Koch, E. Magvas, L. Pusse and E. Spitznagel 2002, 'Der Arbeitsmarkt 2002 und 2003', *IAB Kurzbericht 8*, April 2002: 1–7.

Bachrach, P. and M. Baratz 1963, 'Decisions and Non-Decisions: an Analytical Framework', *American Political Science Review* 57: 641–51.

Bade, K. (ed.) 1994, *Ausländer, Aussiedler, Asyl in der Bundesrepublik Deutschland*. Bonn: Bundeszentrale für politische Bildung.

Baring, A. 1969, *Außenpolitik in Adenauers Kanzlerdemokratie*. Munich: Oldenbourg.

Bawn, K. 1999, 'Money and Majorities in the Federal Republic of Germany: Evidence for a Veto Players Model of Government Spending', *American Journal of Political Science* 43/3: 707–36.

Bayerischer Landtag 2002, *Bericht der Enquete-Kommission des Bayerischen Landtags 'Reform des Föderalismus – Stärkung der Landesparlamente'*, Drucksache 14/8660.

Bean, C. 1991, 'Are Australian Attitudes to Government Different? A Comparison with Five Other Nations', in F. Castles (ed.), *Australia Compared: People, Policies and Politics*. North Sydney: Allen and Unwin.

Beauftragte der Bundesregierung für Ausländerfragen 2002, *Bericht der Beauftragten der Bundesregierung für Ausländerfragen über die Lage der Ausländer in der Bundesrepublik Deutschland*. Berlin and Bonn, available via: http://www.integrationsbeauftragte.de (accessed 27 March 2003).

2004, *Migrationsbericht der Integrationsbeauftragten im Auftrag der Bundesregierung*. Berlin and Bonn, available via: http://www.integrationsbeauftragte.de (accessed 12 June 2004).

Beck, U. 1996, 'Die Subpolitik der Globalisierung. Die neue Macht der multinationalen Unternehmen', *Gewerkschaftliche Monatshefte* 47: 673–80.

Benz, A. 1996, 'Beyond the Public–Private Divide: Institutional Reform and Cooperative Policy-Making', in A. Benz and K. Goetz (eds.), *A New German Public Sector*. Aldershot: Dartmouth/ASGP.

1999, 'From Unitary to Asymmetric Federalism in Germany: Taking Stock after 50 Years', *Publius: The Journal of Federalism* 29/4: 55–78.

2001a, *Der moderne Staat: Grundlagen der politologischen Analyse*. Munich: Oldenbourg.

2001b, 'Interadministrative Relations in the Federal System', in K. König and H. Siedentopf (eds.), *Public Administration in Germany*. Baden-Baden: Nomos.

Benz, A. and K. Goetz 1996, 'The German Public Sector: National Priorities and the International Reform Agenda', in A. Benz and K. Goetz (eds.), *A New German Public Sector*. Aldershot: Dartmouth/ASGP.

Bergner, J. 1991, *The New Superpowers: Germany, Japan, the US, and the New World Order*. New York: St Martin's Press.

Berliner Zeitung, 9 August 2003, 'Arbeitsbienen und Drohnen. Interview mit Bert Rürup'.

Beyme, K. von 2000, *Parteien im Wandel: Von den Volksparteien zu den professionalisierten Wählerparteien*. Wiesbaden: Westdeutscher Verlag.

Bickerich, W. (ed.) 1985, *SPD und Grüne: Das neue Bündnis?* Hamburg: Spiegel-Buch.

Bischoff, D. and W. Teubner 1992, *Zwischen Einbürgerung und Rückkehr: Ausländerpolitik und Ausländerrecht in der Bundesrepublik Deutschland*. Berlin: Hitit Verlag.

Bispinck, R. 1997, 'Deregulierung, Differenzierung und Dezentralisierung des Flächentarifvertrags. Eine Bestandsaufnahme neuerer Entwicklungstendenzen', *WSI-Mitteilungen*: 551–61.

Blancke, S. 2003, 'Die Diffusion von Innovationen im deutschen Föderalismus', in *Jahrbuch des Föderalismus 2003*. Baden-Baden: Nomos.

Blanke, B. and C. Perschke-Hartmann 1994, 'The 1992 Health Reform: Victory over Pressure Group Politics', *German Politics* 3/2: 233–48.

Bluhm, K. 1993, 'Regionale Unterstützungsnetzwerke in der ostdeutschen Industrie', in H. Wiesenthal (ed.), *Einheit als Interessenpolitik*. Frankfurt am Main: Campus.

Bogumil, J. 2001, *Modernisierung lokaler Politik*. Baden-Baden: Nomos.

2002, 'Kommunale Entscheidungsprozesse im Wandel–Stationen der politik- und kommunalwissenschaftlichen Debatte', in J. Bogumil (ed.), *Kommunale Entscheidungsprozesse im Wandel*. Opladen: Leske+Budrich.

Bönker, F. and H. Wollmann 2000, 'Sozialstaatlichkeit im Übergang. Entwicklungslinien der bundesdeutschen Sozialpolitik in den Neunzigerjahren', in R. Czada and H. Wollmann (eds.), *Von der Bonner zur Berliner Republik. 10 Jahre Deutsche Einheit*. Wiesbaden: Westdeutscher Verlag.

Bowler, S. 2000, 'Parties in Legislatures: Two Competing Explanations', in R. Dalton and M. Wattenberg (eds.), *Parties without Partisans: Political Change in Advanced Industrial Democracies*. Oxford: Oxford University Press.

Brettschneider, F. 2001, 'Candidate-voting. Die Bedeutung von Spitzenkandidaten für das Wählerverhalten in Deutschland, Großbritannien und den USA von 1960 bis 1998', in H.-D. Klingemann and M. Kaase (eds.), *Wahlen und Wähler: Analysen aus Anlass der Bundestagswahl 1998*. Wiesbaden: Westdeutscher Verlag.

Budge, I., H.-D. Klingemann, J. Bara, E. Tanenbaum and A. Volkens 2001, *Mapping Policy Preferences: Estimates for Parties, Electors, and Governments 1945–1998*. Oxford: Oxford University Press.

Bulmer, S. 1989a, 'Territorial Government', in G. Smith, W. Paterson and P. Merkl (eds.), *Developments in West German Politics*. London: Macmillan.

1989b, 'Unity, Diversity and Stability: the "Efficient Secrets" behind West German Public Policy?', in S. Bulmer (ed.), *The Changing Agenda of West German Public Policy*. Aldershot: ASGP/Dartmouth.

1997, 'Shaping the Rules? The Constitutive Politics of the European Union and German Power', in P. Katzenstein (ed.), *Tamed Power: Germany in Europe*. Cornell: Cornell University Press.

Bulmer, S. and P. Humphreys 1989, 'Kohl, Corporatism and Congruence: the West German Model under Challenge', in S. Bulmer (ed.) *The Changing Agenda of West German Public Policy*. Aldershot: ASGP/Dartmouth.

Bulmer, S. and W. Paterson 1987, *The Federal Republic of Germany and the European Community*. London: Allen and Unwin.

Bulmer, S., C. Jeffery and W. Paterson 2000, *Germany's European Diplomacy: Shaping the Regional Milieu*. Manchester: Manchester University Press.

Bundesanstalt für Arbeit 2001, *Haushaltsplan: Haushaltsjahr 2001*. Nuremberg: Bundesanstalt für Arbeit.

(ed.) 2003, *Aufbau Ost – Der Beitrag der Bundesanstalt für Arbeit 1990 bis 2002*. Nuremberg: Bundesanstalt für Arbeit.

Bundesministerium für Arbeit und Sozialordnung 2000, *Arbeit für soziale Gerechtigkeit*. Berlin: BMAS.

Bundesministerium der Finanzen 2000, *Arbeitsplätze Schaffen – Zukunftsfähigkeit Gewinnen. Jahreswirtschaftsbericht 2000 der Bundesregierung*. Berlin: BMF.

2002, *Vor einem neuen Aufschwung – Verlässliche Wirtschafts- und Finanzpolitik fortsetzen. Jahreswirtschaftsbericht 2002*. Berlin: BMF.

Bundesministerium für Gesundheit und Soziale Sicherung 2004, *Statistisches Taschenbuch. Arbeits- und Sozialstatistik*. Berlin: BMGS.

Bundesministerium des Innern 1997, 'Aktionsprogramm zur weiteren Steigerung von Effektivität und Wirtschaftlichkeit der Bundesverwaltung. Kabinettsbeschluß vom 18. Juni 1997', reproduced in: Sachverständigenrat Schlanker Staat (ed.), *Abschlußbericht, Band 2: Materialband*. Bonn: BMI.

2002, *Moderner Staat – Moderne Verwaltung. Bilanz 2002*. Berlin: BMI.

2003, *The Public Service in Germany*. Berlin: BMI.

2004, 'Details of the Immigration Act (18 June 2004)', available at: http://www.eng.bmi.bund.de/Annex/en_25624/Details_of_the_Immigration_Act_18_June_2004.pdf (accessed 30 June 2004).

Bundesministerium für Wirtschaft 1997, *Reformen für Beschäftigung. Jahreswirtschaftsbericht der Bundesregierung*. Bonn: BMWi.

Bundesregierung 1999, *Moderner Staat – Moderne Verwaltung. Kabinettsbschluß vom 1. Dezember 1999*, available via: http://www.staat-modern.de (accessed 2 June 2002).

Bundestagsdrucksachen 13/3923, 14/3556, 14/4696, 15/110, available via: http://www.bundestag.de (accessed 10 November 2003).

Bundesverfassungsgericht, *Entscheidungen*, vol. 7. Tübingen: Mohr.

Burchardt, M. 1992, 'Die Praxis des aktuellen Länderfinanzausgleichs und das Problem der Integration der neuen Bundesländer', *WSI Mitteilungen* 45/9: 577–90.

Busch, A. 1991, 'Die deutsch-deutsche Währungsunion: Politisches Votum trotz ökonomischer Bedenken', in U. Liebert and W. Merkel (eds.), *Die Politik zur deutschen Einheit. Probleme – Strategien – Kontroversen*. Opladen: Leske +Budrich.

1993, 'The Politics of Price-Stability: Why the German-speaking Nations are Different', in F. Castles (ed.), *Families of Nations: Patterns of Public Policy in Western Democracies*. Aldershot: Gower.

1994, 'The Crisis in the EMS', *Government and Opposition* 29/1: 80–96.

1995, *Preisstabilitätspolitik. Politik und Inflationsraten im internationalen Vergleich*. Opladen: Leske+Budrich.

Busch, P.-O. and H. Jörgens 2001, 'Breaking the Deadlock – Voluntary Agreements and Regulatory Measures in German Waste Management', paper presented at 29th ECPR Joint Sessions, Grenoble, 6–11 April 2001.

Busse, V. 2001a, *Bundeskanzleramt und Bundesregierung. Aufgaben, Organisation, Arbeitsweise*. Heidelberg: Hüthig Verlag.

2001b, 'The Structure of Federal Administration', in K. König and H. Siedentopf (eds.), *Public Administration in Germany*. Baden-Baden: Nomos.

Castles, S. 1985, 'The Guests who Stayed – The Debate on "Foreigners Policy" in the Federal Republic of Germany', *International Migration Review* 19/3: 517–34.

Chayes, A. and A. Chayes 1995, *The New Sovereignty: Compliance with International Regulatory Agreements*. Cambridge, MA: Harvard University Press.

Chemnitzer Freie Presse, 6–7 November 1993, 'Für frischen Wind'.

Conradt, D. 2001, *The German Polity*. New York: Longman.

Conzelmann, T. 1998, '"Europeanisation" of Regional Development Policies? Linking the Multi-Level Governance Approach with Theories of Policy Learning and Policy Change', *European Integration Online Papers* 2, No. 4, available via: http://eiop.or.at/eiop/ (accessed 5 August 2004).

Cox, R. 1993, 'Creating Welfare States in Czechoslovakia and Hungary', *Government and Policy* 11: 349–64.

Czada, R. 1993a, 'Die Treuhandanstalt im Umfeld von Politik und Verbänden', in W. Fischer, H. Hax and H.-K. Schneider (eds.), *Treuhandanstalt. Das Unmögliche wagen*. Berlin: Akademie-Verlag.

1993b, 'Konfliktbewältigung und politische Reform in vernetzten Entscheidungsstrukturen', in R. Czada and M. Schmidt (eds.), *Verhandlungsdemokratie, Interessenvermittlung, Regierbarkeit*. Wiesbaden: Westdeutscher Verlag.

1995, 'Der Kampf um die Finanzierung der deutschen Einheit', *MPIfG Discussion Paper* 95/1. Cologne: Max-Planck-Institut für Gesellschaftsforschung.

2000, 'Die Tragweite des Eigentums. Vereinigungspolitik, marktwirtschaftliche Transformation und offene Vermögensfragen', in R. Czada and H. Wollmann (eds.), *Von der Bonner zur Berliner Republik. 10 Jahre Deutsche Einheit*. Wiesbaden: Westdeutscher Verlag.

2002, 'The German Political Economy in Flux', in J. Leonhard and L. Funk (eds.), *Ten Years of German Unification*. Birmingham: University of Birmingham Press.

2003, 'Der Begriff der Verhandlungsdemokratie und die vergleichende Policy-Forschung', in R. Mayntz and W. Streeck (eds.), *Die Reformierbarkeit der Demokratie: Innovationen und Blockaden*. Frankfurt am Main: Campus.

Czada, R. and H. Wollmann (eds.) 2000, *Von der Bonner zur Berliner Republik: 10 Jahre Deutsche Einheit*. Wiesbaden: Westdeutscher Verlag.

Dalton, R. 2000, 'The Decline of Party Identifications', in R. Dalton and M. Wattenberg (eds.), *Parties without Partisans: Political Change in Advanced Industrial Democracies*. Oxford: Oxford University Press.

2003, 'Voter Choice and Electoral Politics', in S. Padgett, W. Paterson and G. Smith (eds.), *Developments in German Politics 3*. Basingstoke: Palgrave.

Dalton, R. and M. Wattenberg (eds.) 2000, *Parties without Partisans: Political Change in Advanced Industrial Democracies*. Oxford: Oxford University Press.

Dalton, R., S. Flanagan and P. Beck 1984, *Electoral Change in Advanced Industrial Democracies*. Princeton, NJ: Princeton University Press.

de Rynck, S. 2002, *Changing Public Policy: the Role of the Regions*. Brussels: P. I. E.-Peter Lang.

Decker, F. and J. von Blumenthal 2002, 'Die bundespolitische Durchdringung der Landtagswahlen. Eine empirische Analyse von 1970 bis 2001', *Zeitschrift für Parlamentsfragen* 33/1: 144–65.

Derlien, H.-U. 2000, 'Germany', in H. Kassim, G. Peters and V. Wright (eds.), *The National Coordination of EU Policy*. Oxford: Oxford University Press.

2001a, 'Personalpolitik nach Regierungswechseln', in H.-U. Derlien and A. Murswieck (eds.) *Regieren nach Wahlen*. Opladen: Leske+Budrich.

(ed.) 2001b, *Zehn Jahre Verwaltungsaufbau Ost – eine Evaluation*. Baden-Baden: Nomos.

Derlien, H.-U., S. Heinemann and S. Lock 1998, *The German Public Service – Structure and Statistics*. Bamberg: Bamberger Verwaltungswissenschaftliche Beiträge No. 34.

Detterbeck, K. and W. Renzsch 2003, 'Multi-level Political Competition: the German Case', *European Urban and Regional Studies* 10/3: 257–70.

Deutsche Bundesbank 1995, *Die Geldpolitik der Deutschen Bundesbank*. Frankfurt am Main: Deutsche Bundesbank.

2002, 'Zahlungsbilanzstatistik', December 2002.

Deutsche Gesellschaft für Auswärtige Politik (ed.) 1973, *Regionale Verflechtung der Bundesrepublik Deutschland: Empirische Analysen*. Munich: Oldenbourg.

Deutscher Bundestag Plenarprotokoll 12/214, 4 March 1994.

Deutscher Bundestag 2002, *Stand der Gesetzgebung des Bundes, 14. Wahlperiode (GESTA-online)*, available via: http://dip.bundestag.de/gesta/14/Statistischer Uberblick.pdf (accessed 5 May 2003).

Directorate-General for Economic and Financial Affairs 2002, *Germany's Growth Performance in the 1990s*. Brussels: European Commission.

Döhler, M. and P. Manow 1967, *Strukturbildung von Politikfeldern: Das Beispiel bundesdeutscher Gesundheitspolitik seit den fünfziger Jahren*. Opladen: Leske +Budrich.

Dreyhaupt, F., W. Dierschke, L. Kropp, B. Prinz and H. Schade 1979, *Handbuch zur Aufstellung von Luftreinhalteplänen. Entwicklung und Ziele regionaler Luftreinhaltestrategie*. Mainz: TÜV Rheinland GmbH.

Duckenfield, M. 1999, 'The Goldkrieg: Revaluing the *Bundesbank*'s Reserves and the Politics of EMU', *German Politics* 8/1: 106–30.

Dürrenmatt, F. 1956, *Der Besuch der alten Dame: Eine tragische Komödie mit einem Nachwort*. Zurich: Verlag der Arche.

Dyson, K. 1982, 'West Germany: the Search for a Rationalist Consensus', in J. Richardson (ed.), *Policy Styles in Western Europe*. London: Allen and Unwin.

(ed.) 1992, *The Politics of German Regulation*. Aldershot: Dartmouth/ASGP.

1997, 'Policy Transfer in Regional Economic Development: the Case of SME Policy', *The Regional Review* 7:1: 9–10.

1998, 'Chancellor Kohl as Strategic Leader: the Case of Economic and Monetary Union', in C. Clemens and W. Paterson (eds.), *The Kohl Chancellorship*. London: Frank Cass.

2000, *The Politics of the Euro-Zone: Stability or Breakdown?* Oxford: Oxford University Press.

2001, 'The German Model Revisited: From Schmidt to Schröder', in S. Padgett and T. Poguntke (eds.), *Continuity and Change in German Politics: Beyond the Politics of Centrality?* London: Frank Cass.

(ed.) 2002, *European States and the Euro: Europeanisation, Variation and Convergence*. Oxford: Oxford University Press.

2004, 'Economic Policies: From Pacesetter to Beleaguered Player', in K. Dyson and K. Goetz (eds.), *Germany, Europe and the Politics of Constraint*. London: Proceedings of the British Academy, vol. 119/Oxford University Press.

Dyson, K. and K. Featherstone 1999, *The Road to Maastricht: Negotiating Economic and Monetary Union*. Oxford: Oxford University Press.

Ebbinghaus, B. 2002a, 'Dinosaurier der Dienstleistungsgesellschaft? Der Mitgliederschwund deutscher Gewerkschaften im historischen und internationalen Vergleich', *MPIfG Working Paper* 02/3. Cologne: Max-Planck-Institut für Gesellschaftsforschung.

2002b, 'Exit from Labour: Reforming Early Retirement and Social Partnership in Europe, Japan and the USA', habilitation thesis, University of Cologne.

The Economist, 10 April 1999, 'Mirror, Mirror on the Wall'.

14 March 2002, 'In the Dumps Again'.

7 December 2002, 'An Uncertain Giant: a Survey of Germany'.

19 June 2004, 'Mirror, Mirror on the wall'.

Ellwein, T. 1990, 'Koordination ohne Ende. Von den Grenzen der Zusammenarbeit in komplexen Organisationen', in R. Fisch and M. Boos (eds.), *Vom Umgang mit Komplexität in Organisationen*. Constance: Universitätsverlag Konstanz.

Eurostat 2003, *Statistics in Focus: Population and Social Conditions*. Luxembourg: Statistical Office of the EU.

Färber, G. and M. Sauckel 2000, 'Die Krise der förderalen Finanzverfassung', in R. Czada and H. Wollmann (eds.), *Von der Bonner zur Berliner Republik. 10 Jahre Deutsche Einheit*. Wiesbaden: Westdeutscher Verlag.

Fischer, W., H. Hax and H. Schneider (eds.) 1993, *Treuhandanstalt. Das unmögliche Wagen*. Berlin: Akademie Verlag.

Flockton, C. 1996, 'Economic Management and the Challenge of Reunification', in G. Smith, W. Paterson and S. Padgett (eds.), *Developments in German Politics 2*. London: Macmillan.

Flynn, B. 1997, *Subsidiarity and the Rise of Soft Law*, OP-40 Human Capital and Mobility Network. Colchester: University of Essex.

Forschungsgruppe Wahlen 2002, *Bundestagswahl: Eine Analyse der Wahl vom 22. September 2002*. Mannheim: Forschungsgruppe Wahlen.

Frank, M. 2001, 'The Structure of Administration in the Länder', in K. König and H. Siedentopf (eds.), *Public Administration in Germany*. Baden-Baden: Nomos.

Franke, S. 2003, 'Wählerwille und Wirtschaftsreform', *Aus Politik und Zeitgeschichte* B18–19/2003: 32–8.

Frankfurter Allgemeine Zeitung, 19 November 1998, 'Regierung hat 51 Beamte in einstweiligen Ruhestand geschickt'.

24 February 1999, 'Viererrunde soll zentrale Regierungsvorhaben koordinieren'.

11 September 2001, 'Der Haushalt ist in wesentlichen Teilen Makulatur: Interview mit Dietrich Austermann'.

30 July 2003, 'Weitere Kürzungen für Landesbeamte'.

11 August 2003, 'Im Spannungsfeld'.

Friedberg, A. 1994, 'Ripe for Rivalry: Prospects for Peace in a Multipolar Asia,' *International Security* 18/3: 5–33.

Garten, J. 1992, *A Cold Peace: America, Japan, Germany and the Struggle for Supremacy*. New York: Times Books.

Garton-Ash, T. 1993, *In Europe's Name: Germany and the Divided Continent*. London: Random House.

1994, 'Germany's Choice', *Foreign Affairs* 73/4: 65–81.

Geiß, B. (2001), 'Die Ausländerbeauftragten der Bundesregierung in der ausländerpolitischen Diskussion', in E. Currle and T. Wunderlich (eds.), *Deutschland – ein Einwanderungsland? Rückblick, Bilanz und neue Fragen*. Stuttgart: Lucius & Lucius.

Geppert, D. 2003, *Maggie Thatchers Rosskur – Ein Rezept für Deutschland? Ein Essay*. Berlin: Siedler.

Giersch, H., K.-H. Paque and H. Schmieding 1992, *The Fading Miracle: Four Decades of Market Economy in Germany*. Cambridge: Cambridge University Press.

Gladwell, M. 2000, *The Tipping Point: How Little Things Make a Big Difference*. London: Abacus.

Goetz, K. 1993, 'Rebuilding Public Administration in the New German Länder: Transfer and Differentiation', *West European Politics* 16/4: 447–69.

1999, 'Senior Officials in the German Federal Administration: Institutional Change and Positional Differentiation', in E. Page and V. Wright (eds.), *Bureaucratic Elites in Western European States: a Comparative Analysis of Top Officials in Eleven Countries*. Oxford: Oxford University Press.

2000a, 'European Integration and National Executives: a Cause in Search of an Effect?', *West European Politics* 23/4: 211–31.

2000b, 'The Development and Current Features of the German Civil Service System', in H. Bekke and F. van der Meer (eds.), *Civil Service Systems in Western Europe*. Cheltenham: Edward Elgar.

2003a, 'Executives in Comparative Context', in J. Hayward and A. Menon (eds.), *Governing Europe*. Oxford: Oxford University Press.

2003b, 'Government at the Centre', in S. Padgett, G. Smith and W. Paterson (eds.), *Developments in German Politics 3*. Basingstoke: Palgrave.

2004, 'The Federal Executive: Bureaucratic Fusion versus Governmental Bifurcation', in K. Dyson and K. Goetz (eds.), *Germany, Europe and the Politics of Constraint*. London: Proceedings of the British Academy, vol. 119/ Oxford University Press.

Goetz, K. and S. Hix (eds.) 2000, *Europeanised Politics? European Integration and National Political Systems*. Portland, OR: Frank Cass.

Granovetter, M. 1978, 'Threshold Models of Collective Behaviour', *American Journal of Sociology* 83: 1420–43.

Green, S. 1999, 'The 1998 German Bundestag Election: the End of an Era', *Parliamentary Affairs* 52/2: 306–20.

2000, 'Beyond Ethnoculturalism? German Citizenship in the New Millennium', *German Politics* 9/3: 105–24.

2001, 'Immigration, Asylum and Citizenship in Germany: the Impact of Unification and the Berlin Republic', *West European Politics* 22/4: 82–104.

2002, 'Immigration to the UK and Germany: a Panacea for Declining Labour Forces?', in L. Funk and S. Green (eds.), *New Aspects of Labour Market Policy*. Berlin: Verlag für Wissenschaft und Forschung.

2003, 'Towards an Open Society: Citizenship and Immigration', in S. Padgett, W. Paterson and G. Smith (eds.), *Developments in German Politics 3*. Basingstoke: Palgrave.

2004, *The Politics of Exclusion: Institutions and Immigration Policy in Contemporary Germany*. Manchester: Manchester University Press.

Grube, N. 2001, 'Föderalismus in der öffentlichen Meinung der Bundesrepublik Deutschland', in *Jahrbuch des Föderalismus 2001*. Baden-Baden: Nomos.

Gunlicks, A. 1986, *Local Government in the German Federal System*. Durham, NC: Duke University Press.

2000, 'Financing the German Federal System: Problems and Prospects', *German Studies Review* 23/3: 532–55.

2003, *The Länder and German Federalism*. Manchester: Manchester University Press.

Haas, P. 1992, 'Knowledge, Power and International Policy Co-ordination', *International Oganisation* 46/1: 1–35.

Hagedorn, H. 2001, *Wer darf Mitglied werden? Einbürgerung in Deutschland und Frankreich im Vergleich*. Opladen: Leske+Budrich.

Hagen, J. and R. Strauch 2001, 'German Public Finances: Recent Experiences and Future Challenges', *Working Paper B13*. Bonn: Zentrum für Europäische Integrationsforschung.

Hailbronner, K. 2001, 'Reform des Zuwanderungsrechts. Konsens und Dissens in der Ausländerpolitik', *Aus Politik und Zeitgeschichte* B43/2001: 7–19.

Hall, P. 1986, *Governing the Economy: the Politics of State Intervention in Britain and France*. Cambridge: Polity Press.

1989, *The Power of Economic Ideas*. Princeton: Princeton University Press.

Hall, P. and D. Soskice (eds.) 2001, *Varieties of Capitalism: the Institutional Foundations of Comparative Advantage*. Oxford: Oxford University Press.

Hamilton, W. (ed.) 1964, *The Transfer of Institutions*. Durham: Duke University Press.

Hampton, M. and C. Soe (eds.) 1999, *Between Bonn and Berlin: German Politics Adrift*. Lanham, MD: Rowman and Littlefield.

Hanrieder, W. 1967, *West German Foreign Policy 1949–1963: International Pressure and Domestic Response*. Stanford, CA: Stanford University Press.

Harding, R. and W. Paterson 2000, 'Germany in a Global Era', in R. Harding and W. Paterson (eds.), *The Future of the German Economy*. Manchester: Manchester University Press.

Hartrich, E. 1980, *The Fourth and Richest Reich*. New York: Macmillan.

Hartwich, H.-H. 1992, 'Die Beziehungen zwischen Bundesregierung und Bundesbank im deutschen und westeuropäischen Einigungsprozeß', in H.-H. Hartwich and G. Wewer (eds.), *Regieren in der Bundesrepublik IV: Finanz- und wirtschaftspolitische Bestimmungsfaktoren des Regierens im Bundesstaat – unter besonderer Berücksichtigung des deutschen Vereinigungsprozesses*. Opladen: Leske+Budrich.

2003, 'Arbeitsmarktreform im Bundestagswahlkampf 2002. Eine Fallstudie zum Thema "Demokratie und Arbeitslosigkeit"', *Gesellschaft – Wirtschaft – Politik* 52/1: 113–42.

Hartz, P. et al. 2002, *Moderne Dienstleistungen am Arbeitsmarkt. Vorschläge der Kommission zum Abbau der Arbeitslosigkeit und zur Umstrukturierung der Bundesanstalt für Arbeit*. Berlin: BMAS.

Hassel, A. 1999, 'The Erosion of the German System of Industrial Relations', *British Journal of Industrial Relations* 37/3: 483–505.

Hassel, A. and B. Rehder 2001, 'Institutional Change in the German Wage Bargaining System: the Role of Big Companies', *MPIfG Working Paper* 01/9. Cologne: Max-Planck-Institut für Gesellschaftsforschung.

Hay, C. 1999, 'Crisis and the Structural Transformation of the State: Interrogating the Process of Change', *The British Journal of Politics and International Relations* 1/3: 317–44.

2002, *Political Analysis: a Critical Introduction*. Basingstoke: Palgrave.

Hayward, J. 1973, *Governing France: the One and Indivisible Republic*. London: Weidenfeld and Nicolson.

Heclo, H. and H. Madsen 1987, *Policy and Politics in Sweden: Principled Pragmatism*. Philadelphia: Temple University Press.

Heineck, G. and J. Schwarze 2001, 'Auswirkungen der Einführung der Sozialversicherungspflicht für geringfügige Beschäftigung: Eine Evaluation des "630-DM-Jobs" -Reformgesetzes', *Mitteilungen aus der Arbeitsmarkt- und Berufsforschung* 34/3: 314–27.

Heinze, R. 1998, *Die blockierte Gesellschaft. Sozioökonomischer Wandel und die Krise des 'Modell Deutschland'*. Opladen: Westdeutscher Verlag.

Helby, P. 2001, 'The *Quid Pro Quo* of Environmental Agreements: Reflections on Industrial Efficiency Agreements from Five Countries', paper presented at 29th ECPR Joint Sessions, Grenoble, 6–11 April 2001.

Hertel, W. 2001, 'Kulturföderalismus in Deutschland: Verfassungsfolklore oder Verfassungsrecht', in *Jahrbuch des Föderalismus 2001*. Baden-Baden: Nomos.

Hesse, J. and K. Goetz 1992, 'Early Administrative Adjustments to the Federal Communities: the Case of the Federal Republic of Germany', *Jahrbuch für Europäische Verwaltungsgeschichte* 4: 181–206.

Hickel, R. 1992, 'Föderaler Finanzausgleich im vereinten Deutschland nach 1995', *WSI-Mitteilungen* 45/9: 563–76.

Hirschman, A. 1970, *Exit, Voice, and Loyalty*. Cambridge, MA: Harvard University Press.

Hoffmann, S. 1968, *Gulliver's Troubles, Or the Setting of American Foreign Policy*. New York: McGraw-Hill.

Holtmann, E. 2000, 'Gesetzgebung in der Wohnungspolitik des Bundes: Zur Rolle des parteipolitischen Faktors', in E. Holtmann and H. Voelzkow (eds.), *Zwischen Wettbewerbs- und Verhandlungsdemokratie: Analysen zum Regierungssystem der Bundesrepublik Deutschland*. Wiesbaden: Westdeutscher Verlag.

Holtmann, E. and H. Voelzkow (eds.) 2000, *Zwischen Wettbewerbs- und Verhandlungsdemokratie. Analysen zum Regierungssystem der Bundesrepublik Deutschland*. Wiesbaden: Westdeutscher Verlag.

Hough, D. 2001, 'Die PDS: Ein Zeichen ostdeutscher Andersartigkeit', *Deutschland Archiv* 34/2: 284–7.

2002, *The Fall and Rise of the PDS in Eastern Germany, 1989–2000*. Birmingham: Birmingham University Press.

Hough, D. and C. Jeffery 2003, 'Landtagswahlen: Bundesprotestwahlen oder Regionalwahlen', *Zeitschrift für Parlamentsfragen* 34/1: 79–94.

http://www.bamf.de (accessed 10 January 2005).

http://www.destatis.de (accessed 18 June 2004).

http://www.unhcr.ch (accessed 20 March 2003).

http://www.bundesrat.de (accessed 20 June 2004).

http://www.bva.bund.de (accessed 19 June 2004).

Hülsberg, W. 1988, *The German Greens: a Social and Political Profile*. London: Verso.

Hunold, C. 2001, 'Nuclear Waste in Germany: Environmentalists between State and Society', *Environmental Politics* 10/3: 127–33.

Hüther, M. 1993, 'Reform des Finanzausgleichs: Handlungsbedarf und Lösungsvorschläge', *Wirtschaftsdienst* 73/1: 43–52.

Inglehart, R. 1990, *Culture Shift in Advanced Industrial Society*. Princeton: Princeton University Press.

ISG 1999, 'Geringfügig Beschäftigte nach der Neuregelung des "630-DM-Gesetzes"', *Studien der ISG Sozialforschung und Gesellschaftspolitik* 27. Cologne and Düsseldorf: Institut für Sozialforschung und Gesellschaftspolitik.

Iversen, T., J. Pontusson and D. Soskice (eds.) 2000, *Unions, Employers, and Central Banks: Macro-economic Co-ordination and Institutional Change in Social Market Economies*. Cambridge: Cambridge University Press.

Jacoby, W. 2000, *Imitation and Politics: Redesigning Modern Germany*. Ithaca: Cornell University Press.

2001, 'Tutors and Pupils: International Organizations, Central European Elites, and Western Models', *Governance* 14/2: 169–200.

2002, 'Das Wettrennen um die EU-Mitgliedschaft: Warum die Osterweiterung für Makroökonomen von Bedeutung ist', *WSI-Mitteilungen* May 2002: 292–9.

Jäger, W. and W. Link 1987, 'Republik im Wandel 1974–1982: Die Ära Schmidt', in *Geschichte der Bundesrepublik Deutschland*, vol. v/II. Stuttgart: Deutsche Verlags-Anstalt and Mannheim: Brockhaus.

Jeffery, C. 1995, 'The Non-Reform of the German Federal System after Unification', *West European Politics* 18/2: 252–72.

1999, 'Party Politics and Territorial Representation in the Federal Republic of Germany', *West European Politics* 22/2: 130–66.

2002a, 'Uniformity and Diversity in Policy Provision: Insights from the US, Germany and Canada', in J. Adams and P. Robinson (eds.), *Devolution in Practice: Public Policy Differences within the UK*. London: IPPR.

2002b, 'German Federalism from Cooperation to Competition', in M. Umbach (ed.), *German Federalism Past, Present and Future*. Basingstoke: Palgrave.

2003, 'Cycles of Conflict: Fiscal Equalization in Germany', *Regional and Federal Studies* 13/4: 22–41.

2004, 'The German Länder: From Milieu-Shaping to Territorial Politics', in K. Dyson and K. Goetz (eds.), *Germany, Europe and the Politics of Constraint*. London: Proceedings of the British Academy, vol. 119/ Oxford University Press.

Jeffery, C. and D. Hough 2001, 'The Electoral Cycle and Multi-Level Voting in Germany', *German Politics* 10/2: 73–98.

Jeffery, C. and A. Hyde-Price 2001, 'Germany in the European Union', *Journal of Common Market Studies* 30/4: 689–718.

Jeffery, C. and W. Paterson 2001, 'Germany's Power in Europe', in H. Wallace (ed.), *Interlocking Complexities of European Integration*. Basingstoke: Palgrave.

2004, 'Germany and European Integration: the Shifting of Tectonic Plates', in H. Kitschelt and W. Streeck (eds.), *Germany: Beyond the Stable State*. London: Frank Cass.

Johnson, C. 1995, 'Die rolle intermediärer Organisationen beim Wandel des Berufsbildungssystems', in H. Wiesenthal (ed.), *Einheit als Interessenpolitik*. Frankfurt am Main: Campus.

Joppke, C. 1999, *Immigration and the Nation-State: the United States, Germany and Great Britain*. Oxford: Oxford University Press.

Joppke, C. and E. Morawska (eds.) 2003, *Towards Assimilation and Citizenship*. Basingstoke: Palgrave.

Jun, U. 2002, 'Professionalisiert, medialisiert und etatisiert. Zur Lage der deutschen Großparteien am Beginn des 21. Jahrhunderts', *Zeitschrift für Parlamentsfragen* 33/4: 770–89.

Kädtler, J., G. Kottwitz and R. Weinert 1997, *Betriebsräte in Ostdeutschland: Institutionenbildung und Handlungskonstellationen, 1989–1994*. Opladen: Westdeutscher Verlag.

Kaiser, K. 1971a, 'Transnational Relations as a Threat to the Democratic Process,' *International Organization* 25/3: 706–20.

1971b, 'Transnational Politics: Toward a Theory of Multinational Politics,' *International Organization* 25/4: 790–817.

Kania, H. and B. Blanke 2000, 'Von der "Korporatisierung" zum "Wettbewerb". Gesundheitspolitische Kurswechsel in den Neunzigerjahren', in R. Czada and H. Wollmann (eds.), *Von der Bonner zur Berliner Republik. 10 Jahre Deutsche Einheit*. Wiesbaden: Westdeutscher Verlag.

Karrasch, P. 1995, 'Gewerkschaftliche und gewerkschaftsnahe Politikformen in und mit der Kommune', in S. Benzler, U. Bullmann and D. Eißel (eds.), *Deutschland-Ost vor Ort*. Opladen: Leske+Budrich.

Kaser, M. 1996, 'Post-Communist Privatization: Flaws in the *Treuhand* Model', *Acta Oeconomica* 48: 59–75.

Katz, R. and P. Mair 1995, 'Changing Models of Party Organization and Party Democracy: the Emergence of the Cartel Party', *Party Politics* 1: 5–28.

——— 2002, 'The Ascendancy of the Party in Public Office: Party Organizational Change in Twentieth-Century Democracies', in R. Gunther, J. Ramó-Montero and J. Linz (eds.), *Political Parties: Old Concepts and New Challenges*. Oxford: Oxford University Press.

Katzenstein, P. 1978, 'Conclusion: Domestic Structures and Strategies of Foreign Economic Policy,' in P. Katzenstein (ed.), *Between Power and Plenty: Foreign Economic Policies of Advanced Industrial States*. Madison, WI: University of Wisconsin Press.

——— 1984, *Corporatism and Change: Austria, Switzerland and the Politics of Industry*. Ithaca: Cornell University Press.

——— 1985, *Small States in World Markets*. Ithaca: Cornell University Press.

——— 1987, *Policy and Politics in Germany: the Growth of a Semisovereign State*. Philadelphia: Temple University Press.

——— (ed.) 1989, *Industry and Politics in West Germany: Toward the Third Republic*. Ithaca: Cornell University Press.

——— (ed.) 1997a, *Tamed Power: Germany in Europe*. Ithaca: Cornell University Press.

——— 1997b, 'The Smaller European States, Germany and Europe', in P. Katzenstein (ed.), *Tamed Power: Germany in Europe*. Ithaca: Cornell University Press.

——— 1997c, 'United Germany in an Integrating Europe,' in P. Katzenstein (ed.), *Tamed Power: Germany in Europe*. Ithaca: Cornell University Press.

Kelly, E. 1987, *Policy and Politics in the United States: the Limits of Localism*. Philadelphia: Temple University Press.

Kemmler, M. 1994, *Die Entstehung der Treuhandanstalt. Von der Wahrung zur Privatisierung des DDR-Volksvermögens*. Frankfurt am Main: Campus.

Kennedy, E. 1991, *The Bundesbank: Germany's Central Bank in the International Monetary System*. London: Pinter.

Keohane, R. 2003, 'Ironies of Semisovereignty: the EU and the US', in J. Weiler, I. Begg and J. Peterson (eds.), *Integration in an Expanding European Union: Reassessing the Fundamentals*. Oxford: Blackwell.

Kern, H. 1994, 'Intelligente Regulierung', *Soziale Welt* 1: 11–13.

Key, V. 1964, *Politics, Parties, and Pressure Groups*. New York: Crowell.

King, D. 1995, *Actively Seeking Work: the Politics of Unemployment and Welfare Policy in the United States*. Chicago: University of Chicago Press.

Kirchheimer, O. 1966, 'The Transformation of the Western European Party Systems', in J. LaPalombara and M. Weiner (eds.), *Political Parties and Political Development*. Princeton: Princeton University Press.

Kitschelt, H. 1986, 'Political Opportunity Structures and Political Protest: Anti-Nuclear Movements in Four Democracies', *British Journal of Political Science* 16/1: 57–85.

——— 2000, 'Citizens, Politicians, and Party Cartellization: Political Representation and State Failure in Post-Industrial Democracies', *European Journal of Political Research* 37: 149–79.

Kitschelt, H. and W. Streeck (eds.) 2004a, *Germany: Beyond the Stable State*. London: Frank Cass.

2004b, 'From Stability to Stagnation: Germany at the Beginning of the 21st Century', in H. Kitschelt and W. Streeck (eds.), *Germany: Beyond the Stable State*. London: Frank Cass.

Kleinert, H. 1992, *Aufstieg und Fall der Grünen: Analyse einer alternativen Partei*. Bonn: Dietz.

Klusmeyer, D. 2001, 'A "Guiding Culture" for Immigrants? Integration and Diversity in Germany', *Journal of Ethnic and Migration Studies* 27/3: 519–32.

Knuth, M. 1997, 'Active Labor Market Policy and German Unification: the Role of Employment and Training Companies', in L. Turner (ed.), *Negotiating the New Germany: Can Social Partnership Survive?* Ithaca: Cornell University Press.

Koch, R. 2001, 'Sozialhilfe – eine zweite Chance, kein Lebenstil', available at www.rolandkoch.de/home_cdu.nsf/$pages/content_sozialhilfe (accessed 13 March 2002).

Kommission Mitbestimmung 1998, *Mitbestimmung und neue Unternehmenskulturen: Bericht der Kommission Mitbestimmung der Bertelsmann Stiftung und der Hans-Böckler-Stiftung*. Gütersloh: Verlag der Bertelsmann Stiftung.

König, K. (ed.) 1999, *Verwaltungsmodernisierung im Bund*. Speyer: Speyerer Forschungsberichte 196.

2000, *Zur Managerialisierung und Ökonomisierung der öffentlichen Verwaltung*. Speyer: Speyerer Forschungsberichte 209.

2002, *Verwaltetes Regieren. Studien zur Regierungslehre*. Cologne: Heymann.

König, K. and Siedentopf, H. (eds.) 2001, *Public Administration in Germany*. Baden-Baden: Nomos.

König, T. 1998, 'Regierungswechsel ohne politischen Wandel? Ein Vergleich des wirtschaftspolitischen Handlungsspielraums der Regierung Kohl, einer Regierung Schröder, einer Großen Koalition und einer SPD-Alleinregierung', *Zeitschrift für Parlamentsfragen* 29/33: 478–95.

Koole, R. 1996, 'Cadre, Catch-All or Cartel? A Comment on the Notion of the Cartel Party', *Party Politics* 2: 507–34.

Korte, K.-R. 2000, 'Solutions for the Decision Dilemma: Political Styles of Germany's Chancellors', *German Politics* 9/1: 1–22.

2002, 'In der Präsentationsdemokratie: Schröder's Regierungsstil prägt die Berliner Republik', *Frankfurter Allgemeine Zeitung*, 26 July 2002.

Krasner, S. 1988, 'Approaches to the State: Alternative Conceptions and Historical Dynamics', *Comparative Political Studies* 21: 223–46.

Krause-Burger, S. 2000, *Wie Gerhard Schröder regiert: Beobachtungen im Zentrum der Macht*. Stuttgart: Deutsche Verlags-Anstalt.

Kürschners Volkshandbuch 1995, *Deutscher Bundestag 13. Wahlperiode*. Darmstadt: Neue Darmstädter Verlagsanstalt.

Laakso, M. and R. Taagepera 1979, 'Effective Number of Parties: a Measure with Applications to Western Europe', *Comparative Political Studies* 12: 3–27.

Labrousse, A. and J.-D. Weisz (eds.) 2001, *Institutional Economics in France and Germany: German Ordoliberalism versus the French Regulation School*. Berlin: Springer.

Lafontaine, O. and C. Müller 1998, *Keine Angst vor der Globalisierung*. Bonn: Dietz.

Lane, J.-E. and S. Ersson 1999, *Politics and Society in Western Europe*. London: Sage.

Laver, M. and N. Schofield 1990, *Multiparty Government: the Politics of Coalition in Europe*. Oxford: Oxford University Press.

Lees, C. 1995, 'Bringing the PDS into the Coalition Equation', *German Politics* 4/1: 150–4.

1998, 'SPD-Green Coalitions in the Federal Republic of Germany: Models of Formation and Maintenance', PhD thesis, University of Birmingham.

1999, 'The SPD-Green Coalition', in S. Padgett and T. Saalfeld (eds.), *Bundestagswahl 98: the End of an Era*. London: Frank Cass.

2000a, *The SPD-Green Coalition in Germany: Politics, Personalities and Power*. Manchester: Manchester University Press.

2000b, 'Paradise Postponed: an Assessment of Ten Years of Governmental Participation by the Green Party in Germany', in S. Young (ed.), *Ecological Modernisation*. London: Routledge.

2001, 'Coalitions: Beyond the Politics of Centrality?', *German Politics* 10/2: 117–34.

Lehmbruch, G. 1976, *Parteienwettbewerb im Bundestaat*. Stuttgart: Kohlhammer.

1979, 'Liberal Corporatism and Party Government', in P. Schmitter and G. Lehmbruch (eds.), *Trends Towards Corporatist Intermediation*. London: Sage.

1992, 'Institutionentransfer im Prozeß der Vereinigung: Zur politischen Logik der Verwaltungsintegration in Deutschland', in W. Seibel, A. Benz and H. Mäding (eds.), *Verwaltungsintegration und Verwaltungspolitik im Prozeß der deutschen Einigung*. Baden-Baden: Nomos.

1996a, 'Die ostdeutsche Transformation als Strategie des Institutionentransfers: Überprüfung und Antikritik', in A. Eisen and H. Wollmann (eds.), *Institutionenbildung in Ostdeutschland*. Opladen: Leske+Budrich.

1996b, 'Die korporative Verhandlungsdemokratie in Westmitteleuropa', *Schweizerische Zeitschrift für Politische Wissenschaft* 2/4: 19–41.

1998, 'Zwischen Institutionentransfer und Eigendynamik: Sektorale Transformationspfade und ihre bestimmungsgründe', in R. Czada and G. Lehmbruch (eds.), *Transformationspfade in Ostdeutschland*. Frankfurt am Main: Campus.

2000, 'Institutionelle Schranken einer ausgehandelten Reform des Wohlfahrtsstaates: Das Bündnis für Arbeit und seine Erfolgsbedingungen', in R. Czada and H. Wollmann (eds.), *Von der Bonner zur Berliner Republik: 10 Jahre deutsche Einheit*. Wiesbaden: Westdeutscher Verlag.

2002, *Parteienwettbewerb im Bundesstaat* (first edition 1976). Wiesbaden: Westdeutscher Verlag.

Lehmbruch, G., M. Döhler, E. Grande and O. Singer 1988, 'Institutionelle Bedingungen ordnungspolitischen Strategienwechsels im internationalen Vergleich', in M. Schmidt (ed.), *Staatstätigkeit*. Opladen: Westdeutscher Verlag.

Lenkungsausschuss Verwaltungsorganisation 1998, '*Schlanker Staat': Bilanz und Ausblick. Zweiter Bericht zum Aktionsprogramm zur weiteren Steigerung von Effektivität und Wirtschaftlichkeit in der Bundesverwaltung. Kabinettsbeschluß vom 17. Juni 1998*. Bonn: BMI.

Leonardy, U. 2001, 'Parteien im Föderalismus der Bundesrepublik Deutschland. Scharniere zwischen Staat und Politik', *Zeitschrift für Parlamentsfragen* 33/1: 180–95.

Levy, J. 2002, 'The State after Statism: French Economic and Social Policy in the Age of Globalization', paper presented at the International Conference of the Europeanists, Chicago, 14 May 2002.

Lichtblau, K. 1995, *Von der Transfer- in die Marktwirtschaft: Strukturpolitische Leitlinien für die neuen Länder.* Cologne: Deutscher Instituts-Verlag.

Lightfoot, S. and D. Luckin 2000, 'Research Note: the 1999 Ecological Tax Reform Law', *German Politics* 9/1: 139–52.

Lijphart, A. 1984, *Democracies.* New Haven: Yale University Press.

Lindblom, C. 1978, *Politics and Markets.* New York: Basic Books.

Linder, W. 1999, *Schweizerische Demokratie. Institutionen – Prozesse – Perspektiven.* Berne: Haupt.

Longhurst, K. 2004, *Germany and the Use of Force: the Evolution of German Security Policy 1990–2003.* Manchester: Manchester University Press.

Luckin, D. and S. Lightfoot 1999, 'Environmental Taxation in Contemporary European Politics', *Contemporary Politics* 5/3: 243–61.

Luft, S. 2003, *Ausländerpolitik in Deutschland.* Gräfeling: Resch.

Lupia, A. and K. Strøm 1995, 'Coalition Termination and the Strategic Timing of Parliamentary Elections', *American Political Science Review* 89/3: 648–65.

McAdams, A. 1993, *Germany Divided: From the Wall to Reunification.* Princeton: Princeton University Press.

McAnulla, S. 2002, 'Structure and Agency', in D. Marsh and G. Stoker (eds.), *Theory and Methods in Political Science.* Basingstoke: Palgrave.

Mackscheidt, K. 1993, 'Die Transferaktivität der Bundesanstalt für Arbeit nach der Deutschen Einigung – Dynamik und Effizienz', in K. Hansmeyer (ed.), *Finanzierungsprobleme der deutschen Einheit II.* Berlin: Duncker & Humblot.

McMichael, P. 1990, 'Incorporating Comparison within a World-Historical Perspective: an Alternative Comparative Method', *American Sociological Review* 55: 385–97.

Maier, C. 1997, *Dissolution: the Crisis of Communism and the End of East Germany.* Princeton: Princeton University Press.

Manow, P. 1996, 'Informalisierung und Parteipolitisierung – Zum Wandel exekutiver Entscheidungsprozesse in der Bundesrepublik', *Zeitschrift für Parlamentsfragen* 27/1: 96–107.

  2002, 'Consociational Roots in German Corporatism: the Bismarckian Welfare State and the German Political Economy', *Acta Politica* 37/1–2: 195–212.

Mardegant, U. 2003, 'Die Föderalismusdiskussion in Deutschland', *Aus Politik und Zeitgeschichte* B29–30/2003: 6–13.

Markovits, A. (ed.) 1982, *The Political Economy of West Germany: Modell Deutschland.* New York: Praeger.

Markovits, A. and P. Gorski 1993, *The German Left: Red, Green and Beyond.* Cambridge: Polity Press.

Marsh, D. 1992, *The Bundesbank: the Bank that Rules Europe.* London: Mandarin.

Matheson, G. and M. Wearing 1999, 'Within and Without: Labour Force Status and Political Views in Four Welfare States', in S. Svallfors and P. Taylor-Gooby (eds.), *The End of the Welfare State? Responses to State Retrenchment.* London: Routledge.

Maurer, A. 2003, 'Germany: Fragmented Structures in a Complex System', in W. Wessels, A. Maurer and J. Mittag, *Fifteen into One? The European Union and its Member States.* Manchester: Manchester University Press.

Mayntz, R. and F. Scharpf, 1975, *Policy-Making in the German Federal Bureaucracy.* Amsterdam: Elsevier.

Mearsheimer, J. 1990, 'Back to the Future: Instability in Europe after the Cold War', *International Security* 15/1: 5–57.

Mehl, P. and R. Plankl 2002, 'Regionale Agrarpolitik in Deutschland – Handlungsspielräume in einem verflochtenen Politikfeld', *Jahrbuch des Föderalismus 2002.* Baden-Baden: Nomos.

Menz, G. 2003, 'Regulating the Single Market: National Varieties of Capitalism and their Responses to Europeanisation', *Journal of European Public Policy* 10/4: 532–56.

Merkel, W. 2003, 'Institutionen und Reformpolitik: Drei Fallstudien zur Vetospieler-Theorie', in C. Egle, T. Ostheim and R. Zohlnhöfer (eds.), *Das rotgrüne Projekt. Eine Bilanz der Regierung Schröder 1998–2002.* Wiesbaden: Westdeutscher Verlag.

Mershon, C. 1999, 'The Costs of Coalition: a Five-Nation Comparison', in S. Bowler, D. Farrell and R. Katz (eds.), *Party Discipline and Parliamentary Government.* Columbus: Ohio State University Press.

Mertes, M. 2000, 'Führen, koordinieren, Strippen ziehen: Das Kanzleramt als Kanzlers Amt', in K.-R. Korte and G. Hirscher (eds.), *Darstellungspolitik oder Entscheidungspolitik?* Munich: Hanns-Seidel-Stiftung.

Mettke, J. 1982, *Die Grünen: Regierungspartner von Morgen?* Hamburg: Spiegel-Buch.

Migration und Bevölkerung 4/2001, 'Bericht der Süssmuth Kommission', available via: http://www.migration-info.de (accessed 28 March 2003).

Miskimmon, A. and W. Paterson 2004, 'Foreign and Security Policy: On the Cusp between Transformation and Accommodation', in K. Dyson and K. Goetz (eds.), *Germany, Europe and the Politics of Constraint.* London: Proceedings of the British Academy, vol. 119/Oxford University Press.

Moravcsik, A. 1998, *The Choice for Europe: Social Purpose and State Power from Messina to Maastricht.* Ithaca: Cornell University Press.

Moreno, L. 2003, 'Public Policy in the Spanish Autonomous Communities', *Regional and Federal Studies* 13/3: 133–6.

MPK (Ministerpräsidentenkonferenz) 2003, 'MPK in Berlin: Nächste Verfahrensschritte bei Föderalismusreform und Digitalfunk', Pressemeldung at http://fhh.hamburg.de/stadt/Aktuell/pressemeldungen/2003/juni/27/pressemeldung-20 (accessed 18 August 2003).

Müller, E. 1989, 'Sozial-liberale Umweltpolitik. Von der Karriere eines neuen Politikbereichs', *Aus Politik und Zeitgeschichte* B47–48/1989: 3–15.

Müller, W. 2000, 'Political Parties in Parliamentary Democracies: Making Delegation and Accountability Work', *European Journal of Political Research* 37/3: 309–33.

Müller, W. and K. Strøm (eds.) 1999, *Policy, Office, or Votes? How Political Parties in Western Europe Make Hard Choices*. Cambridge: Cambridge University Press.

Müller-Rommel, F. 1994, 'The Chancellor and His Staff', in S. Padgett (ed.), *Adenauer to Kohl: the Development of the German Chancellorship*. London: Hurst.

Münch, U. 1992, *Asylpolitik in der Bundesrepublik Deutschland*. Opladen: Leske +Budrich.

1998, 'Entflechtungsmöglichkeiten im Bereich der Sozialpolitik', in U. Männle (ed.), *Föderalismus zwischen Konsens und Konkurrenz*. Baden-Baden: Nomos.

Muniak, D. 1985, 'Policies that Don't Fit', *Policy Studies Journal* 14: 1–19.

Münz, R. and R. Ohliger 1998, 'Long Distance Citizens: Ethnic Germans and their Immigration to Germany', in P. Schuck and R. Münz (eds.), *Paths to Inclusion: the Integration of Migrants in the United States and Germany*. Oxford: Berghahn.

Muramatsu, M. and F. Naschold, (eds.) 1996, *State and Administration in Japan and Germany*. Berlin: de Gruyter.

Murray, L. 1994, 'Einwanderungsland Bundesrepublik Deutschland? Explaining the Evolving Positions of German Political Parties on Citizenship Policy', *German Politics and Society* 33: 23–56.

Nägele, F. 1996, *Regionale Wirtschaftspolitik im kooperativen Bundesstaat: Ein Politikfeld im Prozess der deutschen Vereinigung*. Opladen: Westdeutscher Verlag.

Naschold, F. and J. Bogumil, 2000, *Modernisierung des Staates: New Public Management in deutscher und internationaler Perspektive*. Opladen: Leske+ Budrich.

Nicholls, A. 1994, *Freedom with Responsibility: the Social Market Economy in Germany 1918–63*. Oxford: Clarendon Press.

Niedermayer, O. 2003, *Die öffentliche Meinung zur zukünftigen Gestalt der EU: Bevölkerungsorientierungen in Deutschland und den anderen EU-Staaten*, Analysen zur europäischen Verfassungsdebatte der ASKO EUROPA-STIFTUNG und des Instituts für Europäische Politik. Bonn: Europa Union Verlag.

Norris, F. 2001, 'The Good Old Days were not as Good as We Thought,' *New York Times*, 30 November.

O'Riordan, T. (ed.) 1996, *Ecotaxation*. London: Earthscan.

OECD 1993, *OECD Environmental Performance Reviews: Germany*. Paris: OECD.

2000, *Taxing Wages in OECD Countries 1998/1999*. Paris: OECD.

Olson, M. 1982, *The Rise and Decline of Nations: Economic Growth, Stagflation, and Social Rigidities*. New Haven: Yale University Press.

Osborne, D. 1988, *Laboratories of Democracy*. Boston: Harvard Business School Press.

Padgett, S. 1993, 'The New German Electorate', in S. Padgett (ed.), *Parties and Party Systems in the New Germany*. Aldershot: Dartmouth/ASGP.

1999, *Organizing Democracy in Eastern Germany: Interest Groups in Post-Communist Society*. Cambridge: Cambridge University Press.

2000, 'The Boundaries of Stability: the Party System Before and After the 1998 Bundestagswahl', in S. Padgett and T. Saalfeld (eds.), *Bundestagswahl '98: End of an Era?* London: Frank Cass.

2001, 'The German *Volkspartei* and the Career of the Catch-all Concept', *German Politics* 10/2: 51–72.

2003, 'Political Economy: The German Model under Stress', in S. Padgett, W. Paterson and G. Smith (eds.), *Developments in German Politics 3*. Basingstoke: Palgrave.

Page, E. 2003, 'Europeanization and the Persistence of Administrative Systems', in J. Hayward and A. Menon (eds.), *Governing Europe*. Oxford: Oxford University Press.

Panebianco, A. 1988, *Political Parties: Organization and Power*. Cambridge: Cambridge University Press.

Papadakis, E. 1993, 'Class Interests, Class Politics and Welfare State Regime', *British Journal of Sociology* 44/2: 249–70.

Paterson, W. 1973, 'Foreign Policy and Stability in West Germany', *International Affairs* 49/2: 413–30.

1989, 'Environmental Politics', in G. Smith, W. Paterson and P. Merkl (eds.), *Developments in West German Politics*. London: Macmillan.

1994, 'The Chancellor and Foreign Policy', in S. Padgett (ed.), *Adenauer to Kohl: the Development of the German Chancellorship*. London: Hurst.

1998, 'Helmut Kohl, the "Vision Thing" and Escaping the Semisovereignty Trap', *German Politics* 7/1: 17–36.

2003, 'Germany and Europe', in S. Padgett, W. Paterson and G. Smith (eds.), *Developments in German Politics 3*. Basingstoke: Palgrave.

Paterson, W. and G. Smith (eds.) 1981, *The West German Model: Perspectives on a Stable State*. London: Frank Cass.

Paterson, W. and D. Southern 1991, *Governing Germany*. Oxford: Blackwell.

Patzelt, W. 2003, 'Chancellor Schröder's Approach to Political and Legislative Leadership', *German Politics* 13/2: 268–99.

Pearce, D., A. Markandya and E. Barbier 1989, *Blueprint for a Green Economy: a Report for the UK Department of the Environment*. London: Earthscan.

Pedersen, M. 1979, 'The Dynamics of European Party Systems', *European Journal of Political Research* 7: 1–26.

Pehle, H. and A.-I. Jansen 1998, 'Germany: the Engine in European Environmental Policy?', in K. Hanf and A.-I. Jansen, *Governance and Environmental Quality: Environmental Politics, Policy and Administration in Western Europe*. Harlow: Addison Wesley Longman.

Pempel, T. 1982, *Policy and Politics in Japan: Creative Conservatism*. Philadelphia: Temple University Press.

Pierre, J. and G. Peters 2000, *Governance, Politics and the State*. London: Macmillan.

Pierson, P. 1996, 'The New Politics of the Welfare State', *World Politics* 48: 143–79.

Pigou, A. 1920, *The Economics of Welfare*. London: Macmillan.

Poguntke, T. 1994, 'Parties in a Legalistic Culture: the Case of Germany', in R. Katz and P. Mair (eds.), *How Parties Organize: Change and Adaptation in Party Organizations in Western Democracies*. London: Sage.

2002, 'Zur empirischen Evidenz der Kartellparteien-These', *Zeitschrift für Parlamentsfragen* 33/4: 790–806.

Pollitt, C. and G. Bouckaert 2000, *Public Management Reform: a Comparative Analysis*. Oxford: Oxford University Press.

Presse- und Informationsamt der Bundesregierung, 21 October 1998, 'Bulletin No. 69'.

Preusche, E. 1993, '"Hilfe zur Selbsthilfe"', *WISOC Informationsblatt* 21.

Puhle, H.-J. 2002, 'Still the Age of Catch-allism? Volksparteien and Parteienstaat in Crisis and Re-equilibration', in R. Gunther, J. Ramó-Montero and J. Linz (eds.), *Political Parties: Old Concepts and New Challenges*. Oxford: Oxford University Press.

Reichard, C. 2001, 'New Approaches to Public Management', in K. König and H. Siedentopf (eds.), *Public Administration in Germany*, Baden-Baden: Nomos.

Renzsch, W. 1991, *Finanzverfassung und Finanzausgleich: Die Auseinandersetzungen um ihre politische Gestaltung in der Bundesrepublik Deutschland zwischen Währungsreform und deutscher Vereinigung (1948 bis 1990)*. Bonn: Dietz.

1994, 'Föderative Problembewältigung: Zur Einbeziehung der neuen Länder in einen gesamtdeutschen Finanzausgleich ab 1995', *Zeitschift für Parlamentsfragen* 25/1: 116–38.

1999, 'Party Competition in the German Federal State: Variations on an Old Theme', *Regional and Federal Studies* 9/3: 180–92.

2000, 'Bundesstaat oder Parteienstaat: Überlegungen zu Entscheidungsprozessen im Spannungsfeld von föderaler Konsensbildung und parlamentarischem Wettbewerb in Deutschland', in E. Holtmann and H. Voelzkow (eds.), *Zwischen Wettbewerbs- und Verhandlungsdemokratie: Analysen zum Regierungssystem der Bundesrepublik Deutschland*. Wiesbaden: Westdeutscher Verlag 2000.

2001, *Finanzausgleich und die Modernisierung des Bundesstaates: Perspektiven nach dem Urteil des Bundesverfassungsgerichts*. Bonn: Friedrich-Ebert-Stiftung.

Reutter, W. (ed.) 2004, *Germany on the Road to 'Normalcy': Policies and Politics of the Red-Green Federal Government (1998–2002)*. Basingstoke: Palgrave.

Robischon, T., A. Stucke, J. Wasem and H.-G. Wolf 1995, 'Die politische Logik der deutschen Vereinigung und der Institutionentransfer', *Politische Vierteljahresschrift* 36/3: 423–59.

Rock, D. and S. Wolff (eds.) 2002, *Coming Home to Germany? The Integration of Ethnic Germans from Central and Eastern Europe in the Federal Republic since 1945*. Oxford: Berghahn.

Rosenfeld, M. 2002, 'Die Wirtschaftsentwicklung in den neuen Ländern', in *Jahrbuch des Föderalismus 2002*. Baden-Baden: Nomos.

Roth, D. and M. Jung 2002, 'Ablösung der Regierung vertagt: Eine Analyse der Bundestagswahl 2002', *Aus Politik und Zeitgeschichte* B49–50/2002: 3–17.

Rüdig, W. 2000, 'Phasing out Nuclear Energy in Germany', *German Politics* 9/3: 43–80.

Rudzio, W. 2000, *Das politische System der Bundesrepublik Deutschland*. Opladen: Leske+Budrich.

Saalfeld, T. 1995, *Parteisoldaten und Rebellen*. Opladen: Leske+Budrich.

1997, 'Deutschland: Auswanderung der Politik aus der Verfassung?', in W. Müller and K. Strøm (eds.), *Koalitionsregierungen in Westeuropa: Bildung, Arbeitsweise und Beendigung*. Vienna: Signum.

2000a, 'Germany: Stable Parties, Chancellor Democracy, and the Art of Informal Settlement', in W. Müller and K. Strøm (eds.), *Coalition Governments in Western Europe*. Oxford: Oxford University Press.

2000b, 'Court and Parties: Evolution and Problems of Political Funding in Germany', in R. Williams (ed.), *Party Finance and Political Corruption*. London: Macmillan.

2002, 'The German Party System – Continuity and Change', *German Politics* 11/3: 99–130.

Sabatier, P. and H. Jenkins-Smith 1993, *Policy Change and Learning: an Advocacy Coalition Approach*. Boulder: Westview Press.

Sachverständigenrat zur Begutachtung der gesamtwirtschaftlichen Entwicklung 1989, *Weichenstellungen für die neunziger Jahre. Jahresgutachten des Sachverständigenrates zur Begutachtung der gesamtwirtschaftlichen Lage*. Stuttgart: Metzler-Poeschel.

2002, *Zwanzig Punkte für Beschäftigung und Wachstum. Jahresgutachten 2002/03*. Stuttgart: Metzler-Poeschl.

Sachverständigenrat 'Schlanker Staat' 1997a, *Abschlußbericht Band 1*. Bonn: BMI.

1997b, *Abschlußbericht Band 2: Materialband*. Bonn: BMI.

Sachverständigenrat für Umweltfragen 1974, *Die Abwasserabgabe – Wassergüterwirtschaftliche und Gesamtökologische Wirkungen. 2. Sondergutachten*. Wiesbaden: Rat von Sachverständigen für Umweltfragen.

Sally, R. and D. Webber 1994, 'The German Solidarity Pact: a Case Study in the Politics of the Unified Germany', *German Politics* 3/1: 19–46.

Sartori, G. 1976, *Parties and Party Systems: a Framework for Analysis*. Cambridge: Cambridge University Press.

1987, *The Theory of Democracy Revisited. Part One: The Contemporary Debate*. Chatham, NJ: Chatham House.

Scarrow, S. 2000, 'Parties without Members? Party Organization in a Changing Electoral Environment', in R. Dalton and M. Wattenberg (eds.), *Parties without Partisans: Political Change in Advanced Industrial Democracies*. Oxford: Oxford University Press.

Scharf, T. 1994, *The German Greens: Challenging the Consensus*. Oxford: Berghahn.

Scharpf, F. 1988, 'Joint-Decision Trap: Lessons from German Federalism and European Integration', *Public Administration* 66: 239–78.

1991, *Crisis and Choice in European Social Democracy*. Ithaca: Cornell University Press.

1993, 'Verhandeln, wo nicht regiert werden kann: Handlungsfähigkeit und Legitimation der Politik am Ende des 20. Jahrhunderts', in *30 Jahre Beirat für Wirtschafts- und Sozialfragen: Daten, Fakten, Perspektiven*. Vienna: Beirat für Wirtschafts- und Sozialfragen 68: 23–41.

1997, *Games Real Actors Play: Actor-Centered Institutionalism in Policy Research*. Boulder: Westview.

Scharpf, F., B. Reissert and F. Schnabel 1976, *Politikverflechtung: Theorie und Empirie des kooperativen Föderalismus in der Bundesrepublik*. Berlin: Cornelsen.

Schattschneider, E. E. 1960, *The Semisovereign People: a Realist's View of Democracy in America*. New York: Holt, Rinehart, and Winston.

Schäuble, W. 1991, *Der Vertrag: Wie ich über die deutsche Einheit verhandelte*. Stuttgart: Deutsche Verlags-Anstalt.

Schelling, T. 1978, *Micromotives and Macrobehaviour*. New York: W. W. Norton.

Schiller, T. and V. Mittendorf (eds.) 2002, *Direkte Demokratie: Forschung und Perspektiven*. Wiesbaden: Westdeutscher Verlag.

Schindler, P. 1983, *Datenhandbuch zur Geschichte des Deutschen Bundestages 1949 bis 1983*. Bonn: Presse- und Informationszentrum des Deutschen Bundestages.

1994, *Datenhandbuch zur Geschichte des Deutschen Bundestages 1983 bis 1991*. Baden-Baden: Nomos, 1994.

1999, *Datenhandbuch zur Geschichte des Deutschen Bundestages 1949 bis 1999*. Baden-Baden: Nomos.

Schluchter, W. and P. Quint (eds.) 2001, *Der Vereinigungsschock. Vergleichende Betrachtungen zehn Jahre danach*. Weilerswist: Velbrück Wissenschaft.

Schmid, J. 1990, *Die CDU: Organisationsstrukturen, Politiken und Funktionsweisen einer Partei im Föderalismus*. Opladen: Leske+Budrich.

Schmid, J. 2001, 'Bevölkerungsentwicklung und Migration in Deutschland', *Aus Politik und Zeitgeschichte* B43/2001: 20–30.

Schmid, J. and S. Blancke 2003, 'Bilanz der Bundesregierung Schröder im Bereich der Arbeitsmarktpolitik 1998–2002: Ansätze zu einer doppelten Wende', in C. Egle, T. Ostheim and R. Zohlnhöfer (eds.), *Das rot-grüne Projekt. Eine Bilanz der Regierung Schröder 1998–2002*. Wiesbaden: Westdeutscher Verlag.

Schmidt, H. 1993, *Handeln für Deutschland. Wege aus der Krise*. Berlin: Rowohlt.

Schmidt, M. 1987, 'West Germany: the Policy of the Middle Way', *Journal of Public Policy* 7/2: 135–77.

1989, 'Learning from Catastrophes: West Germany's Public Policy', in F. Castles (ed.), *The Comparative History of Public Policy*. Cambridge: Polity Press.

1993, *Erwerbsbeteiligung von Frauen und Männern im Industrieländervergleich*. Opladen: Leske+Budrich.

2000a, 'Immer noch auf dem "mittleren Weg"? Deutschlands Politische Ökonomie am Ende des 20. Jahrhunderts', in R. Czada and H. Wollmann (eds.), *Von der Bonner zur Berliner Republik. 10 Jahre Deutsche Einheit*. Wiesbaden: Westdeutscher Verlag.

2000b, *Demokratietheorien*. Opladen: Leske+Budrich.

2002a, 'The Impact of Political Parties, Constitutional Structures and Veto Players on Public Policy', in H. Keman (ed.), *Comparative Democratic Politics*. London: Sage.

2002b, 'Germany: the Grand Coalition State', in J. Colomer (ed.), *Political Institutions in Europe*. London: Routledge.

2003, *Political Institutions in the Federal Republic of Germany*. Oxford: Oxford University Press.

Schmidt, S. 1996, 'Privatizing the Federal Postal and Communications Services', in A. Benz and K. Goetz (eds.), *A New German Public Sector.* Aldershot: Dartmouth/ASGP.

Schmidt, V. 2002, *The Futures of European Capitalism.* Oxford: Oxford University Press.

Schmidt-Preuß, M. 1997, 'Die Treuhand-Verwaltung', in J. Isensee and P. Kirchhof (eds.), *Handbuch des Staatsrechts der Bundesrepublik Deutschland.* Heidelberg: C. F. Müller.

Schmitter, P. 1979, 'Still the Century of Corporatism?', in P. Schmitter and G. Lehmbruch (eds.), *Trends towards Corporatist Intermediation.* London: Sage.

Schneider, H.-P. 1999, 'German Unification and the Federal System: the Challenge of Reform', in C. Jeffery (ed.), *Recasting German Federalism: the Legacies of Unification.* London: Pinter.

Schoen, H. and J. W. Falter 2001, '"It's Time for a Change!" – Wechselwähler bei der Bundestagswahl 1998', in H.-D. Klingemann and M. Kaase (eds.), *Wahlen und Wähler: Analysen aus Anlass der Bundestagswahl 1998.* Wiesbaden: Westdeutscher Verlag.

Schroeder, W. 2000, *Das Modell Deutschland auf dem Prüfstand: Zur Entwicklung der industriellen Beziehungen in Ostdeutschland (1990–2000).* Wiesbaden: Westdeutscher Verlag.

Schroeder, W. and B. Ruppert 1996, 'Austritte aus Arbeitgeberverbänden. Motive – Ursachen – Ausmaß', *WSI-Mitteilungen* 11: 316–29.

Schudlich, E. 1982, 'Kooperation statt Korporatismus', in U. Billerbeck (ed.), *Korporatismus und gewerkschaftliche Interessenvertretung.* Frankfurt am Main: Campus.

Schwarz, H.-P. 1994, *Die Zentralmacht Europas: Deutschlands Rückkehr auf die Weltbühne.* Bonn: Siedler.

Seeleib-Kaiser, M. 2002, 'A Dual Transformation of the German Welfare State?', *West European Politics* 25/4: 25–48.

Sinn, G. and H.-W. Sinn 1992, *Jumpstart: the Economic Reunification of Germany.* Cambridge, MA: MIT.

Sinn, H.-W. 2000, *Germany's Economic Unification: an Assessment after Ten Years.* Munich: Ifo-Institute.

Sinn, H.-W. and F. Westermann 2001, 'Two Mezzogiornos', *Rivista di Diritto Finanziario e Scienza de la Finanze* 60: 29–54.

Skocpol, T. 1992, *Protecting Soldiers and Mothers: the Political Origins of Social Policy in the United States.* Cambridge, MA: Belknap Press.

Skou Andersen, M. 1994, *Governance by Green Taxes: Making Pollution Prevention Pay.* Manchester: Manchester University Press.

Smith, G. 1976, 'West Germany and the Politics of Centrality', *Government and Opposition* 11/4: 387–407.

1982, 'The German *Volkspartei* and the Career of the Catch-all Concept', in G. Smith and H. Döring (eds.), *Party Government and Political Culture in Western Germany.* London: Macmillan.

1991, 'The Resources of a German Chancellor', in G. Jones (ed.), *West European Prime Ministers.* London: Frank Cass.

Société Générale 2002, 'Germany's Potential Growth Rate – A Matter of Concern', *SG Euro Economy,* September 2002.

SPD-Greens 1998, *Aufbruch und Erneuerung – Deutschlands Weg ins 21. Jahrhundert. Koalitionsvereinbarung zwischen der Sozialdemokratischen Partei Deutschlands und Bündnis 90/Die Grünen.* Bonn: SPD/Bündnis 90/Die Grünen.

2002, *Erneuerung – Gerechtigkeit – Nachhaltigkeit: Koalitionsvertrag 2002–2006.* Berlin: SPD/Bündnis 90/Die Grünen.

Der Spiegel, 21 August 1995 (34/1995), 'Der Mann mit der Ölkanne'.

17 July 2000 (29/2000), 'Da habe ich ja gesagt'.

11 September 2000 (37/2000), 'Zynischer Umgang'.

4 March 2002 (10/2002), 'Die Rückseite der Republik'.

2 September 2002 (36/2002), '"Lasst uns hier abhauen"'.

21 September 2002 (39/2002), 'Die blockierte Republik'.

20 January 2003 (3/2003), 'Sieger auf verlorenem Posten'.

24 February 2003 (9/2003), 'Sozialer Sprengstoff'.

19 July 2004 (30/2004), 'Langer Anlauf, kurzer Sprung'.

Stamm, B. 1998, 'Wettbewerbsföderalismus in der Sozialversicherung', in U. Männle (ed.), *Föderalismus zwischen Konsens und Konkurrenz.* Baden-Baden: Nomos.

Steingart, G. 2004, *Deutschland: Abstieg eines Superstars.* Munich: Piper.

Stern, K. 1998, 'Die Bundesbank im Staatsgefüge', in Deutsche Bundesbank (ed.), *Fünfzig Jahre Deutsche Mark. Notenbank und Währung in Deutschland seit 1948.* Munich: Beck.

Stolorz, C. 1997, 'Bedrückende Perspektiven des Föderalismus im vereinigten Deutschland', *Zeitschrift für Parlamentsfragen* 28/2: 311–34.

Streeck, W. 1991, 'On the Institutional Conditions of Diversified Quality Production', in E. Matzner and W. Streeck (eds.), *Beyond Keynesianism: the Socio-Economics of Production and Employment.* London: Edward Elgar.

2001a, 'Introduction: Explorations into the Origins of Nonliberal Capitalism in Germany and Japan', in W. Streeck and K. Yamamura (eds.), *The Origins of Nonliberal Capitalism.* Ithaca: Cornell University Press.

2001b, 'High Equality, Low Activity: the Contribution of the Social Welfare System to the Stability of the German Collective Bargaining Regime', *Industrial and Labour Relations Review* 54/3: 698–706.

2001c, 'Tarifautonomie und Politik: Von der Konzertierten Aktion zum Bündnis für Arbeit', in Gesamtverband der metallindustriellen Arbeitgeberverbände (eds.), *Die deutschen Arbeitsbeziehungen am Anfang des 20. Jahrhunderts.* Cologne: Deutscher Institutsverlag.

Streeck, W. and P. Schmitter 1984, 'Community, Market, State and Associations? The Prospective Contribution of Interest Governance to Social Order', *European Sociological Review* 1: 119–38.

Strøm, K. 2000, 'Parties at the Core of Government', in R. Dalton and M. Wattenberg (eds.), *Parties without Partisans: Political Change in Advanced Industrial Democracies.* Oxford: Oxford University Press.

Strøm, K. and W. Müller 1999, 'Political Parties and Hard Choices', in W. Müller and K. Strøm (eds.), *Policy, Office, or Votes? How Political Parties in Western Europe Make Hard Choices.* Cambridge: Cambridge University Press.

Strübin, M. 1997, 'Ecological Tax Reform in Germany', *German Politics* 6/2: 168–80.

Sturm, R. 1990, 'Die Politik der Deutschen Bundesbank', in K. von Beyme and M. G. Schmidt (eds.), *Politik in der Bundesrepublik Deutschland*. Opladen: Westdeutscher Verlag.

1999, 'Der Föderalismus im Wandel. Kontinuitätslinien und Reformbedarf', in E. Jesse and K. Löw (eds.), *50 Jahre Bundesrepublik Deutschland*. Berlin: Duncker & Humblot.

2003, 'Policy-Making in a New Political Landscape', in S. Padgett, W. Paterson and G. Smith (eds.), *Developments in German Politics 3*. Basingstoke: Palgrave.

Süddeutsche Zeitung, 27 June 2002, '"Ich möchte keine zweisprachigen Ortsschilder haben." Otto Schily zum Zuwanderungs- und Integrationsgesetz'.

9 July 2004, 'Föderalismus-Kommission fährt sich fest'.

Suh, J., P. Katzenstein and A. Carlson (eds.) 2004 *Rethinking Security in East Asia: Identity, Power and Efficiency*. Stanford, CA: Stanford University Press.

Tarrow, S. 1994, *Power in Movement: Social Movements, Collective Action and Politics*. Cambridge: Cambridge University Press.

Tewes, H. 2001, *Germany, Civilian Power and the New Europe: Enlarging NATO and the European Union*. Basingstoke: Palgrave.

Thies, M. 2000, 'On the Primacy of Party in Government: Why Legislative Parties Can Survive Party Decline in the Electorate', in R. Dalton and M. Wattenberg (eds.), *Parties without Partisans: Political Change in Advanced Industrial Democracies*. Oxford: Oxford University Press.

Trampusch, C. 2002, '*Die Bundesanstalt für Arbeit und das Zusammenwirken von Staat und Verbänden in der Arbeitsmarktpolitik von 1952 bis 2001*', MPIfG Working Paper 02/5. Cologne: Max-Planck-Institut für Gesellschaftsforschung.

2003a, 'Dauerproblem Arbeitsmarkt: Reformblockaden und Lösungskonzepte', *Aus Politik und Zeitgeschichte* B18–19/2003: 16–23.

2003b, 'Ein Bündnis für die nachhaltige Finanzierung der *Sozialversicherungssysteme*: Interessenvermittlung in der deutschen Arbeitsmarkt- und Rentenpolitik', *MPIfG Discussion Paper* 03/1. Cologne: Max-Planck-Institut für Gesellschaftsforschung.

Tsebelis, G. 1995, 'Decision Making in Political Systems: Veto Players in Presidentialism, Parliamentarism, Multicameralism, and Multipartism', *British Journal of Political Science* 25: 289–326.

1999, 'Veto Players and Law Production in Parliamentary Democracies: an Empirical Analysis', *American Political Science Review* 93/3: 591–608.

2002, *Veto Players. How Political Institutions Work*. Princeton/New York: Princeton University Press/Russell Sage Foundation.

Tuohy, C. 1992, *Policy and Politics in Canada: Institutionalized Ambivalence*. Philadelphia: Temple University Press.

Turek, J. 1996, 'Treuhandanstalt', in W. Weidenfeld and K.-R. Korte (eds.), *Handbuch zur deutschen Einheit*. Frankfurt am Main: Campus.

Unger, F. 1993, 'Landnahme im Osten', *Neue Gesellschaft – Frankfurter Hefte* 40/3: 221–8.

Vail, M. 2003, 'Rethinking corporatism and Consensus: the Dilemmas of German Social-Protection Reform', *West European Politics* 26/3: 41–66.

Vesper, D. 1998, 'Länderfinanzausgleich: Neuer Verteilungsstreit zwischen West und Ost', *DIW-Wochenbericht* 12 February 1998: 133–41.

Wagschal, U. 2001, 'Der Parteienstaat der Bundesrepublik Deutschland. Parteipolitische Zusammensetzung seiner Schlüsselinstitutionen', *Zeitschrift für Parlamentsfragen* 32/4: 861–86.

Waldrauch, H. and D. Çinar 2003, 'Staatsbürgerschaftspolitik und Einbürgerungspraxis in Österreich', in I. Stacher and H. Fassmann (eds.), *Österreichischer Migrations- und Integrationsbericht*. Klagenfurt: Drava.

Weale, A. 1992a, *The New Politics of Pollution*. Manchester: Manchester University Press.

1992b, 'Vorsprung durch Technik? The Politics of German Environmental Regulation', in K. Dyson (ed.), *The Politics of German Regulation*. Aldershot: Dartmouth/ASGP.

Weale, A., T. O'Riordan and L. Kramme 1991, *Controlling Pollution in the Round*. London: Anglo-German Foundation.

Wehling, H.-G. 2003, 'Rat und Bürgermeister in der deutschen *Kommunalpolitik*', in A. Kost and H.-G. Wehling (eds.), *Kommunalpolitik in den deutschen Ländern*. Wiesbaden: Westdeutscher Verlag.

Weidner, H. 1995, *25 Years of Modern Environmental Policy in Germany: Treading a Well-Worn Path to the Top of the International Field*. Berlin: Wissenschaftszentrum Berlin für Sozialforschung, FS II 95–301.

Die Welt, 31 July 2004, 'Die Deutschen sind sauer – Risiken und *Nebenwirkungen* der Gesundheitsreform'.

Wey, K-G. 1982, *Umweltpolitik in Deutschland: Kurze Geschichte des Umweltschutzes in Deutschland seit 1900*. Opladen: Westdeutscher Verlag.

Wiesendahl, E. 2000, 'Changing Party Organisations in Germany: How to Deal with Uncertainty and Organised Anarchy', in S. Padgett and T. Saalfeld (eds.), *Bundestagswahl '98: End of an Era?* London: Frank Cass.

Wildenmann, R. 1969, *Die Rolle des Bundesverfassungsgerichts und der Deutschen Bundesbank in der politischen Willensbildung. Ein Beitrag zur Demokratietheorie*. Stuttgart: Kohlhammer.

Wilke, H. 1983, *Entzauberung des Staates: Überlegungen zu einer sozietalen Steuerungstheorie*. Königstein: Athenäum.

Wingens, M. and R. Sackmann 2000, 'Evaluation AFG-finanzierter Weiterbildung. Arbeitslosigkeit und Qualifizierung in Ostdeutschland', *Mitteilungen aus der Arbeitsmarkt- und Berufsforschung* 33/1: 39–53.

Wollmann, H. 2000, 'Local Government Systems: From Historic Divergence towards Convergence? Great Britain, France, and Germany as Comparative Cases in Point', *Environment and Planning C: Government and Policy* 18: 33–55.

2001, 'Die Transformation der politischen und administrativen Strukturen in Ostdeutschland – zwischen "schöpferischer Zerstörung", Umbau und Neubau', in H. Bertram and R. Kollmorgen (eds.), *Die Transformation Ostdeutschlands*. Opladen: Leske+Budrich.

2002, 'Recent Democratic and Administrative Reforms in Germany's Local Government: Persistence and Change', in J. Caulfield and H. Larsen (eds.), *Local Government at the Millennium*. Opladen: Leske+Budrich.

Wollmann, H. and R. Roth (eds.) 1999, *Kommunalpolitik: Politisches Handeln in den Gemeinden*. Opladen: Leske+Budrich.

Wollmann, H. and E. Schröter (eds.) 2000, *Comparing Public Sector Reform in Britain and Germany*. Aldershot: Ashgate.

Wright, V. 1989, *The Government and Politics of France*. London: Hutchinson.

Wurzel, R. 2004, 'Environmental policy: a Leader State under Pressure?', in K. Dyson and K. Goetz (eds.), *Germany, Europe and the Politics of Constraint*. London: Proceedings of the British Academy, vol. 119/Oxford University Press.

Wurzel, R., A. Jordan, T. Zito and L. Brückner 2003, 'From High Regulatory State to Social and Ecological Market Economy? "New" Environmental Policy Instruments in Germany', *Environmental Politics* 12/1: 115–36.

Die Zeit, 16 November 1984 (46/1984), 'Späte Einsicht'.

4 April 2002 (14/2002), 'Angsthasen und Panikmacher'.

9 January 2003 (2/2003), 'Die vergreiste Republik'.

Zentralbankrat der Deutschen Bundesbank 1999, 'Überlegungen und Vorschläge zur künftigen Organisationsstruktur der Deutschen Bundesbank', *Bundesbankmagazin* 3: 3–8.

Ziblatt, D. 2001, 'Just How Powerful are Ideas? The Failed Push for Fiscal Decentralization and the Persistence of Germany's Federal System', paper presented at the Annual Conference of the American Political Science Association Conference, San Francisco, 1 September 2001.

Zohlnhöfer, R. 1999, 'Die große Steuerreform 1998/99: Ein Lehrstück für Politikentwicklung bei Parteienwettbewerb im Bundesstaat', *Zeitschrift für Parlamentsfragen* 30/2: 326–45.

2000, 'Der Parteienwettbewerb, die kleinen Koalitionspartner und das Scheitern der Steuerreform. Eine Erwiderung auf Wolfgang Renzsch', *Zeitschrift für Parlamentsfragen* 31/3: 719–24.

2001a, *Die Wirtschaftspolitik der Ära Kohl. Eine Analyse der Schlüsselentscheidungen in den Politikfeldern Finanzen, Arbeit und Entstaatlichung, 1982–1998*. Opladen: Leske+Budrich.

2001b, 'Parteien, Vetospieler und der Wettbewerb um Wählerstimmen: Die Arbeitsmarkt- und Beschäftigungspolitik der Ära Kohl', *Politische Vierteljahresschrift* 42: 655–82.

2003, 'Institutionelle Hemmnisse für eine kohärente *Wirtschaftspolitik*', *Aus Politik und Zeitgeschichte* B18–19/2003: 9–15.

Index